Illiberal Constitutionalism in Poland and Hungary

This book theorizes illiberal constitutionalism by interrogation of the Rule of Law, democratic deterioration, and the misuse of the language and relativization of human rights protection, and its widespread emotional and value-oriented effect on the population.

The work consists of seven Parts. Part I outlines the volume's ambitions and provides an introduction. Part II discusses the theoretical framework and clarifies the terminology adopted in the book. Part III provides an in-depth insight into the constitutional identity of Poles and Hungarians and argues that an unbalanced constitutional identity has been moulded throughout Polish and Hungarian history in which emotional traits of collective victimhood and collective narcissism, and a longing for a charismatic leader have been evident. Part IV focuses on the emergence of illiberal constitutionalism, and, based on both quantitative and qualitative analyses, argues that illiberal constitutionalism is neither modern authoritarianism nor authoritarian constitutionalism. This Part contextualizes the issue by putting the deterioration of the Rule of Law into a European perspective. Part V explores the legal nature of illiberal legality when it is at odds and in compliance with the European Rule of Law, illiberal democracy, focusing on electoral democracy and legislative processes, and illiberalization of human rights. Part VI investigates whether there is a clear pattern in the methods of remodelling, or distancing from constitutional democracy, how it started, consolidated, and how its results are maintained. The final Part presents the author's conclusions and looks to the future.

The book will be an invaluable resource for scholars, academics, and policy-makers interested in Constitutional Law and Politics.

Tímea Drinóczi is Visiting Professor at the Faculty of Law at Federal University of Minas Gerais, Brazil. Since 2017, she has also been a Doctor of the Academy of Sciences of Hungary. Professor Drinóczi has been a visiting professor in law schools in Plzen, Brno, Cologne, Graz, Istanbul, and Osijek, and has presented papers at several conferences all over Europe, in Hong Kong, Nanjing, Seoul, and Santiago. She served as a professor at the University of Pécs, Faculty of Law, Hungary, and Kenyatta University School of Law, Nairobi, Kenya.

Agnieszka Bień-Kacała is Professor within the Department of Constitutional Law, Faculty of Law and Administration at Nicolaus Copernicus University in Toruń, Poland. Professor Bień-Kacała has been a visiting professor in law schools in Athens, Prague, and Maastricht. Together, Professors Drinóczi and Bień-Kacała have presented papers at several conferences all over Europe, and in Hong Kong and Santiago de Chile.

Comparative Constitutional Change

Comparative Constitutional Change has developed into a distinct field of constitutional law. It encompasses the study of constitutions through the way they change and covers a wide scope of topics and methodologies. Books in this series include work on developments in the functions of the constitution, the organization of powers and the protection of rights, as well as research that focuses on formal amendment rules and the relation between constituent and constituted power. The series includes comparative approaches along with books that focus on single jurisdictions, and brings together research monographs and edited collections which allow the expression of different schools of thought. While the focus is primarily on law, where relevant the series may also include political science, historical, philosophical and empirical approaches that explore constitutional change.

Series editors:

Xenophon Contiades is Professor of Public Law, Panteion University, Athens, Greece and Managing Director, Centre for European Constitutional Law, Athens, Greece.

Thomas Fleiner is Emeritus Professor of Law at the University of Fribourg, Switzerland. He teaches and researches in the areas of Federalism, Rule of Law, Multicultural State; Comparative Administrative and Constitutional Law; Political Theory and Philosophy; Swiss Constitutional and Administrative Law; and Legislative Drafting. He has published widely in these and related areas.

Alkmene Fotiadou is Research Associate at the Centre for European Constitutional Law, Athens.

Richard Albert is Professor of Law at the University of Texas at Austin.

Also in the series:

Illiberal Constitutionalism in Poland and Hungary
The Deterioration of Democracy, Misuse of Human Rights and Abuse of the Rule of Law
Tímea Drinóczi and Agnieszka Bień-Kacała

Courts and Judicial Activism under Crisis Conditions
Policy Making in a Time of Illiberalism and Emergency Constitutionalism
Edited by Martin Belov

For more information about this series, please visit: www.routledge.com/Comparative-Constitutional-Change/book-series/COMPCONST

Illiberal Constitutionalism in Poland and Hungary

The Deterioration of Democracy, Misuse of Human Rights and Abuse of the Rule of Law

Tímea Drinóczi and Agnieszka Bień-Kacała

Routledge
Taylor & Francis Group
LONDON AND NEW YORK

First published 2022
by Routledge
2 Park Square, Milton Park, Abingdon, Oxon OX14 4RN

and by Routledge
605 Third Avenue, New York, NY 10158

Routledge is an imprint of the Taylor & Francis Group, an informa business

British Library Cataloguing-in-Publication Data
A catalogue record for this book is available from the British Library

Library of Congress Cataloging-in-Publication Data
Names: Drinóczi, Tímea, author. | Bień-Kacała, Agnieszka, author.
Title: Illiberal constitutionalism in Poland and Hungary : the deterioration of democracy, misuse of human rights and abuse of the rule of law / Tímea Drinóćzi and Agnieszka Bień-Kacała.
Description: Abingdon, Oxon ; New York, NY : Routledge, 2021. | Series: Comparative constitutional change | Includes bibliographical references and index.
Identifiers: LCCN 2021008954 (print) | LCCN 2021008955 (ebook) | ISBN 9781032007304 (hardback) | ISBN 9781032007366 (paperback) | ISBN 9781003175353 (ebook)
Subjects: LCSH: Rule of law–Poland. | Rule of law–Hungary. | Civil rights–Poland. | Civil rights–Hungary. | Populism–Poland. | Populism–Hungary. | Poland–Politics and government–21st century. | Hungary–Politics and government–21st century.
Classification: LCC KJC4426 .D75 2021 (print) | LCC KJC4426 (ebook) | DDC 340/.11–dc23
LC record available at https://lccn.loc.gov/2021008954
LC ebook record available at https://lccn.loc.gov/2021008955

ISBN: 978-1-032-00730-4 (hbk)
ISBN: 978-1-032-00736-6 (pbk)
ISBN: 978-1-003-17535-3 (ebk)

DOI: 10.4324/9781003175353

Typeset in Galliard
by Taylor & Francis Books

Contents

Illustrations

Tables

Figures

Foreword

Rosalind Dixon

In this important new book, Drinóczi and Bien-Kacała explore recent constitutional changes in Hungary and Poland and provide valuable insights into the nature and origins of these developments, and how they should be conceptualized within the broader comparative constitutional literature.

Both Hungary and Poland, the authors suggest, have witnessed a sustained attack on a range of independent oversight bodies, including courts, and a retreat from liberal commitments to inclusion, openness, and transnational engagement. Yet, according to the authors, neither country has descended into full-scale authoritarianism, or a wholly arbitrary system of government. Each retains some commitment to limited government through adherence to national and European legal norms, or at least a partial willingness to apply and implement EU law. Drinóczi and Bien-Kacała thus suggest that these systems are neither wholly constitutionally democratic nor wholly authoritarian in character, but rather a form of hybrid regime. They label the current model of government in Hungary and Poland as "illiberal constitutional" in nature.

The authors offer important insights about both the erosion of liberal constitutional norms in Hungary and Poland, and its causal origins. Following Schwartz and Bardi, they argue that the "value profile" common in eastern European countries is ill-suited for the development of democracy,[1] and they go on to argue that "an unbalanced constitutional identity has been moulded throughout the Polish and Hungarian history in which emotional traits of collective victimhood and collective narcissism, and a longing for a charismatic leader is noticeable" and that this is a key contributor to the illiberal constitutional turn in these countries.

Methodologically, Drinóczi and Bien-Kacała explore both the similarities and differences between the two countries, and ultimately apply what in Ran Hirschl's terms could be regarded as principles of case-selection based on the "most different cases principle".[2] They note that Poland has been influenced by Hungary in

1 See Part III: Identity. See also SH Schwartz and A Bardi, "Influences of Adaptation to Communist Rule on Value Priorities in Eastern Europe," *Political Psychology* 2(385) (1997) 407–408.

2 R Hirschl, *Comparative Matters: The Renaissance of Comparative Constitutional Law* (Oxford University Press, 2014).

this context, and therefore recognize the complexities of treating them as two independent cases. But they do an excellent job in highlighting a range of important differences between the two countries, including the degree to which the legislature is bicameral versus unicameral (Poland is bicameral, Hungary is unicameral), the nature of presidential power, the role of the Catholic Church, and the strength and make-up of civil society.

In doing so, they also challenge many of our existing notions of the kinds of countries most likely to be suited to application of the most different cases principle: these are two neighbouring and quite similar countries socio-culturally, and yet there may be sufficient structural constitutional differences to make it plausible to consider them as different, not similar, cases for the purposes of causal inference. This is a question that no doubt readers will debate, and disagree on, in engaging with the book, but raising it is one of the great contributions it makes.

Similarly, some may contest the empirical determination that underlies their label and the choice of specific terms, but again their use and justification of those terms is valuable for the discussion it is sure to provoke. There is clearly some ongoing commitment to rule by law in both countries, and the maintenance of at least a superficial commitment to electoral democracy. But there is an equally live question as to whether there is in fact an ongoing commitment to the rule of law, or the kinds of checks and balances necessary for true constitutionalism, in either country,[3] and using "constitutionalism" in the label could be understood to convey that there is some real – not just formal or pretextual – commitment to limited, non-arbitrary forms of government.[4]

Furthermore, the authors see liberalism, not democracy, as having suffered the greatest harm in recent processes of "abusive" constitutional change in Hungary and Poland,[5] but attacks on liberalism and democracy often go together.[6] The authors adopt a relatively thin or minimalist definition of democracy, which is capable of attracting agreement among all reasonable political and constitutional theorists and democratic actors worldwide.[7] But even this relatively minimalist definition of democracy must include a commitment to a range of political rights

3 See M Krygier, "The Challenge of Institutionalisation: Post-Communist 'Transitions', Populism, and the Rule of Law", *European Constitutional Law Review* 15(544) (2019); W Sadurksi, *Poland's Constitutional Breakdown* (Oxford University Press, 2019).

4 See, e.g., M Tushnet, "Authoritarian Constitutionalism", *Cornell Law Review* 100 (391) (2014). See also Krygier, n. 3.

5 See D Landau, "Abusive Constitutionalism", *UC Davis L Review* 47(189) (2013); R Dixon and D Landau, "1989–2019: From Democratic to Abusive Constitutional Borrowing", *International Journal of Constitutional Law* 17(489) (2019).

6 See Dixon and Landau, n. 5.

7 Landau and I adopt a similar approach, in suggesting that there is value to adopting a "minimum core" definition of democracy as the benchmark for making judgments about abusive constitutional change or borrowing: D Landau and R Dixon, "Constraining Constitutional Change", *Wake Forest Law Review* 50(859) (2015); D Landau and R Dixon, "Abusive Judicial Review: Courts against Democracy", *UC Davis Law Review* 53(1313) (2019); Dixon and Landau, n. 5.

and freedoms and institutional checks and balances necessary to ensure truly free and fair, multi-party elections conducted on the basis of open debate and universal participation.[8] On this definition, Poland and Hungary have seen a slide towards illiberal *and* undemocratic government.

The book provides an extremely useful account of recent constitutional developments in Hungary and Poland, but it is not just about Hungary and Poland. It is about a broader set of challenges to constitutional democracy worldwide, and the use of the different cases principle or methodology allows the authors to offer insights and lessons about national psychology and self-understanding and their relationship to abusive forms of constitutional change, which have the potential to speak to a much broader range of cases of democratic backsliding.

I commend the book to readers and encourage an ongoing debate about both the terminology it uses and the causal explanatory variables it points to. The debate we have will be much richer for the contribution made by this important new work.

8 Landau and Dixon, "Constraining Constitutional Change", n. 7; Landau and Dixon, "Abusive Judicial Review", n. 7; Dixon and Landau, n. 5.

Acknowledgements

We offer our profound thanks to the series editors of Comparative Constitutional Change who supported us throughout the process, and especially Prof. Richard Albert, who encouraged us to keep going at the right moment.

The main gratitude goes to Routledge and its editors for the opportunity to work together again and publish this book.

We are grateful to the National Science Centre, Poland (2018/29/B/HS5/00232, 'Illiberal constitutionalism in Poland and Hungary') for the financial support of our research project. The final result of our research is this book – may it be an inspiration and a premonitory sign for those who believe that constitutional democracy should be saved.

I Introduction

Ambitions and comparison

The title of this book is Illiberal Constitutionalism in Poland and Hungary: The Deterioration of Democracy, Misuse of Human Rights and Abuse of the Rule of Law. For many, even this title might cry out for explanation – "Why it is only Hungary and Poland?", "How can constitutionalism be illiberal?" – an explanation we offer in two sections of the book: this Introduction and Part II, "Terms".

I Ambitions

This book aims to offer a comprehensive and theoretically substantiated framework within which the Hungarian and Polish constitutional remodelling that has occurred between 2010/2015 and the end of 2020 can be conceptualized. We propose to call the result of this remodelling "illiberal constitutionalism", and that in Member States of the European Union (EU) it should be viewed as a separate concept from the perspective of constitutional studies. We also go further in conceptualizing the term as a reality (and not only as a theoretical possibility as Mark Tushnet does[1]) and elaborate more on its actual implementation (based on Graham Walker[2]) by using qualitative analyses and quantitative data.

In our view, illiberal constitutionalism is a stage in the process of authoritarianization of EU Member States (illiberalization of constitutionalism), mainly in the post-socialist region that has been "hit" by autocrat populist leaders in the second decade of the 21st century. They have brought about the deterioration of constitutional democracy and the hollowing out of its components, which was hardly an easily preventable development. The gradualness of the deterioration and the embeddedness of EU law (*acquis*) and human rights commitments (regardless of their weakness and flaws) in the daily adjudication of law have kept these states from turning to (modern) authoritarianism. This phenomenon constitutes one element of the concept of illiberal constitutionalism. On the other hand, we propose that the normative appeal of the regime for the population

1 M Tushnet, "The Possibility of Illiberal Constitutionalism?", *Florida Law Review* 69 (1997) 1367–1384.

2 G Walker, "The Idea of Nonliberal Constitutionalism", *Ethnicity and Group Rights* 39 (1997).

DOI: 10.4324/9781003175353-1

could find its roots more in an unbalanced constitutional identity that longs for a charismatic leader than in a particular political philosophy. Consequently, it is also suggested that this appeal could be satisfied by the application of a patchwork of ideologies in so far as they can be invoked by a charismatic leader for satisfying the current emotional needs of the polity. This, in turn, allows the regime to form the constitutive features of illiberal constitutionalism, which are illiberal legality, illiberal democracy, and illiberalization of human rights.

Due to their unbalanced constitutional identity, illiberal constitutionalism is certainly a good fit for Hungarian and Polish societies, but it has not been always like this – as the history of transition at the beginning of the 1990s proves. Nevertheless, illiberal constitutionalism seems to be the legal and social reality, and it seems to claim stability. It could continue to remain like this as long as Hungary and Poland are still Member States of the EU and continue to enjoy the benefits of membership.

The emergence of a new type of constitutionalism (illiberal constitutionalism) in the form of illiberal legality, illiberal democracy, and misuse of the language of human rights accompanied by diminishing protection cannot be denied. We also cannot ignore the fact that this system, along with these characteristics, is maintained and supported by the voters. The electoral victories of 2010, 2014, and 2018 in Hungary cannot be explained solely by the manipulation of electoral laws, increasing electoral irregularities, and further monopolization of the media. In Poland, where the electoral playing field was not corrupted to the extent seen in Hungary, the PiS (Law and Justice Party) was also supported in parliamentary elections in 2015 and 2019, though to a different extent (it lost the *Senat* in 2019), and its candidate won the presidential election in 2020. It also does not mean that the population, en masse, is content with the politics of Fidesz and the PiS, or that the opposition could not achieve some measure of victory (the election of mayors in 2019 in Hungary and local elections in 2018 in Poland) or that discontent cannot be expressed. But what is true is that the possibility to express dissent has continuously been narrowed down. Regardless, people still seem to support, or at least do not oppose, populist autocrats and their policies – in the sense that people tend to be comfortable with the system in which they find themselves. People behaved in the same manner during and after the democratic transition (1989/1990): they welcomed systemic changes, supported them, felt comfortable – until they got receptive to the complete opposite, to the extent that we have been experiencing since 2010 and 2015.

Therefore, in this book, we argue that illiberal constitutionalism within the EU is a coherent concept and can be distinguished from other similar notions of constitutionalism. We also argue that this is a negative concept: when the preconditions exist (historical and emotional trajectory, EU membership) and the autocratic populist leader starts a remodelling exercise, which leads in the direction of authoritarianism, illiberal constitutionalism emerges and entails more backsliding.[3] We propose that, in agreement with most of the scholars criticizing these

3 For the avoidance of repetition, in this book, "backsliding" is used interchangeably with other terms (e.g., deterioration, democratic decay, retrogression, and autocratization in

changes, illiberal constitutionalism is destructive of the common European project, manipulatively exaggerating and exploiting the existing value-orientation of the people in a way that is not compatible with liberal constitutionalism and that ultimately could – or even should – result in these states leaving the EU or being isolated within the EU. Nevertheless, the bottom line is that an EU Member State should not develop illiberal constitutionalism (though it could occur in conformity with the will of the voters); and the EU should not allow this type of remodelling. Illiberal constitutionalism within the EU represents standards of wrong actions on the part of both the EU and the Member States concerned.

Illiberal constitutionalism today – we must add, fortunately – is found only in Hungary and Poland. Its seeds, however, have already been noted from time to time in other Member States, too, for example in Romania or the Czech Republic. Therefore, it seems to be vital to understand the constitutional characteristics of illiberal constitutionalism and its root causes, which, we believe, emerge from the historical and emotional characteristics of these nations. Beyond investigating this, we primarily engage with a comparative constitutional law inquiry. We also consider the measurements of the World Justice Project (WJP),[4] the Bertelsmann Transformation Index (BTI), the Varieties of Democracy Index (V-Dem), Freedom House, and the Economist Intelligence Unit (EIU) Democracy Index,[5] which provide for a variety of labels (from "hybrid" to "free") to describe Hungary and Poland in a particular year and from a specific perspective. We study the effects of membership of the EU and Council of Europe (CoE), along with the locked-in nature of EU and international human rights law. These investigations require both a universal and a more regional or contextualized analysis from the

democracy or authoritarianization), even though it does not precisely describe the process. Backsliding does not express the fact that the "sliding" is not directed back to a previously known non-democratic or non-constitutionalist state – which is in our case socialism. It also does not properly indicate that the deterioration is voluntary, which is the opposite to the involuntary action we would associate with "sliding". Similarly, see A Lührmann and SI Lindberg, "A Third Wave of Autocratization Is Here: What Is New About It?" *Democratization* 7 (2019) 1099. For more insight on democratic decay, see e.g., TG Daly, "Diagnosing Democratic Decay", Conference paper, Comparative Constitutional Law Round-table, Gilbert and Tobin Centre for Public Law, UNSW Law School, 7 August 2017; on the term "constitutional retrogression", see e.g., AZ Huq and T Ginsburg, "How to Lose a Constitutional Democracy" *UCLA Law Review* 65(95) (2008); on authoritarianization, see e.g., E Frantz and A Kendall-Taylor, "The Evolution of Autocracy: Why Authoritarianism Is Becoming More Formidable", *Survival: Global Politics and Strategy* 59(57) (2017); and on autocratization, see the above-mentioned article by Lührmann and Lindberg (1095–1113).

4 https://worldjusticeproject.org/our-work/research-and-data/wjp-rule-law-index-2020. The WJP Rule of Law Index, notwithstanding its imperfections, produces more definitive and authoritative measures of the Rule of Law across the globe. See e.g., M Versteeg and T Ginsburg, "Measuring the Rule of Law: A Comparison of Indicators", *Law and Social Inquiry* 1 (2017) 101.

5 www.bti-project.org/en/home.html?&cb=00000; www.v-dem.net/en/publications/democracy-reports/; https://freedomhouse.org/; www.eiu.com/topic/democracy-index.

perspective of a civil law jurisdiction, and at the same time try to utilize the academic achievements of other disciplines as well.

The book thus fits into the series of efforts by the scholarly community to offer strategies and constitutional designs to save constitutional democracy[6] and assist in the fight against further deterioration, democratic decay,[7] and illiberalization.[8] This is so, even if we are more pessimistic but – at the same time maybe – more realistic than other proponents of constitutional democracy and liberal constitutionalism when assessing the possibilities for re-transformation. It is so mostly because we base our theory on the historical and emotional trajectories and past and current value orientations of our respective nations. With this unique and, without doubt, subjective approach, we mean to refresh the discussion on constitutionalism and offer new insights into the Hungarian and Polish models. We hope that we can also create a rudimentary link between two disciplines, comparative public law and social psychology, for a better understanding of current constitutional changes in Europe and worldwide.

II Why Hungary and Poland?

Even though there are similarities between Hungary and Poland that would genuinely generate a need for comparison, one might ask why we consider them together, especially when there are notable differences.[9] It could be argued that there is an evident difference in the constitutional system of government, the role of presidents, the characteristics of the opposition and civil society, and the institutional influence of the Catholic Church; and therefore, that the difference in the starting point renders the comparison unbalanced. When, however, we take a deeper look at the essence of these differences and how they are present in the current regimes, we could reach another conclusion. These differences have in fact not considerably impacted either the emergence of the current political and legal situation or its apparent stability in either country; that is, these differences do not really matter[10] when it comes to illiberal constitutional remodelling, making Hungary and Poland comparable. Let us explain why.

6 See e.g., T Ginsburg and AZ Huq, *How to Save Constitutional Democracy?* (University of Chicago Press, 2018).

7 TG Daly, "Democratic Decay: Conceptualising an Emerging Research Field", https://link.springer.com/article/10.1007/s40803-019-00086-2.

8 See e.g., S Hanley, "Understanding the Illiberal Turn: Democratic Backsliding in the Czech Republic", www.tandfonline.com/doi/full/10.1080/21599165.2018.1493457.

9 See e.g., W Sadurski, "How Democracy Dies (in Poland): A Case Study of Anti-Constitutional Populist Backsliding", *Sydney Law School Legal Studies Research Paper No 18/01* (2018) 4–8; W Sadurski, *Poland's Constitutional Breakdown* (Oxford University Press, 2019) 3–5. A Bozóki and D Hegedűs, "An Externally Constrained Hybrid Regime: Hungary in the European Union", *Democratization* 25(1173) (2018).

10 See also W Sadurski, "Constitutional Democracy in the Time of Elected Authoritarians", *International Journal of Constitutional Law* 2 (2020) 331.

1 *Differences*

1.1 Do they matter?

It could be argued that the structure of a bicameral parliament (Poland) allows for more balance in exercising power than a unicameral (Hungarian) system. It is indeed true: bicameralism has its advantages, in terms of, for example, inclusion and the avoidance of additional constraint. These goals are best served in a strong bicameral system and less so in the face of weak bicameralism. Poland exercises the latter system: its bicameralism is asymmetric (the *Senat*'s powers are not equal to those of the *Sejm*, the lower chamber of Polish parliament) and congruent (there is no overrepresentation of minorities in the *Senat*). On the other hand, both the *Senat* and the *Sejm* are elected by the people, so the *Senat* can use its legitimacy to compensate for its lack of formal power, to an extent.[11] As Hungary has a unicameral parliament, these advantages do not feature there.

Another claim could be that the presumed stronger constitutional position of the Polish President could serve as a counter-weight to the power-grabbing of the political forces. Indeed, one might argue that the position of the Polish president is stronger than that of his/her Hungarian counterpart. It would also mean a difference in the governmental system, which, as per the design, is parliamentary in Hungary. Generally, the Polish academia label the governmental system as a rationalized parliamentary system, which is based on the German chancellor system. Because of this, the Polish variation is sometimes called a "semi-chancellor" system. It follows that the Polish governmental system is based on the decisive role of parliament, with the influence of government on the effective lawmaking process. The position of the government and the prime minister vis-à-vis ministers is strong. The 1997 Constitution provides for a constructive vote of no confidence, which terminates the mandate of the whole government, not just that of the Prime Minister. Therefore, by design, the government is bound by the political trust of and is politically responsible to the majority of the Parliament – and not to the President.[12] The constitutional design in both Poland and Hungary is similar, and the role and powers of the presidents are adjusted to the parliamentary system of government.

What is truly distinctive, however, is the way in which the presidents are elected. In Hungary, it is the parliament that elects the President, while in Poland, she/he is elected directly by the voters. This distinction creates strong popular legitimation of the Polish President and higher expectations of voters. It does not, however, translate into more power for the President to control and determine policy-making, but could translate into revoking the legitimacy to compensate for his/her lack of power. It also makes the presidential election more partisan, in that two

11 For the classification, see A Lijphart, *Patterns of Democracy – Government Forms and Performance in Thirty-Six Countries* (Yale University Press, 2012) 192.

12 M Granat and K Granat, *The Constitution of Poland. A Contextual Analysis* (Hart Publishing, 2019) 32–33.

main political parties, two world views, are clashing. So, the Polish President indeed has more potential for political mobilization than the Hungarian one.

The character of the political (parliamentary and extra-parliamentary) opposition also varies, which leads to visible differences in the opportunities for big Polish and Hungarian cities, and also to the different characteristics of the protest movements, their mobilizing forces, and their effectiveness. The extra-parliamentary opposition and the protest movements, their mobilizing forces, have always been more visible in Poland (*Solidarność*) than in Hungary. Thus, the opposition is weak in Hungary but still strong in Poland.

It is also proposed, as a characteristic difference between Hungary and Poland, that the Catholic Church is traditionally more involved in politics in Poland; consequently, its legitimizing force is stronger for the current government.[13]

Furthermore, when we look at the timeline of changes, it may be noted that the illiberal change of direction started in 2010 in Hungary and in 2015 in Poland. This is another difference that could be considered. Indeed, the year marking the starting point of transformation suggests its own reasons and has its own consequences, but the difference does not make these two states incomparable or make the comparison unbalanced. It was Hungary that pointed out the goal and paved the way to illiberal remodelling for Poland. Fidesz grabbed the political opportunity offered by the political crisis in Hungary before 2010, which coincided with the world financial crises. In 2010, Orbán declared explicitly the illiberal state-building. That year was also when the Smoleńsk plane crash happened, which served as a fertile political point of reference for populist sentiments awakened by Jarosław Kaczyński and the PiS in Poland. They succeeded in the parliamentary elections in 2015. For the first couple of years thereafter, the undeniable existing differences translated into differences in speed and areas of deterioration – which, however, have been fading away.

1.2 How the differences translated into the post-2010 and 2015 periods

1.2.1 CONSTITUTIONAL DESIGN

The difference as regards the constitutional design of the of the two countries' presidents became visible during the Polish electoral campaign of 2020, when the Mayor of Warszawa, Rafał Trzaskowski, supported by Civic Platform, entered the campaign as the strongest candidate against the incumbent President Andrzej Duda, supported by PiS. Nevertheless, regardless of their constitutional positions, in neither Poland nor Hungary is the President recognized as an elected official who can act as a counterbalance to power-grabbing; they are not equipped to do so. They are also not political leaders or "strong" presidents. The leaders behind the systemic changes have been Prime Minister Viktor Orbán in Hungary and, initially, "an ordinary MP" and the President of the PiS party, and since October 2020 Vice Prime Minister, Jarosław Kaczyński in Poland. Nevertheless, while the

13 Sadurski, n. 9 (2019) 5.

positions of the populist leaders within the formal constitutional settings have been different, their role in inducing and controlling constitutional design has been the same. Therefore, in these circumstances, it is doubtful whether a President could be a meaningful actor facilitating re-transformation, even if he/she wanted to be. The presidents could express their views and opinions about certain policies by exercising their powers, such vetoing and requesting constitutional review, but they could not substantially influence the original political will of PiS and Fidesz. However, we should add that since the beginning of the remodelling process, the presidents and the parliamentary majority (since 2019, in Poland, only in the *Sejm*) have been from the same political parties. No changes can be expected in this regard.

When combining the character of the opposition with the structure of parliaments, we may note that a *Senat* with a majority made up of opposition parties can slow down the remodelling and bring more quality to the legislative process. Still, the *Senat* can be, and usually is, outvoted by the *Sejm*, as the *Sejm* has a decisive position within the lawmaking procedure. The weak Polish bicameralism, in combination with different majorities in the houses of parliament, gives rise to the opportunity for a variety of voices and opinions to be heard in public. Thus, the *Senat* informs Polish society about the possible consequences of legislative actions in Poland. The question is its efficiency, which, to a great extent, is dependent on how the extra-parliamentary opposition, other movements, and society itself are able to act on the information provided.

1.2.2 THE CHARACTER OF THE OPPOSITION, CIVIL SOCIETY, AND THE VERTICAL DIVISION OF POWER (BIG CITIES)

The effectiveness of the extra-parliamentary opposition and protest movements seems no stronger in Poland than in Hungary. In Poland, no claim formulated by protesters appears to have caused any significant[14] changes to the decisions of the ruling majority, not even those relating to Polish judicial reform;[15] in Hungary, protests failed to prevent the kicking out of the Central European University,[16] not to mention any other reform affecting, for example, higher education.[17] Even if one might consider the so-called "black protest" in 2016 (women against a proposed stricter abortion law[18]) in Poland an effective one, we should remember

14 Except the internet tax in Hungary, www.bbc.com/news/world-europe-29846285. But it is fairly correct to say that this withdrawal did not overturn the illiberal system.

15 The march of a thousand robes: www.reuters.com/article/us-poland-judiciary-toga-march/thousands-protest-against-polands-plan-to-discipline-judges-idUSKBN1ZA0PD

16 www.ceu.edu/content/mass-protest-budapest-against-law-targeting-ceu

17 https://insighthungary.444.hu/2020/06/25/fearing-for-its-autonomy-university-holds-protest-against-privatization-plan

18 The ban on so-called eugenic abortion (if the foetus is irreparably damaged) and the possibility of lifting the obligation on physicians to inform a woman about places where a pregnancy can be legally terminated were discussed within the legislative process in April 2020. The legislative process is still pending.

that the same talks have been taking place about future anti-abortion actions during the COVID-19 pandemic. Eventually, the protesting women's position was weakened by the decision of the Constitutional Tribunal of Poland (CT) in October 2020.[19]

One might also suggest that local government in major cities (e.g., Gdańsk, Wrocław, Warszawa) is stronger in Poland than in Hungary, which could more easily facilitate the creation of political alliances against the central government. On the one hand, it is true that the opposition is concentrated in the big Polish cities, and that its members have been able to claim victory in the local and *Senat* elections. However, this does not seem to be a characteristic of the Polish situation alone; to a certain extent it pertains in Hungary[20] as well. On the other hand, in both states, the stronger opposition centred in local government has generated a demand for strong centralization and practices against the opposition-led local governments. This seems to be a characteristic of the illiberal turn in both countries.

Hungarian opposition has not been able to secure meaningful power in elections since 2010, even though it won a moderate "victory" at local government elections in 2019. The strength and political possibilities and influence of the opposition are relative, as the opposition is bound to function within the constitutional and legislative framework adopted by the Fidesz-led parliament and government according to their actual political needs. These kinds of tactics have not been experienced in Poland until recently. The changes in relation to the National Electoral Commission, which became a political rather than a judicial organ, entered into force after the 2019 parliamentary election, played some role in the presidential election in 2020, and could potentially affect the next parliamentary election in 2023. Another reason for the weakness of the opposition is the monopolization of the media, which makes the playing field quite uneven. On the other hand, parliamentary opposition in both states has been sidelined by both formal measures, such as standing order rules, and informal practices. The apparent inability of the Hungarian opposition to successfully unite against Fidesz before a parliamentary election is another characteristic. On the other hand, the local elections in 2019 saw the joining of forces, which led to some success on the side of the opposition. Polish opposition also united before local elections in 2018 and the parliamentary election in 2019, leading to a win in the *Senat.* In the 2020 presidential election, however, the opposition parties decided to compete separately, and subsequently Duda won. It seems that if and when the opposition unite, they have a chance. This possibility was taken away from the Hungarian opposition by the electoral reform of December 2020, which made it even more difficult to have a party list in the national election (2022) and force opposition parties to formally cooperate and create joint lists.

19 See in Part V, Limits – Constitutional design and identity, point III.

20 In the 2019 local elections, 12 out of 23 big cities in Hungary were led by a mayor supported by Fidesz-KDNP; 7 mayoral positions were won out of 23 districts in the capital by a Fidesz-KDNP candidate. The capital is led by an opposition politician.

1.2.3 THE INFLUENCE OF THE CHURCH

The Catholic Church in Poland is not as united in its support for the PiS government as it might seem at first sight. There are pro-government and pro-opposition voices, and opinions demanding neutrality as well. After the presidential election (2020), analyses linked the support for PiS to the religiousness of the voters: PiS voters are recruited from villages and from people in their 50s and above and these people are said to be more religious than others. The narratives of both the Catholic Church and the PiS are directed at these types of people. One of the most influential radio and television broadcasters is led by the powerful clergyman Tadeusz Rydzyk, who supports the PiS and has a strong connection (including a financial one) with the government. It is, however, questionable if this connection has anything to do with the remodelling of the constitutional system, as the support and political engagement of some clergy do not translate into a (constitutional) majority in Poland, where about 90 per cent of the people declare themselves to be Roman Catholic.[21] What might bolster government endeavours more are those politically active priests who use their masses to call for support for the government (mobilization by clergy). It is not a uniquely Polish phenomenon, however, but has been a practice in Hungary too. In Hungary, the typical Fidesz voter is a conservative and right-wing supporter who does not live in the big cities or the capital. Just over half the population of Hungary profess to be Christians; the majority of them are Catholic. Most acknowledge that their religious identity is largely a matter of national culture or family tradition, but only around one in ten attend the obligatory weekly mass.[22] So, it might be safe to assume that there are likely to be factors other than religion behind the political support for rulers.

1.2.4 DIFFERENCE IN THE YEARS OF REMODELLING

The most significant reason for taking a different path in remodelling is that, in Hungary, the Fidesz has been able to preserve its constitutional majority almost continuously since 2010, while in Poland the PiS only secured an absolute majority in both houses of parliament in 2015 and achieved a majority in the *Sejm* alone in the election in 2019. Consequently, Hungary has passed a new illiberal constitution; Poland has not, but the constitutional system that has been created informally does seem to be supported by the population. A different constitutional design and different electoral results slowed down the illiberalization process in Poland, and also made it harder to accelerate it to the Hungarian extent – in the beginning. In this sense, Poland has been lagging behind Hungary. The differences (lack of a constitutional majority and the majority of the opposition in the

21 While only about 40 per cent attend holy mass: W Sadłoń, "Differentiation, Polarization and Religious Change in Poland at the Turn of 20th and 21st Century", *Przegląd Religioznawczy – The Religious Studies Review* 4(262) (2016) 33, 35. According to Sadłoń's research, the decline in religious practice among Poles during the last 30 years is evident, but it is slower than in other European states.

22 https://budapestbeacon.com/political-christianity-in-orbans-hungary/,www.pewforum.org/wp-content/uploads/sites/7/2017/05/CEUP-FULL-REPORT.pdf

Senat) could affect the path of illiberalization, while the goal (consolidation of power by an autocratic leader[23]) and the potential end (upholding illiberal constitutionalism within the EU) remain the same. Poland's judicial reform, which goes beyond that in Hungary, means that in that regard Poland has caught up with Hungary; thus the "lagging", that is, the consequence of the five-year difference in the remodelling, lies mainly in the level of deterioration of democracy and human rights. Let us give an example: the Istanbul Convention was ratified in 2015 by Poland before the illiberal changes commenced. Hungary, already an illiberal state, refused to ratify the Convention. After just five years of illiberalization, in 2020 Poland expressed its willingness to withdraw from the Convention and questioned the constitutionality of the Convention before the CT.[24]

2 *Similarities*

From a historical perspective, Hungarians and Poles share similar experiences. Beyond having the same king and being bound by their personal union in the Middle Ages,[25] the socialist countries of Hungary and Poland, under the influence zone of the Soviet Union, were forced to adopt a communist constitution that introduced the socialist model of state and legal systems. In the late 1980s, Hungary and Poland underwent similar transition processes from socialism to democracy. By using different approaches towards constitution-making, they created new constitutional regimes, which were based on the Rule of Law, democracy, and human rights.[26] Hungary and Poland created liberal constitutionalism – the need to constrain public power and defend human rights through the idea of the Rule of Law as prescribed in a written constitution – and democracy – rule by the people, usually but not exclusively through elected representatives who, to a certain extent and without disregarding minority opinions, represent the view of the majority – as a package, as opposed to their gradual development in the Western polities.[27] Therefore, in the newly established constitutional system, which we call constitutional democracy,[28] liberal constitutionalism and democracy were not conflicting values but rather were meant to complement each other.

Nevertheless, as Thomas Humphrey concluded in 2008, without a rigorous Rule of Law or commitment to constitutionalism, defended and, in practice,

23 In a more detailed manner this involves: distancing themselves from common European values, claiming to be the fighters for sovereignty and independence, and a strong national state that needs to be respected, while gradually dismantling the constitutional democracy.

24 Case K 11/20; it is still pending.

25 The personal union between the Kingdom of Hungary and the Kingdom of Poland was achieved twice: in 1370–1382 under Louis I of Hungary, and in 1440–1444 under Vladislaus III of Poland.

26 Both states joined the Council of Europe – Hungary in 1990, Poland in 1991 – and ratified the European Convention on Human Rights (ECHR).

27 Classic constitutionalism was born before democracy in its modern form with universal suffrage taking root.

28 See Part II, Terms.

enriched by constitutional courts, the democratic transition might not have been successful, because without the Rule of Law, liberal and democratic rights are not safe, and the equal dignity of all citizens is endangered.[29] Indeed, the transformation process was facilitated and actively assisted by the constitutional courts. Both the Hungarian Constitutional Court (CC) and the Polish CT embraced an activist approach towards constitutional interpretation, which was required by both the fact and the fragility of the transition, as well as some vague constitutional provisions. Both states joined the EU in 2004, which meant that they acknowledged mutual interests and values shared by the then Member States and adapted their legal systems to the accession.

Despite differences in their constitutional history, the historical particularities and the emotional trajectories of both Hungarians and Poles seem to create a receptiveness to populism and a call for a strong(er) autocratic leader. The unsettled and vulnerable identities of both have created a longing for stability, which they, more usually than not, find in a right-wing autocratic leader.[30] Various narrative psychological studies,[31] Schwartz and Bardi's findings from 1997 on the value priorities in the region after the communist rule, and the value research results published in 2019[32] also support comparability. Schwartz and Bardi concluded that the value profile common in Eastern European countries, which lacks the commitment to egalitarianism and autonomy values, is ill-suited to the development of democracy.[33]

29 T Humphrey, 'Democracy and the Rule of Law: Founding Liberal Democracy in Post-Communist Europe', *Colum. J. E. Eur. L.* 2(94) 124 (2008). Due to this development, GJ Jacobsohn and Y Roznai call the Hungarian and Polish events of 1989/1990 "constitutional revolution". GJ Jacobsohn and Y Roznai, *Constitutional Revolution* (Yale University Press, 2020).

30 T Hajdu, *A magyar identitás szabadságharcos – interjú Szabó Zsolttal, az ELTE Szociálpszichológia tanszékének adjunktusával*, Mindset Pszichologia (18 November 2017), http://mindset.co.hu/a-magyar-identitas-szabadsagharcos-interju-szabo-zsolttal-az-elte-szocialpszichologia-tanszekenek-adjunktusaval/.

31 Narrative psychology provides a dynamic approach to understanding human identity and the process of making sense of our ever-changing world. See generally, U Popp-Baier, *Narrative Psychology*, in ALC Runehov and L Oviedo (eds), *Encyclopedia of Sciences and Religions* (2013); É Fülöp et al., "Emotional Elaboration of Collective Traumas in Historical Narratives" (2014), http://real.mtak.hu/20201/3/emotional_elaboration_of_collective_traumas.pdf; A Jefferys, *What is Narrative Psychology*?, Pen & the Pad (10 March 2017), https://penandthepad.com/narrative-psychology-3393.html; J László, *Narratív pszichológia*, Pszichológia 28 (2008), http://real.mtak.hu/2385/1/49413_ZJ1.pdf; M Murray, "Narrative psychology and narrative analysis" in PM Camic et al. (eds), *Qualitative Research in Psychology: Expanding Perspectives in Methodology and Design* (2003), www.researchgate.net/publication/274889276_Chapter_6_Narrative_psychology_and_narrative_analysis.

32 J Eichhorn et al., "How European Publics and Policy Actors Value an Open Society: Key Insight across Countries" (Open Society European Policy Institute, 2019), http://voicesonvalues.dpart.org/images/finalreports/OSI-019-18-Key-Insights_v5.pdf.

33 SH Schwartz and A Bardi, "Influences of Adaptation to Communist Rule on Value Priorities in Eastern Europe", *Political Psychology* 2 (1997) 407–408. See also in Part III, Identity.

The Hungarian and Polish cases are unique because of the transformative power of populism, which, from being a "permanent shadow over representative politics",[34] has become the authentic part of illiberal constitutional politics. Populist parties in both states won the general election after political crises. Just after creating the new government, populist leaders Viktor Orbán – Hungarian Prime Minister, formal authority – and Jarosław Kaczyński – Polish President of the PiS party, at that time informal authority – started to transform the then existing constitutional democracies. Since then, they have enjoyed continuous popular support. Because of the different general election results, these leaders used different means of transformation. The Hungarian way was more formal, based on constitutional measures such as adoption and amendments to the constitution that, occasionally, have been abusive. Poland uses informal tools of transformation, breaching and bypassing constitutional provisions, especially in connection to the CT and judiciary. In effect, the Hungarian system is based on an illiberal constitution – the 2011 Fundamental Law – whereas the Polish system is based on the delegitimization and, later, the relegitimization of the still-binding Constitution of 1997,[35] and on the continuously constructed illiberal invisible constitution. This difference, however, does not alter the fact that Hungarian and Polish decision-makers have undeniably created new illiberal constitutional systems. They have introduced new laws and changed others in the fields of, for example, elections, the judiciary and court systems, and civil society. They have provided less and less protection to individuals by restricting their freedoms of assembly, expression, the press, and other means of social communication, while starting to create a more communitarian and less egalitarian and liberal understanding of human rights. These measures have met with strong, yet unsuccessful, reactions from international and supranational organizations and different non-governmental organizations (NGOs), and even from the Hungarian and Polish judiciaries.

This transformative effect and the apparent inability of the international and supranational community to directly address similar illiberal challenges emerging from both countries support our opinion that the Hungarian and Polish cases are unique in the world and, at the end of 2020, even in Europe. Nevertheless, their example could potentially be contagious.

Democratic decay appears to be affecting liberal democracies[36] that face major economic and financial crises, and that are struggling with migration challenges,

34 J-W Müller, *What is Populism?* (University of Pennsylvania Press, 2016) 16. Jan-Werner Müller observes the worldwide wave of populism and argues that populism cannot be perceived as an authentic part of modern democratic politics, or as a kind of pathology caused by irrational citizens, but is a permanent shadow over representative politics.

35 Until 2019, the liberal 1997 Constitution had been delegitimized in the official narrative. In the 2019 general election, a constitutional majority was not achieved by the PiS, therefore passing a new illiberal constitution remains impossible. Consequently, after 2019, the 1997 Constitution is no longer delegitimized in the official rhetoric as it already has its illiberal content.

36 See e.g., TG Daly, "Diagnosing Democratic Decay", Conference paper, Comparative Constitutional Law Round-table, Gilbert and Tobin Centre for Public Law, UNSW

terror threats, and the global pandemic. Yet even if we are able to see the results of the undeniable populist influence, there are remarkable differences between the states in democratic decay. Compare, for example, the unpopularity of Brazilian politicians, and the new role of the judiciary in fighting against corruption[37] and the actions of the President during the COVID-19 pandemic,[38] with the continuing popularity of the Fidesz in Hungary or the popular support the PiS receives in Poland – without any serious judicial challenge. Further, while in Hungary and Poland the judiciary, including the constitutional courts, has already been compromised, the United States continues to enjoy an uncompromised judicial system. The different historical roots of constitutional development in these states, the more-or-less unified commitment towards the same constitutional principles in Europe, and the different attitudes to military *coups d'état* should also be taken into account. In addition, this powerful and concentrated transformation of the system that occurred in Hungary and Poland has not been observed – yet – in other countries where populist parties won general elections, such as Czech Republic, Slovakia, Austria, and Italy. It is also true, however, that the Czech Republic and Romania are flirting with different layers of illiberalism, such as corruption and reforms affecting the judiciary.[39]

III Insight into the book

We believe that the fundamentals of constitutional democracy (liberal constitutionalism) should be the standard implemented within the Hungarian and Polish societies and in their constitutions. Unfortunately, however, we have realized that we can identify and outline a pattern of constitutional conduct in Hungary and Poland that has distanced these states more and more from the constitutional conduct generally expected of a constitutional democracy (liberal constitutionalism). We were interested in the extent of the deterioration and wanted to see if it both quantitatively and qualitatively approaches the state of "authoritarianism", as many in scholarly literature claim. These points are captured in Part II on "Terms" and Parts IV and V on "Limits" ("Comparative perspective" and "Constraint in constitutional design and identity").[40]

Law School, 7 August 2017, www.academia.edu/34052302/Diagnosing_Democratic_Decay.

37 FJG Acunha and JZ Benvindo, "Democratic Decay in Brazil and the New Global Populism", INT'L ASS'N CONST. L. BLOG (6 June 2017), https://blog-iaclaidc.org/test-3/2018/5/26/democratic-decay-in-brazil-and-the-new-global-populism.

38 VM Pinheiro, M Ilarraz, and MT Mestriner, "The Impacts of the COVID-19 Crisis on the Brazilian Legal System: A Report on the Functioning of the Branches of the Government and On the Legal Scrutiny of Their Activities", *The Theory and Practice of Legislation* 8(1–2) 193–212.

39 See e.g., Hanley, n. 8.

40 These two parts draw heavily on our findings already presented in T Drinóczi and A Bień-Kacała (eds), *Rule of Law, Common Values and Illiberal Constitutionalism. Poland and Hungary within the European Union* (Routledge, 2020). Nevertheless, in this book, we have extended our perspective and take a more holistic view compared

In Part II on "Terms", we discuss some of the theoretical framework, that is, the notions of constitutionalism and constitutional democracy, in the light of which and because of which we felt it necessary to develop the concept of illiberal constitutionalism. We also explain our reasons for using the term "constitutionalism", what separates this notion from other descriptions already applied to Hungary and Poland, and what the word "illiberal" might mean in the term "illiberal constitutionalism". We consider studies on isms, which show that old notions of ideology have been stretched, providing renewed motivation to rethink isms and their relationship to ideology.[41] Thus, the "constitutionalism", in the term "illiberal constitutionalism", can also be seen as enhancing the universal character of the ism itself – in constitutionalism (constitutional design) – "as this kind of rhetoric presents sub-categories of an ism rather than questioning its prominence".[42]

We also observed that these kinds of detrimental changes have received steady and continuous political support. As many have already discussed, one of the reasons is the rise of nationalism and right-wing populist politics combined with autocratic leaders. It has led us to investigate further why this transformation, which is completely different from the democratization process after the fall of communism, is so appealing to the population.

Partly following the argument set forth in Part II, in Part III on "Identity" we argue that an unbalanced constitutional identity has been moulded throughout Polish and Hungarian history, in which emotional traits of collective victimhood and collective narcissism, and a longing for a charismatic leader, are noticeable. In the discussion on the states' historical and emotional trajectories, we dedicate separate sections to their history before and after the Second World War, because this global conflict marked the beginning of the influence of the former Soviet Union. It also led to the same urge for transformation and re-joining the Western part of Europe. After a review of the historical and emotional trajectories of the remote past, we continue with an investigation of the value-orientation of Poles and Hungarians in the post-communist past and beyond, which shows distinct features as compared to the societies in Western states.

Again, following the arguments presented in the previous Parts (clarification of terminology, in-depth insight into the constitutional identity of Poles and Hungarians), we have asked whether there were some limits on the public power at the times examined (2010/2015–2020). To answer that, we needed to understand the starting point of the backsliding; therefore, we have explored the emergence of

to the one we employed in the edited volume, which focused on the Rule of Law and investigated the question of whether it is still a common European value.

41 "While both the concept of ideology and the isms have changed over time, the overall association of isms with ideology has become somewhat weaker, though definitely not lost and definitely not in all contexts. Both have changed historically and have been contested in particular debates." J Kurunmäki and J Marjanen, "Isms, Ideologies and Setting the Agenda for Public Debate", *Journal of Political Ideologies* 23(3) (2018) 256–282.

42 Ibid.

illiberal constitutionalism. We have also put the regression into a regional (European) and broader context (in contrast to authoritarianism), to see how Hungary and Poland fare in a comparative analysis, whether they (still) maintain some characteristics that make them constitutionalist.

This complex issue is discussed in Parts IV and V. Part IV, "Limits – comparative perspective", focuses on the emergence of illiberal constitutionalism, and, based on both quantitative and qualitative analyses, argues, for instance, that illiberal constitutionalism is neither (modern) authoritarianism nor authoritarian constitutionalism. The third section of this Part contextualizes the issue by putting the Rule of Law deterioration into a European perspective. For the analysis of the Rule of Law, which is delivered in the section on illiberal legality (in Part V, "Limits – Constraints in constitutional design and identity"), we propose the introduction of the concept of European Rule of Law, as in our view it could be considered a (regional) constraint on public power. When conceptualizing the European Rule of Law, we draw on the idea that the Rule of Law is a context-related notion, and we also explain what "European" and "Rule of Law" mean in that term.

Part V finds these constraints in the Hungarian and Polish versions of the European Rule of Law, democracy and human rights protection – mainly due to all of the factors mentioned in the previous Parts on "Identity" and "Limits". To express the difference, we propose the use of terms "illiberal legality", "illiberal democracy", and "illiberalization of human rights protection" to express the results of the abuse of the Rule of Law, deterioration of democracy, and misuse of human rights. In these sections, we explore the legal nature of illiberal legality (when it is at odds and in compliance with the European Rule of Law) and illiberal democracy (focusing on electoral democracy and legislative processes). In the field of human rights, we briefly review the steps towards illiberalization and common challenges that have to be faced by all European states (as regards which they either succeed or not), the visions that inform the populist autocrats, and the emerging concept in Hungary that assumes that the state could be a holder of fundamental rights.

Being able to collect these characteristics of illiberal constitutionalism could also suggest some sort of stability of the system. Therefore, we have started to investigate whether it is possible to detect a clear pattern regarding the methods by which the remodelling (i.e., distancing from constitutional democracy) commenced, was consolidated, and through which its results are maintained. Part VI on "Stability – How 'illiberal limits' emerge and work" elaborates on this.

We have identified four such patterns. The first is capturing the constitution and constitutionalism, which has been done gradually through formal (Hungary) and informal (Poland) constitutional changes and their combination (Hungary) – each showing the paradox of unconstitutional formal and unconstitutional informal constitutional amendments. This has been extended to the occupation of key positions in every sphere of the constitutional system.

We have also noted that, besides the political branches, the other major player is each country's constitutional court. Considering the regulatory alterations to the constitutional courts and the role they play in our civil law jurisdictions, we propose to view the changes, and thus the method of remodelling, as amounting to illiberal judicialization of politics, instead of juristocracy and political constitutionalism.

Another method of remodelling is pushing the limits to achieve certain goals. It is a political and legal game, comprising a cynical approach to criticism, and it features a combination or different variations of backing off.

Comparative constitutional scholars have already identified some exit strategies that could assist in the re-transformation of the backsliding regimes. We must report sadly, though, that rendering these measures or design elements or strategies ineffective has greatly contributed to the consolidation of illiberal constitutionalism. We see this phenomenon as something that could contribute to the stability of illiberal constitutionalism in our countries. We briefly conclude in Part VII.

II Terms

Constitutionalism, illiberal(ism), and constitutional democracy

Before starting to defend our position that the Hungarian and Polish systems can best be described by the term "illiberal constitutionalism", we need to back up our assertion that constitutionalism can be something other than liberal. The notion that constitutionalism cannot be anything else was not questioned in the Western legal system until Fidesz and the PiS came to power in Hungary and Poland, respectively, in 2010 and 2015. Based on the constitutional development of our region, in this chapter we challenge this idea and clarify some terms that we use, such as "constitutionalism", the adjective "illiberal", and "constitutional democracy".

I Constitutionalism in the term "illiberal constitutionalism"

1 The need for a new term

Scholars, en masse, seem to be puzzled about how best to label the events in Hungary and Poland. We list some of them here: Paul Blokker refers to "populist constitutionalism",[1] Kim Lane Scheppele proposes "authocratic legalism",[2] and Wojciech Sadurski uses the terms "constitutional breakdown", "anti-democratic system", "plebiscitary autocracy", and "populist authoritarianism".[3] Many others describe the events that led to the "backsliding" in Hungary and Poland and put them in a wider Central and Eastern European,[4] European,[5] or global[6] context.

1 P Blokker, *Populist Constitutionalism*, VerfBlog (4 May 2017), https://verfassungsblog.de/populist-constitutionalism/
2 KL Scheppele, "Autocratic Legalism", *U. Chi. L. Rev.* 85(545) (2018).
3 W Sadurski, *Poland's Constitutional Breakdown* (Oxford University Press, 2019) 25, 243.
4 B Bugarić, "A Crisis of Constitutional Democracy in Post-Communist Europe: 'Lands In-Between' Democracy and Authoritarianism", *Int'l J. Const. L.* 13(219) (2015); P Blokker, *New Democracies in Crisis?* (Routledge, 2015).
5 J Ruprik, "The Specter Haunting Europe: Surging Illiberalism in the East", *J. Democracy* 27(77) (2016) 137.
6 S Levitsky and LA Way, "The Myth of Democratic Recession", *Democracy* 26(45) (2015) 48.

DOI: 10.4324/9781003175353-2

The labelling of this phenomenon varies widely.[7] References are made to "borderline authoritarianism",[8] "illiberal regimes", "grey-zone" countries,[9] the "transition away from democracies" and "democracies in regression",[10] "competitive authoritarianism",[11] or "authoritarian constitutionalism".[12] The Hungarian events have even been considered to amount to a "counter-constitutional revolution"[13] and "abusive constitutionalism".[14] Poland has been described as indulging in "anti-constitutional populist backsliding"[15] and as a "dual state".[16] Political scientists call the Hungarian political system a hybrid regime, standing between democracy and authoritarianism,[17] a diffusely defective democracy,[18] and a plebiscitary leader democracy.[19] Lately, Freedom House has labelled Hungary as a transitional or hybrid regime (based on its democracy score).[20] We have collected the most important views together in Table II.1 to show the varieties of conceptual frameworks developed by others.

We have felt that the framework of liberal constitutionalism might have prevented scholars from appreciating the gradualness of the deterioration and the implications of the regional context within which the constitutional systems of Hungary and Poland are studied. What we have also assumed is that the undeniable democratic degeneration of the two systems had not reached the extent of that seen in Turkey or Russia, the two countries commonly

7 Levitsky and Way, n. 6, 45.
8 Levitsky and Way, n. 6, 47.
9 L Diamond, "Facing Up to the Democratic Recession", *J. Democracy* 26(142) (2015).
10 Ruprik, n. 5, 133, 77.
11 Bugarić, n. 4, 223; Diamond, n. 9, 148.
12 M Tushnet, "Authoritarian Constitutionalism", *Cornell Law Review* 100 (2015).
13 Blokker, n. 4, 171.
14 D Landau, "Abusive Constitutionalism", *U.C. Davis L. Rev.* 47(189) (2013). Rosalind Dixon and David Landau explain how democratic constitutional borrowing could turn to be an abusive one and where we can detect abusive judicial review in both states. See R Dixon and D Landau, *Abusive Constitutional Borrowing: Legal Globalization and the Subversion of Liberal Democracy* (Oxford University Press, 2021).
15 W Sadurski, "How Democracy Dies (in Poland): A Case Study of Anti-Constitutional Populist Backsliding", *Sydney Law School Legal Studies Research Paper No 18/01* (2018).
16 J Zajadło, Podwójne państwo, http://konstytucyjny.pl/jerzy-zajadlo-podwojne-panstwo/ (20.10.2020).
17 A Bozóki and D Hegedűs, "An Externally Constrained Hybrid Regime: Hungary in the European Union", *Democratization* 25(1173) (2018) 1175.
18 M Bogaards, "De-democratization in Hungary: Diffusely Defective Democracy", *Democratization* 8 (2018) 1491.
19 A Körösényi, G Illés, and A Gyulai, *The Orbán Regime. Plebiscitary Leader Democracy in the Making* (Routledge, 2020).
20 ZS Csaky, *Nations in Transition: Dropping the Democratic Façade* (Freedom House, 2020), https://freedomhouse.org/report/nations-transit/2020/dropping-democratic-facade#Facade. See also Part IV, Limits.

Table II.1 The variety of labels used by scholars for characterizing Hungary and Poland

Who …	*what to call …*	*how …*	*in connection with which country …*	*based on the (conceptual) framework of …*
Wojciech Sadurski	constitutional system	populist authoritarianism (2018)	Poland	liberal constitutionalism (rejection of terms illiberal, democracy, constitutionalism in connection with Hungary)
		plebiscitary autocracy (2018)		Issacharoff (linking completely controlled elections by a party and the plebiscite)
Gábor Attila Tóth	constitutional system	modern authoritarian (2017)	Hungary	liberal constitutionalism
Gábor Halmai	constitutional system	authoritarian totalitarian (2020)	Hungary	liberal constitutionalism (rejection of terms illiberal, democracy, constitutionalism in connection with Hungary)
Kim Lane Scheppele	the law-making practice of autocrats	autocratic legalism (2018)	Hungary Poland	liberal constitutionalism
David Landau	constitutional amendment practice	abusive constitutionalism (2013)	Hungary	comparative constitutional law
Rosalind Dixon and David Landau	constitutional change constitutional justice	abusive constitutional borrowing abusive judicial review	Hungary Poland	comparative constitutional law
Cesare Pinelli	constitutional democracy	competitive authoritarianism (2017)	Hungary, impliedly Poland	Levitsky and Way (competitive authoritarianism) and Zakaria (in opposition to illiberal democracy)

(*Continued*)

Table II.1 (Cont.)

Who …	*what to call …*	*how …*	*in connection with which country …*	*based on the (conceptual) framework of …*
Paul Blokker	constitutional democracy	populist constitutionalism	Hungary, Poland	a form of constitutional critique and "counter-constitutionalism", not a denial of liberal constitutionalism and the Rule of Law. It is related to a Schmittian understanding of the constitution and the Rule of Law. Opposite to democratic constitutionalism
Körösényi András, Gábor Illés, Attila Gyulai	leadership	plebiscitary leader democracy (hybrid regime) (2020)	Hungary	Weber (Weberian model of plebiscitary leader democracy)
Bozóki, Hegedüs	governance	externally constrained hybrid regime (2018)	Hungary	
Matthijs Bogaards	the state of constitutional democracy	diffusely defective democracy (2018) – combining features of exclusive, delegative, illiberal, and tutelary democracy	Hungary	Merkel et al. (defective democracy) BTI Transformation Index
Anna Lührmann, Staffan I Lindberg	process of changes	autocratization in a democracy that has not yet led to a complete breakdown to authoritarianism but where this possibility is still an open question (2019)[21]	Hungary	V-Dem, which is based on Dahl's concept of electoral democracy

Source: authors.

21 In our book, we use "autocratization" and "authoritarianization" in the following way. Autocratization is an antithesis of democratization and features a gradual process that can occur in both autocracies and democracies in a clandestine way. A Lührmann and SI Lindberg, "A Third Wave of Autocratization is Here: What is New About It?"

mentioned together with Hungary and Poland as examples of modern authoritarianism.[22] Therefore, we put forward that, when trying to understand the democratic decay in Hungary and Poland, one should not forget that sometimes the matter of degree is a matter of kind.[23]

Furthermore, we took it as it decisive that Hungary and Poland, due to their EU and CoE membership and their interconnectedness, embrace multilevel constitutionalism to a greater extent than the other two states. Also, insofar as regional community membership is maintained by both parties, for example between the EU and the two states, Hungary and Poland should be considered constitutional democracies even if in a flawed, thin or merely formal version, which we propose to call "illiberal constitutionalism".

We have also assumed that we could consider these factors only if we disentangle liberalism and constitutionalism.

2 *Entangling or disentangling*

The generally and traditionally accepted view of the term "constitutionalism" is that it cannot be anything but liberal, which is why the expression "illiberal constitutionalism" is opposed. Another reason is that constitutionalism entails constraints on public power, which are seen, by liberal constitutionalists, in neither Hungary nor Poland.[24] Consequently, when a state, like Hungary or Poland, fails to display the attributes of its former "liberal" self, and weakens its former constitutionalism along with its constraint on public power, it is called a (modern) authoritarian[25] or anti-democratic regime.[26] Authors usually argue that the term "illiberal", or even "constitutionalism", should not be used; some authors have declared themselves uncertain whether it is still correct to refer to the Hungarian and Polish legal orders as embracing "constitutionalism". It does not strike us as

Democratization 7 (2019) 1097, 1098. Authoritarianization is the autocratization process (cf. autocratization) in a democracy. Authoritarianization is a gradual erosion of democratic norms and practices by democratic leaders, elected at the ballot box through reasonably free and fair elections. E Frantz and A Kendall-Taylor, "The Evolution of Autocracy: Why Authoritarianism is Becoming More Formidable?", *Survival: Global Politics and Strategy* 59 (2017) 57.

22 GA Tóth, "Authoritarianism" in R Grote, F Lachenmann, and R Wolfrum (eds), *Max Planck Encyclopedia of Comparative Constitutional Law* (Oxford Constitutional Law; online resource, 2017); A Puddington, "Breaking Down Democracy: Global Strategies, and Methods of Modern Authoritarians", https://freedomhouse.org/sites/default/files/June2017_FH_Report_Breaking_Down_Democracy.pdf, June 2017. For Turkey, see e.g., M Somer, "Understanding Turkey's Democratic Breakdown: Old vs. New and Indigenous vs. Global Authoritarianism", *Southeast European and Black Sea Studies* 16 (2016) 481–503.

23 Part IV, Limits elaborates on this.

24 For a collection of terms used to describe democratic decay and backsliding, see www.democratic-decay.org/.

25 G Halmai, "Populism, Authoritarianism, and Constitutionalism", *German Law Journal* 20 (2019) 296–313; Tóth, n. 22; Scheppele, n. 2.

26 Sadurski, n. 3, 243.

surprising that our proposed term ("illiberal constitutionalism") has been rejected as a concept or dealt with cautiously. Nevertheless, authors such as Kim Lane Scheppele, Gábor Halmai, and Gábor Attila Tóth either avoid using the term, or, when they do use it, call it an oxymoron or state that "it does not exist".[27] For them, neither Hungary nor Poland is a democracy, nor, from a strictly liberal constitutionalist point of view, can those states be described as constitutionalist. As said, the authors' primary reason is that, for them, constitutionalism is intrinsically liberal; it cannot be anything else. From that perspective, we might even agree that our term could be seen as oxymoronic.

Consequently, many comparative constitutional law scholars tend to see Hungary and Poland as modern authoritarian regimes. For them, constitutionalism, as presented above, is either liberal or non-existent. We do understand their position. It is, however, a predominantly American scholarly view – as we can learn from, for example, Graham Walker.[28] We view constitutionalism differently, as we (Poles and Hungarians) received it as a package as a result of the transition:[29] we, similarly to other non-American scholars, prefer to refer to the constitutionalism that emerged in 1989/1990 as "constitutional democracy", which embodies the Rule of Law, democracy, and human rights at the same time.[30] After the transition, liberal thought – as opposed to the previously socialist one – dominated the discussion.

In our region, where constitutional development has been continually disrupted, democracy and liberalism and constitutionalism did not need to "fight" for prevalence. Addressing issues arising in this region without considering this difference would lead to a simplified and restricted understanding of the recent constitutional remodelling. We could, again, here quote Graham Walker: the conflation of liberalism and constitutionalism "has impoverished the idea of constitutionalism and made it almost impossible to conceive of constitutional

27 See e.g., G Halmai, "The Making of 'Illiberal Constitutionalism' With or Without a New Constitution: The Case of Hungary and Poland" in D Landau and H Lerner (eds), *Comparative Constitution Making* (Edward Elgar, 2019); or "Illiberal Constitutionalism in East-Central Europe", *EUI Working Paper LAW 2019/05.* To our best knowledge, these authors do not engage with the discussion of the term of "illiberal constitutionalism" that has already been used for describing the type of constitutionalism in illiberal polities. In this case, "illiberal" refers to the mere fact that the polity is illiberal. L-A Thio, "Constitutionalism in illiberal polities" in M Rosenfeld and A Sajó (eds), *Oxford Handbook of Comparative Constitutional Law*, Online Publication Date: Nov 2012, DOI: 10.1093/oxfordhb/9780199578610.013.0001.

28 G Walker, "The Idea of Nonliberal Constitutionalism", *Ethnicity and Group Rights* 39 (1997).

29 See in point III below.

30 For further details, see J Elster, "Constitutionalism in Eastern Europe: An Introduction", *The University of Chicago Law Review* 58(2) (1991) 447–482; C Pinelli, "Illiberal Regimes in the Perspective of Comparative Constitutionalism", *Revista di diritti comparati* 1 (2017) 5, 6. This approach also resonates with political science's conceptual framework on defective democracy. See Bogaards, n. 18, 1481–1499, whose framework is Merkel et al., *Defekte Demokratie: Band 1; Merkel et al., Defekte Demokratie: Band 2* (Verlag, 2006).

arrangements that do not pivot on liberal values".[31] Li-Ann Thio, referring to Walters, also reiterates that "liberal constitutionalism is often treated as synonymous with constitutionalism itself";[32] for interrogating the structures, regimes, or polities that are not liberal, the "concepts of constitutionalism and liberalism must be disentangled".[33]

Indeed, we have observed that in both theory (Walker,[34] Tushnet,[35] Thio,[36] Alviar, Frankenberg,[37] Stopler,[38] Ip[39]) and real life (e.g., Hungary, Poland, Israel, Singapore, Hong Kong) this conflation of the notions of constitutionalism and liberalism has become less evident. We could even challenge the view that assumes that both Hungary and Poland accommodated liberal constitutionalism after the transition. This claim could be based on non-liberal values that were inherently present in their constitutionalism in different forms. We could mention, for example, the role of the churches, the limitation test for fundamental rights that has allowed for the consideration of weighting in the constitutional interest and values other than fundamental rights, and the expressed positive obligation of the state to act in promoting rights and liberties. One could identify this as liberal constitutionalism, but "liberalism" in that term should mean "modern liberalism" as opposed to the "classical" version, or we could label it as "mixed constitutionalism".[40] It does not change the fact, however, that until the 21st century liberalism dominated the intellectual mainstream – and in the constitutional courts too. In this book, we do not wish to investigate what we can best call a regime whose demise we have been experiencing since 2010 and 2015. Instead, what we intend to show is that this particular constitutionalism transformed into something qualitatively new, which, for now, appears to be stable. Therefore, when we refer to the transition or pre-2010/2015 era, we will use "liberal constitutionalism" as a descriptive tool.

3 *Words disentangled*

Some scholars[41] have distanced themselves from the view that constitutionalism can only be liberal (e.g., referring to authoritarian constitutionalism, hybrid

31 Walker, n. 28, 164.
32 Thio, n. 27, 133.
33 Thio, n. 27, 134.
34 Walker, n. 28.
35 M Tushnet, "The Possibility of Illiberal Constitutionalism", *Fla L. Rev.* 69 (2017).
36 Thio, n. 27.
37 H Alviar and G Frankenberg (eds), *Authoritarian Constitutionalism* (Edward Elgar, 2019).
38 G Stopler, "Semi-liberal Constitutionalism", *Global Constitutionalism* 8 (2019) 94–122.
39 EC Ip, *Hybrid Constitutionalism: The Politics of Constitutional Review in the Chinese Special Administrative Region* (Cambridge University Press, 2019).
40 Thio, n. 27, 136.
41 See Tushnet, n. 12, n. 35; Alviar and Frankenberg (eds), n. 37. Gingsburg and Huq, *How to Save Constitutional Democracy?* (University of Chicago Press, 2018). Another alternative view can be seen in DS Law, "Alternatives to Liberal Constitutional Democracy", *Md. L. Rev.* 77(223) (2017); BP Frohnen, "Is Constitutionalism Liberal?", *Campbell L. Rev.* 33(529) (2011); JM Farinacci-Fernós, "Post-Liberal Constitutionalism", *Tulsa L. Rev.* 54(1) (2018).

constitutionalism, non-liberal constitutionalism, illiberal constitutionalism in an illiberal polity, semi-liberal constitutionalism, mixed constitutionalism). They do not necessarily claim that the non-liberal version of constitutionalism is normatively attractive, or reject the "ideal-type ideal" of liberal constitutionalism. They do not really confuse constitutionalism with the constitution either – which is the criticism usually voiced by liberal constitutionalists.[42] Instead, they are more open to inviting non-liberal ideas that seem to be normatively acceptable in a polity and could serve as an internal model of justification of a certain type of constitutionalism. Of course, if we believe that constitutionalism can only be "thick" (Tushnet), that is, liberalism is built into the definition, we have to believe that this justification can only be the liberal ideology (liberalism). In this sense, the word "constitutionalism" is related more to a specific ideology and philosophy. Nevertheless, for example, for Louis Henkin, constitutionalism requires the legitimacy that a government enjoys when it acts according to the constitution, checks and balances that limit the room for manoeuvre of the government, judicial review, and human rights.[43] It might follow that liberal constitutionalism does mean not only the ideology, but also the existence of a certain constitutional design. It includes the institutions that have emerged from this ideology (most importantly, check and balances, judicial review, a demand for constraint on public power, inclusion in decision-making processes, etc.).

Tushnet[44] differentiates between "thick constitutionalism" (liberal constitutionalism) and "thin constitutionalism", which include a space for civil society, freedom of expression, the inclusion of people in governmental decisions, through, for example, elections, and the thin concept of the Rule of Law (after Fuller). He attempted to see whether illiberal constitutionalism is theoretically possible. Through exploring settings that represent a moving away from liberal constitutionalism, he concluded that it could be possible, in so far as thin constitutionalism and the thin Rule of Law prevail – in his example, in the case of second-class citizens, as he calls those who are not treated equally by the central state. He adds that one of the major difficulties of the theoretical conceptualization of illiberal constitutionalism is the question of how stable this system might be. Incumbents want to maintain the system, while first-class citizens enjoying full-scale liberal constitutionalism could start to seriously criticize the system. Maintaining power could become difficult without resort to violence; and once violence is used, a slide into authoritarianism is the most probable result, which makes this system prone to (swift) failure. Tushnet notes, thus, that the line between illiberal constitutionalism and authoritarianism is thin.

Walker[45] also warns that non-liberal constitutionalism is inclined to slip into non-constitutionalist illiberalism, which he calls fascism. He proposes that

42 Halmai about Walker in "Illiberal Constitutionalism in East-Central Europe", *EUI Working Paper LAW 2019/05*, 19–20.
43 See e.g., L Henkin, "Constitutionalism, Democracy and Foreign Affairs", *Indiana Law Journal* 4 (1992) 885, 886.
44 Tushnet, n. 35. 1367–1384.
45 Walker, n. 28.

constitutionalism is a broader category than liberal constitutionalism, and conceives of the latter and of non-liberal constitutionalism as subcategories of constitutionalism. In his view, constitutionalism consists of two limits. The first is the structural limit on the power. The second is the normative or aspirational limits, which are the normative frames of reference for intra-polity discussions and which could cover a variety of moralities. The differences, thus, between liberal and non-liberal constitutionalism are threefold. The first is the value source (individual per se vs. individual as a participant in a given system to which allegiance is naturally owed) and, consequently, the difference in the vision of character (liberal vs. non-liberal character). The second is the type of norms that are in focus (liberal norms vs. non-liberal norms). The third is that non-liberal constitutionalism is more local than universal, while the reverse pertains in liberal constitutionalism. Non-liberal constitutionalism, to be able to preserve its constitutionalist status, should be neither "totalist" in its aspirations nor "tyrannist" in its exercise of power.

We might conclude here that "thick constitutionalism" (liberal constitutionalism) is ideologically driven, making it impossible to disentangle constitutionalism from liberalism. In contrast, the idea of non-liberal constitutionalism is less ideology-driven and gives more relevance to constitutional identity and constitutional design. Here, the constitutional design does require a government to be similarly limited by the same sort of tools as are demanded by liberal constitutionalism.

When discussing the term "constitutionalism", we would also recall Walter's view, along with the definitions found in online encyclopaedias, that, in essence, "constitutionalism is about fettered power".[46] In this most restrictive understanding of the term, it translates into the Rule of Law. Unlike Tushnet (see his concept of thick and thin constitutionalism and the role of the Rule of Law), we define the Rule of Law as a thick concept (see in Part IV, Limits), but we do not equate it with either democracy or human rights. We do not deny their intrinsically intertwined nature either. Instead, we base our theory on the term "constitutional democracy" and its constitutive elements. Therefore, if we wish to describe the nature of the constitutionalism that Hungary and Poland have, we need to study what has happened to the Rule of Law, how the weakening of the Rule of Law affected democracy and human rights protection (as they are intertwined), and how (and into what) the remodelling exercise changed the previously existing understanding of (liberal) constitutional democracy, constitutionalism, and human rights commitment, and how these are connected to the constitutional identities of Poles and Hungarians.

4 *Conceptual differences*

As said, we argue that there has been gradualness in the deterioration of the Hungarian and Polish systems, the end of which could be, first, modern and then full-scale or hard authoritarian regimes. Based on qualitative analysis and

46 Walker, n. 28, 164.

quantitative data,[47] we argue that Hungary and Poland are not there yet. We do not claim that the end-game of the populist autocratic leaders is authoritarianism. We merely state the obvious: at the end of any deterioration, one may find authoritarianism. We conceptualize the degree of backsliding against the features of constitutional democracy in two liberal polities, that is, the Hungarian and Polish ones, that, at the determining moment of change (during the transition and on the path to EU membership), showed more commitment towards liberal values (as compared with their unbalanced constitutional identity).

In the following, we engage in finding the conceptual features that distinguish illiberal constitutionalism from the other conceptualizations listed in Table II.1 above.

4.1 … from competitive, modern authoritarianism, authoritarianism, and "illiberal democracy"

The stage at which Hungary and Poland find themselves is certainly "in-between"; thus, it displays some evidence of hybridity. Autocratic practices and authoritarian visions certainly corrupt the formerly and routinely applied mechanisms and institutions. The hybridity itself, though, indicates that we cannot talk about its being the opposite of liberal constitutionalism, that is, authoritarianism or modern authoritarianism. Moreover, categorization as a "hybrid regime" does not tell us much about a regime's essence. For that, we need to investigate to what extent and why the Rule of Law, democracy, and human rights protection have deteriorated. This even more so because political scientists have identified a distinct type of hybrid regime: competitive authoritarianism.[48] Competitive authoritarianism refers to a regime, authoritarianism, that does not organize periodic free and fair elections. Marlies Glasius draws our attention to the fact that "when attempting to investigate all authoritarian regimes … scholars still fall back on classic definitions of *democracy*, as formulated by Schumpeter and Dahl, to delineate their field".[49] He recalls Jason Brownlee[50] when he writes that even though the Dahl-based formulation explains more about what authoritarianism is actually like, and gives rise to in-between categories such as hybrid regimes or defective democracies, the "'core is still the vacuum', since the definition continues to rely on absence, on lack of elections and freedoms, rather than on a positive definition of what authoritarianism actually is and what it does".[51]

47 Both in this Part of the book and in Part IV, Constraints.
48 S Levitsky and LA Way, "The Rise of Competitive Authoritarianism", *Journal of Democracy* 2 (2002).
49 M Glasius, "What Authoritarianism Is … and Is Not: A Practical Perspective", *International Affairs* 3 (2018) 519.
50 J Brownlee, "Authoritarianism After 1989", *Harvard International Review* 4 (2010).
51 Glasius, n. 49, 519. Lately, a different term has been suggested to cover regimes from hybrid to authoritarian, that is "new despotism", John Keane, *New Despotism* (Harvard University Press, 2020).

When it comes to the conceptualization of competitive authoritarianism (Levitsky and Way) and that of authoritarianism by comparative constitutional scholars (Ginsburg and Huq, Halmai, Tóth), Glasius is only partly right. These concepts do give a positive definition of what the term comprises. However, we do not think that they can serve as a useful conceptual framework for analysing and understanding the constitutional changes in Hungary and Poland. We claim that, despite the continuous backsliding and more and more ways of institutional dismantling, the turn to authoritarianism has not yet happened.

Discussing the differences between liberal constitutional democracy and competitive authoritarianism, Ginsburg and Huq describe pure authoritarian regimes as occurring in countries where there is a complete absence of effective political competition and power cannot be lost in elections. At the same time, however, there is a written constitution, courts, and other Rule-of-Law accoutrements.[52] Gábor Attila Tóth contrasts authoritarian constitutional systems with illiberal democracies and liberal autocracies, and admits that there are no conceptual criteria for distinguishing these systems from one another. Still, he lists five defining elements of authoritarianism (authoritarian ruler, façade constitution, hegemonic voting practices, shortfall of institutional checks, and restricted individual and collective rights),[53] which partly coincide with the description given by Arch Puddington (below). Gábor Attila Tóth thus also defines authoritarianism by referring to an absence.[54] Still, his definition further covers value and institutional preferences, such as official ideology, or traditional norms of a certain religion, a pragmatic decision-making style, and unconstrained and indefinite competences allocated to the executive either formally or informally. Modern authoritarianism is a regime that is the contemporary counterpart of the historical authoritarianism.[55] Puddington refers to previously authoritarian regimes that have engaged in liberalizing measures as a strategic approach towards enhancing their legitimacy and retaining the power to engage with an international order. While writing about goals, strategies, and methods of modern authoritarians, he discusses Hungary and Poland, along with Russia, Turkey, China, calling them illiberal democracies.[56] Puddington defines modern authoritarianism as the 21st-century, more enlightened version of the authoritarianism of the previous century, in terms of its pretension to be something else, especially being less authoritarian. He also admits that the modern authoritarian systems sometimes revert to the methods applied by

52 T Ginsburg and AZ Huq, *How to Save Constitutional Democracy?* (University of Chicago Press, 2018) 22–23.

53 Tóth, n. 22.

54 “Narrowed political pluralism, absent or inadequate democratic institutions, denied or unenforceable fundamental rights, lack or shortfall of constitutional checks and balances, and oppression of non-governmental-organizations.” Tóth, n. 22.

55 Tóth, n. 22.

56 A Puddington/Freedom House, *Breaking Down Democracy: Goals, Strategies, and Methods of Modern Authoritarians* (Freedom House, June 2017). See also, Tóth, n. 22.

their former counterparts.[57] Both authors, thus, provide quite an extensive conceptual framework for theorising the systems that Hungary and Poland are nurturing, and seem to include these countries under the label (modern) authoritarianism.

Günter Frankenberg views authoritarianism as a wide range of autocratic practices that combine to create regimes of governance, and marks the distinguishing elements of authoritarian constitutionalism. These include authoritarian political technology and constitutional opportunism, power as private property, participation as complicity, and a culture of immediacy. For him, Hungary's regime, Orbánism, is to be viewed only as a "temptation of authoritarianism",[58] with which view we wholeheartedly agree. Similarly, Lührmann and Lindberg have assessed the deterioration in Hungary as an autocratization process in a democracy that has not (yet) led to complete breakdown, that is, the turn to autocracy has not happened yet. They also note that it is an open question whether this turn will occur in the future.[59] Lührmann and Lindberg describe the democratic erosion as a tactic in the autocratization process in democracies, similar to the constituent elements of modern authoritarianism: power is legally accessed, there is a legal façade, and democratic norms are substantially undermined without abolishing key democratic institutions. The overlapping of the conceptualizations of Tóth, and Lührmann and Lindberg, and the apparent tension between them are not caused by their different methodologies and perspectives alone but by the binary code necessitated by thick constitutionalism (its "entangled" nature).

Levitsky and Way explain that competitive authoritarian regimes must be distinguished from democracy and full-scale authoritarianism.[60] When talking about

57 There is, for instance, economic openness and, to a certain extent, pluralist media, political competition, civil society and the Rule of Law. There is also, however, retained or direct control of the economy or media outlets, co-opted political opposition, the legal harassment of politicians, and the employment of instruments for keeping a close watch on civil society as a (almost) daily practice. Puddington, n. 56.

58 G Frankenberg, "Authoritarian Constitutionalism: Coming to Terms with Modernity's Nightmares" in H Alviar and G Frankenberg (eds), *Authoritarian Constitutionalism* (Edward Elgar, 2019) 18–24, 36.

59 Lührmann and Lindberg, n. 21. 1097, 1098–1099.

60 Distinction from democracy: "Although elections are regularly held and are generally free of massive fraud, incumbents routinely abuse state resources, deny the opposition adequate media coverage, harass opposition candidates and their supporters, and in some cases manipulate electoral results. Journalists, opposition politicians, and other government critics may be spied on, threatened, harassed, or arrested. Members of the opposition may be jailed, exiled, or – less frequently – even assaulted or murdered." Distinction from full-scale authoritarianism: "Although incumbents in competitive authoritarian regimes may routinely manipulate formal democratic rules, they are unable to eliminate them or reduce them to a mere façade. Rather than openly violating democratic rules (for example, by banning or repressing the opposition and the media), incumbents are more likely to use bribery, co-optation, and more subtle forms of persecution, such as the use of tax authorities, compliant judiciaries, and other state agencies to 'legally' harass, persecute, or extort cooperative behavior from critics. Yet even if the cards are stacked in favor of autocratic incumbents, the persistence of meaningful democratic institutions creates arenas through which opposition forces

the latter, they rely heavily on a democracy concept. In our view, even if Hungary is now labelled a hybrid system,[61] this label only qualifies the democracy component of constitutional democracy (liberal constitutionalism), that is, its diminishing content. For this component we suggest the term "illiberal democracy"[62] – another expression that more often than not[63] faces rejection in the literature. For instance, Halmai calls "illiberal democracy" an oxymoron,[64] and Pinelli views it as a misnomer. Pinelli argues that the term suggests that illiberal democracy is substantially democratic despite its being illiberal. Pinelly thus advises the use of the term "competitive authoritarian system" instead.[65] Our illiberal democracy concept, however, is not restricted to electoral democracy issues, including party system and media coverage implications, which are the cornerstones of the term "democracy".[66] Even if it were so, we still could not use the general label "competitive authoritarian system" for Hungary and Poland, as they have not seemed, so far, to feature all the criteria required for a competitive authoritarian system. Besides, they do not share the constitutional development of states in relation to the term that was introduced by Levitsky and Way.[67] Illiberal democracy, as we see it, also covers[68] the wider non-involvement of people in public discourse and its causes. We find these causes in the rise of nationalist populism and the value-orientation of the population, which is connected to their national and constitutional identities. The term "illiberal democracy" indeed has a democratic bias: it seeks to remind us that a fully-fledged democracy has been transforming into something else, and not that something else has been transforming into a fully-fledged democracy – which has given rise to the creation of the term "competitive authoritarianism". Besides, membership of the EU is a strong argument also in this case.[69]

may – and frequently do – pose significant challenges. As a result, even though democratic institutions may be badly flawed, both authoritarian incumbents and their opponents must take them seriously." Levitsky and Way, n. 48, 53, 54.

61 Poland is still recognized as a democracy; however, it dropped from being a consolidated democracy in 2019 to a semi-consolidated democracy in 2020.

62 See also Part V, Limits.

63 Puddington uses the term. Puddington, n. 56.

64 G Halmai, "Illiberal Constitutionalism in East-Central Europe", *EUI Working Paper LAW 2019/05*, 20.

65 Pinelli, n. 30.

66 Modern democratic regimes all meet four minimum criteria: 1) executives and legislatures are chosen through elections that are open, free, and fair; 2) virtually all adults possess the right to vote; 3) political rights and civil liberties are broadly protected, including freedom of the press, freedom of association, and freedom to criticize the government without reprisal; and 4) elected authorities possess real authority to govern, in that they are not subject to the tutelary control of military or clerical leaders. Levitsky and Way, n. 48, 53.

67 Levitsky and Way, n. 48, 51.

68 We do not use the term to indicate the violation of civil liberties, as seems to be the case in the concept of "diffusely defective democracy". Bogaards, n. 18, 1487.

69 See Part IV, Limits.

Comparative constitutional law scholars label the democratic decay in Hungary as "modern authoritarianism", while Poland's anti-democratic regimes have been referred to as "populist authoritarianism" or "plebiscitary autocracy". For the sake of terminological clarity, we propose a more nuanced approach instead of these categorizations and the suggestion of calling Hungary and Poland's regimes "competitive authoritarianism" or "modern authoritarianism".[70] The term "illiberal constitutionalism" captures, on the one hand, an illiberalization process (authoritarianization or autocratization in a democracy), which is a thicker understanding of democratic recession or erosion, as it also indicates a distancing from the previously accepted liberal values and understanding of constitutional affairs. On the other hand, it also means a concept in which we can find certain constraints and which is informed by a unique constitutional identity.

4.2 … *from mixed and hybrid and authoritarian constitutionalism*

Mixed constitutionalism has not been discussed in the literature as illiberal constitutionalism that is accommodated in an illiberal polity but as a term that juxtaposes liberal and non-liberal principles and institutions, for example, as in the case of the German Basic Law. Mixed constitutionalism is used for describing post-Communist East European constitutions, where it has been used as a moderating strategy.[71] It is also connected to a society with a strong illiberal orientation that incorporates some liberal values in its non-liberal constitutions.[72] In the first decade of the 21st century, Hungary and Poland could still fit into this category, but this term fails to grasp the process and the result of the remodelling that at the time of writing has been going on for a decade in Hungary and for five years in Poland. Nevertheless, it could describe constitutionalism in the East Asian context, where mixed constitutionalism is "neither wholly liberal nor wholly Confucian".[73]

Hybrid constitutionalism is connected to the constitutional system of Hong Kong, which is described as not fully democratic (the Chief Executive is selected by a pro-Beijing committee; only half the legislature is returned by direct elections, the other half by pro-Beijing functional constituencies), but where, at least up to 2020,[74] human rights were generally and rigorously protected and the Rule of Law was in place.[75] In contrast, in Hungary and Poland, parliaments are directly

70 Indices seem to support our position (Part IV).
71 Thio, n. 27, 136.
72 Walker, n. 28.
73 BN Son, *Confucian Constitutionalism in East Asia* (Routledge, 2016) 174.
74 www.hrw.org/news/2020/07/29/china-new-hong-kong-law-roadmap-repression. https://thediplomat.com/2020/08/hong-kongs-cancelled-elections-paved-the-way-for-the-latest-arrests/
75 C Chan, "Thirty Years from Tiananmen: China, Hong Kong, and the Ongoing Experiment to Preserve Liberal Values in an Authoritarian State", *International Journal of Constitutional Law* 17(2) (2019) 443. EC Ip, *Hybrid Constitutionalism: The Politics of Constitutional Review in the Chinese Special Administrative Region* (Cambridge University Press, 2019).

elected by voters while the Rule of Law is degraded, and one can see serious irregularities in human rights protection.

In authoritarian constitutionalism, as Tushnet explains, liberal freedoms are protected at an intermediate level, elections are reasonably free and fair, and there is a normative commitment to constraints on public power. Against this background, Tushnet differentiates between the abusive constitutionalism of Hungary and the authoritarian constitutionalism of Singapore. He speculates that the "normative commitment to constraints on public power", which he extracted from the "description of how constitutionalism operates in Singapore, might be a truly distinguishing characteristic of authoritarian constitutionalism".[76] One can argue, however, that a "normative commitment to constraints on public power" is somewhat missing in Poland and Hungary. Exercise of public power remains almost unconstrained; political leaders do not respect the idea of constitutionalism.[77] Nevertheless, the system they have must respect, to the extent desirable, EU law, which apparently functions as an internal and implied constraint. If we consider EU law as part of the legal systems of the Member States, any constraint on its daily application, at politically irrelevant or less relevant levels, and possible influence on the populist agenda, needs to be seen as an internal, constitutional constraint.[78] This type of constraint only exists within the EU. Thus, based on Tushnet's position, the new systems in Hungary and Poland cannot be labelled authoritarian constitutionalism.

4.3 … from populist constitutionalism

As far as populist constitutionalism is concerned, as advocated by, for example, Paul Blokker and Jan-Werner Müller,[79] we would not consider it a legal concept but mainly a sociological phenomenon. As such, it is a sociological characteristic of the constitutional system and forms the sociological basis for either an illiberal or an authoritarian regime. Populism is a political program, movement, ideology,

76 Tushnet, n. 12.

77 It is shown in the indexes as well if one compares the Rule-of-Law commitment of Singapore, with a global rank of 13, and Hong Kong, with a global rank of 16, with that of Poland (global rank of 27) and Hungary (global rank of 57). These figures changed in 2020, as follows: Singapore, 12; Hong Kong, 16; Hungary, 60; Poland, 51. World Justice Project, *Rule of Law Index 2019* (2019), https://worldjusticeproject.org/sites/default/files/documents/WJP-ROLI-2019-Single%20Page%20View-Reduced_0.pdf; World Justice Project, *Rule of Law Index 2020* (2020), https://worldjusticeproject.org/our-work/research-and-data/wjp-rule-law-index-2020. See more in Part IV, Limits.

78 It could be viewed as external constraint if we take a more nationalistic perspective; but it would not make any difference to its meaning.

79 See e.g. Blokker, n. 1; P Blokker, "Populist Constitutionalism, Popular Engagement, and Constitutional Resistance", https://reconnect-europe.eu/blog/blokker-populist-constitutionalism/, 7 February 2019; JW Müller, "Populism and Constitutionalism" in C Rovira Kaltwasser et al. (eds), *The Oxford Handbook on Populism* (Oxford University Press, 2017).

worldview, a governing style, or a rhetoric about legitimate authority and where power should lie.[80] It is also viewed as a form of extreme majoritarianism, being democratic but not liberal democratic, a critique of elites, and a claim to be the sole, authentic representative of a single, homogeneous, authentic people.[81] It could lead to authoritarianism,[82] which is considered a "bad" regime. Likewise, from a liberal perspective we could distinguish "bad" populism, a demand for popular hegemony, from "good" populism, which is a critique of under-inclusiveness and under-representation.[83]

It follows that "populist constitutionalism" is, again, a contested concept, which, instead of describing a distinct form of constitutionalism, indicates a "populist approach to constitutionalism"[84] and constitutions.[85] The ideology and governing style of the leaders are at the core of "populist constitutionalism", which makes it more of a sociological than a legal phenomenon – it is different from our more constitutional law- and constitutional studies-oriented approach.

The populist attitude of rulers is a tool to gain popular support for them to govern and achieve either "bad" or "good" policy goals. What helps them achieve their goals is the rhetoric, which claims that legitimate authority flows directly from the people and points to an enemy, who happens to be the corrupt (former) "establishment" that has betrayed the public trust.[86] Later, to maintain power, this "enemy" will be any group that is different from the current populist establishment and against which the people need to be protected.[87] Nevertheless, and this is what we focus on more in this book, populist leaders still need to transform[88] the system peacefully. They do it within the framework of a broader and

80 See e.g., P Norris, "Measuring Populism Worldwide", *Harvard Kennedy School, Faculty Research Working Paper Series RWP 20–002*, 2.

81 See Populism, www.democratic-decay.org/index; P Norris, "Is Western Democracy Backsliding? Diagnosing the Risk", *Journal of Democracy* 28(2) (2017) 14–15; C Mudde and C Rovira Kaltwasser, *Populism: A Very Short Introduction* (Oxford University Press, 2017) 34; JW Müller, *What is Populism?* (University of Pennsylvania Press, 2016) 3, respectively.

82 Mudde and Kaltwasser, n. 81, 34; Norris, n. 81, 15.

83 R Howse, "Populism and its Enemies", *Workshop on Public Law and the New Populism*, Jean Monnet Center, NYU Law School, 15–16 September 2017; M Tushnet and B Bugaric, *Populism and Constitutionalism: An Essay on Definitions and Their Implications* (21 April 2020), http://nrs.harvard.edu/urn-3:HUL.InstRepos:42660123

84 This seems to be evident from scholarly works, even if authors do not explicitly admit it. See e.g. Blokker, n. 79 (2017 and 2019) and Müller, n. 81.

85 D Landau, "Populist constitutions", *University of Chicago Law Review* 85 (2018) 521.

86 Norris, n. 81, 3.

87 See e.g., the Polish and Hungarian rhetoric against the "enemies" of the state and nation, such as George Soros, migrants, and sometimes Brussels.

88 As Pippa Norris explains: "In the political sphere, the rhetoric claims that legitimacy lies with the 'people', a powerful claim echoing core democratic values. In practice, however, the language may often be weaponized as a façade by strongman leaders with authoritarian values who claim a direct mandate to act on behalf of 'the people' while they actively seek to dismantle checks and balances on executive power. This

supranational community, and with the support of the people through legal measures, such as adopting a new constitution, creating an invisible constitution, and introducing retrograde abusive amendments and unconstitutional legislation, just as happened in Hungary and Poland. This leads us to the investigation of other terms, such as "abusive constitutionalism", "abusive legalism", and "autocratic legalism".

4.4 … from constitutionalism with other adjectives

For us, abusive constitutionalism is not a separate type of constitutionalism, for two reasons.[89] First, it simply means the use of mechanisms of constitutional change to erode the democratic order[90] (as happened in Hungary[91]), and seems to be contrary to "the orthodox view of constitutionalism", which, besides being a complex liberal ideology and practice, requires effective constraints on public power.[92] Second, abusive constitutionalism is about, among other things, the successful use of unconstitutional constitutional amendments. The constitution thus does not include any constraint on public power, which is the prerequisite for the title "constitutionalism". Combined with a populist leader, the term "populist constitutionalism" can also be criticized on this very account.

Both abusive legalism and autocratic legalism, similarly to abusive constitutionalism, refer to the use of law by autocratic leaders in a particular constitutional system. Abusive legalism, as Cheung describes it, features in Singapore and Hong Kong, where ordinary law is used in a way that seems to be consistent with the formal and procedural aspects of the Rule of Law but in order to frustrate the latter and consolidate power.[93] Autocratic legalism in Venezuela, according to Corrales, embodies the use (enacting laws empowering the executive), abuse (inconsistent and biased implementation of laws), and non-use of the law in the service of the executive branch.[94] Scheppele uses the term to describe how

includes attacking the legitimacy of elected representatives and political opponents, as well as the courts, judges, and rule of law, state officials and mainstream media, along with the broader range of policy technocrats, professional think tanks, academic opinion-formers, and scientific consultants." Norris, n. 81, 3.

89 The content of abusive constitutionalism is viewed as illiberal constitutionalism by Pablo Castillo-Ortiz, but he uses the term interchangeably with illiberalism. Castillo-Ortiz, "The Illiberal Abuse of Constitutional Courts in Europe", *European Constitutional Law Review* 15(1) (2019) 48–72.

90 Landau, n. 14.

91 T Drinóczi, "Constitutional Politics in Contemporary Hungary", *Vienna Journal on International Constitutional Law* 1 (2016) 63–98.

92 Frankenberg, n. 58, 7; W Waluchow, "Constitutionalism" in EN Zalta (ed), *The Stanford Encyclopedia of Philosophy* (Spring 2018 Edition), https://plato.stanford.edu/archives/spr2018/entries/constitutionalism/; R Bellamy, "Constitutionalism", www.britannica.com/topic/constitutionalism

93 A Cheung, "'For My Enemies, the Law': Abusive Legalism", *Candidacy Paper, JSD Program, NYU School of Law*, 15 January 2018.

94 J Corrales, "The Authoritarian Resurgence: Autocratic Legalism in Venezuela", *Journal of Democracy* 26 (2015) 38–43.

consolidated democracies, especially Hungary, are turning to "autocratic constitutionalism", without revealing the content of this term. She explains how "legalistic autocrats" use mainly constitutional law to hollow out the democratic system, not only in Hungary but in Turkey as well. She further shows how they borrow tactics from one another.[95]

These terms and their conceptualization offer a valuable contribution to the description of how illiberal constitutionalism or degradation to an authoritarian system (Venezuela) has been achieved, or how autocrats like sharing their experiences but say little about the systems created.

4.5 … from the dual state

Jerzy Zajadło,[96] embarking on a theoretical adventure, asks the question whether a dual state exists in Poland or not. He uses Ernst Fraenkel's concept, built on the Nazi regime operating under the Weimar Constitution, which assumes the simultaneous existence of two distinct states. One is "normative" and the other is "prerogative". In the first, the administrative and judicial bureaucracies operate according to rules (to protect the legal order as expressed in legislation, decisions of the courts, and decisions of administrative bodies); while in the second, the party operates free of any ultimate legal restraint – there are no rules operating on the political sphere, so the jurisdiction of party and state officials is not subject to general regulation.[97]

We appreciate the comparison of Polish events with those that led Ernst Fraenkel to construct the concept of a dual state. We can also report that the observations of Polish academia sometimes go even further and acknowledge the alteration of constitutional bodies and the establishment of "parallel public institutions" (judges of the CT, vice-president of the CT, president of the Supreme Court, National Council of Radio Broadcasting and Television).[98]

In our opinion, however, the Poland that operates under the informally changed Constitution 1997 and the Hungary that operates under the Fundamental Law (FL)[99] qualify neither as dual states, nor as ones in which parallel institutions have emerged. What is observable in Hungary and Poland is that there are rules on the political sphere (power was not grabbed in an emergency), and we can also observe some constraint on powers due to membership of the EU and CoE. The state structures are indeed compromised, infiltrated, and occupied by the ruling parties (Fidesz and PiS) and their members, without, however, doubling the

95 The expression "autocratic constitutionalism" appears only in the abstract. Scheppele, n. 2, 545, 550–552, 571–581.

96 Zajadło, n. 16.

97 E Fraenkel, *The Dual State: A Contribution to the Theory of Dictatorship* (Oxford University Press, 1941) 3–7, https://archive.org/details/in.ernet.dli.2015.13142/page/n1/mode/1up

98 M Bernatt and M Ziółkowski, "Statutory Anti-Constitutionalism", *Wash. Int'l L.J.* 28 (487) (2019) 505–516.

99 See more on this in Part VI, Stability.

institutions. Therefore, the day-to-day practice of every state organ is more subordinate to partisan expectations than to constitutional rules and values. Yet these expectations are more usually than not translated into legal measures (in both states), or appear in the invisible abstract constitutional norms (Poland). In the case of both Hungary and Poland, the dual state concept might describe better a socialist totalitarian state, rather than being a crucial phenomenon of the recent changes.

II Illiberal(ism)

We use "illiberal" to qualify both constitutionalism and one of its components, democracy. The "illiberal" component of our terms has not really been explored in the literature[100] either – because, to the best of our knowledge, the term "illiberal constitutionalism" itself (connected to Poland and Hungary) has not been contested with arguments that go beyond mere denial. "Illiberal democracy", however, as can be seen above, has been viewed through the lens of illiberal regimes and illiberal polities. As said, Pinelli rejects the use of the term "illiberal democracy" and proposes "competitive authoritarian regime" instead.

1 Illiberal polity and constitutionalism

Thio, on the other hand, identifies illiberal polities, which could be "illiberal, preliberal, non-liberal, or semi-liberal societies, producing 'communitarian' and 'theocratic' forms of constitutionalism".[101] It is argued that the main features of illiberal polities and illiberal constitutionalism are that: (1) there is a common enemy, that is, liberal constitutionalism; (2) there are limiting constitutive norms; and (3) the state is expressly non-neutral, privileging a substantive vision of the good, informed by ethnicity, religious or communal morality. Therefore, illiberal constitutionalism is a conceptual framework already developed for illiberal polities, that is, Islamic constitutionalism, and in polities where the community plays a role in forming personal identity and moral choice[102] – which belongs to the "non-Western type cultures", including legal culture, as well. We can agree that neither the Hungarian nor the Polish polity is like these. In both polities, there is a strong feeling of belonging to the Western world and culture (with its individualistic approach), despite the wildly developed illiberal value preferences (hierarchy, majoritarianism and family). Value-orientation studies, history, historical and emotional trajectories present in different narratives, and social psychology interrogations of emotions over the past couple of years prove our point.[103]

The word "illiberal" in the term "illiberal constitutionalism", as we use it, does not explicitly refer to the quality of polities; instead, it expresses the U-turn in the

100 Tushnet stayed in the arena of theoretical thinking. Tushnet, n. 35.
101 Thio, n. 27, 134.
102 Thio, n. 27, 138–143.
103 See Part III, Identity.

constitutional development of Hungary and Poland in the context of the EU that has been allowed by the constitutional and national identities of Hungarians and Poles, informed by their historical experiences and emotional trajectories. "Illiberal" means for us, first and foremost, that the three pillars of the formerly existing constitutional democracy (the Rule of Law, democracy, and human rights protection) have eroded to a palpable extent. Constitutional courts that were established to protect settings of liberal constitutionalism have become servants of the politicians rather than custodians of the constitution, and operate within the concept of illiberal judicialization of politics. As for the polity, "illiberal" indicates that illiberal constitutionalism can be established in a polity that is susceptible to transformative change in a less liberal (illiberal) direction (e.g., people are more willing to trade off their liberties) by manipulative and populist-nationalist rhetoric expressed by a charismatic leader. "Illiberal" also means that there are illiberal practices connected to human rights, such as prioritizing the rights of the community (majority) over minority rights, making the recognition of human rights conditional on the fulfilment of civic duties, a communitarian vision, a less egalitarian perspective. Even if the Hungarian and Polish remodelling does not mean that these are polities in which "the community plays a role in forming personal identity and moral choice",[104] this is what populist autocratic leaders intend to introduce in a top-down manner, or, rather, appeal to, enlarge and trigger an already existing illiberal value-orientation. As it turns out, society is not entirely averse to this – as has been evidenced in the elections since 2010 (Hungary) and 2015 (Poland).

2 *Illiberal in the term "illiberal constitutionalism"*

2.1 *The origin*

Political slogans such as "an illiberal democracy is being built"[105] appeared and led to the reformation and demolition of the formerly existing Hungarian and Polish constitutional and legal frameworks.

The choice of the word "illiberal" is based on a speech by the Hungarian Prime Minister, Viktor Orbán, which was later, in terms of content, used by the leader of the PiS, Jarosław Kaczyński, in Poland as well. Even if Kaczyński did not describe his vision of the new Polish system as illiberal, he said that "there will be Budapest in Warsaw",[106] expressing his willingness to follow Orbán's vision as much as possible.

104 Thio (n. 27) on illiberal constitutionalism in illiberal polities.

105 Prime Minister Viktor Orbán's Speech at the 25th Bálványos Summer Free University and Student Camp, Tusnádfürdő (Băile Tuşnad) on 26 July 2014, www.kormany.hu/en/the-prime-minister/the-prime-minister-s-speeches/prime-minister-viktor-orban-s-speech-at-the-25th-balvanyos-summer-free-university-and-student-camp

106 This is what he said in 2011 when the Law and Justice Party, PiS, lost the parliamentary election, *see Przyjdzie dzień, że w Warszawie będzie Budapeszt*, TVN24 (9 October 2011), www.tvn24.pl/wiadomosci-z-kraju,3/przyjdzie-dzien-ze-w-warszawie-bedzie-budap

Orbán, in 2014, told his audience that he envisions "an illiberal state, a non-liberal state [that] does not reject the fundamental principles of liberalism such as freedom … but it does not make this ideology the central element of state organisation, but instead includes a different, special, national approach". He mentioned that liberal doctrine holds that "everything is permitted that is not forbidden", while illiberal doctrine says "don't do what you don't want to be done to you".[107] Orbán used the expression "illiberal state", referred to the concept that democracy can be illiberal, and later used it to legitimize the constitutional remodelling in his political communication.[108] The term "illiberal democracy", described by Fareed Zakaria[109] as another but alarming possibility in the path of constitutional and democratic development,[110] was thus used and revitalized by the Hungarian Prime Minister as an adaptable and desirable version of democracy. We simply regard it as a political slogan, which we borrow and try to conceptualize from a constitutional law perspective. For us, the term expresses the main idea of how Orbán's and Kaczyński's states work, and how this political declaration led to the reformation and demolition of the formerly existing Hungarian and Polish legal frameworks. The fact that Orbán began to use the term "Christian democracy" instead of "illiberal democracy" in 2019[111] does not affect the core of his vision and political endeavour, nor the direction of the remodelling exercise.

Nevertheless, Jan-Werner Müller, in the context of systemic degradation of Hungarian and Polish constitutionalism, opposes the term "illiberal" and suggests "undemocratic" instead.[112] What he describes as the problem with the term "illiberal democracy", that is, it is used to justify the "undemocratic" actions of governments, such as the attack on democracy's very foundations – assembly, media and thus hindering political opposition – is indeed a problem. However, these governments are not acting in an undemocratic way. Democratic mechanisms are used, democratic rules are observed – at least formally – and political

eszt,186922.html;www.ft.com/content/0a3c7d44-b48e-11e5-8358-9a82b43f6b2f. After 2015, when PiS won the election, it was made clear that the expression was not restricted to the election result but had become a programme, Program PiS 2014, Law & Justice 7, 12 (31 October 2017), http://pis.org.pl/dokumenty

107 Orbán, n. 108. The features of this politics are collected by Gábor Halmai in G Halmai, "Illiberalism in East-Central Europe", *EUI Working Paper LAW* 2019/05, 2–12.

108 Orbán, n. 105.

109 "Democratically elected regimes, often ones that have been reelected or reaffirmed through referenda, are routinely ignoring constitutional limits on their power and depriving their citizens of basic rights and freedoms." F Zakaria, "The Rise of Illiberal Democracy", *Foreign Affairs* 6 (1997) 22; F Zakaria, *The Future of Freedom: Illiberal Democracy at Home and Abroad* (W. W. Norton and Company, 2007).

110 Zakaria, n. 109 (1997), 24.

111 Orbán's full speech at Tusványos: political philosophy, upcoming crisis and projects for the next 15 years, 29 July 2019, https://visegradpost.com/en/2019/07/29/orbans-full-speech-at-tusvanyos-political-philosophy-upcoming-crisis-and-projects-for-the-next-15-years/

112 J-W Müller, *The Problem With "Illiberal Democracy"*, Soc. Eur. (27 January 2016), www.socialeurope.eu/the-problem-with-illiberal-democracy

actors and governments have legitimacy as well. If we get rid of the terms "illiberalism" and "democracy", the observance of formal democratic rules and others that we discuss in this book does not seem to be taken into consideration. What Müller sees as undemocratic is rather, from a legal perspective,[113] unconstitutional but democratic in a formal sense.[114] In our theory, however, illiberal democracy, as a version of democracy, is only one component of illiberal constitutionalism. Illiberal constitutionalism refers not only to the fact that democratically elected leaders misuse their power; it also encompasses the almost smooth and undisturbed remodelling of the entire liberal constitutional system (constitutional democracy) within a European cultural and legal community represented by the Western ideal of legal and democratic development that appears under the aegis of the CoE and, most prominently, the EU. Illiberal constitutionalism is characterized by an illiberal type of democracy (as opposed to liberal democracy, which implies competitive and repetitive elections, inclusion, respect of political and other related rights, etc.), misuse of the language of human rights (as opposed to the theory of human rights that implies individualism and protection of group rights, high respect for human dignity and equality, inclusion, institutional and procedural protection against the state and any actors having actual power over the individual), and an illiberal version of the Rule of Law, which we propose should be called "illiberal legality". For that, an illiberal constitution is essential in the form of either a formal new constitution – like the Hungarian FL – or an informal one – like the Polish informally changed, invisible constitution, which is preferred to the 1997 Constitution. These constitutions and the system they remodel create governance and a constitutional culture that acts against formally accepted liberal values and the ideals of constitutionalism. Indeed, they embrace and transmit illiberal values, based on which illiberal constitutionalism emerges by disrupting the structures and mechanisms of the former substantive constitutional democracy. Illiberalism, in this sense, is both the Hungarian and Polish governance itself and its ideological base,[115] which is accompanied by an unbalanced constitutional identity and the longing for a charismatic leader.

2.2 *Identity and leader*

The coincidence of many factors prompts the association of the adjective "illiberal" with constitutionalism in Hungary and Poland. The first of these is the

113 What makes a constitutional law analysis difficult, however, is that what is evidently unconstitutional will not necessarily be declared unconstitutional by a constitutional court. This disagreement on the constitutionality of a law goes beyond the usual disagreements that we experience regarding court decisions. Thus, unconstitutionality may be upheld in a constitutional way. On the paradox of constitutional amendments, see Part VI.

114 It is thus clear that legal and the political analysis are often interwoven, but in this book, we give more weight to the legal analysis.

115 Slightly differently, see L Csink, "Rule of Law in Hungary: What Can Law and Politics Do?" in T Drinóczi and A Bień-Kacała (eds), *Rule of Law, Common Values and Illiberal Constitutionalism. Poland and Hungary within the European Union* (Routledge, 2020).

vector of changes coupled with strong opposition to, even rejection of, the formerly employed liberal values and the acceptance of an illiberal way of doing things. The second is the historical and still present longing for a charismatic leader. This leader, right now, happens to be a populist, nationalist and autocratic leader who is able to address and capture the unbalanced constitutional identity and, thus, offer visions and justifications with which people can easily identify, or that appeal to their nonchalance.

The "illiberal" part of the term "illiberal constitutionalism" thus neither refers directly to the polity itself (like in Thio's work) nor entails a coherent political philosophy – despite the attempts in works written by pro-government scholars (e. g., political constitutionalism, which is addressed in Part VI on "Stability"). Instead, what we see is a patchwork of some components of some (political) philosophy (e.g., communitarianism, conservativism, political realism and pragmatism, neoliberalism) and ideologies (e.g., nationalism)[116] – all of them being heavily influenced and determined by right-wing populism and identity politics. The adaptive ground for these is the unbalanced constitutional identity, the illiberal value-orientation, and the emotional trajectories of Poles and Hungarians: they, in their desire to reach genuine independence and sovereignty, are

116 For the presence of these terms, see, e.g., A Buzogány and M Varga, "The Ideational Foundations of the Illiberal Backlash in Central and Eastern Europe: The Case of Hungary", *Review of International Political Economy* 25(6) (2018) 811–828 (political illiberalism in the region has intellectual underpinnings in the Western critique of liberalism, the assumption of the lack of willingness of the post-communist liberals of breaking with the past); P Stubbs and N Lendvai-Bainton, "Authoritarian Neoliberalism, Radical Conservativism and Social Policy within the European Union: Croatia, Hungary and Poland", *Development and Change* 51(2) (2019) 554; and A Fabry, *The Political Economy of Hungary: From State Capitalism to Authoritarian Neoliberalism* (Springer, 2019) (authoritarian neoliberalism); G Sheiring, www.tni.org/en/article/hungarys-regime-is-proof-that-capitalism-can-be-deeply-authoritarian (authoritarian capitalism); G Halmai, "Illiberalism in East-Central Europe", *EUI Department of Law Research Paper No. 2019/05* (on ideas of the idealogues of the Kaczyński and Orbán regimes); D Bunikowski, The crisis in Poland, Schmittean questions and Kaczyński's political and legal philosophy (the author claims that (1) Kaczyński's political and legal philosophy is not a democratic political and legal philosophy in the sense of Western democracies but an illiberal political and legal philosophy which is an eclectic but pragmatic ideology informed by Rousseau's volonte general; (2) this also embraces the political practice of Schmitt visible in the theory of the sovereign and the selected ideas of Stanisław Ehrlich without due regard to pluralism; (3) Orbán is a cynical pragmatist); J Sanecka-Tyczyńska, "Prawa i Sprawiedliwości krytyka Konstytucji Rzeczypospolitej Polaskiej z 1997 r." ["Law and Justice Criticism of the Constitution of the Republic of Poland of 1997"], *Przegląd Sejmowy* 4(147) (2018) 83–88 (the author emphasises "nation" as a concept based on common cultural, language, history, political tradition); abstract of A Gyulai, "Reality Free of Ideology: Viktor Orbán's Realism and Illiberalism", https://ecpr.eu/Events/Event/PaperDetails/41864 (on that the illiberalism of Orbán is different from anti-liberalism because of realism; realism emerged in Hungary not as a coherent political theory against the mainstream liberal political philosophy but an implicit understanding of politics against a technocratic, deterministic and depoliticizing approach to politics).

historically more receptive to paternalism, clientelism, nationalism and leadership featuring authoritarian personalities, or even being autocratic.

Historically, the coincidence of a historical moment of unbalanced identity and the emergence of an illiberal and charismatic leader has shown more durability in Hungary and Poland than the liberal constitutional period after the transition. It might be assumed that there is a historically held belief and applied practice that these countries are better run if there is a charismatic leader, whose charisma is more important than their ideology – due to the unbalanced constitutional identity. It would require further study to establish if this could create a basis for a distinct ideology, or a more coherent political philosophy for illiberalism itself.[117] What we propose here is that, at this moment in time, illiberal constitutionalism is a reality that seems to be attractive for the Polish and Hungarian polities.

This justification will most certainly convince neither those who apply the thick understanding of constitutionalism (conflating liberalism and constitutionalism), nor those who would emphasize the "illiberalism" part of the term. They would miss a coherent political philosophy for justifying the ism in illiberalism. Our conceptualization could, however, be more appealing to those who do not conflate "constitutionalism" and "liberalism", and would not equate constitutionalism (which would remain if we remove the ideology of liberalism from the constitutional design) with any other particular ideology.

3 The term "illiberal(ism)" in the economic and social sphere

The illiberal constitutionalism that has been developed in Hungary and Poland is based on the pillars of liberal constitutionalism (the Rule of Law, democracy, human rights protection), thus on the political and private sphere of liberalism. Political changes are often translated into changes in the economic model, moving away from liberal to a highly coordinated variety of capitalism or something else. While we appreciate the economic reasons and, most importantly, the consequences of the remodelling, it does not make these the focal point of our research. Still, it is difficult to disconnect the political, economic, social, cultural, and environmental reasons, but in this book, our perspective only allows us to briefly list some of the views of the economic and social system of Hungary and Poland. These conceptualizations of changes in the other subsystems of society encourage us to argue that the Hungarian and Polish regimes can best be called "illiberal constitutionalism". Probably, the most telling clue is visible inequality. On the one hand, it contributes to the rise of clientelism, which facilitates the emergence of oligarchs in Hungary and the putting of Polish loyalists into critical positions. On the other hand, it turns welfare support into political support.

117 These enquiries from a more social and political science perspective have already begun. See the findings of the authors mentioned in the previous footnote, and e.g., G Mészáros, "Carl Schmitt in Hungary: Constitutional Crisis in the Shadow of Covid-19", MTA LWP 2020/17, https://jog.tk.mta.hu/mtalwp/carl-schmitt-in-hungary-constitutional-crisis-in-the-shadow-of-covid-19 (emergence of Schmitt's theory of the sovereign during the COVID-19 constitutional emergency).

Gábor Scheiring notes that in Hungary it is not economic liberalism but authoritarian capitalism which has arisen as a new economic model. Authoritarian capitalism was built on positioning the state against the coalition of transnational companies and their centrist-liberal political allies. This way the support of the national capitalist class was secured.[118]

Csaba László also observes that the

> 2010–2018 period has shown a series of unconventional measures, both in the economy and in the broader political context. Analysts supportive of the line of the government apply the term "unorthodox" policy mix. They mean a series of measures that are contrary to conventional wisdom. We shall see in some detail, if and to what degree, ad-hoc regulatory interventionism, nationalisation sometimes followed by privatisation to friends, marginalising foreign ownership in banking, energy sector and trade, and super lax monetary policy together has indeed been successful in bringing about sustainable and high rates of growth, real convergence to the core EU.[119]

Adam Fabry conceives of the changes in the political economy of Hungary as a fusion of authoritarianism and neoliberalism, and calls the system that has emerged "authoritarian neoliberalism".[120] Paul Stubbs and Noémi Lendvai-Bainton, when comparing Hungary, Poland, and Croatia, add that, beyond their embrace of authoritarian neoliberalism per se, what unites the leading parties in these countries even more in their effort to maintain a grip on power is the combination of welfare chauvinism, layered social welfare, and national populism.[121]

As Edit Zgut explains, in Poland, the effect of illiberal political remodelling on the economic sphere of liberalism is not so advanced and took a different path to that in Hungary. While the phenomenon of the "mafia state"[122] seems to be a characteristic of Hungarian events, state-controlled corruption appears not only in the economy but in political life as well. This system of oligarchs is based on personal relationships, political and economic dependence, and loyalty. Such practices form a systemic reality in both states, but Poland has not developed this kind of relationship with the entrepreneur environment. However, even in Poland, there

118 www.tni.org/en/article/hungarys-regime-is-proof-that-capitalism-can-be-deeply-authoritarian

119 L Csaba, "Unorthodoxy in Hungary: An Illiberal Success Story?" *Post Communist Economies*, www.tandfonline.com/doi/full/10.1080/14631377.2019.1641949. See also www.bti-project.org/en/index/economic-transformation.html. The development in this respect seems to be uneven in both states and still the quality of economic transformation is high. While Hungary is acknowledged as advanced, with 7.18 points (rank 22/136), Poland remains highly advanced with 8.36 points (rank 12/136). Russia and Turkey are both limited (6.11 points, rank 50/136), and Singapore is highly advanced (8.82 points, rank 6/136).

120 A Fabry, *The Political Economy of Hungary: From State Capitalism to Authoritarian Neoliberalism* (Springer, 2019).

121 Stubbs and Lendvai-Bainton, n. 116, 554.

122 B Magyar, *Post-Communist Mafia State: The Case of Hungary* (CEU Press, 2016).

are strong connections between PiS supporters and state-owned businesses and banks.[123] The Government controls high and well-paid positions to which it appoints its loyalists. There is strong pressure on economic nationalism and the repolonization of the economy (including media). The amendment of the Civil Service Act of 2016 (removing barriers to fill top positions in ministries with party members) has brought about important changes. After entering into force, a large-scale personnel exchange took place in public administration, state-owned enterprises, and banks. In consequence, state funds are used to pay PiS acolytes as they are employed for only a few months, with huge payments one after another.

Zgut also draws our attention to the fact that "while Orbán's new crony clientelist system is fixed around the uncontested prime minister, Kaczyński has to deal with several competing networks which might limit his effectiveness in the long run".[124] That is why the PiS has been pursuing the 500+ program – creating mass clientelism by turning welfare support into political support. The same tactic is followed by Orbán, who was quick to introduce the reduction of utility prices and to make it the companies' monthly duty to inform clients about how much money they have saved due to this governmental intervention. This information is now an inseparable part of all utility bills.

III Constitutional democracy

1 Substantive constitutional democracy

We have already mentioned that, considering the constitutional development of the region, for us, a constitutional democracy is a constitutional regime in which the Rule of Law and the protection and promotion of human rights as such prevail.[125] Constitutional democracy is thus not only a constitutionalized form of democracy, it also embodies constitutionalism (in which no power can be exercised without constraints) and democracy (the rule of the people) at the same time. Therefore, they cannot be mutually exclusive or competing factors, either at a constitutional design level or in terms of constitutional interpretation.

As a counter-effect of the socialist regime, legal procedures and legal constitutions were preferred in Central and Eastern Europe (CEE) over any other political considerations and approaches to the exercise of public power. The newly adopted (in most of the post-socialist countries, including in Poland) or substantially modified (as in Hungary) constitutions, based on the Kelsenian tradition and relying on the very notion and function of the legal understanding of a constitution, were seen as senseless, unless able to be defended and enforced. A constitution or a constitutional setting without a written constitution, as in the UK, or the

123 E Zgut, "Authoritarian Regime Durability: The Bread and Butter of Hungarian and Polish Backsliding during COVID-19", https://visegradinsight.eu/authoritarian-regime-durability-hungary-poland/

124 Ibid.

125 See also Ginsburg and Huq, n. 52, 224.

treaties that we consider to be like a constitution for the EU, may be defended and enforced in many ways. Depending on the type of constitution, that is, whether it is a political concept, as defined by Bellamy as regards the UK, or a legal notion, which applies in most of the European states, different procedures may be used for these purposes. We might think of, for instance, political processes such as elections and public discourse in the UK, or institutions, such as constitutional courts, in Hungary or Poland, ordinary courts in the Nordic countries or the United States, or even council-of-state-type institutions or a high degree of respect for international treaties as in the Netherlands. In states with common law traditions, such as the UK, Canada, and New Zealand, the human rights charters or provisions are defended by the ordinary courts.[126] Nonetheless, the new constitutional democracies, as established after the transition in the CEE region, required a written constitution, in a legal sense, that encompassed all of its essential principles and defense mechanisms. These principles included the Rule of Law, human rights and democracy, in the form in which they have arisen during (Western European) constitutional development, as the core values of modern societies and political systems. In this way, the content of democracy has been enriched and has moved away from a minimalist to a maximalist understanding. This regional approach, in fact, has come to encompass all that is usually labelled a liberal democracy, liberal constitutionalism, and, later, liberal constitutional democracy or constitutional liberal democracy.[127]

The proliferation of adjectives attached to constitutionalism is indeed the result of a centuries-long Western constitutional development, which, however, in recent decades has featured conceptually tightly braided democracy and constitutionalism.[128] The ideas of democracy and constitutionalism certainly originate in liberalism. This raised human beings to the forefront of any public action, which triggered a demand for constrained authority that originates its legitimacy in democratic means.[129] Nevertheless, insofar as the above-mentioned constitutional defense mechanisms and instruments focus on the defense of individual human rights, a compliant state could be called liberal, but this adjective just states the obvious. The ideological base has already interwoven the claim for democracy and the demand for the Rule of Law. It has also already been absorbed by constitutional provisions rendering democracy, the Rule of Law, and the protection of human rights of the utmost concern to the state, the main principles of the constitutional order and entitlements or rights of the people. It follows that if a state is a constitutional democracy in Europe today, theoretically, it does not need any adjective to express its commitment towards the Rule of Law, human rights (not only civil and political), and democracy.[130]

126 S Gardbaum, "The Case for the New Commonwealth Model of Constitutionalism", *German L.J.* 14(2229) (2013).
127 For the varieties of these expressions, see the index www.democratic-decay.org/index
128 See the index at www.democratic-decay.org/index
129 Scheppele, n. 2, 558–559.
130 See it differently at Dem Dec Index, www.democratic-decay.org/index

As there exists a perfect realization of neither constitutionalism nor its three main components, different monitoring and enforcing mechanisms have been established at international, supranational, and national levels. Indeed, after the transition, those post-socialist states in the CEE earnestly pursued compliance with or, depending on their national needs, even exceeded the minimum standards laid down by the Rule of Law, human rights, and democracy requirements of the CoE and the EU.[131] As there is neither perfect state organization nor public power, or a faultless political force, the legal principles and elements of the Rule of Law, democracy, and human rights have always been prone to infringement. Mainly at the national state level, these violations could range from "innocent" or honest mistakes, due to institutional design, wrong answers to some new challenges, and a transition to a constitutionalist state,[132] to deliberate ones.[133] As long as the legal and political defense mechanisms are in place, for example constitutional courts and regularly organized and competitive elections, any wrongdoing to constitutional democracy can eventually be eliminated.

2 Formal constitutional democracy and illiberal constitutionalism

The "deliberate mistakes", however, could amount to dismantling a previous and commonly accepted level of constitutional democracy (liberal constitutionalism), including the Rule of Law, democracy, and human rights, especially when neither constitutional nor political dialogue can reconcile the diverging views and find the least common denominator. This occurs when, mainly, the reformist populist leaders and, partly, the newly restructured and packed institutions straightforwardly reject the different views and the need for compromise – as has been happening in both Hungary and Poland. Dismantling the Rule of Law and manipulating the procedural safeguards of democracy most definitely affects the human rights regime of a particular state. This first phase of illiberalization of human rights could eventually lead to an obviously misunderstood but politically demanded reformation of the language and theory on human rights that is at odds with the core tenets of legal regimes dedicated to

131 On these impacts in general, see RR Ludwikowski, "Supreme Law or Basic Law? The Decline of the Concept of Constitutional Supremacy", *Cardozo Journal of International & Comparative Law* 9 (2001) 253–296.

132 On these types of mistakes in the field of the Rule of Law, see e.g., D Kochenov and A Jakab (eds), *The Enforcement of EU Law and Values* (Oxford University Press, 2017); in the field of human rights, see e.g., A Nusserger, "The European Court of Human Rights and the Rule of Law – A Tale of Hopes and Disillusions" in M Zubrik (ed), *Human Rights in Contemporary World. Essays in Honor of Professor Leszek Garlicki* (Wydawnictwo Sejmowe, 2017).

133 See e.g., Gingsburg and Huq, *How to Save Constitutional Democracy?* (University of Chicago Press, 2018), Sadurski, n. 3; Freedom in the World 2019, Democracy in retreat, https://freedomhouse.org/report/freedom-world/2019/democracy-retreat; GA Tóth, "Illiberal Rule of Law? Changing Features of Hungarian Constitutionalism" in M Adams et al. (eds), *Constitutionalism and the Rule of Law* (Cambridge University Press, 2017).

human rights and their protection.[134] Hungary and Poland, in their illiberal turn since 2010 and 2015,[135] have dismantled the substantive elements of the constitutional democracy described above. What is left is its shell, with a hollowed-out Rule of Law concept (illiberal legality), illiberal democracy, and a reduced level of human rights protection with the misuse of its language and ideas. This is only formal constitutional democracy, which is better called "illiberal constitutionalism".

Illiberal constitutionalism is thus a particular state in the process of democratic decay or backsliding from (liberal) constitutionalism, that is, from a substantive constitutional democracy to an authoritarian regime. Illiberal constitutionalism is not yet an authoritarian system, but it is heading in that direction. Membership of the EU makes it possible to keep "constitutionalism", and the actual legal remodelling, legislative and other legal actions and political behaviours call for the label "illiberal". The palpable oxymoron in the term "illiberal constitutionalism" forms a thick constitutionalism point of view, thus highlighting the paradox affecting Hungary, Poland, and the EU. First, the EU, which is built on certain principles, still has two Member States that keep disrespecting those very same principles. Second, it seems that both the EU and Hungary and Poland are comfortable with the regime-sustaining and legitimizing role of the EU.[136] Third, the populist leaders of Hungary and Poland act like children testing the boundaries of their actions, and keep pushing as far as they can.

In this context, based on the Polish and Hungarian experiences, as opposed to the term "illiberal constitutionalism"[137] as used to describe the constitutionalism in an illiberal polity, we suggest the following. The term indicates a process of deterioration that has not resulted (yet) in an autocracy or modern authoritarianism because there is still a weak constraint on public power (illiberalization of constitutionalism). Beyond this characteristic, illiberal constitutionalism as a concept is proposed to mean a retained constitutionalist structure (as a result of the process and the existing constraints) and the combination of the unbalanced constitutional identity and a charismatic leader. This identity is moulded and designed in a way that tends to accept and support illiberal (non-liberal) visions and ideas, and thus makes the maintenance of liberal constitutionalism more difficult – though not impossible.

The following Parts elaborate on these points.

134 We will discuss it in Part V, Limits.
135 See below.
136 These functions are borrowed from Bozóki and Hegedűs, n. 18, 1174.
137 Thio, n. 27.

III Identity

Unbalanced constitutional identity: emotions and values

Hungary and Poland emerged from a troubled history, which left its mark on the emotional trajectory of their populations. An unbalanced constitutional identity has been moulded throughout Polish and Hungarian history, in which emotional traits of collective victimhood and collective narcissism, and the accompanying resentment,[1] plus a longing for a charismatic leader emerged. This state of emotions could easily and quickly be intensified and exploited by today's populist leaders.[2] These feelings, and the populist politics based on them, are why the current populist autocrats emphasize and trigger, and at the same time are dependent upon, the currently aggrandized features of the constitutional identity of Poles and Hungarians. Hungarian and Polish populist leaders, starting from 2010,[3] have, with increased intensity, exploited the emotional needs of their compatriots and used different techniques to gain political support for remodelling constitutional settings. This support seems to be stable because it originates from a historically shaped value-orientation connected to the group identification so widely shared by Hungarians and Poles.[4] These emotions also explain the fact that Hungary and Poland are the most renegade members of the EU, and why the EU seems not to be entirely successful in adequately addressing populist and illiberal leaders, notwithstanding the Article 7 procedure and the Rule of Law conditionality.

1 TT Koncewicz, "Unconstitutional Capture and Constitutional Recapture: Of the Rule of Law, Separation of Powers and Judicial Promises", *Jean Monnet Ctr. for Int'l & Regional Econ. L. & Just., Working Paper 3/17.*

2 Similarly see G Rajcsányi, "Viktor Orbán's Hungary: Orbanist Politics and Philosophy from a Hungarian Perspective", www.kas.de/c/document_library/get_file?uuid=8e914238-5bca-e235-e176-f8d502f4a33f&groupId=288143, 123, M Toomey, "History, Nationalism, and Democracy: Myth and Narrative in Viktor Orbán's Illiberal Hungary", *New Perspectives* 26(1) (2018).

3 2010 was the year when the Fidesz Party won the parliamentary elections and started to develop an illiberal Hungary, and when the tragic plane crash happened in Smoleńsk. The latter event is a continual point of emotional reference for the PiS Party in Poland.

4 A Cichocka and A Cislak, "Nationalism as Collective Narcissism" *ScienceDirect Current Opinion in Behavioral Sciences* 34 (2020) 69–74.

DOI: 10.4324/9781003175353-3

I Historical and emotional trajectory

1 Framework of investigation

Narrative psychology provides a dynamic approach to understanding human identity and the process of making sense of our ever-changing world.[5] Thinking in narratives is everywhere: narratives are embedded in social interactions, in the works of professional authors, and in stories of ordinary people. Many branches of psychology, such as cognitive studies of narratives and hermeneutic studies of narratives, deal with narratives.[6] Scientific narrative psychology presumes a strong relationship between narrative and identity, and focuses on qualitative methods, such as the life-story interview. It helps the identification of inner states and representations of social relations by connecting narrative compositions to psychological processes in individuals and groups. The interrelations between the development and shaping of individual identity and the role of the narrative in this process have also been studied in the context of group identity. Éva Fülöp and her co-authors[7] have proposed not only that individuals have a "life trajectory", which sequentially represents the positively or negatively evaluated events of their lives, but also that this evaluative sequence of salient historical events – the "historical trajectory" – characterizes the identity of nations, including their emotional life.[8] They also explain that

> narrative social psychology claims that states and characteristics of group identity that govern people's behaviour when they act as group members as

5 M Murray, "Narrative Psychology and Narrative Analysis" in PM Camic, JE Rhodes, and L Yardly (eds), *Qualitative Research in Psychology: Expanding Perspectives in Methodology and Design* (American Psychological Association, 2003) 110.

6 J László, Narratív pszichológia, *Pszichológia* 4 (2008), http://real.mtak.hu/2385/1/49413_ZJ1.pdf, 5.

7 They have conducted empirical research with regard to Hungary: see É Fülöp, I Csertő, B Ilg, Zs Szabó, B Slugoski, and J László, "Emotional Elaboration of Collective Traumas in Historical Narratives", http://real.mtak.hu/20201/3/emotional_elaboration_of_collective_traumas.pdf

8 Poles as a group are described in the scope of societal psychology, social psychology, and narrative psychology by e.g., B Wojciszke (ed), *Jacy są Polacy? Badania opinii społecznej jako źródło wiedzy psychologicznej* [*What Are Poles Like? Social Feedback Survey as a Source of Psychological Knowledge*] (Wydawnictwo Instytutu Psychologii PAN, 1995); D Doliński and T Grzyb, *Posłuszni do bólu. O uległości wobec autorytetu w 50 lat po eksperymencie Milgrama* [*Painfully Obedient. On the Submission to Authority 50 years After Milgram's Experiment*] (Smak Słowa, 2017); M Drogosz (ed), *Jak Polacy przegrywają, jak Polacy wygrywają* [*How the Poles Lose, How the Poles Win*] (Gdańskie Wydawnictwo Psychologiczne, 2005). Polish historical and time perspectives are elaborated in A Zajenkowska (ed), *Polska na kozetce: Siła obywatelskiej refleksyjności* [*Poland on the Couch: The Power of Civic Reflexivity*] (Smak Słowa, 2016); W Wrzesiński, *Charakter narodowy Polaków: Z rozważań historyka* [*National Character of Poles: From the Historian's Reflections*] (Wydawnictwo Uniwersytetu Wrocławskiego, 2004); P Augustyniak, *Homo Polacus: Eseje o polskiej duszy* [*Homo Polacus: Essays about Polish Soul*] (Znak, 2015).

> well as the elaboration of traumatic experiences which affect the group as a whole can be traced objectively, that is, empirically in the narrative composition and narrative language of different forms of group histories.[9]

Group or national identity is thus assumed to be constructed by a genuinely narrative group history. Group or national identity construction has three main channels: historiography, collective memory, and history textbooks and historical novels. Fülöp et al. found that if these sources are studied, they can help "empirically operationalize the concept of historical trajectory and explore emotional aspects of national identity through a narrative analysis of the emotional entailments" of the historical trajectory of a group or a nation.[10] The history of the group through recurring experiences makes collectives more sensitive to certain emotions, and, as a consequence, every nation has its own characteristic emotional repertoire and norms of emotional expression.[11]

As the term "achievements of the historical constitution" appears in the Fundamental Law of Hungary (FL),[12] it seems justified to conduct a brief overview of theories on the Hungarian historical constitution and the nation's ancient constitutionalism.[13] Due to the lack of a similar provision in the Polish Constitution 1997, such a perspective has not developed in relation to Polish constitutional history and constitutional research. There have been, however, several poets, writers, and theorists who, in Hungarian and Polish *belles lettres*, with their own artistic and scholarly methods, have expressed the Hungarian and the Polish identities and changes in those identities. By doing so, they also have tried to interpret and explain these alterations, and the underlying emotional attitudes and national characteristics.

9 Éva Fülöp et al., "Emotional Elaboration of Collective Traumas in Historical Narratives" (2014), http://real.mtak.h/020//emotional_elaboration_of_collective_traumas.pdf, 5.

10 Historiography provides the most canonized form of historical experiences by attempting to ascertain the objective facts of events and to diminish ambiguities. Collective memory (e.g. diaries, family accounts, oral history) tends to represent history in a biased, i.e. a group-serving, way from the perspective of the in-group. History textbooks and historical novels represent transitional forms of memory lying between historiography and collective memory, since in these narratives concrete acts of history are saturated with the psychological aspects of the episodes (e.g. intentions, perspectives, evaluations, emotions, agency, etc.). See Fülöp et al., n. 9, 3.

11 Fülöp et al., n. 9, 8.

12 Article R) FL.

13 A Cieger, "Alkotmányosság és nemzeti identitás – a magyar történelem kontextusában. Vázlat" ["Constitutionalism and National Identity – in the Context of Hungarian History. Draft"], http://atelier.org.hu/upload/category/mta_elte_atelier/kotoerok1.3_cieger_andras.pdf; M Zászkaliczky, "Eszmetörténeti szempontok a történeti alkotmányosság közép- és kora újkori magyarországi történetéhez" ["Some Considerations on the Hungarian Mediaeval and Modern History of the Historical Constitutionalism, from the Perspective of History of Ideas"] *Közjogi Szemle* 3 (2015).

Below, we offer a brief collection of these descriptions from historical sources (reports, poems, and novels) and the empirical results of narrative psychology, and, in the case of Hungary, legal accounts regarding the term "historical constitution". We have decided to discuss Hungary and Poland in separate sections, to emphasize that different historical events can cause different emotions and features. However, those emotions supported by similar value-orientation lead to the same result, that is, the emergence of components of illiberal constitutionalism – an unbalanced constitutional identity and a longing for a charismatic leader. Then they have been translated into populist rhetoric, the lack of political self-restraint, and the inability or unwillingness of the people to form a strong and capable civil society, or to forcefully raise their voice against extreme views or firmly resist an aggressive and clearly unfounded political campaign.

2 Hungarian national identity – more than a stereotype

2.1 Historical sources: reports, poems, and novels

In the light of today's polemics about European values, commitments, and compliance, the thoughts of Francesco Massaro, Secretary of Venice, and many others to whom we refer below, could not be more topical. He visited the court of King Matthias as early as 1523, and he noted:

> Hungarians are the worst kind in the world. They do not like or respect any nation in the world, nor do they like one another. Everyone thinks of his own comfort, steals from the public purse, and there are few who care about it. The secretly nurtured hatred and hostility [of Hungarians] against one another are almost unbelievable. Nonetheless, every day they eat together and one could almost believe they are brothers. There is no obedience; they are proud and arrogant, they cannot rule or govern, but they do not accept counsel from someone who is an expert. They always boast of their own achievements, they are ready to swear on anything, but they are very slow to act. They deal with very little other than feasting and robbing the public. These are things in which they are sedulous.[14]

This description is supported by historical accounts of Hungarian society in the Middle Ages. Noblemen (gentry) living in towns are characterized by their arrogant, high-minded one-upmanship, which is viewed as an antecedent of the lifestyles of the communist and socialist elite during socialism.[15] Therefore, wangling

14 Translation by the authors.

15 "Nemesi mentalitás: Magyar néprajz VIII" ["Mentality of Noblemen: Hungarian Folklore"], http://mek.oszk.hu/02100/02152/html/08/96.html; "Chapter XIV: The Decline of the Gentry and the Novel", www.arcanum.hu/hu/online-kiadvanyok/MagyarIrodalom-magyar-irodalomtortenet-1/a-history-of-hungarian-literature-from-the-earliest-times-to-the-mid-1970s-lorant-czigany-47D8/chapter-xiv-the-decline-of-the-gentry-and-the-novel-4B1D/-

(a kind of manipulation), sloth, and fogydom (the tendency to obscurantism and insistence on outworn ideas) are generally assumed as fixed national characteristics of Hungarians.

These features appear in poems and novels, and in various articles as well:[16] fogydom and laziness appear in a poem by Sándor Petőfi (*A magyar nemes* [17]) and in the writings of the nobleman and politician István Széchenyi (19th century). Mihály Babits emphasized the persistent tendency of Hungarians to postpone making decisions, while Sándor Karácsony depicts them as representative of the Asian sense of time: no one acts to relieve suffering, other than those who are the subject of it; there is a tendency to expect to benefit without making any effort. There is dissension and a lack of co-operation and trust. Koestler asserts that being Hungarian is a collective neurosis. Péter Müller recalls the text of the national hymn, which blames God for every bad event in Hungarian history.[18] Endre Ady, in 1905, viewed Hungary as a "ferry nation, which even in its most formidable dreams only runs between two shores, from East to West, but preferably backshore".[19] According to Ákos Kertész, Hungarians are "genetically dependent", due to the historical determination stemming from the long centuries of feudalism, which is a culturally embedded behaviour. They feel no guilt for the most grievous historical crimes and shift the blame on to someone else.[20]

Indeed, it seems that in Hungary there has always been a disagreement between pro-Western and pro-Eastern movements, ideologies and political figures, starting with the first Hungarian king, (Saint) Stephan I, who, in the context of the dichotomy used, represented the pro-Western approach as opposed to the pro-Eastern one that still followed paganism and traditional views on succession to the throne. Historically, pro-Westerners have been, since the beginning of the Hungarian statehood, Christians, maintainers of feudalism, then later on supporters of the Habsburgs and, from the end of the 19th century, liberals, progressives, leftists, or Western conservatives. A more "Eastern-focused" approach was taken by those who put more emphasis on nationalism and patriotism.[21]

16 For the collection of opinions set out below, see J Ladányi, *Önpusztító nemzeti habitus* [*Self-destructive National Habitus*] (L'Harmattan, 2015) 19–23.

17 See, e.g., S Petőfi, "The Magyar Noble", http://mek.oszk.hu/06500/06567/06567.htm#49

18 The literal and poetic translation (William N Loew, 1881) can be found at https://en.wikipedia.org/wiki/Himnusz

19 E Ady, "Ismeretlen Korvin-kódex margójára" ["Side-note to the Unknown Korvin-Codex"] *Figyelő* (1905). In English see D Boyd and I Salusinszky (eds), *Re-reading Frye* (University of Toronto Press, 1999); G Csordás, "A Farewell to Central Europe" (July 2016), www.literaturhauseuropa.eu/en/observatory/blog/a-farewell-to-central-europe

20 "Kertész Ákos nyílt levele az Amerikai Népszavához" ["Open Letter of Ákos Kertész to the American Népszava"], www.nepszava.com/2011/08/velemeny/kertesz-akos-nyilt-levele-az-amerikai-nepszavahoz.html

21 Rajcsányi, n. 1, 124.

The political theorist István Bibó characterized Hungarians as a nation with a "distorted mentality".[22] He studied the period between 1848 and 1948 and found that during this 100-year timeframe, the fixations of the Old World, such as a hierarchal view of society, the obsession with ranks in society, the prevalence of control over service in the exercise of power, had become endemic. These fixations pervaded the whole of society, and no political and personal changes could obliterate them. This situation was seen to compromise the transformation of society. Bibó also asserted that since the end of the 19th century, Hungarian society and the political elite had been unable to form a clear vision of their own position and possibilities, or to adopt adequate policies. Society was unable to find and empower those leaders who could recognize its needs and identify the measures necessary to face the challenges. He added that other nations had instinctively acted in a more proper manner. At historical moments, the French and British chose to turn, to a certain extent, against their previous orientation as communities and commenced a different national endeavour. Here Bibó was referring to the French Revolution, and to the Reformation and the emergence of Puritanism in England. Both nations experienced the abandonment of their previous national arrangements. For Bibó, it proved that the French and the British had something different in their national characteristics or identity,[23] which resulted in different collective behaviour from that attributed to Hungarians.[24] When studying the Hungarian remodelling in the first couple of years after the 2010 election, István Pogány stated that the elements that Bibó described as the "deformed" political culture of the period preceding the Second World War, had reasserted themselves.[25]

2.2 The legal conceptualization of the "historical" in the term "historical constitution"

Hungary did not have a written constitution before the Communist Constitution adopted in 1949. The previous era was governed by the concept of the "historical constitution". Márton Zászkaliczky is of the opinion that historical constitutionalism, through reforms, was not able to form the basis and direct antecedent of modern democracy, because it was not facilitated by historical development (the medieval structure of the political power remained and historical discontinuity was experienced). If, following András Cieger, we identify the notion he called "ancient constitutionalism", which became a central issue in the constitutional struggles of the 18th century, with the "historical constitution", we

22 I Bibó, *Válogatott tanulmányok I–IV*, Második kötet: *Eltorzult magyar alkat, zsákutcás magyar történelem* [*Selected Papers I–IV, 2nd vol: Distorted Hungarian Character, Hungarian History with a Dead End*] (1948), http://mek.oszk.hu/02000/02043/html/350.html

23 Though he never used identity in his work cited.

24 Bibó, n. 22.

25 I Pogány, "The Crisis of Democracy in East Central Europe: The 'New Constitutionalism' in Hungary", *European Public Law* (2013) 341–367.

reach results that are confusing but supported by the descriptions of poets and novelists and social scientists (above), and those of social psychology studies (below). At that time, the reference to ancient constitutionalism was significant, because it meant that the country had a system of customs that formed the uniformly and steadily developing 900- and, later, 1,000-year-old unwritten constitution of which Hungarians are so proud. This constitutional development was identical to the history of the nation; but at that time, "the nation" meant the nobility. Consequently, the protection and preservation of constitutional customs, rights, and privileges were both obligations and basic conditions of national existence. Throughout history, reference to the country's ancient constitutionalism was used to achieve different and sometimes conflicting goals.[26] In the second half of the 19th century, the cult of constitutionalism reached a certain degree of maturity. However, its content became meaningless, because the establishment of constitutional institutions and the pursuit of European standards fell short and national traditions dominated.[27] The Hungarian Soviet Republic (Hungarian Republic of Councils, 1919), during its existence of less than half a year, presented a sharp break with the preceding interpretation of constitutionalism. Compared to this, the restoration of civilian constitutionalism in the Horthy era between the two World Wars – although incapable of developing constitutional consciousness – again came as a novelty. The general identity crisis of this era had an impact on the legal and political system, the constitutionalism and interpretation of the past. In the 1930s, the reference to constitutional traditions increasingly provided arguments[28] for restrictions in the area of equality before the law and parliamentarism. The 1949 Communist Constitution, by establishing that Hungarian constitutionalism started with the liberation of the country by Soviet troops, meant another rupture with earlier constitutionalism. So does the constitutional amendment of 1972, which refers once more to Hungary's 1,000-year-old history and rejects the former understanding of historical events. Against this background, it is not surprising that parallel interpretations of the past exist following the democratic transition; a new constitutional patriotism could not emerge; and a chaotic mixture of traditions and values could be observed.[29] The FL (2011) also represents a total repudiation of the former 20 years. This controversy may also be problematic as, according to social psychology studies, the remembered past becomes social and cultural knowledge and practice, which creates an identity.[30]

26 See, e.g., medieval order relations v. liberal programme of extension of rights, freedom fights against Vienna v. compromise with Vienna in 1867. Cieger, n. 13, 56.

27 Cieger, n. 13, 61.

28 Democratic liberalism and Europe's ceasing to be a world power, Parliament's negotiating at too much length and too much, and liberal achievements (as of 1848) are incompatible with the constitutional traditions of the Hungarian nation, etc. Cieger, n. 13, 67, 70–71.

29 Cieger, n. 13, 76, 78, 80.

30 É Fülöp, B Péley, and J László, "A történelmi pályához kötött érzelmek magyar történelmi regényekben" ["History-related Emotions in Hungarian Historical Novels"], http://real.mtak.hu/2385/1/49413_ZJ1.pdf, 65.

2.3 *Narrative psychology and other interpretations*

Scientific narrative psychology, as already mentioned, supports the emotional attitude displayed in reports, novels, and poems. Orsolya Vincze and János László, when studying history textbooks for students in high schools between 1900 and 2006, found that in those volumes, fear, hope, enthusiasm, and disappointment were the feelings used to describe the emotional characteristics of the Hungarian nation. They also asserted that during negative historical events, Hungarians were portrayed as inefficient actors.[31] Éva Fülöp, Bernadette Péley, and János László identified the typical emotional patterns in four historical novels written by authors of different times as fear, hope, enthusiasm, disappointment, and sadness. Depressive types of feeling were dominant, with some self-criticism, such as shame and guilt, towards the ingroup. In outgroup relations, these emotions were more critical and included anger and disdain.[32]

All these results point to the depressive dynamics of the Hungarian national identity.[33] From the perspective of narrative psychology,[34] in the Hungarian collective memory, positively evaluated events belong to the medieval period. This is especially true regarding the defence of Christian Europe against the Ottoman Turks, which seems to be part of the national ideology and identity.[35] Historical events occurring in later centuries, for example wars of independence and revolutions (1703, 1848, 1956[36]), were always followed by defeat and repression. The pattern recurred in the World Wars; both wars were lost by Hungary, and this loss is preserved in the collective memory.[37] Passive resistance featured in the period after 1849, which also seems to be integrated into the collective memory, as was implemented after the Revolution of 1956.[38] Collective victimhood, mainly due

31 O Vincze and J László, "A narratív perspektíva szerepe a történelemkönyvekben" ["The Role of Narratives in History Textbooks"], http://real.mtak.hu/2385/1/49413_ZJ1.pdf, 33.

32 Fülöp, Péley, and László, n. 30, 58.

33 Fülöp et al., n. 9, 5.

34 Fülöp et al., n. 9, 4. For more about Hungarian history in English, see P Lendvai, *The Hungarians: A Thousand Years of Victory in Defeat* (Princeton University Press, 2004).

35 This appears even in the preamble to the FL.

36 Rákóczi's War of Independence (1703–11) was the first significant attempt to overthrow the Habsburgs. The insurrection was unsuccessful, but the Hungarian nobility still managed to partially satisfy Hungarian interests. The Hungarian Revolution of 1848 was closely linked to other revolutions of that year in the Habsburg territories, and grew into a war for independence from the Austrian Empire. The repression of the war was followed by a consolidation period, called passive resistance, which ended with the Austro-Hungarian Compromise of 1867. The Hungarian Revolution of 1956 was a nationwide revolt against the Socialist Government and its Soviet-imposed policies. Soviet troops put an end to the Revolution, which was followed by great retaliation.

37 Fülöp et al., n. 9, 4.

38 Gy Spiró, "Két középkelet-európai mentalitás az államiság szempontjából" *2000 Irodalmi és Társadalmi havi lap* 6 (2007) 7.

to oppression by the Turks in the Middle Ages, by the Habsburgs later on, by the Soviets in the 20th century, under the Trianon peace treaty[39] and, as György Spiró explains, as a result of the recurring and experienced disloyalty of the state mainly in the 20th century,[40] also seems to be an integrated part of the national identity.[41] Collective victimhood is more likely to arise when people feel the sense of victimhood not because of the harm experienced by themselves, but because of the loss or suffering of their group. Victimization in the history of a group can cause substantive changes in group identity.[42] People thus have continuously been disappointed in the efficiency of state institutions and their operation. Citizens were abandoned in their disappointment by all regimes throughout Hungarian history. This has led to the attraction of an autocratic leader, which also may have been integrated into the national identity.[43]

The sense of collective victimhood also immunizes the group, just as it does abused persons. For Zsolt Szabó, it explains why Hungary is not a host nation.[44] It was also Hungary that adopted the first legal measures against the Jewish population based on Nazi examples, and Hungary that actively collaborated with Nazi Germany in implementing their policies.[45] These events caused collective guilt, which triggered varying degrees of amnesia and an urge for self-justification.[46] Furthermore, anti-Jewish laws were criticized at that time, amongst other reasons on the ground that they would justify the position that no hard work and personal responsibility were needed to acquire goods. It may have amplified the fixed national characteristics featured in the literature – laziness and wangling, and so on.[47]

39 The Treaty of Trianon was the peace agreement of 1920 to formally end World War I, between most of the Allies and the Kingdom of Hungary, which was at that time, until 1946, a "monarchy without a monarch". Around two-thirds of the territory of the country were allocated to neighbouring countries, along with the population of those parts; one-third of Hungarians were left outside post-Trianon Hungary.

40 The Hungarian Soviet Republic (1919), by its own nature, betrayed its citizens based on their social class background. In the 1940s, the state betrayed all those citizens it claimed to be Jewish, i.e. 10 per cent of its population; the socialist regime betrayed all its people except the nomenclature (protégées of the system). Spiró, n. 38, 10.

41 Fülöp et al., n. 9, 7, 19; Spiró, n. 38, 6, 10.

42 Fülöp et al., n. 9, 7. "A magyar identitás szabadságharcos – interjú Szabó Zsolttal, az ELTE Szociálpszichológia tanszékének adjunktusával" ["Freedom Fighter of the Hungarian Identity – Interview with Zsolt Szabó, lecturer from the ELTE Social Psychology Department"], http://mindset.co.hu/a-magyar-identitas-szabadsagharcos-interju-szabo-zsolttal-az-elte-szocialpszichologia-tanszekenek-adjunktusaval/

43 Spiró, n. 38, 5.

44 "A magyar identitás szabadságharcos", n. 42.

45 In return, revision of the Trianon peace treaty was hoped for.

46 Spiró, n. 38, 5.

47 Spiró, n. 38, 7.

3 National identity and Poland

3.1 Brief historical overview

In the case of Poland, the national trauma is connected to the loss of statehood and freedom. However, freedom is perceived more in relation to state sovereignty and independence than in relation to individuals.[48]

Since the beginning of its statehood in the 10th century and the adoption of Western Christianity by Mieszko I in AD 966 (baptism), Poland has constantly developed and expanded, especially in the 14th–17th centuries. During the Jagiellonian dynasty, Poland established the Polish–Lithuanian Commonwealth with the Grand Duchy of Lithuania in 1569. During this period, a unique form of political system – noble democracy (republican monarchy, *monarchia mixta*)[49] – was created. The most important values were freedom (free election of the king and *liberum veto*[50]) and reference to the Res Publica (First Polish Republic). Republicanism was strongly developed during the era of romanticism, especially by the poet, dramatist, and essayist Adam Mickiewicz.[51]

However, starting from the end of the 17th century, Poland faced a period of decline caused by devastating wars and the deterioration of the political system (especially because of the active use of the *liberum veto*). The most traumatic event in Polish history was the First Partition in 1772. The desperate attempt to save and strengthen the Commonwealth resulted in the Constitution of 3 May 1791 (3 May Constitution), but it could not prevent the Second (1793) and the Third (1795) Partitions of Poland by the Russian Empire, the Kingdom of Prussia, and the Austrian Habsburg Monarchy. In consequence, the "great Polish nation" was mashed up by neighbouring empires, with the assistance of certain Polish noblemen who opposed the 3 May Constitution. This period can be characterized by the feelings of loss (statehood, freedom, sovereignty, and independence) and betrayal from both inside (by various Polish noblemen) and outside (by the neighbouring empires). This is why the 3 May Constitution is a strong Polish myth and symbolizes the unfulfilled dream of a liberated Poland.[52] The feeling of

48 M Granat and K Granat, *The Constitution of Poland: A Contextual Analysis* (Hart Publishing, 2019) 13–14.

49 A Tarnowska, "The Sovereignty Issue in the Public Discussion in the Era of the Polish 3rd May Constitution (1788–1792)" in U Müßig (ed), *Reconsidering Constitutional Formation I, National Sovereignty, A Comparative Analysis of the Juridification by Constitution* (Springer International Publishing, 2016) 233.

50 *Liberum veto* was a parliamentary device in the Polish–Lithuanian Commonwealth. It was a form of the legal right of each member of the Sejm to defeat by his vote alone any measure under consideration, or to dissolve the Sejm and nullify all acts passed during its session. See www.britannica.com/topic/liberum-veto

51 C Miłosz, *Historia literatury polskiej* [*History of Polish Literature*] (Znak, 1993) 263–264.

52 Tarnowska, n. 49, 218.

collective victimhood was born,[53] as Poles have been the victims of the political actions of their neighbouring states, and has grown systematically as a result of subsequent unsuccessful uprisings,[54] as well as during and after the Second World War.

Between 1795 and 1918, Poland did not exist as an independent state.[55] In 1918, the Second Polish Republic was established. The young state was multiethnic, but anti-Semitism was widespread in society. At that time, Poland was trying to rebuild its statehood and its identity. Circumstances were not favourable, however: Poland was surrounded by totalitarian ideologies (Nazi, Fascist, and Soviet) and experienced its own autocratic period (especially after the coup of 1926[56] and under the 1935 Constitution[57]). Obviously, Poland was not prepared for another traumatic defeat, which eventually happened in September 1939 when Germany (1 September) and the Soviet Union (17 September) occupied her territory. During the Second World War, Poles witnessed the Holocaust, but they did not collaborate institutionally as did Hungary. The Soviet Union also caused unthinkable harm in Katyń in 1940.[58]

The feeling of collective victimhood was strengthened by the events of the 20th century. Poland remained under Soviet influence until 1989, and, like the Hungarians in 1956, felt that Western Europe had betrayed her. During socialism, several mass demonstrations were organized and bloodily repressed in 1956, 1968, 1970, and 1980. Except for the protest of 1968,[59] these events were more economically than politically driven; but still, in 1981, even martial law was introduced to defend the socialist regime. The martial law proclamation was explained as being to prevent Soviet "help" in fighting against the demonstrators, as happened in Hungary in 1956 when Soviet troops "came to assist". In the national collective memory, it is viewed as a betrayal of Poles and Poland by Poles.

In 1989, the Third Polish Republic was founded. The decision to organize the Round Table Talks was made in September 1988 by the Opposition, Catholic Church, and the Government. It made the transition to (liberal constitutional)

53 D Bar-Tal, L Chernyak-Hai, N Schori, and A Gundar, "A Sense of Self-perceived Collective Victimhood in Intractable Conflicts", *International Review of the Red Cross* 91(874) (2009) 237.

54 See e.g. 1794: Kościuszko's; and in November 1830 and January 1863.

55 The remnants of the Polish state were established as non-independent entities. First, it was The Duchy of Warsaw 1807–15 and then the Kingdom of Poland 1815–1914.

56 It was a coup d'état carried out by Marshal Józef Piłsudski between 12 and 14 May 1926. The coup provided authoritarian means to restore moral "health" to public life. The weakness of the Polish parliamentary system was the background to the events in 1926.

57 It introduced a presidential system with certain elements of authoritarianism.

58 The Katyń massacre comprised a series of mass executions of Polish nationals (about 22,000, mainly officers and police officers) carried out by the NKVD ("People's Commissariat for Internal Affairs", the Soviet Secret Police) in April and May 1940.

59 See the events of March 1968 (or "the March events") – a major series of protests against the Government by students, intellectuals, and others. They were also connected to the mass emigration of Polish citizens of Jewish origin as a consequence of an anti-Semitic campaign.

democracy possible.[60] This event was of exceptional importance, a very rare situation in Polish history, when Poles holding opposing views were cooperating peacefully to transform the state and its political system and achieved consensus. After 30 years, this consensus is once again assessed as the betrayal of Poles by Poles.

3.2 Historical and other sources – explanations of the emotional trajectory of Poles

Collective victimhood based on the loss of statehood, defeat, and the trauma of war is specifically preserved in the literature of romanticism and connected to messianism ("Poland is a messiah of nations", said Mickiewicz in "Dziady").[61] As a result, the claim that Poles deserve better has been constantly and strongly heard. The notion of messianism has been strengthened and developed by Catholicism and the Catholic Church, which has played the role of a consolidating institution for the Polish nation and for preserving its culture, especially during partition. As historical background, the defence of Christian Europe against the Ottoman Turks is used to highlight the relevance of Poles in European history and culture. Poles view themselves, just like the Hungarians, as the "defenders of Europe", and strongly embrace this myth. Obviously, "messianism" refers not only to the nation as a messiah. Such a fate also demands a messiah who would lead the state against adversity. This romantic vision of the independent Poles and Poland as the messiah of nations was, however, not the only one developed at that time. The second concept was the hard work required to promote the well-being of individual Poles, which was seized upon by Polish positivism as a reaction to the failure of the uprisings.[62] These two movements (romanticism and Polish positivism) created a double identity for Poles, connected with the co-existence of contradicting features, aspirations, and concepts. It is clear when we consider how the Polish nation was born. During the period of partition (at the end of the 18th century and throughout the 19th century), a general concept of the Polish nation and its sovereignty was developed. The concept was founded, first, on the pre-revolutionary noble-based community.[63] Nobles were familiar with revolutionary ideas, such as the American concept of "independence" and the French concept of "equality". The idea of independence in particular was developed by Polish revolutionaries (e.g. Tadeusz Kościuszko),[64] as well as by the romantic poets (e.g. Juliusz Słowacki).[65] However, the modern Polish nation emerged under foreign

60 A Bień-Kacała, "Informal Constitutional Change: The Case of Poland", *Przegląd Prawa Konstytucyjnego* 6(40) (2017), 199–218.
61 Miłosz, n. 51, 263–264.
62 Polish positivism encompasses the period in philosophy and literature from 1863–late 19th century. The main Polish propagators of hard work and the economic development of the Polish nation were Maria Konopnicka, Bolesław Prus, and Henryk Sienkiewicz (the last also propagated patriotism).
63 Tarnowska, n. 49, 29–34.
64 Tarnowska, n. 49, 216.
65 Miłosz, n. 51, 281–282.

oppression when there was no independent state.[66] Therefore, the struggle for freedom and equality was combined with the fight for an independent state. In consequence, Poles are constantly torn between the importance of the community (an independent Poland – the Motherland, the Polish nation as ideals of romanticism) and the value of hard work for personal freedom and happiness (associated with Polish positivism). However, historical events have shown that the Poles could not establish a strong independent state and the reforms undertaken could not bring individual well-being. Failure on these two grounds has given rise to the feeling of national weakness. In order to deal with this weakness, two visions of Poland have emerged and been identified by sociologists.[67] The first is a conservative vision, which is related to retreating to "ourness", while the second is a liberal and left-wing approach. The latter recommends openness and the adoption of ideas from abroad to counter the weakness of the reforms undertaken. However, psychologists have identified an obstacle to such openness.[68] According to their findings, Poles represent a strong negative auto-stereotype (exhibiting a low level of pride in political and societal achievements); but at the same time, they display a high level of positive identification with the national ingroup (a high level of pride in being Polish). Such a psychological profile creates specific simultaneous feelings. On the one hand, Poles need to reform and change the country; and on the other hand, they want to live within an imagined, idealistic, and great Poland. The grounds for polarization and two divergent visions of Poland can be seen here.

In the context of the transition from and to democracy, Poland is depicted "as pure and innocent – a victim of historical circumstances dictated and imposed by foreign rulers".[69] Such a perception strongly affects the sense of common identity, even if involvement in the communist state has never been disputed. Therefore, the description of Poles as collaborators with the Nazi regime or as perpetrators encounters a very strong reaction,[70] even if presented in an artistic sense.[71] Nowadays, certain intellectuals and artists are referred to as "anti-Polish". In such emotional circumstances, the need for the "defence of the honour of Poland and

66 Z Wojciechowski, *Nacjokratyzm, czyli rządy sejmikowe* [*Natiocratism, Sejmiks' Ruling*] (Drukarnia Uniwersytetu Poznańskiego Poznań, 1936) 20–21.

67 A Leszczyński, *No dno po prostu jest Polska: Dlaczego Polacy tak bardzo nie lubią swojego kraju i innych Polaków* [*Poland Hits Rock Bottom: Why Poles Do Not Like Their Country and Other Poles*] (W.A.B., 2017) 255–264.

68 M Bilewicz, *Być gorszymi* [*To Be Worse*] (Uniwersytet Warszawski, 2008) 43–47.

69 A Gliszczyńska-Grabias and A Śledzińska-Simon, "Victimhood of the Nation as a Legally Protected Value in Transitional States – Poland as a Case Study", https://ssrn.com/abstract=3120407, 5.

70 Especially to JT Gross's books: *Neighbors: The Destruction of the Jewish Community in Jedwabne, Poland* (Princeton University Press, 2001); *Fear: Anti-Semitism in Poland After Auschwitz* (Random House, 2006); *Złote żniwa: Rzecz o tym, co się działo na obrzeżach zagłady Żydów* [*Golden Harvest: What Was Happening On the Outskirts of the Extermination of the Jews*] (Znak, 2011).

71 See the strong reaction to the film *Ida* and to the winning of an Oscar in 2015, e.g. at www.theguardian.com/film/2015/jan/30/pawel-pawlikowski-ida-criticism-film

the Poles" arises and is promoted, especially by right-wing politicians and their milieu.[72] In 2006, a new crime of "defamation of the Polish Nation" (*lex Gross*) was introduced to the criminal code, but it was annulled by the Constitutional Tribunal in 2008.[73] Ten years later Poles faced the same emotional rollercoaster, and a new version of the previous offence was introduced.[74] The background to the provision was the homogeneous perception of the Polish nation, which also includes the view that during the Holocaust, the Poles were saviours not perpetrators. Again, the new provision was challenged. The official message was that Poles can only act in a positive way. Therefore, the enactment may be linked to Poles' willingness to secure a positive perception of themselves. This situation triggered a sharp reaction from Israel, and the provision was repealed on 27 June 2018.[75] From sociological and psychological points of view, two extreme attitudes may be observed in reaction to a historical crime: a reduction of nationalism and openness to strangers; or an increase in nationalism and a retreat from openness.[76] It can therefore be concluded that in Poland there are two visions of the nation (homogeneous or heterogeneous). They have been shaped by historical events; and, depending on the events, one takes precedence over the other. The aforementioned offence defined the Polish nation as a homogeneous entity consisting of only good people. Such an approach is directly connected to the narrative of the education of Polish history, which promotes an idealized vision of the Poles.[77]

The social order in Poland has comprised parochialism and a folwark-like[78] societal structure.[79] As a result, Poles organize themselves by establishing a hierarchy;[80] thus, a democratic method of decision-making is almost impossible. Consequently, Poles need a type of strong leader – or, better, a "messiah" – who will tell them what is good or bad and what they deserve (see mythological persons and similar figures, such as Józef Piłsudski and Lech Kaczyński[81]). Every

72 Gliszczyńska-Grabias and Śledzińska-Simon, n. 69, 5–9.

73 CT judgment of 8 September 2008, K 5/07.

74 The Law on the Institute of National Remembrance, 26 January 2018.

75 See both statutes at https://ipn.gov.pl/pl/o-ipn/ustawa/24216,Ustawa.html

76 Leszczyński, n. 67, 252–254.

77 M Bilewicz, *Między idealizacją a hiperkrytycyzmem: Polska niepamięć historyczna i jej źródła* [*Between Idealization and Hypercriticism: Poland Historical Oblivion and Its Sources*], Instytut Studiów Zaawansowanych, Warszawa, Seria ANALIZY, September 2018, 1–8.

78 A folwark was a primarily serfdom-based farm and agricultural enterprise. Folwarks originated as land belonging to a feudal lord and not rented out to peasants but worked by his own hired labour. The peasants toiled on the lots they rented from the lord, but in addition were obliged to provide complimentary labour for the lord on his folwark.

79 E Michalik and J Santorski, *Polska na kozetce* [*Poland on the Couch*] (Książki Burda, 2016).

80 A Bień-Kacała, *Równość czy hierarchiczność? Kilka słów o wartościach w państwie, prawie i społeczeństwie [Equality or Hierarchy? A Few Words about Values in the State, Law and Society*], *Gdańskie Studia Prawnicze* XL (2018) 17–30.

81 After a plane crash in 2010, in which Lech Kaczyński died, his authority was transferred to Jarosław Kaczyński (Lech's twin brother). A Bień-Kacała and A Tarnowska,

decision of such a leader is acceptable and undisputable. Reasoning is not needed because of the people's strong belief in the leader's infallibility.

II Post-communist past and beyond

The third wave of democratization in Poland and Hungary was based on the naïve belief that the Western European development of values could be implemented almost overnight in 1989/1990 by the use of institutional implantation, disregarding the necessity for the lengthy process of transformation and the evident existence of the communist or socialist past.[82] By using different approaches towards constitution-making, Poland and Hungary created new constitutional regimes, which were based on the Rule of Law, democracy, and human rights. The Western concept of the Rule of Law was needed for a new legal design after over 40 years of communism. It had to go hand in hand with the newly established constitutional democracy, however, which again was formed based on Western experiences. In the emerging democracies in the region at the beginning of the 1990s, the Rule of Law had to be viewed as a necessary safeguard from a descent into illiberalism – which happened in Russia and Romania.[83]

In 1989, it was believed that Eastern Europe would be able to implement all the values building constitutional democracy. Almost 30 years after the fall of communism, the opinion is shared that only an imitation of and a longing for a (Western type of) "normality" could be observed instead of actual implementation.[84] During the last 30 years, however, the Western "normality" has changed, a fact which has gone unnoticed in Eastern Europe. This region has somehow remained stuck at the beginning of the transition period in the 1990s, with the demand for a strong "national normality", instead of embracing the emerging need for diversity. One of the reasons for this may be found in the particular national identity that was also shaped during the Soviet era,[85] and another could be the memory of conflicts in Europe. Michal Stambulski argues that there are

82 G Skąpska, "Law and Society in a Natural Laboratory: The Case of Poland in the Broader Context of East-Central Europe" in M Kaase, V Sparschuh and A Wenninger (eds), *Three Social Science Disciplines in Central and Eastern Europe: Handbook on Economics, Political Science and Sociology (1989–2001)* (Informationszentrum Sozialwissenschaften; GESIS Servicestelle Osteuropa; Collegium Budapest, Institute for Advanced Study, 2002) 597.

83 For further details, see T Humphrey, "Democracy and the Rule of Law: Founding Liberal Democracy in Post-Communist Europe", *Colum J. E Eur. L* 2(94) (2008) 116.

84 I Krastev and S Holmes, "Explaining Eastern Europe: Imitation and its Discontents", *Journal of Democracy* 3 (2018) 118–122.

85 See further in Lendvai, n. 34; A Zamoyski, *The Polish Way: A Thousand-Year History of the Poles and Their Culture* (Hippocrene Books, 2012); A Bień-Kacała, A Tarnowska, and W Włoch, "Nation – Delegation – Constitution: Reconsidering the Role of Religion in Polish Identity Development", *Bratislava Law Review* 1 (2019) 6–25, and A Bień-Kacała, A Tarnowska, and W Włoch, "The Nation, Delegation, and Constitutional Change in Poland", *Hungarian Journal of Legal Studies* 4 (2018) 355–377; T Drinóczi and A Bień-Kacała, "Extra-legal Particularities and Illiberal

different drives for contemporary constitutional identities. Rejecting the past that produced Nazism and colonialism would not advocate reconstructing the past but would focus on constructing a common good. On the other hand, in a post-socialist setting, the rejection of the communist past would lead to the rejection of a utopian and common future, and demand the reconstruction of the abandoned past, that is, the one that existed before communism.[86]

Social science research[87] shows that neither the Hungarian nor the Polish historical trajectory provides favourable ground on which to build an emotionally stable identity.[88] Hungarians experience a feeling of collective victimhood, primarily because of the Trianon peace treaty (1918), and of being abandoned, to their disappointment, by all regimes throughout Hungarian history.[89] Poles are also traumatized because of the loss of statehood and independence.[90] These particularities were strengthened during the Soviet era in both states. Schwartz and Bardi's findings from 1997 on the value priorities in the region after communist rule seem to be supported by the value research results published in 2019.[91] They concluded that the value profile common in Eastern European countries, which lacks the commitment to egalitarianism and autonomy values, is ill-suited for the development of democracy.[92]

Both nations feel disappointed with democracy[93] and share distrust in public institutions.[94] It seems that traumatization and low trust in institutions, as well as

Constitutionalism: The Case of Hungary and Poland", *Hungarian Journal of Legal Studies* 4 (2018) 338–354.

86 M Stambulski, "Nostalgic Constitutional Identity", *Journal of the Polish section of IR* 3 (2019) 104.

87 See e.g. works in nn 4–8 and 70.

88 Fülöp et al., n. 9, 11.

89 Spiró, n. 38; A Schmidt, "Challenges of the Illiberal Democracy in Hungary: Some Aspects to the 2018 Elections", *Polski Przegląd Politologiczny* 6(2) (2008) 88.

90 See Drinóczi and Bień-Kacała, n. 85, 346–347.

91 Reports are available at https://dpart.org/voices-on-values/. See n. 110.

92 SH Schwartz and A Bardi, "Influences of Adaptation to Communist Rule on Value Priorities in Eastern Europe", *Political Psychology* 2 (1997) 407–408. Similarly, Skąpska, n. 82, 597.

93 For Hungarians, democracy seems to be associated more with economic well-being than with democratic freedoms (of speech, assembly, and association). Only 49 per cent of Hungarians see democracy as a better system than others. However, they still believe that the type of the form of government that guides their lives does not make much difference to them, see: A Bíró-Nagy, "Illiberal Democracy in Hungary: The Social Background and Practical Steps of Building an Illiberal State", www.cidob.org/en/articulos/monografias/illiberals/illiberal_democracy_in_hungary_the_social_background_and_practical_steps_of_building_an_illiberal_state, (2017) 35. Economic support by the state is very important for Poles, and it has been one of the most important issues during electoral campaigns.

94 Around 40–50 per cent of the Polish population/voters/those who participated in a study do not trust in political institutions, such as the government or parliament, www.cbos.pl/SPISKOM.POL/2018/K_035_18.PDF, 9.

reliance on the state's support, provide fertile ground for trading off freedom. This is supported by abovementioned research on value-orientation. Research on value-orientations during communism in our region ascertained that people can indeed gradually acclimate their values to changed circumstances, upgrade the importance of values that become attainable, and downgrade the importance of those whose pursuit is no longer achievable.[95] The question is how long this acclimation takes, and whether it can happen again at all to the extent that it could have transformative force in society. It is intriguing, especially in the Eastern part of Europe, as scholars have identified distinctively Western European values.[96] They found that, when comparing them with those more commonly shared in Eastern Europe, the following stand out in Western Europe: low importance is given to mastery values;[97] most importance is given to affective autonomy values and least importance to conservative values; more appreciation is accorded to initiative and achievement; and more tolerance is shown to outgroups and post-material values, such as freedom and social responsibility. In contrast to the West, it was found that, in our region, mastery values are even less important, while conservativism and hierarchy are more important.[98]

As much as politicians are using similar political means to achieve the very same goal of building illiberal constitutionalism in Poland and Hungary, based on a strong and effective state governed by a populist leader who also governs a (in their view) "homogeneous nation", differences stemming from current constitutional and political context matter less. What seems to be more important here is the specific value-orientation of the ordinary citizen who is still an enthusiastic supporter of the Hungarian or Polish populist leaders, notwithstanding the controversial national politics and explicit xenophobia displayed towards fellow human beings.

It is still the people who tolerate, accept, and even support the changes and populist politics. It seems that people want, or at least do not substantially oppose, the remodelling of constitutionalism in Hungary and Poland. Recent election results, in 2019, in Poland and Hungary could give hope, as the PiS lost its majority in the *Senat*, and in the Hungarian local elections opposition candidates won control in 11 of Hungary's 23 larger cities, including Budapest.[99] Nevertheless, even though these results could bring about a healthier vertical division of

95 Schwartz and Bardi, n. 92, 394. During socialism, and especially during the years called Gulash-communism, people acclimated to the one-party system and socialism, in exchange for relative well-being and foreseeable but slow prosperity and growth.

96 From a different perspective, see M Weber, *The Protestant Ethic and the Spirit of Capitalism* (Routledge, 1930); Wrzesiński, n. 8.

97 "Mastery values emphasize getting ahead through active self-assertion, through changing and mastering the natural and social environment. Exemplary values are ambition, success, and daring." Schwartz and Bardi, n. 92, 390.

98 Schwartz and Bardi, n. 92, 406.

99 B Novak, "Setback for Orban as Opposition in Hungary Gains Ground in Elections", (14 October 2019), www.nytimes.com/2019/10/14/world/europe/hungary-elections-orban.html

power and more quality in legislation,[100] in the Hungarian and Polish illiberalism, respectively, these expectations, unfortunately, could prove to be too high. First, autonomy at the local levels is limited, and local governments need to work within the national, and thus illiberal, framework. Second, the Polish *Senat*, given its powers, cannot significantly influence legislative content and avert any informal (and usually unconstitutional) constitutional change. What the election results showed, on the other hand, was, first, that the Hungarian opposition could organize itself, and had one common candidate against a Fidesz candidate, and people appreciated this at the local level. Second, Poles still support the illiberal turn of the PiS but, at the same time, do not fully accept further reduction of pluralism.[101] They do support other political groups that are consolidated on the left (SLD, Wiosna, Razem) and the farther right (Konfederacja Wolność i Niepodległość) of the political spectrum.

What this result cannot address, and most probably what did not change, is the value attitude of people. Results of scientific narrative psychology and other social psychological empirical studies support our presumption that the emotional attitudes of the people and the community can be found behind the illiberal transformation and the degree of tolerance of disrespect for the Rule of Law. Regardless of the 20 or 25 years of liberal constitutionalism in Hungary and Poland, what we seem to have, to possibly differing degrees, is as follows: lack of respect for others; compromised self-confidence; the feeling of being a victim, with all the attached sensations of inferiority; a strong desire for stability, which is the reason why they are willing to trade off liberal and democratic values and are in need of a strong leader; prioritizing values of conservativism and hierarchy, which leads to a tendency towards conservativism and authoritarianism; reluctance regarding or controversial attitudes towards the values of a liberal constitutional democracy or open society; a majoritarian understanding of democracy.[102] All of

100 On the quality in legislation see T Drinóczi, "Concept of Quality in Legislation – Revisited: Matter of Perspective and a General Overview", *Statute Law Review* 3 (2015).

101 https://poledialogu.org.pl/wp-content/uploads/2019/09/Political-cynicism-Resume-in-English.pdf, 16.

102 See the summary of the Value Research: J Eichhorn et al., "How European Publics and Policy Actors Value an Open Society: Key Insight Across Countries" (Open Society European Policy Institute 2019), http://voicesonvalues.dpart.org/images/finalreports/OSI-019-18-Key-Insights_v5.pdf. The reports on Hungary (by Bulcsú Hunyadi, Csaba Molnár, Veszna Wessenauer), Poland (by Filip Pazderski), Italy, Germany, and France are available at http://voicesonvalues.dpart.org/. It is of interest that Italians, who dealt with a populist governmental crisis in August 2019, share similar value attitudes toward open society values as Hungarians and Poles. Additionally, Zygmunt Bauman opines that it is rather the pluralism of moral rules that instils feelings and fear of uncertainty and ambivalence in the people. Thus, pluralism has brought about chaos among moral values; the world is full of almost unlimited freedom, and an overwhelming responsibility for peoples' own choices created the crisis of morality. Therefore, a strong need arises for stable, solid, and firm values provided by authority. Z Bauman, *Etyka ponowoczesna* [*The Late Modern Ethics*] (Wydawnictwo Aletheia, 2012). Schwartz and Bardi, n. 92, 398.

these identity-related phenomena, which have apparently already been internalized, eventually combine to form a national and constitutional identity.[103] This illiberal mentality, consciously, through direct actions such as constitutional amendments or constitutional court decisions,[104] or subconsciously, through elections[105] and due to the lack of effective social resistance and automatic submission to unquestionable authority, extends to the area of law.[106] Societies thus accept the created illiberal constitutions, which can either be enacted (Poland 1935, Hungary 2011) or remain invisible (Poland 2015). In this latter case, the constitution consists of illiberal practices and unconstitutional rules instead of legitimate legal provisions. This type of group identity, at certain historical moments, seemed and still seems to be fertile soil for populist leaders who have an illiberal vision of society and state. Nevertheless, it does not offer the best conditions for developing the civic virtues necessary for upholding a substantive constitutional democracy. Moreover, the societal illiberal value-orientation also has an impact on notions of democracy, sovereignty, and attitudes towards human rights protection – as we will discuss them in the following parts.

III Possible root cause: the combination of the above

These specific emotional and historical trajectories, value-orientations, and attitudes are seriously aggravated by populism, and overlap with collective narcissism.[107] "Collective narcissism" is defined as "a belief that one's own group (the

103 For constitutional identity, see M Rosenfeld, "Constitutional Identity" in M. Rosenfeld and A Sajó (eds) *The Oxford Handbook of Comparative Constitutional Law* (Oxford University Press, 2012) 756–776; G Jacobsohn, *Constitutional Identity* (Harvard University Press, 2010). For a European perspective, see, e.g., T Drinóczi, "Constitutional Identity in Europe: The Identity of the Constitution. A Regional Approach", *German Law Journal* 21(2) (2020) 105–130. On Hungary and Poland, see Drinóczi and Bień-Kacała, n. 85, 338–354.

104 See the Hungarian amendment to the Fundamental Law (FL) on constitutional identity, the decision of the Constitutional Court (CC) on the constitutional identity from 2016, and the Polish Constitutional Tribunal (CT) on the sovereignty of Poland that shall be defended against EU law and enforceable CJEU decisions from April 2020; T Drinóczi, "Hungarian Constitutional Court: The Limits of EU Law in the Hungarian Legal System", *Vienna Journal On International Constitutional Law* 1 (2017) 139–151; A Bień-Kacała, "Polexit is Coming or is it Already Here? Comments on the Judicial Independence Decisions of the Polish Constitutional Tribunal", *Int'l J. Const. L. Blog*, 28 April 2020, at www.iconnectblog.com/2020/04/polexit-is-coming-or-is-it-already-here-comments-on-the-judicial-independence-decisions-of-the-polish-constitutional-tribunal

105 See all the Hungarian elections from 2010 and the Polish ones since 2015 – with some fallback (Hungarian local elections in 2019 and the election to the Polish *Senat* 2019), both Fidesz and the PiS claimed victory.

106 Similarly see A Sajó, "The Constitution of Illiberal Democracy as a Theory About Society", *Polish Sociological Review* 4 (2018) 405–410.

107 A Golec de Zavala, K Dyduch-Hazar, and D Lantos, "Collective Narcissism: Political Consequences of Investing Self-Worth in the Ingroup's Image", *Advances in Political Psychology* 40(1) (2019) 46, Cichocka and Cislak, n. 4, 69–74; JP Forgas and D

ingroup) is exceptional and entitled to privileged treatment, but others do not sufficiently recognize it. Thus, central to collective narcissism is resentment that the ingroup's exceptionality is not sufficiently externally appreciated".[108] This seems to overwhelmingly direct the Hungarian and Polish populist autocrats, who exploit the unbalanced constitutional identity of their polity and, at the same time, aggrandize this feature of identity, along with the accompanying sense of collective victimhood.

1 Populism – playing with emotions

Populist rhetoric and identity politics seem to be the primary forms of political legitimization in use at present. Today's populists tend to see the people or the nation as a homogeneous or uniform group.[109] Those who are different are viewed as enemies,[110] and are treated accordingly by the use of exclusion, criminalization, demonization, and victimization. These tools and measures also contribute to forge unity, a sense of belonging, and appeal to the unbalanced constitutional identity. In Hungary and Poland, the ground base for this is facilitated by the constitutions themselves, and these tools appear in practise and in legal measures as well.

The preambles to the constitutions are formulated to express the greatness of the nations and their historical victories. However, while the (liberal) Polish Constitution 1997 is more egalitarian and future-oriented, the (illiberal) Hungarian FL is anchored in the past, and links the identity of the members of the Hungarian nation to the historical constitution of Hungary and to religious faith. The FL was meant to be a new beginning, a rupture with the previous 20 years, and also used as a tool for appealing to certain elements of constitutional identity and to offer an alternative narrative for historical events.[111]

The constitutions also encapsulate both the political nation[112] and the cultural nation.[113] Membership of the cultural nation and national ethnicity – Hungarian

Lantos, "Understanding Populism: Collective Narcissism and the Collapse of Democracy in Hungary", www.sydneysymposium.unsw.edu.au/2019/chapters/ForgasSSSP2019%20.pdf, 28.

108 Golec de Zavala, Dyduch-Hazar, and Lantos, n. 107, 37.

109 JW Müller, *What is Populism?* (University of Pennsylvania Press, 2016); J Plattner, "Populism, Pluralism, and Liberal Democracy", *Journal of Democracy* 1(21) (2010) 88.

110 Plattner, n. 109; L Diamond, "Facing Up to the Democratic Recession", *Journal of Democracy* 1 (2015) 149.

111 See further, K Miklóssy and H Nyyssönen, "Defining the New Polity: Constitutional Memory in Hungary and Beyond", *Journal of Contemporary European Studies* (2018) 5–9; H Nyyssönen and J Metsälä, "Highlights of National History? Constitutional Memory and the Preambles of Post-Communist Constitutions", *European Politics and Society*, (2020).

112 Hungarian Fundamental Law art. B (regarding people); Polish Constitution art. 4 (regarding nation).

113 Preambles and other constitutional provisions concerning Polish/Hungarian ethnicity.

or Polish – was repeatedly emphasized during the migration crisis of 2015 and in the years following, and when drafting new laws.[114] In Hungary, the redesign of the electoral rules with the assistance of the CC, and the highly preferential acquisition of Hungarian citizenship by those having Hungarian origin living abroad, led to the two-thirds election victory of the Fidesz Party in 2014.[115]

While Hungary successfully demonizes migrants, in Poland the parliamentary opposition has been excluded from participating in the working sessions of the *Sejm* due to its allegedly obstructive actions. Recently in both states, the LGBTQIA+ community has been made not welcome. Victimization is also a common practice: there have been legal proceedings against Hungarian civil society upon the order of the Prime Minister, and legal procedures against Polish protesters too, who are occasionally harassed by the police. There is also criminal legislation that criminalizes the assistance provided to asylum-seekers by NGOs and violates the human rights of those who enter Hungary illegally. There has been visible violence in Poland towards foreigners – for example, entrepreneurs and students – especially those who look different or who speak other languages. Nowadays, however, that hostility has been more powerfully expressed towards the LGBTQIA+ and women, especially those voicing pro-choice opinions.[116]

The measures used for such demonization and victimization, save for the street violence, are formally legal. This legal fight against migrants and foreigners, or against those who hold opposing views, is presented as a legitimate counteraction against the chaos caused by these individuals and the threat they allegedly pose to security and stability. Populist leaders put themselves forward as being able to restore order – the disorder itself usually being generated by those same populist leaders with their nationalist politics.[117] As the problem is often incorrectly

114 See, e.g., the new billboard campaign against the Soros Plan to relocate migrants from Africa and the Middle East; "Hungarian gov't begins all-out assault on Soros", *Budapest Business Journal* (28 September 2017), https://bbj.hu/politics/hungarian-govt-begins-all-out-assault-on-soros_139438; and the accompanying legislation, and the law on foreign-funded non-governmental organizations (NGOs) of 2017, which introduces new obligations for certain categories of NGOs receiving annual foreign funding above HUF7.2 million – approximately €24,000 – to register and label themselves in all their publications, websites, and press material as "organizations supported from abroad", and to report specific information about the funding they receive from abroad to the Hungarian authorities. These organizations face sanctions if they fail to comply with the new reporting and transparency obligations. This law triggered an infringement procedure; the CJEU condemned Hungary in Case C-78/18 *European Commission v Hungary*. In the case of Poland, such an approach can be seen in connection to the crime of "defamation of Polish nation" as described above.

115 Republikon Institute, *Hungarian Elections 2014: Turnout and the Impact of the Electoral System*, 4 liberty.eu (9 May 2014), http://4liberty.eu/republikon-institute-election-2014-turnout-and-the-impact-of-the-electoral-system, Constitutional Court Dec. 5, 2016, MK.3141/2014 (Hung.).

116 See in more detail in Part V, Limits, point III.

117 It is visible especially in an international or a national context. DW Drezner, "The Angry Populist as Foreign Policy Leader: Real Change or Just Hot Air", *Fletcher F. World Aff.* 41 (2017) 23.

identified, because there might not be a problem at all, or because its focal point lies elsewhere, challenges cannot be adequately addressed, and a legal solution acceptable to the wider environment, that is, the international community or the EU, cannot be found.

A ramification of populism is a new form of identity politics, which is emerging especially in Hungary, and which finds its legal basis in Article 4(2) of the TEU and in the FL.[118] The main message of the FL is that Hungarian constitutional identity is to be found in the past through the historical constitution, and it should be defended against undue influences such as EU legislation, or against any exaggerated and unrealistic attempt to alter the "ethnic map" of Hungary.[119] Identity politics thus have an ethnic implication and an exclusive character as well. Its success may also be supported by historical and societal factors. As Ruprik states, it has deep historical resonance in the CEE societies, because there, as opposed to in Western Europe, no post-colonial integration was experienced that would have opened up society to diversity.[120]

Both populist nationalism and identity politics play with the emotions and exclude rationality.[121] According to András Sajó, "emotional politics refers to a situation where the politics is shaped by emotional manipulation of the masses".[122] This kind of politics has been described as one of the threats to the CEE after the transition period,[123] but, as can be seen, it features in today's politics as well. Such emotional politics allows for the replacement of the Rule of Law with the "verdict of the people". Instead, the Weberian sense of rationalism should be a component of a constitutional democracy, as it limits and even moulds the decision-making process. This is present neither in Hungary nor in Poland, where there is no sign of pursuit of rational, or even constitutional, legislation. It is apparently not demanded by the population, whose value-orientation prioritizes authoriarianism, in the sense of blind submission to authority and a preference for hierarchy and stability.

118 Decision of the CC: 22/2016. (XII. 5.) ABH.

119 "We insist on the ethnic and cultural composition of Hungary", said the Prime Minister. See www.kormany.hu/hu/a-miniszterelnok/beszedek-publikaciok-interjuk/orban-viktor-beszede-a-kulkepviselet-vezetok-ertekezleten-2015

120 J. Ruprik, "The Specter Haunting Europe: Surging Illiberalism in the East", *J. Democracy* 27(77) (2016) 84.

121 C Miller-Idriss (2019) "The Global Dimensions of Populist Nationalism", *The International Spectator* 54(2) 17–34, DOI: 10.1080/03932729.2019.1592870; F Fukuyama, "The Rise of Populist Nationalism", www.credit-suisse.com/about-us-news/en/articles/news-and-expertise/francis-fukuyama-the-rise-of-populist-nationalism-201801.html (2018); MA Waterburg, "Populist Nationalism and the Challenges of Divided Nationhood: The Politics of Migration, Mobility, and Demography in Post 2010 Hungary", *East European Politics and Societies* 34(4) (2020) 962–983; M Feischmidt and B Majtényi, *The Rise of Populist Nationalism: Social Resentment and Capturing the Court in Hungary* (Central European University Press, 2019).

122 A Sajó, "Militant Democracy and Emotional Politics", *Constellations* 19 (2012) 563.

123 A Sajó, "Militant Democracy and Transition Towards Democracy" in A Sajó (ed) *Militant Democracy* (Eleven International Publishing, 2004) 217, 218.

2 Collective narcissism and collective victimhood

As said previously, collective narcissism is a core source of political choices that undermine constitutional democracy. In particular, it is linked to intergroup hostility and aggression, voting behaviour, political conservatism, and conspiratorial thinking. It is related to the biased perception of intergroup reality, in which events are selectively seen and remembered in the service of the ingroup's image and linked to a divisive social identity.[124] It seems that Hungarians and Poles share such a belief and raise political demands on it.[125]

The continual references to the achievements of Hungarians who became famous after leaving the country, and the historical role of Hungary in defense of Europe against the Ottoman Empire, which appears in the FL and political speeches, indicate a pride that is not recognized by others to a sufficient extent. Poles share similar feelings of pride and refer to the defense of Christian Europe against Ottoman (Muslim) culture. Poles were able to preserve national and Catholic values to a greater extent than Western countries. Western states abandoned Hungary and Poland after the Second World War and contributed to their becoming "occupied" by the Soviet Union. There is a demand in political communications for respect to be shown to Hungarians and Poles. Voters' sympathy can easily be gained when calling out EU institutions for acting disrespectfully against Hungarians and Poles when they criticize government actions.[126] Thus, as far as voting behaviour is concerned, collective narcissism is associated with the support of populists worldwide, not only in Poland and Hungary.[127] Another phenomenon, the divisive social identity, just follows on from this. Especially in political communications, we can see that there are true members of the ingroup and those less worthy, which could increase the bond between the "true members" and secure a feeling of belonging.

This could also be connected to the conspiratorial thinking that, in Hungary, is clearly present in the hate campaign against George Soros, the NGOs, and those supporting and promoting human rights and diversity. In Poland, it was clear in relation to the Smoleńsk plane crash in 2010, claiming that former Prime Minister Donald Tusk and Russia were to blame. Conspiratorial thinking is associated with the fictional aggression of outgroups, which leads to physical aggression against members of the outgroup (e.g., attacks on people of colour, including physical attacks or spitting on them) because they speak differently and look different, or are associated with political opposition.

As for the biased perception of intergroup reality, it could be connected in both states to the way in which they dealt with their past in between the two World Wars, and during the Second World War when collaborating with Nazi Germany

124 Golec de Zavala, Dyduch-Hazar, and Lantos, n. 107, 44.

125 Forgas and Lantos, n. 107, 6–7.

126 Lately, see the 2020 Rule of Law Report, *The Rule of Law Situation in the European Union*, Brussels, 30.9.2020 COM(2020) 580 final and country reports on Hungary and Poland.

127 Golec de Zavala, Dyduch-Hazar, and Lantos, n. 107, 55.

and playing their part in the Holocaust, even if we consider that Poland never institutionally collaborated with Nazi Germany. An example in Poland is the aforementioned crime of "defamation of the Polish Nation". In Hungary, there is the revival of nostalgia towards the Horthy regime and the refusal to face this element of the past.

Hungarian and Polish collective narcissism also claims for itself exceptional national moral characteristics, such as honesty, decency, fairness, kindness, or hospitality. Such a constructed "perfect" picture of a nation is then exploited by state propaganda. The notion of the "nation" is exaggerated, abused, and based on the specific importance of nationalism that is bound to freedom.[128] As we have already mentioned, in both states, the fight for personal freedom in the mid-19th century was connected with a claim for a sovereign state. Moreover, Polish – and, we might add, Hungarian – collective narcissism is linked to religious fundamentalism,[129] misogyny,[130] and homophobia.[131] Being Polish, stereotypically, means being a male, heterosexual, Catholic person.[132] By the same token, being Hungarian, stereotypically, means being a male, heterosexual Christian.

It seems that even during the COVID-19 pandemic, Orbán has taken advantage of the emotional characteristic of the Hungarian constitutional identity when playing the role of the sole saviour of the nation. The same was done by Kaczyński, when he kept pushing for the presidential election to be organized as soon as possible in the changing circumstances caused by the same pandemic.[133] This health crisis has also proved to be a useful time to push the illiberal value system in the face of an EU that is reported to abandon states in their time of need and attack Hungary and Poland with irrelevant and overpoliticized claims of implementing Rule of Law considerations built into the Rule of Law conditionality mechanism.[134] This context could have been the reason why almost no one in Poland protested against decisions of the CT on the non-applicability of the CJEU's rulings, which inevitably may push Poland away from the European community.[135]

128 I Krastev and S Holmes, "Explaining Eastern Europe: Imitation and Its Discontents" *Journal of Democracy* 29(3) (2018) 120.
129 Golec de Zavala, Dyduch-Hazar, and Lantos, n. 107, 44.
130 See e.g., the underrepresentation of women in the public sphere, especially in Hungary. Women's place is in the kitchen, the role of the women in society is to give birth – speeches of MPs in the Hungarian Parliament; a Polish PiS MP during the 2019 electoral campaign used similar rhetoric: "If a woman first gave birth at the age of 30, how many children can be born? These are the consequences of telling women that they do not have to do what God has called them to do."
131 See the attitude towards LGBTQIA+ communities in constitutional amendments, CT decisions, and local governments resolutions. More on this in Part V, Limits, point III.
132 Golec de Zavala, Dyduch-Hazar, and Lantos, n. 107, 44.
133 See more in Part V, Limits, point II.
134 2018/0136(COD) Protection of the Union's budget in case of generalised deficiencies as regards the rule of law in the Member States.
135 Bień-Kacała, n. 104. Protests come from abroad rather than Poland, https://ruleoflaw.pl/call-to-jourova-and-reynders-act-to-save-democracy-in-poland/

At the same time, the effort to build the CEE identity based on an alternative vision of European values has gone almost unnoticed.[136] In Poland, attitudes towards the EU are not very optimistic;[137] while in Hungary, the population is told that the EU does not provide financial help during the crisis. Again, collective narcissism creates a demand to appreciate particular values as against common ones. The newest example of the demand to appreciate Hungary and Poland is the new common project to establish a Rule of Law Institute to counter the "EU attack" and stop the EU applying "double standards towards Hungary and Poland".[138] The way the Hungarian Minister for Foreign Affairs addressed the issue is quite telling, in terms of emotions: "The aim of this institute of comparative law would be that we should not be taken for fools", adding that he had "had enough of some Western European politicians using us as a punchbag". The stereotypical view on the polities and the accompanying national populist politics have also been reinforced by describing the Hungarian and Polish governmental policies as patriotic, based on Christian values, and as focusing on national interests as opposed to the international liberal mainstream.[139]

Consequently, the assumed victimized past that has remained unresolved, the present victimhood that has been aggrandized, and the intense feeling of exceptionality have created an environment that is friendly towards illiberal remodelling, including the transformation of the components of constitutionalism to illiberal legality, illiberal democracy, and the misuse and lowering of human rights protection.

136 https://rmx.news/article/v4/poland-hungary-czechia-and-slovakia-need-a-joint-treaty-that-presents-alternative-vision-of-european-values?fbclid=IwAR1A7AhiboVppMkFMPZcGButa1gk6onRM61suynHwotGxj6t5y8MKBVqjgc

137 https://oko.press/konsensus-polakow-w-sprawach-europejskich-sie-skonczyl-nowe-badania/

138 https://notesfrompoland.com/2020/09/28/poland-and-hungary-to-create-institute-for-assessing-rule-of-law-in-eu-countries/;https://www.reuters.com/article/instant-article/idUKKBN26J1RU

139 https://hungarytoday.hu/hungary-poland-new-comparative-law-institute/

IV Limits

Comparative perspective

States undergoing democratic backsliding change from their "original state" to something new that is perceived to be worse. Democratic decay, however, has been seen to affect constitutional democracies.[1] Some of these states face significant economic and financial crises; others struggle with migration challenges, the threat of terror, and currently the COVID-19 pandemic. Populist politicians tend to amplify each of these challenges. Even where the results of populist influence are undeniable, there are remarkable differences among states in democratic decay, not only in terms of institutional and structural mechanisms[2] but also due to the circumstances of their emergence as constitutional democracies, which is usually referred to as the third wave of the democratization process.

I The emergence of illiberal constitutionalism

As is well known, this process led to three results. The first was a constitutional democracy, which still has not shown any sign of regression.[3] Second, it resulted in an authoritarian (re)consolidation, which, according to Steven Levitsky and Lucan Way, is not to be viewed as a democratic rollback.[4] Third, democracy in some other states has reverted to a more or less authoritarian form, as Alina Rocha Menocal and others observe, relying on Latin-American and African experiences. While authoritarian (re)consolidation (the second result) does not typify the CEE states, because those in power in the regime from which the democratic transition emerged (the communist-socialist party) differ from those that hold power now (right-wing parties, conservatives), the authoritarian form (the third result) could fit the CEE

1 See e.g. TG Daly, "Diagnosing Democratic Decay", www.academia.edu/34052302/Diagnosing_Democratic_Decay
2 See Introduction, point II. 2.
3 See, e.g. the Baltic states, especially Estonia.
4 S Levitsky and LA Way, "The Myth of Democratic Recession", *Democracy* 26(45) (2015) 46–48.

DOI: 10.4324/9781003175353-4

context[5] regardless of the label we attach. The reason is simple, as stated by Menocal et al. about the countries in which they are interested: the leading political players, forces, and institutions do not accept democracy as "the only game in town".[6]

We partly disagree with this view because, as argued below, we contest the categorization of Hungary and Poland as authoritarian states. We see the events as follows: from 1989/1990, a vector of changes led towards a fully fledged constitutional democracy; as from 2010 (in Hungary) and 2015 (in Poland) this vector turned "down" and now points towards authoritarianism (Figure IV.1).[7] Based on qualitative and quantitative arguments, we claim that in the continuum from liberal democracy toward an authoritarian regime, these two states must have already passed the midway point but still have not reached the far end signalled by authoritarianism. This also means that in Hungary and Poland, due to the constitutional and historical development of the European states, constitutionalism, the Rule of Law, the ideal of democracy and the EU, constitutional democracy and multilevel constitutionalism should be the only game in town. This playing field, however, seems to be taken seriously by Hungarian and Polish actors only in one instance. It occurs when they have already "hit the wall" and receive immediate or prolonged political and legal reminders about the extent of the boundaries that are still tolerated by the political and legal actors of the EU. Thus, illiberal constitutionalism is not the opposite of liberal constitutionalism but rather a state of relativization.[8] This relativization technique, that is, pushing the limits game, has been increasingly utilized, but only until it reaches the tolerance threshold of either the population or the EU – for example, until it feels that transformative reforms can be made while still remaining politically unpunished.[9]

The constitutional remodelling in Hungary and Poland is the result of a peaceful constitutional development that features the selective and arbitrary application of the constitutions in both states, the non-inclusive character of the constitution-making process in Hungary, and the abusive and unconstitutional

5 AR Menocal, V Fritz, and L Rakner, "Hybrid Regimes and the Challenge of Deepening and Sustaining Democracy in Developing Countries", *South African Journal of International Affairs* 1 (2008) 15–30.

6 Ibid., 31. See also A von Bogdandy et al. (eds), *Transformative Constitutionalism in Latin America: The Emergence of a New Jus Commune* (Oxford University Press, 2017).

7 This is what Anna Lührmann and Staffan I Lindberg call democratic recession, as a form of the third wave of autocratization, which mainly affects democracies. A Lührmann and SI Lindberg, "A Third Wave of Autocratization Is Here: What Is New about It?" *Democratization* 7 (2019) 1103–1104.

8 Similarly, see MF Plattner, "Populism, Pluralism, and Liberal Democracy", *J. Democracy* 21(81, 91) (2010).

9 We elaborate on this in Part VI, Stability, point III.

informal constitutional changes in Poland. This understanding of constitutional democracy suggests that the Rule of Law, human rights, and democracy may have been defectively worded in a constitution, poorly implemented, or poorly enforced. The precise problem lies here: these states are still constitutional democracies in a formal sense. Each one still has a constitution, which is more than the formal constitution of an autocratic system, as it, for example, maintains and allows the functioning, to a certain extent, of constitutional review mechanisms and is less oppressive than those of even the modern authoritarian regimes. Both constitutions still contain EU clauses and formally maintain the Rule of Law and formal democracy in the majoritarian sense, though with no patience for procedural guarantees and individual rights. These states misuse the language of fundamental rights mainly for two reasons. First, these matters might contradict the will of the majority, as argued by the leading populist parties. Second, they might slow down the decision-making process, which is expected to be fast and efficient in order to prove the capability and strength of the state and thus its populist leader.[10] Both constitutions still provide for the constitutional protection of fundamental rights, but either offer a lower level of protection than the previous constitution[11] or contradict international and European human rights standards.[12] Nonetheless, these issues are politically important ones; there is either no or considerably less depletion of the constitutional protection over the rights, with minimal political implications.

II A comparative perspective – looking for constraints

It worth repeating here that, in our view, when we are studying systemic deterioration, the matter of degree (what is indicated by different types of indices) is a matter of kind.

We have reviewed the figures set out in the most important indices, and while appreciating their different conceptual framework and methodology, we found that, from a holistic and quantitative perspective, we can support our claim that neither Hungary nor Poland is in as bad a shape as Turkey or Russia – the states with which Hungary and Poland are usually paired. Nevertheless, they are doing much worse than their European counterparts. For the sake of terminological clarity, we have extended our comparison with Singapore (authoritarian constitutionalism) and Hong Kong (hybrid constitutionalism) as well.[13] The holistic approach has allowed us to construct a more complex picture in which we could

10 Plattner, n. 8, 88.

11 See in Hungary, for example, family, social security, and the right to assembly, which can be restricted by the enjoyment of privacy, family life, and home; Arts L, XIX(1), VI, Fundamental Law (FL). The new Art VI was introduced by the Seventh Amendment in 2018.

12 See Part V, Limits, point III.

13 We would not think it important to contrast the Hungarian and Polish figures with European states because it is not debated at all that they do much better.

combine and consider the overall results of figures, assessments, and analyses from more rule-of-law oriented (WJP), more democracy-induced (EIU Democracy Index, V-dem), human-rights-focused (Freedom House), and "combined" (BTI) indices. Based on these, and supported with qualitative arguments,[14] we believe that we can make a case that there is a tangible, though continuously weakening and eroding, constraint on public power, which still keeps Hungary and Poland away from authoritarianism and preserves their constitutionalist identity.

Based on the WJP Rule of Law Index Summary Table (Table IV.1),[15] we can detect some distinctive differences between Hungary and Poland, on the one hand, and Russia and Turkey, on the other. According to that table, the overall score of Hungary and Poland has been decreasing since 2015,[16] but has never dipped below 0.5, while Russia and Turkey have stayed within the range 0.42 and 0.47. The overall score for Hungary has firmly decreased from 0.58 to 0.53, while for Poland the decrease is within the range from 0.72 (2015) to 0.66 (2019). The WJP measures the Rule of Law in eight categories, but for now, we focus on the sub-category of constraints on government power. A steady decrease can be seen in the case of Hungary and Poland, while Russia scores around 0.4, reaching 0.36 in 2020. Turkey experienced backsliding from 0.37 (2015) to 0.30 (2020). In the region, Hungary, with its score changing from 0.49 (2015) to 0.40 (2020), was ranked 23rd out of 24 for three years (2015–2018), falling to last position in 2019, and staying there in 2020. It is notable that it scored 0.63 in 2012–2013. Poland fell back 0.2 points from 2015: in that year, it scored 0.77, dropping to 0.58 by 2020. Simultaneously, its regional rank dropped from 15th to 21st. In 2020, the WLP Index explained that in a five-year period, Hungary and Poland declined the most in the region. Hungary scored the lowest in many categories, including constraints and open government – the latter of which we would view as a component of democracy. Poland dropped the most in 2019: it fell from position 27 to 51, while Hungary fell three positions and is now ranked 60.

Conversely, Singapore, which exercises authoritarian constitutionalism, obviously performs better in the WJP Rule of Law Index, but, according to the EIU Democracy Index and the reports of Freedom House (Table IV.4 on the assessment of Freedom House), it does not do so in other fields. The reason is that in authoritarian constitutionalism, liberal freedoms are protected at an intermediate level, elections are reasonably free and fair (but without genuine party competition), and there is a normative commitment to constraints on public

14 Part II, Terms.

15 See directly at https://worldjusticeproject.org/our-work

16 We have chosen 2015 as a baseline for two reasons. First, the reports are more comparable from 2015, despite the fact that they include more and more countries to be measured: the number increased from 102 (2015) to 126 (2019), while in the years 2016–2018 the number of countries studied was 113. Second, Polish deterioration started in 2015, when the Hungarian one was already ongoing.

Table IV.1 WJP Rule of Law Index Summary table[17]

	2015		*2016*		*2017–2018*		*2019*		*2020*	
	Overall score	*Con-straints*	*Overall score*	*Con-straints*	*Overall score*	*Con-straints*	*Overall score*	*Con-straints*	*Overall score*	*Con-strain-ts*
Hun-gary	0.58	0.49	0.57	0.46	0.55	0.44	0.53	0.41	0,53	0,40
Poland	0.71	0.77	0.71	0.68	0.67	0.61	0.66	0.58	0,66	0,58
Russia	0.47	0.39	0.45	0.4	0.47	0.39	0.47	0.45	0,47	0,36
Turkey	0.46	0.37	0.43	0.32	0.42	0.3	0.42	0.32	0,43	0,30
Singa-pore	0.81	0.76	0.82	0.75	0.8	0.7	0.8	0.69	0,78	0,67
Hong Kong	0,76	0,71	0,77	0,7	0,77	0,66	0,77	0,65	0,76	0,65

Source: authors, revised version of the Table in T Drinóczi and A Bień-Kacała (eds), *Rule of Law, Common Values and Illiberal Constitutionalism: Poland and Hungary within the European Union* (Routledge, 2021) 29.
Note: The rating ranges from 0 (weaker adherence to the Rule of Law) to 1 (stronger adherence to the Rule of Law).

power.[18] This is supported by the WJP Rule of Law Index: Singapore's overall score is around 0.8, and in the sub-category of constraints on government power it scores around 0.7 (with a range of 0.77 and 0.67), which makes it a better performer than Hungary and Poland (Table IV.1). This characteristic does not feature in the BTI Political Transformation Index (Table IV.2), which, in its Rule of Law section, labels both Hungary and Singapore as highly defective democracies. Considering the other states, the difference is palpable: Poland retains its defective democracy status, while Russia and Turkey are considered moderate autocracies.

To sum up: Poland and Hungary have not been labelled as moderate autocracies in neither the mentioned categories, while Singapore is considered to be a highly defective democracy and hard-line autocracy, and Russia and Turkey are called either highly defective democracies or moderate autocracies in the categories that interest us most.

Nevertheless, the BTI Index (Table IV.3 on the BTI Index) also warns that Hungary is on the edge of a turn, especially where the threshold of "Free and fair elections" is concerned. The threshold value there is 6, and Hungary scored 6 in 2020. In the categories "Freedom of expression" and "Separation of powers", Hungary has almost reached the threshold value. Threshold value is important in the assessment of whether a country is a democracy or an autocracy. A country is

17 Venezuela is not indicated as it finds itself at the bottom of the lists with its overall score of 0.32 in 2015 and 0.28 in 2019. Corrales argues that Venezuela's shift from competitive authoritarianism towards authoritarianism has been facilitated by authoritarian legalism. J Corrales, "The Authoritarian Resurgence: Autocratic Legalism in Venezuela", *Journal of Democracy* 26 (2015) 38.
18 M Tushnet, "Authoritarian Constitutionalism", *Cornell Law Review* 100 (2015) 72.

Table IV.2 The BTI Political Transformation Index

Which index …		*how to call …*	*the country of …*	*within the (conceptual\analytical) framework of …*
BTI Political Transformation Index	Value	defective democracy	Hungary	https:\\www.bti-project.org\en\methodology.htmlDemocracy is measured against these five indicators. • democracy in consolidation • defective democracy • highly defective democracy • moderate autocracy • hard-line autocracy
			Poland	
		moderate autocracy	Russia	
			Turkey	
			Singapore	
		n\d	Hong Kong	
	Stateness	democracy in consolidation	Hungary	
			Poland	
		defective democracy	Russia	
			Turkey	
		democracy in consolidation	Singapore	
		n\d	Hong Kong	
	Political participation	defective democracy	Hungary	
		democracy in consolidation	Poland	
		moderate autocracy	Russia	
		highly defective democracy	Turkey	
		moderate autocracy	Singapore	
		n\d	Hong Kong	
	Rule of Law	highly defective democracy	Hungary	
		defective democracy	Poland	
		moderate autocracy	Russia	
			Turkey	
		highly defective democracy	Singapore	
		n\d	Hong Kong	
	Stability of government and institutions	highly defective democracy	Hungary	
		defective democracy	Poland	
		moderate autocracy	Russia	
			Turkey	
		hard-line autocracy	Singapore	
		n\d	Hong Kong	
	Political and social integration	defective democracy	Hungary	
		defective democracy	Poland	
		moderate autocracy	Russia	
		highly defective democracy	Turkey	
			Singapore	
		n\d	Hong Kong	

Source: authors.

Table IV.3 The BTI Index

Which index …		*how to call …*	*the country of …*	*within the (conceptual/analytical) framework of …*
BTI democracy vs. autocracy	reaching a threshold or below a threshold	at the threshold: Free and fair elections almost at the threshold: Freedom of expression and Separation of powers	Hungary	https://www.bti-project.org/en/methodology.html a country is classified as an autocracy if even one score falls short of the relevant threshold -Free and fair elections -Effective power to govern -Association/assembly rights -Freedom of expression -Separations of powers -Civil rights -Monopoly on the use of force and Basic administration (average) autocracy is failing country in which the state's monopoly on the use of force and basic administrative structures are lacking to such an extent that the government is severely limited in its capacity to act
		not below since 2010, steady deterioration in all categories (except Effective power to govern), especially in Freedom of expression and Separation of powers	Poland	
		below (not below in Civil rights and Monopoly on the use of force and Basic administration)	Russia	
		below (not below in Effective power to govern and Monopoly on the use of force and Basic administration)	Turkey	
		below (not below in Civil rights and Monopoly on the use of force and Basic administration)	Singapore	
		n/d	Hong Kong	

Source: authors.

classified as an autocracy if even one score falls short of the relevant threshold of "Free and fair elections", "Effective power to govern", "Association/assembly rights", "Freedom of expression", "Separation of powers", "Civil rights", "Monopoly on the use of force" and "Basic administration" (average).

While Russia has never been a fully democratic state, as elections are rather plebiscites and they are not based on a proper electoral programme (they are not "programmatic") and do not even satisfy the minimalistic Schumpeterian meaning, Poland and Hungary both experienced constitutional democracy after the transition, and their elections still have their "programmatic" meaning, are free, even if not necessarily fair or free from undue manipulation, and it is still possible to lose a majority. Even if elections did show some degree of being flawed, as in Hungary, which, in the assessment of

Table IV.4 The assessment of Freedom House

Which index …		*how to call …*	*the country of …*	*within the (conceptual/analytical) framework of …*
Freedom House	freedom score (political rights and civil liberties)	from free (–2018) to partly free (2019–)	Hungary	https://freedomhouse.org/reports/freedom-world/freedom-world-research-methodology
		free	Poland	
		not free	Russia	
			Turkey	
		partly free	Singapore	• free
			Hong Kong	• partly free
	internet freedom	free	Hungary	• not free
		n/d	Poland	
		not free	Russia	
			Turkey	• consolidated democracy
		partly free	Singapore	• semi-consolidated democracy
		n/d	Hong Kong	
	democracy	from semi-consolidated democracy (2019) to transitional/hybrid (2020)	Hungary	• transitional/hybrid • consolidated authoritarian (post-Soviet states in Asia)
		from consolidated democracy (2019) to semi-consolidated democracy (2020)	Poland	
		consolidated authoritarianism	Russia	
		n/d	Turkey	
			Singapore	
			Hong Kong	

Source: authors.

Freedom House in 2020 (Table IV.4), sunk from being a semi-consolidated democracy to a transitional or hybrid regime,[19] or some elements of political influence, as in Poland, which is now labelled a semi-consolidated democracy, political pluralism and political competitiveness are still in place.[20] The electoral process is assessed relatively highly (9 out of 12), while Poland scored 11 out of 12 in 2019 and 2020.[21] The majority still has the power to rewrite electoral rules to favour themselves, as occurred in 2020 in Hungary – which could eventually, in 2022, eliminate the chances of changing the reigning elite. However, it has not happened in Poland, not even during the COVID-19 pandemic – even though there were attempts to do so.[22] There is always a possibility to further monopolize the media – which is an ongoing practice in both states. Still, the index scores reflect significant differences in this regard too.[23]

Similarly to the assessment of Freedom House in the category "Democracy", V-Dem's assessment (Table IV.5), which is focused on Dahl's concept of electoral democracy (clean election, universal suffrage, elected executive, freedom of expression and association, alternative sources of information), shows that Hungary deteriorated from being a liberal democracy to embracing non-democracy, which is also labelled as being an "electoral authoritarian regime" (2020) or "electoral autocracy" (2020). Poland has dropped from being a liberal democracy to an electoral democracy, and is following in the footprints left by Hungary (2020). Within the theoretical framework used, this assessment places Hungary, together with Turkey, Russia and Singapore, under the heading "electoral autocracy". Poland is on its way to joining.

However, if we take a look at the other indexes measuring democracy (the three Tables IV.6–8 on EIU and the one on Freedom House), Hungary and Poland still perform better compared to these other countries. According to the EIU Democracy Index (2006–2016, and 2020, Tables 7–8), which designates countries as full democracies if they score between 8 and 10, Hungary and Poland are flawed democracies,[24] because they score greater than 6 but less than or equal to 8. Turkey is a hybrid state (scores greater than 4, and less than or equal to 6),[25] Russia, as it scores less than or

19 Bozóki and Hegedűs, who already labelled Hungary a hybrid regime in 2018. A Bozóki and D Hegedűs, "An Externally Constrained Hybrid Regime: Hungary in the European Union", *Democratization* 25(7) (2018).

20 According to Freedom House, both countries deteriorated in 2020. Hungary scored 49, Poland 65, while Russia reached 7, https://freedomhouse.org/countries/nations-transit/scores

21 For a comparison, in 2019, Russia scored 0 and Turkey scored 5, https://freedomhouse.org/countries/freedom-world/scores

22 T Drinóczi and A Bień-Kacała, "COVID-19 in Hungary and Poland: Extraordinary Situation and Illiberal Constitutionalism", *The Theory and Practice of Legislation* 8(1–2) (2020) 171–192.

23 Freedom House 2019 and 2020, media freedom: 2 out of 4 for Hungary and 3 for Poland, while Russia scored 0, Turkey 1, and Singapore 2.

24 A flawed democracy respects civil liberties and free and fair elections, but has significant weaknesses in other respects, such as media freedom, low participation, and problems regarding governance.

25 In hybrid regimes, there is a certain degree of pluralism but with frequent harassment of journalists, a non-independent judiciary, and substantial electoral irregularities, including government pressure on opposition parties.

Table IV.5 The assessment of V-Dem

V-Dem	• *from liberal democracy to* • *non-democracy* • *electoral authoritarian regime (2020)* • *electoral autocracy (2020)*	*Hungary*	*Dahl's concept of electoral democracy (clean election, universal suffrage, elected executive, freedom of expression and association, alternative sources of information)https://www.v-dem.net/media/filer_public/f0/5d/f05d46d8-626f-4b20-8e4e-53d4b134bfcb/democracy_report_2020_low.pdf*
	• from liberal democracy to • electoral democracy • autocratizing country • steps in the footprints of Hungary have been taken (2020)	Poland	• *liberal democracy* • *electoral democracy* • *electoral autocracy* • *closed autocracy*
	electoral autocracy	Russia	
		Turkey	
		Singapore	
	closed autocracy	Hong Kong	

Source: authors.

Table IV.6 EIU Democracy Index

EIU Democracy Index • electoral process and pluralism • civil liberties • the functioning of government • political participation • political culture	flawed democracy (2006-)	Hungary	Democracy Index 2019A year of democratic setbacks and popularprotest 52–55 • full democracy • flawed democracy • hybrid regimes • authoritarian regimes
		Poland	
	authoritarian	Russia	
	hybrid	Turkey	
	flawed democracy	Singapore	
		Hong Kong	

Source: authors.

Table IV.7 EIU Democracy Index 2006–2016

	EIU Democracy Index 2006–2016
	(from–to)
Hungary	7.53–6.72
Poland	7.3–6.83
Russia	5.02–3.24
Turkey	5.7–5.04
Singapore	5.89–6.38
Hong Kong	6.42 (2016)

Source: authors.

Table IV.8 EIU Democracy Index 2020

	EIU Democracy Index 2020 on 2019						
	Overall score	*Rank*	*Electoral process and pluralism*	*Functioning of the government*	*Political participation*	*Political culture*	*Civil liberties*
Hungary	6.63	55=	8,75	6,07	5,00	6,25	7,06
Poland	6.62	57	9,17	6,07	6,11	4,38	7,35
Russia	3.11	134=	2,17	1,79	5,00	2,5	4,12
Turkey	4.09	110	3,08	5,00	5,00	5,00	2,35
Singapore	6.02	75=	3,92	7,86	5,00	6,25	7,06
Hong Kong	6.02	75=	3,58	4,36	6,11	7,5	8,53

Source: authors.

equal to 4, transformed from hybrid to authoritarian (2011), and Singapore has gradually been upgraded from a hybrid to a flawed democracy (2014). EIU Democracy Index 2019 also mentions explicitly that the gap between the Czech Republic, Slovakia, and Slovenia, on the one hand, and Hungary and Poland, on the other hand, is now significant. Poland fell below Hungary for the first time in 2019.[26]

The "freedom" score (political rights and civil liberties) and "internet freedom" score (Table IV.4) measured by Freedom House acknowledges three categories: free, partly free, and not free. As for the "freedom" score, both Hungary and Poland retained their status in 2020 as compared to 2019: Hungary is partly free, Poland is free. In these two years, their "democracy" score became worse than

26 Democracy Index 2019, "A Year of Democratic Setbacks and Popular Protest", A report by The Economist Intelligence Unit. *EIU Democracy Index 2020*, 31.

their "freedom" score. In Hungary, internet freedom is ranked "free".[27] Russia, which is viewed as exercising consolidated authoritarianism ("democracy" score), and Turkey are not free in either category. Singapore is partly free (in both categories) as is Hong Kong ("freedom" score). Thus, consolidated authoritarianism ("democracy score") is not free, in terms of political rights, civil liberties, and internet freedom (Russia). A transitional/hybrid regime is partly free in terms of political rights and civil liberties, while it becomes free if we consider the internet. The semi-consolidated Poland is free.

It is undeniable that the overall effect of systemic changes[28] points in the direction of consolidated authoritarianism (Freedom House – "democracy" score) and/or moderate autocracy (BTI), but the use of an equation mark between Hungary and Poland and these other states is not supported. Nevertheless, it cannot be denied either that the contents of the, for example, Turkish, Russian, Hungarian and Polish toolboxes, are very similar: mass support, elite economic interests, and manipulation of political information. They also share some common features, though to a measurably different degree, such as suppression of NGOs and legalized political repression, with targets punished through vaguely worded laws and politically obedient courts. Without going into detail about what the party system looks like (e.g., in Singapore and Russia), how elections are manipulated by more than regulatory means (Russia and Turkey), how free speech is infringed by harassment, bringing criminal charges based on bogus allegations, and using violence (Singapore, Russia, and Turkey),[29] it seems evident that there is not only a quantitative but a qualitative difference between Poland and Hungary, on the one hand, and Russia, Turkey, and even Singapore, on the other. Thus, what is less characteristic of illiberal constitutionalism is the limited, selective, and typically hidden use of extralegal force or violence, an illusion of pluralism that masks state control over key political institutions, with co-opted or otherwise defanged opposition parties allowed to participate in regular elections.[30] What has not been experienced in either Hungary or Poland, despite their undisputed backsliding in human rights protection, is the extent and gravity of human rights violations seen in Russia, Turkey, and Singapore, according to Freedom House.[31]

27 There are no data available on Poland.

28 We do not list here the result of the V-Dem assessment as it is interested in only a segment of our research.

29 https://freedomhouse.org/report/freedom-world/2019/singapore;https://freedomhouse.org/report/freedom-world/2019/turkey;https://freedomhouse.org/report/freedom-world/2019/russia

30 A Puddington, "Breaking Down Democracy: Global Strategies, and Methods of Modern Authoritarians", https://freedomhouse.org/sites/default/files/June2017_FH_Report_Breaking_Down_Democracy.pdf, June 2017.

31 In the category of "global freedom", Russia, Turkey, and Singapore scored 20 (not free), 32 (not free), and 50 (partly free) out of 100 in 2019, respectively, while Hungary achieved 70 (the same as the previous year; partly free), and Poland 84 (free), https://freedomhouse.org/countries/freedom-world/scores,https://freedomhouse.org/country/hungary/freedom-world/2020

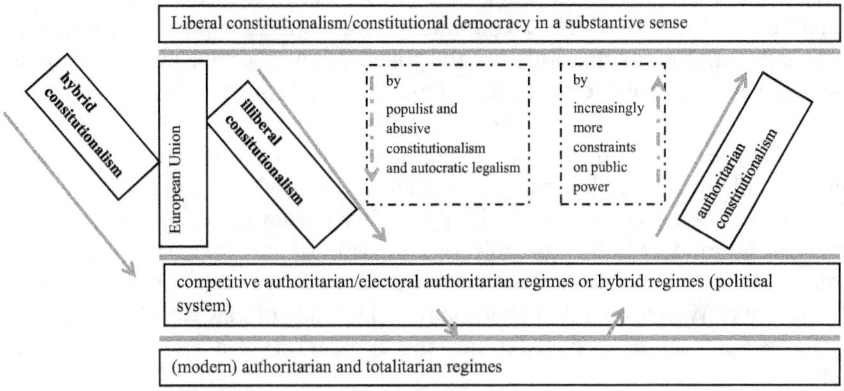

Figure IV.1 Illiberal constitutionalism in comparison
Source: revised version of the Table in T Drinóczi and A Bien´-Kacała (eds), 4 Rule of Law, Common Values and Illiberal Constitutionalism. Poland and Hungary within the European Union (Routledge, 2021) 22.

Nevertheless, it is also true that the Singaporean type of "normative commitment to constraints on public power" is, to a certain extent, missing in Poland and Hungary. However, even the illiberal systems of Poland and Hungary, as Member States of the EU, must respect the EU law. If we consider EU law as part of the legal system of Member States, any constraint on its daily application (in politically not, or less relevant cases) and possible influence on the populist agenda need to be seen as internal, implied constitutional constraints. These types of constraints only exist within the EU. Thus, it follows that the new systems in Hungary and Poland could be labelled as neither (modern) authoritarian regimes nor authoritarian constitutionalism, precisely because of the existence of the European Rule of Law.

III Contextualization: the European Rule of Law as a constraint on public power

1 Rule of Law as a context-related notion

There are many theories and opinions in the literature concerning the Rule of Law. It is viewed as a national, supranational, transnational, or international concept[32] or ideal, or as an applicable and, thus, enforceable legal principle or value.[33]

32 M Adams et al. (eds), *Constitutionalism and the Rule of Law* (Cambridge University Press, 2017); H Krieger, G Nolte, and A Zimmermann (eds), *The International Rule of Law: Rise or Decline?* (Oxford University Press, 2019).

33 J Waldron, "The Concept of the Rule of Law", *Georgia Law Review* 1 (2008) 59–60; D Kochenov and A Jakab (eds), *The Enforcement of EU Law and Values* (Oxford University Press, 2017); C Closa and D Kochenov (eds), *Reinforcing the Rule of Law Oversight in the European Union* (Cambridge University Press, 2016).

There is disagreement on its definition and constituent elements, ranging from a "thin" to a "thick" version in a continuum,[34] or from short positive descriptions to negative definitions that list what the Rule of Law does not mean, and on its measurability and suitable methods.[35] One can recall its recognition throughout history as a rule against the arbitrary use of power, as summarized by, for example, Martin Krygier.[36] Another conceptualization of the term is that "government officials and citizens are bound by and abide by the law", as defined by Brian Z. Tamanaha.[37] Scholars interrogate the Rule of Law from the perspective of international law and examine the role of international law in a changing global order,[38] while others study it from the perspective of axiology,[39] or in the light of the history of Western political philosophy.[40] The Rule of Law can also mean, and its realization can be deduced from, the application of a set of quantitative indices.[41]

Having different approaches, controversies, and uncertainties concerning the notion of the Rule of Law in mind, Jorgen Moller and Adrian Bedner collected the advantages of the thin and thick understandings of the concept and came to the conclusion that the Rule of Law is a context-related concept.[42] The definition of the Rule of Law depends on the purpose of the specific investigation. The thin version is usually supported and used by (communist, illiberal, etc.[43]) states, as it is easier to comply with, and by scholars who use the term for analytical purposes, or who engage with legal historical, legal-philosophical, and pragmatic researches, because they are concerned with the quality of the legal system, therefore they focus on procedural and formal elements. The thick concept is popular among social activists, different (international) organizations, and those who criticize

34 C May and A Winchester (eds), *Handbook of the Rule of Law* (Edward Elgar, 2018).
35 See, e.g. M Versteeg and T Ginsburg, "Measuring the Rule of Law: A Comparison of Indicators", *Law and Social Inquiry* 1 (2017) 100.
36 M Krygier, "The Rule of Law: Pasts, Presents, and Two Possible Futures", *Annual Review of Law and Social Science* 12 (2016).
37 BZ Tamanaha, "The History of the Rule of Law", *Singapore Journal of Legal Studies* (2012) 233.
38 Krieger, Nolte, and Zimmermann (eds), n. 32.
39 A Madeja, "The European Values and the Rule of Law" in T Drinóczi and A Bień-Kacała (eds), *Rule of Law, Common Values and Illiberal Constitutionalism. Poland and Hungary within the European Union* (Routledge, 2021) 45–76.
40 W Włoch, "'Where the Laws Do Not Govern, There is No Constitution': On the Relationship between the Rule of Law and Constitutionalism" in Drinóczi and Bień-Kacała (eds), n. 39, 77–101.
41 Versteeg and Ginsburg, n. 35; https://worldjusticeproject.org
42 J Moller, "The Advantages of a Thin Version" in May and Winchester (eds), n. 34, 33; A Bedner, "The Promise of a Thick View" in May and Winchester (eds), n. 34, 41.
43 The thick concept of the Rule of Law, as explained by Gosalbo-Bono, is either refuted in the socialist regimes, or transformed, as happens in Islamic law. R Gosalbo-Bono, "The Significance of the Rule of Law and its Implications for the European Union and the United States", *University of Pittsburgh Law Review* 72 (2010) 289. Islamic law is not examined here, as it has been an applicable law in neither Hungary nor Poland.

existing authoritarian regimes or states in democratic decay, because this version can strongly support their criticism.[44] The differences in perspectives make us realize that, even if we acknowledge the usefulness and necessity of the idea of the Rule of Law as a universal and, therefore, thin concept,[45] we should differentiate between legal systems (Western, Asian, socialist, etc.[46]), the scholarly fields within whose frameworks we are examining it (e.g., political philosophy or law), and its distinct approaches (e.g., formal and substantive or thin and thick) when we are investigating the extent of compliance with a particular Rule of Law concept. Therefore, we could also say that the Rule of Law is not only a historical and geographical context-related concept, but that its interpretation is enabled by a certain tradition in which both the texts on the principle of the Rule of Law and the interpreter participate.[47]

The Rule of Law, not surprisingly, is also a contested notion, as indeed is the concept of the European Rule of Law, which we introduced in our edited book, *Rule of Law, Common Values and Illiberal Constitutionalism.*[48] There, we offered the use of the latter expression when discussing different deviations from the Rule of Law in European states, especially in states undergoing democratic decay and in the era of the emergence of illiberal constitutionalism. The European Rule of Law is proposed to represent a thick(er) understanding of the Rule of Law that has emerged throughout history as a common European heritage, value, and principle.

2. "European" in the term "European Rule of Law"

As said, the illiberal states emerging in Europe are still constitutional democracies, which are shaped peacefully by populist politicians from a more substantial form of constitutional democracy that prioritizes (liberal) constitutional values, through the use of the methods we noted in Part II, Terms (populist style of governance, abusive constitutionalism, and autocratic legalism). These states are still constitutional democracies in a formal or thin sense. As has already been suggested, each still has a constitution, which is more than the formal (façade) constitution of an autocratic system as it, for example, maintains and allows the functioning of constitutional review mechanisms to a certain extent. Besides, both the constitution and the system are less oppressive than those in the modern and "real" authoritarian regimes. The constitutions "lock in" the European law and international minimum standards.[49]

44 Moller, n. 42, 31–33; Bedner, n. 42, 41.
45 C May, "The Centrality of Predictability to the Rule of Law" in May and Winchester (eds), n. 34, 1.
46 Whichever classification we use, be it based on families (Arminjon, Nolde, and Wolff), multidimensional methodology (Zweiert and Kötz), or ideologically inspired (Rene David), there is always a clear distinction between "Western" and "non-Western" states.
47 Tamanaha, n. 37, 247, A Zanghellini, "The Foundations of the Rule of Law", *Yale Journal of Law & the Humanities* 2 (2016) 216.
48 Drinóczi and Bień-Kacała (eds), n. 39.
49 T Ginsburg, "Locking in Democracy: Constitutions, Commitment, and International Law", 38 *New York University Journal of International Law & Politics* (2006) 757; A Moravcsik, "The Origins of Human Rights Regimes: Democratic Delegation in Post-war Europe", *International Organizations* 54 (2000) 243–244.

We are in agreement with Ricardo Gosalbo-Bono, who calls this phenomenon the "European way" of the Rule of Law, as it "derives from the law of the European Union and from the system established under the European Convention of Human Rights".[50]

Indeed, even though Angelika Nusserger notes that the European Court of Human Rights (ECtHR) was not intended to be a Rule of Law court, given its special relationship with human rights it had no other choice than to acknowledge it, which happened as early as 1975.[51] In *Goden v UK*, the Court pointed out that the Rule of Law is one of the features of the common spiritual heritage of the Member States of the CoE, asserted that the Rule of Law and human rights are intrinsically interwoven, and enumerated those human rights that are essential components of the Rule of Law. The Rule of Law, in the area of human rights[52] and in the jurisprudence of the ECtHR, mainly embodies the right to fair trial by an independent judiciary, the rights to liberty and security, the prohibitions of torture, inhuman and degrading treatment, equality before the law, the principles of *nullum crimen* and *nulla poena*, and *ne bis in idem*, and institutional and substantive safeguards. Among the last category, the independence of the judiciary,[53] legal certainty,[54] proportionality, and the responsibility of a state for human rights violations the particular state has committed or enabled to be committed might be mentioned.[55]

In Europe, there are at least three different kinds of Rule of Law traditions: the French constitutionalism (*l'État de droit*), the English Rule of Law, and the German *Rechtsstaat.* Despite the differences in the national ideas of the Rule of Law, the EU has made efforts to come up with a universal understanding of the term, which represents a thick approach.[56] However, until the Rule of Law conditionality debate, EU legislation failed to define what the Rule of Law really is, instead strongly relying on the findings of the Venice Commission. Undoubtedly, the role and mission of the Venice Commission and those of the EU are different; but as they profess the same values, including the Rule of Law, they do cooperate.[57] In the multilevel constitutionalism, therefore, the Rule of Law, the Rule of Law Checklist of the Venice Commission from 2016, could be used as a benchmark when we assess the Hungarian and Polish approaches to the European Rule of Law as a value.[58] The Rule of Law

50 Gosalbo-Bono, n. 43, 259.

51 *Goden v UK* (App no 4451/70 A/18), 21 February 1975.

52 These rights are covered by Arts 5–7, 14, and Protocol No 7, Art 4.

53 *Okkali v Turkey*, 17 October 2006, App no 52067/99 RJD 2006-XII, para 65.

54 *Malone v UK*, 2 August 1984, App no 8691/79, A82, para 86.

55 *Soering v UK*, 7 July 1989, App no 14038/88, A161; A Nusserger, "The European Court of Human Rights and the Rule of Law – A Tale of Hopes and Disillusions" in M Zubrik (ed), *Human Rights in Contemporary World: Essays in Honor of Professor Leszek Garlicki* (Wydawnictwo Sejmowe, 2017) 162–165.

56 Most recently, see 2020 Rule of Law report, *The Rule of Law Situation in the European Union*, COM(2020) 580 final, 1.

57 See e.g., the new EU Framework to strengthen the Rule of Law, COM(2014) 0158 final; W Hoffmann-Riem, "The Venice Commission of the Council of Europe – Standards and Impact", *European Journal of International Law* 2 (2014) 595.

58 Rule of Law Checklist Adopted by the Venice Commission at its 106th Plenary Session (Venice, 11–12 March 2016).

Checklist mentions the criteria of equality, non-discrimination, and an independent judiciary, which maintains constitutional supremacy and legality, legal certainty, prevention of the abuse (misuse) of power, and access to justice. The Rule of Law concept of the Checklist and the Rule of Law conditionality seem to embrace a more substantive understanding of the Rule of Law, as it fits the European or Western type of (liberal) constitutionalism nurtured by the EU and European states.

Regardless of the EU's legislative silence so far, the Court of Justice of the European Union (CJEU) seems to take the Rule of Law and judicial independence seriously: it has thickened up judicial independence in its decisions on judicial independence in Poland.[59] In *Commission v Poland* (Case C-619/18), the Rule of Law and judicial independence have been linked, the latter having been considered a quasi-absolute value, the restriction of which is subject to scrutiny for proportionality.[60] When the CJEU ruled on the joined cases concerning the independence of the disciplinary chamber of the Polish Supreme Court in November 2019, it further assured that judicial independence, and thus the Rule of Law, has a rather thick understanding.[61] It referred at length to the case-law of the ECtHR, as the applicable provision of the Charter corresponds to the Articles of the Convention (ECHR),[62] which demonstrates a harmony of interpretation in terms of human rights protection and stresses the thorough material content of judicial independence under the ECHR as part of EU law.[63]

The thinner interpretations of the Rule of Law and their use in theory and practice, especially in the Rule of Law measurements and development projects, are equally important. What we argue here is that there is also a value in viewing the Rule of Law in a thick(er) sense, especially when it is connected to European constitutional development.[64] Just briefly mentioning some of the thin approaches: Christopher May argues that the Rule of Law has reached the status of a global common sense,[65] which seems to be in line with the view of

59 MA Simonelli, "Thickening Up Judicial Independence: The ECJ Ruling in Commission v. Poland (C-619/18)", https://europeanlawblog.eu/2019/07/08/thickening-up-judicial-independence-the-ecj-ruling-in-commission-v-poland-c-619-18/; P Zinonos, "The Independence of the Disciplinary Chamber of the Polish Supreme Court or How to Forget about Discipline", https://europeanlawblog.eu/2019/12/02/the-independence-of-the-disciplinary-chamber-of-the-polish-supreme-court-or-how-to-forget-about-discipline/; K Lenaertes, "New Horizons for the Rule of Law Within the EU", *German Law Journal* 21 (2020) 34.

60 *Commission v Poland* (Case C-619/18), paras 46, 47, 58, 76, ECLI:EU:C:2019:531.

61 Joined Cases C-585/18, C-624/18, C-625/18, paras 121–122.

62 The right to effective remedy and fair trial: Art 47 Charter; Arts 6(1) and 13 ECHR.

63 Zinonos, n. 59.

64 See also M Sellers, "What Is the Rule of Law and Why It Is Important?" in JR Silkenat, JRE Hickey Jr, and PD Barenboim (eds), *The Legal Doctrines of the Rule of Law and the Legal State (Rechtsstaat)* (Springer, 2014) 3–6 (the Rule of Law has a Western European origin); D Kochenov, "The EU and the Rule of Law – Naïveté or a Grand Design?", *University of Groningen Faculty of Law Research Paper Series 2018*, 5, 10 (the EU emerged as a particular type of constitutionalism based on the rule of law through national democracies).

65 C May and A Winchester, "Introduction to the Handbook of the Rule of Law" in May and Winchester (eds), n. 34, 1.

Fallon, who opines that a general theory of the Rule of Law needs to be thin and abstract.[66] May also proposes that the Rule of Law could be narrowed down to predictability. Let us briefly mention here the accounts of Fuller and Raz, which are the prototypes of the thinnest concept of the Rule of Law as they only contain principles that describe the characteristics of the law. For Lon Fuller, it comprises the following: generality, publicity, stability, prosperity, clarity, consistency of the law, the possibility of compliance with the law, and congruence between rules announced and their actual administration.[67] According to Raz, the principles of the Rule of Law are that it comprises reasonably clear, reasonably stable, publicly available general rules and standards that are applied prospectively and not retrospectively.[68] For them, these attributes alone are capable of guiding and, to a certain extent, limiting the exercise of power,[69] which phenomenon seems to be a generally accepted primary function and normative foundation of the Rule of Law in the literature.[70] As Moller comprehensively defines formal legality, this term requires the above-mentioned characteristics of the law, a power exercised via law (rule by law), state actions to be subjected to law, and equality before the law.[71]

We would, however, rather refer back to our opinion, according to which the Rule of Law is a context- and geographical-space-related and time-sensitive notion. Zimmermann observes that the Rule of Law is traditionally connected to classical liberalism, that is, the power is limited by the individual rights of the citizen. This perspective is embedded in the concepts of *l'État de Droit* and *Rechtsstaat*, [72] and the Hungarian *jogállam* and the Polish *państwo prawa*. The values that are required to supplement the formal or thin understanding of the Rule of Law are usually viewed as liberal values, such as the effective protection and realization of human rights and governing in a way that promotes a social coexistence in which the state acts for the individual and not vice versa.

Different outcomes concerning the meaning and the components of the Rule of Law can be reached if we stay in the realm of political philosophy or consider the jurisprudence of the constitutional courts. Constitutional interpretation contributes to the implementation of the constitution, including many abstractly stipulated constitutional principles such as the Rule of Law. Constitutional court judges undoubtedly may follow a particular political philosophy with which they can identify, but when interpreting the constitutional text they are supposed to be

66 RM Fallon, Jr, "'The Rule of Law' as a Concept in Constitutional Discourse", *Columbia Law Review* 1 (1997) 7.

67 L Fuller, *The Morality of Law* (Yale University Press, 1969).

68 J Raz, "The Rule of Law and its Virtue", *Law Quarterly Review* 93 (1977).

69 Moller, n. 42, 30.

70 A brief summary is offered by the entry of Rule of Law at https://plato.stanford.edu/entries/rule-of-law/. See also e.g., A Zimmermann, "Understanding the Rule of Law: Conceptions and Perspective", http://alrf.msk.ru/understanding_the_rule_of_law_conceptions_and_perspectives; Krygier, n. 36.

71 Moller, n. 42, 29.

72 Zimmermann, n. 70.

(more) bound by the constitution, the already established case-law, and the rules of constitutional interpretation, however contested and diverse this last exercise may be.[73] The Hungarian Constitutional Court (CC), for instance, from the beginning of its operation, established that it perceives the Rule of Law principle of the Constitution (the one that preceded the FL) in a formal sense; thus, it would not link it to any other existing constitutional provisions, for example, those on fundamental rights, and yet it interpreted it widely.[74] In Poland, before 1997 (the year when the Constitution entered into force), the Constitutional Tribunal (CT) perceived the Rule of Law in a substantive way, linking it with human rights.[75] After most of the human rights were constitutionalized in Constitution 1997, the perception of the Rule of Law in the jurisprudence of the CT become more formal. Nevertheless, the CT still links it to human rights, even if less intensively. Both courts were also engaged with the interpretation of the Rule of Law when deemed necessary to decide on the constitutionality of pieces of legislation.[76]

Scholars adopting different perspectives, including assessment of the jurisdiction of constitutional (supreme) courts, will hardly find themselves on the same page and come to a common understanding on the definition and content of the Rule of Law. Therefore, given the scope of this book, what Michel Rosenfeld notes concerning the conceptualization of the Rule of Law in Germany in the second half of the 20th century is all the more important. As opposed to the positivist *Rechtsstaat*, which emphasized legality and predictability, its contemporary version, called *Verfassungsstaat*, aims at fairness through constitutionalizing substantive norms and values.[77] This constitutionalization and the subsequent jurisprudence of the German Constitutional Court could explain why "some present day positivists are committed to a substantive conception of the rule of law ideal",[78] whatever its exact content may be. As Leighton McDonald observed, it is

73 On the practices of constitutional interpretation in the USA, Germany, and Poland (until 2015), see, e.g., DE Finck, "Judicial Review: The United States Supreme Court Versus the German Constitutional Court", *Boston College International and Comparative Law Review* 1 (1997); DM Beatty, "The Forms and Limits of Constitutional Interpretation", *The American Journal of Comparative Law* 49 (2001); A Bień-Kacała, "Informal Constitutional Change" *Przegląd Prawa Konstytucyjnego*, 6(40) (2017), 199–218; T Groppi, "Constitutional Revision in Italy: A Marginal Instrument for Constitutional Change" in X Contiades (ed), *Engineering Constitutional Change* (Routledge, 2016) 218–220.

74 A Jakab and E Bodnár, "The Rule of Law, Democracy and Human Rights in Hungary: Tendencies from 1989 until 2019" in Drinóczi and Bień-Kacała (eds), n. 39, 105–118; T Drinóczi, "The Rule of Law: The Hungarian Perspective" in Drinóczi and Bień-Kacała (eds), n. 39, 119–132.

75 I Wróblewska, "The Rule of Law: The Polish Perspective" in Drinóczi and Bień-Kacała (eds), n. 39, 133–150.

76 Until 2012, the CC had no power to review the constitutionality of a judicial decision *per se*, i.e., without focusing on the applicable law.

77 M Rosenfeld, "Legitimacy of Constitutional Democracy", *Southern California Law Review* 74 (2001), 1313, 1350.

78 Zanghellini, n. 51, 216.

a misleading simplification to assume that "that various forms of natural law inspired jurisprudence (such as Ronald Dworkin's) are wedded to 'substantive' or 'thick' conceptions of the rule of law, whereas positivist theory is committed to a 'formal' or 'thin' rule of law ideal".[79] As said, constitutional courts are usually not concerned with labelling what they apply as a benchmark of constitutionality; they consider, amongst other things, the text of the constitutions, which usually recognizes the particular state as a Rule of Law state, with or without modifying adjective, and other provisions of the constitution, for example, fundamental rights or other value-related rules. What constitutional courts interpret as the Rule of Law in a particular country comprises its definition and constituent elements in that particular country. The particular text informs their decisions; if it reads "democratic state of the rule of law" [*demokratikus jogállam*] or "a democratic state ruled by law" [*demokratyczne państwo prawa*], as in the case of the Hungarian Constitution (until 2012) and FL (from 2012), and the Polish Constitution 1997, respectively, they might be inclined to give a more value-oriented (more thicker) understanding of the Rule of Law. This is because the noun has received a modifying adjective, that is, "democratic". In the ideal case, the core elements of the domestically interpreted and implemented Rule of Law in the legal sense are in line with the expectations of the supranational and international community to which the state belongs and in whose decision-making processes it participates.

The literature from both Hungary and Poland agrees on the fact that their legal systems have adequately accommodated the international human rights obligations, and that they have been struggling with similar challenges to other states concerning the application of the Charter of Fundamental Rights of the EU. Undeniably, however, as we are dealing with two states detaching themselves from the ingroup of the European community, some issues uniquely feature both Hungary and Poland, which we will discuss later.[80]

3 "Rule of Law" in the term "European Rule of Law"

It has become clear that the (Western) European states and the EU have adopted and nurtured a distinct kind of constitutionalism, which entails a particular understanding of the Rule of Law. The importance of trust underlines the argument that when it comes to assessment of the Rule of Law situation of a particular European state that belongs to a wider supranational and international community, reduction of the examination to the thin version of the Rule of Law cannot bring about a satisfactory result. In the European sphere, thus, it is proposed to view the Rule of Law as a triangle. The two sides joining at the top represent a twin legal obligation that stems from constitutional rules, international human rights obligations, and the EU law to be observed by Member States. These are based on a foundation of shared values and political ideals that derive from the

79 L McDonald, "Positivism and the Formal Rule of Law: Questioning the Connection", *Australian Journal of Legal Philosophy* 26 (2001) 93.

80 Part V, Limits, point III.

common constitutional traditions of the European states.[81] Thus, when compliance of a Member State with the Rule of Law is examined, the term represents the observance of a unique Rule of Law concept in a particular kind of constitutionalism, namely, the Western type of constitutionalism that has been accommodated by Member States (nation-states) and the EU (supranational community).[82]

Consequently, the twin concept of the Rule of Law is seen as having a core common and intertwined normative meaning for both the EU and its Member States. As a political ideal, which is the base line of the triangle, it requires, at least, that no power is exercised arbitrarily. It also implies the demand for respect[83] and protection[84] of the individual. The Rule of Law also translates to an applicable legal concept, which dictates that law binds all, including both the state and the people. The need to obey the law demands that individuals are aware of the law, a prerequisite facilitated by the regulatory state. In this sense and in order to achieve these purposes, the Rule of Law calls for the fullest possible compliance of state power with the rules of "formal legality". Formal legality presupposes the rule by law (power exercised via the law), that state action is subject to law, equality before and under the law, and adherence to specific core characteristics of the law (generality, publicity, predictability, clarity, etc.[85]).[86] Formal legality needs to be enforced by the judiciary, which includes the constitutional courts; otherwise, it loses its constraining power. In

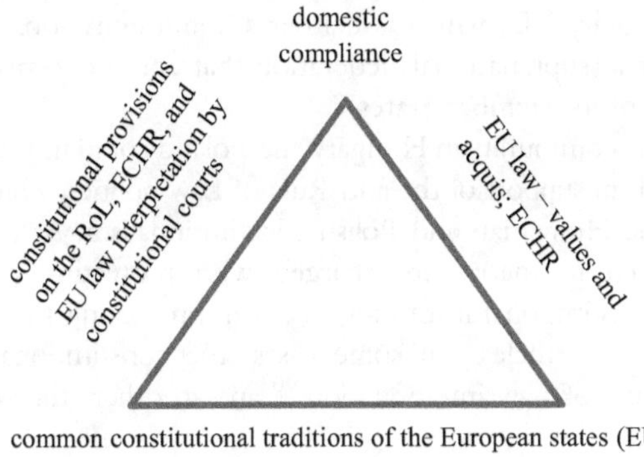

Figure IV.2 The European Rule of Law from the perspective of the national constitutional system

Source: Drinóczi and Bień-Kacała, eds, n. 39. 17.

81 Similarly, see G Palombella, "Beyond Legality – Before Democracy: Rule of Law in the EU Two Level System" in Closa and Kochenov (eds), n. 33.

82 See e.g., Kochenov, n. 64, 10.

83 Respecting the individual is the underlying idea of limiting power. See Waldron, n. 36, 59–60.

84 Protection is an implied component of the prevention of the exercise of arbitrary power, otherwise the underlying idea itself becomes questionable.

85 For this, see Fuller, n. 67; J Raz, "The Rule of Law and its Virtue" in J Raz (ed), *The Authority of Law: Essays on Law and Morality* (Oxford University Press, 1979).

86 Referring to the theories of Raz, Fuller, and Finnis, Moller uses this approach in Moller, n. 42, 29.

this process, it is subject to different forms of interpretation and application, such as respecting the legal hierarchy, allowing the necessary time for adjusting to a new regulation (congruence), and respecting legitimate expectations (predictability).

In domestic legal systems, the national constitutions accommodate EU law and direct state authorities to participate in the EU decision-making process, demanding its enforcement. Suspicion that the Rule of Law is not being enforced in its entirety by a Member State suggests a violation of, first, constitutional norms in the "domestic Rule of Law" and the so-called EU clauses and, second, Article 2 TEU.[87] Therefore, the enforcement of these rules and compliance with EU values is the task of national legislative authorities, adjudicative bodies, constitutional courts, and the EU itself. The observance, maintenance, and enforcement of the Rule of Law, as a political ideal, rest with the political community.

The implementation and application of EU law (*acquis*) have over the years become the daily practice of Member States, including Hungary and Poland.[88] Challenges concerning the observance and enforcement of the value system, including the Rule of Law, democracy, and human rights, on which the European integration project is based, have surfaced in the last decade and have triggered the attention of both EU institutions and scholars.[89] This has been informed by the cumulative effects of the rise of populist nationalism over Europe and the very nature of the contemporary EU, which is neither a community loosely based on economic interests nor a (supranational) federation that could effectively interfere in the domestic affairs of its Member States.

The domestic political community in Hungary and Poland could not resist populist nationalism and remains in support of the anti-Rule of Law politics, which have successfully remodelled the Hungarian and Polish constitutionalism. As a result, constitutional courts, which in theory are charged with protecting constitutional principles, and other constitutional institutions assist in promoting the anti-Rule of Law political agenda. Nevertheless, in some cases, the constitutional courts do uphold their former Rule of Law interpretation,[90] and in others they expand it.[91]

87 See the explanation of the two levels concerning the Rule of Law in a supranational community in Palombella, n. 81.

88 M Varju, "A magyar jogrendszer és az Európai Unió joga: tíz év tapasztalata" ["The Hungarian Legal System and the Law of the European Union: Experiences of Ten Years"] in A Jakab and G Gajduschek (eds), *A magyar jogrendszer állapota* [*The State of the Hungarian Legal System*] (MTA Társadalomtudományi Kutatóközpont, Jogtudományi Intézet, 2016) 143–171; Annual reports on monitoring the application of EU law, https://ec.europa.eu/info/publications/annual-reports-monitoring-application-eu-law_en

89 See, amongst others, the books mentioned in n. 1, and the different rules of law mechanisms the EU has been experimenting with, such as Rule of Law conditionality, the idea of strengthening the Rule of Law through increased awareness, an annual monitoring cycle and more effective enforcement, and the new EU Framework to strengthen the Rule of Law, n. 57.

90 See Jakab and Bodnár, and Wróblewska, nn. 74 and 75, respectively.

91 Part VI, Stability, points I and II.

Other constitutional actors, such as the ombudsman,[92] ordinary judges,[93] the corruption agency or the state audit office,[94] are successfully attempting to maintain some core tenets of constitutionalism, including observance of the Rule of Law.

The enforcement or non-enforcement of the Rule of Law as a value and legal concept are equally complex and confusing at the EU level. Similar to national polities, the EU has been so far ineffective in ensuring that Member States comply with its values and principles. There are many reasons for this: first, the design of the EU is based on the doctrine of delegated powers and mutual trust; second, priority has always been given to the enforcement of the acquis and not to the values. Once a country becomes a Member State, the principle of mutual trust and the presumption that all values and principles are shared, implemented, and enforced internally by the Member States are activated. Therefore, value enforcement has yet to develop effective mechanisms,[95] and to all intents and purposes has not found adequate tools to deal with ideologically induced non-compliance. We are not sure if it is possible at all exactly, because the difference seems to lie in confessing to divergent values in one community, that is, the EU. This discrepancy, sooner or later, has to be resolved one way or another, but we have not reached that point quite yet.

The deviation from the EU acquis can also have Rule of Law implications. These include the careless use of law or the random abuse of political power, which, however, can be corrected with time through the available enforcement mechanisms and the functioning of democracy in any given Member State. The same applies to other types of defiance, such as infringing the provisions of the acquis by non-compliance through errors of judgement or interpretation, and incorrect or non-timely implementation of a directive, taking advantage of the fact that there are grey areas in EU economic regulations. None of these examples of non-compliance, however, is confined to a particular regime; they occur in all Member States.[96] In fact, though,

92 The Hungarian ombudsman's petitions to the CC have been considered admissible, and the Court concurred with the ombudsman concerning the unconstitutionality of the restrictive use of the concept of marriage and family, and the extent of criticism politicians, among others, have to endure in the interests of unfettered democratic public opinion. See 14/2014 (V. 13.) and 6/2014 (III. 7.) CC decisions, respectively. Conversely, the Polish ombudsman ceases to log cases (already diverted to the CT) and withdraws already logged ones (e.g., on the Prosecutor General's competences in 2018, or the status of civil servants in 2019) due to the changes in the adjudication panel of the CT. The panel is composed of judges irregularly appointed by the *Sejm* to the CT, which raises doubts as to the independence and impartiality of the CT and the constitutionality of its decisions. Nevertheless, the ombudsman is quite vocal in his public speeches about violations of the Polish Rule of Law.

93 Both Polish and Hungarian judges use the possibility of preliminary ruling procedures extensively. See e.g. Varju, n. 88; and W Sadurski, *Poland's Constitutional Breakdown* (Oxford University Press, 2019) 211–213.

94 In 2018, these Polish authorities expressed concerns about the use of public money, which triggered investigations and sanctions that turned out to be flawed, https://freedomhouse.org/report/freedom-world/2019/poland.

95 See e.g., Closa and Kochenov (eds), n. 33.

96 A Jakab and D Kochenov, "Introductory Remarks" in Kochenov and Jakab (eds), n. 33, 2–3.

despite the "business-as-usual non-compliances" and the systematic Rule of Law value infringements by the public legislative and regulatory powers, EU law is still applied every day by both the Polish and Hungarian ordinary courts. Moreover, the annual transposition deficits in both countries do not outstandingly deviate from the EU 28[97] average.[98]

4 *The European Rule of Law – a rudimentary concept*

Against this background, the European Rule of Law represents a thick(er) understanding of the Rule of Law that has emerged throughout history as a common European heritage, value, and principle. It comprises a particular political theory, which demands prevention of any arbitrary use of power with all its necessary preconditions and implementation mechanisms. It also means a legally enforceable concept that is present in the national constitutions and the European legal order, and which is distinctively interpreted by national and supranational courts in accordance with their respective positive constitutional law. Thus, the European Rule of Law, in both the European and domestic arenas, is necessarily a less thin (or a thick) concept, as it not only prescribes formal and legal features, but it requires the domestic law to bear some specific content, which would make it a "good domestic law" informed by the political agenda and decisions reached by the EU and, intrinsically, its Member States. The European Rule of Law expresses a limitation on the domestic political decision-maker because there is another positive law (i.e., EU law) that the holder of the domestic rule-making power cannot manipulate and override. No domestic populist leader can hijack the EU law and law-making process in the same way that they might with their national legislation and lawmaking authorities.[99] It would also demand enforcement mechanisms: individuals can report to the EU in order to contest domestic decision-making,[100] and judges can initiate preliminary ruling procedures.[101] The latter

97 The data were collected before Brexit.

98 Varju, n. 88; Annual Reports, n. 88. This is something that can be measured and reported on, and can inform the overall Rule of Law assessment of Member States. How to measure, what type of Rule of Law observance to measure, which kind of indices to use and what conclusions to draw from them, and whether the results should be interpreted alongside those of other states or not, can also be puzzling. There are measurements and reports that indicate the obvious Rule of Law deterioration, and there are views claiming that Hungary and Poland have already deviated from a state of constitutionalism towards authoritarianism. One of the central claims of these views is that the Rule of Law has ceased to constrain the exercise of public power and that authoritarian legality has replaced its understanding. See e.g. G Halmai, "Populism, Authoritarianism, and Constitutionalism", *German Law Journal* 20 (2019); GA Tóth, "Illiberal Rule of Law? Changing Features of Hungarian Constitutionalism" in M Adams et al. (eds), *Constitutionalism and the Rule of Law* (Cambridge University Press, 2017); KL Scheppele, "Autocratic Legalism", *The University of Chicago Law Review* 85 (2018).

99 Palombella, n. 81.

100 Palombella, n. 81.

101 Morten Broberg acknowledges that from a Rule of Law perspective, the importance of the procedure is high, although it has not been designed as an enforcement

require an independent judiciary with judges adopting anti-authoritarian attitudes,[102] who can make responsible decisions as judges of the supranational entity. National judges, despite attempts at their repression, make their voices heard through demonstrations, marches, collaboration, reports, and preliminary procedure requests. The Convention and the case-law of the ECtHR do not and cannot feature constraints in the same manner. They have palpably weaker direct influence, but, indirectly, mainly through the decisions of the CJEU, also compose the European Rule of Law.

mechanism. M Broberg, "Preliminary References as a Means for Enforcing EU Law" in Kochenov and Jakab (eds), n. 33, 111.

102 L Henderson, "Authoritarianism and the Rule of Law", *Indiana Law Journal* 66 (1991) 396.

V Limits

Constraints in constitutional design and identity

Mainly due to the factors mentioned in the preceding Parts of this book, we find constraints on constitutional design and identity – more precisely, on the Hungarian and Polish versions of the European Rule of Law, democracy, and human rights protection – where they incorporate EU law and international human rights law. We propose to refer to these national versions as constituting "illiberal legality", "illiberal democracy", and "illiberalization of human rights protection", as these terms help us to express the results of the abuse of the Rule of Law, deterioration of democracy, and misuse of human rights.

I Illiberal legality

1 The term

Voters in both Hungary and Poland care little about the realisation, implementation, and especially the value content of the Rule of Law, which is unfortunate. As the Venice Commission noted, "The Rule of Law can only flourish in a country whose inhabitants feel collectively responsible for the implementation of the concept, making it an integral part of their own legal, political and social culture."[1] Collective responsibility can hardly be nurtured when the Rule of Law is surrounded by nationalistic and political interpretations. It takes the term out of context, especially when this narrative claims that the Rule of Law is a fluid, mainly political concept, itself ill-fitted or inadequate for use as an objective measure in an official legal procedure (such as Article 7 TEU). It disregards the coexistence of two considerations, and thus misguides the debate: even though legal procedures can politically be assessed, criticized, or even praised, they still stay in the realm of the law informed by legal approaches, guarantees, processes, and legal arguments. The official legal Rule of Law procedures reflect a legal design and content, and draw on the need for cooperation, dialogue, mutual understanding and comparison; and like many other aspects of the law, they are pervaded by

1 Rule of Law Checklist adopted by the Venice Commission at its 106th Plenary Session (Venice, 11–12 March 2016).

DOI: 10.4324/9781003175353-5

political considerations. The error thus is that when legal arguments are rebutted based on exclusively political and populist arguments, and at the same time, the legal context is simply disregarded.

This context is provided by the fact that Hungary and Poland are Member States of the EU, a community whose fundamental and commonly shared values, that is, the Rule of Law, democracy, and human rights, amongst others, form a part of legal instruments, such as the TEU and national constitutions. The enforcement of the legal provisions is the task of the legally established bodies of the national and supranational community. At the same time, all of the above, and the success of the enforcement activity, can later be used for political assessments that are made by political bodies through a legal process that can and shall be designed to make a political decision on the membership of the community. Membership of a community is always a political decision that, in a community that follows the principles of the Rule of Law, should be supported and guided by legal rules and processes. This decision may be based on an assessment of how a member observes a common value when trust in that member is tilted. In the EU, Member States are trusted to follow the shared values and commonly agreed principles and rules.[2]

In the Member States, people trust their politicians and state institutions to follow the legally binding rules, including the national constitution, EU law, and international obligations. In the huge pool of political ideologies, people are free to choose; politicians and parties are free to pursue different political visions in so far as the end result fits the actual and current state of the European project. It seems, however, that in Hungary and Poland, the political atmosphere is different from that in the other Member States, as the majority of the people still trust in illiberal and populist politicians, even if they have seen the results of their political and party activities.

As opposed to the term "European Rule of Law", we propose to call the Hungarian and Polish version "illiberal legality", which is not only partially different from the European Rule of Law but which, paradoxically, forms its perverted version and, as such, is thus similar to it. It has two twin sides too, that is, a European side and a domestic one. Within the context of illiberal constitutionalism, this term can best express the partial hollowed-out character of the concept of the European Rule of Law, and express how it features in the Hungarian and Polish constitutional systems.

Illiberal legality is a nationalistic and overpoliticised conceptualisation of the European Rule of Law, which, in the political narrative, is used to protect the sovereignty of the state that is under attack by external factors, such as supranational and international (legal) communities, and social and economic challenges. Politicisation of the term "European Rule of Law" detaches it from its legally binding nature and takes it out of context, which serves the purposes of illiberal

2 Opinion of the Court (Full Court) of 18 December 2014 in Case 2/13, ECLI:EU:C:2014:2454, para 168; Case C-619/18, *Commission v Poland*, ECLI:EU:C:2019:53.

populism. The detaching exercise from and the nationalistic redesign of the European Rule of Law are always opportunistic: depending on whether it is in the interests of the populist leader, the European Rule of Law is either respected or ignored to a certain extent. Illiberal legality does not respect the basic tenets of constitutionalism but, due to membership of the EU (and other international organizations), it is legally – and politically – forced to recognize some constraints over its exercise of public power. It is the logical consequence and a necessary component of a constitutional remodelling designed and performed by a populist and authoritarian leader who is leading the country in an authoritarian direction within the framework of the EU. Therefore, illiberal legality is the antithesis of the European Rule of Law, in terms of values, the role of a constitution, and the components of the European Rule of Law. Illiberal legality retains formal legality, which is part of each thin concept of the Rule of Law and extends to the application and enforcement of the enforceable EU law. This effect is viewed as a weak internal (supranational) constraint on the domestic powers.

2 *Legal features of illiberal legality*

Illiberal legality emphasizes the instrumental and opportunistic use of the law in both legislation and the application and adjudication of the law. It simply views and uses the law as a tool of political power (rule by law) to achieve its mission at any cost, without understanding the ideal that no one is above the law, that is, the constitution-amending and legislative power and constitutional review competences cannot be abused to the advantage of a selected group of people. Thus, it can also be argued that neither equality (non-discrimination), nor the prevention of abuse (misuse) of power, or the other elements of the benchmark of the Checklist are realized in Hungary and Poland to a sufficient extent. Each segment of the Rule of Law is compromised, and the failure to adhere to the requirements of the European Rule of Law is systematic, politically induced and supported, and widespread in those legal systems. This does not mean, however, that the European Rule of Law is not observed as a legal norm to a certain extent. Rather, it features the opportunistic approach of illiberal constitutionalism towards this concept. The practice of the implementation and everyday application of EU law is, amongst other things, appreciated as a constraint on domestic public power.

2.1 At odds with the European Rule of Law

Nevertheless, it is a well-known fact that in recent years, there have been many accusations concerning both Hungary and Poland because of their non-compliance with the Rule of Law.

Many international organizations, such as the UN Special Rapporteur and Venice Commission, have expressed their concerns, shared their opinions, and formulated recommendations. These, however, being soft law instruments, did not resolve the problem. The illiberal state apparently does not take soft law measures seriously, nor does it pay much attention to hard(er) law measures, highly political in nature as they are, such as the EU mechanisms to safeguard European law and values, and the results of court proceedings. Even after launching "the nuclear option" against Poland and Hungary (2017, 2018), the legal and political landscape has not evinced any change.[3] It is already certain that no other measures, such as infringement procedures, could produce the expected effect in every case.

The reason for the intransigence of illiberal populist states is simple: the actors speak different languages. European and international institutions expect a constructive dialogue to be conducted in an impartial, evidence-based, and cooperative manner. But communicating with populist politicians through dialogue cannot be successful given the very nature of populism – neither consensus-seeking nor compromise, which should result from a dialogue, exists in the populist agenda.[4] There is no space for consideration of the opinions of others, because that would require the illiberal populist leaders to accept legal and constitutional constraints and put themselves in a non-national context in which each actor has its own political, legal, and moral duties and responsibilities. A "normative commitment to constraints on public power", as put by Tushnet when describing a different legal setting (authoritarian constitutionalism), does not feature in Poland and Hungary in the same way as elsewhere.[5] It is enough to think of the unconstitutional constitutional amendments of 2010 and in 2013 (the Fourth Amendment of the FL) in Hungary, and of the continuous breach of the Polish Constitution by informal constitutional changes. Legal arguments are rebuffed by populist slogans, and, considering the populist parties' continuous electoral victories at the national level, this "game" seems to please the voters. On the other hand, due to their membership of the European Union, EU law, paradoxically, still represents a weak but tacitly existing constraint on public power within those polities. Even if its defense mechanisms have not worked so far, and to a certain extent its application at the legislative level is flawed in some areas, the mere existence of EU law and its day-to-day adjudication by national courts may influence the illiberal politicians and keep them from leading their countries into authoritarianism even more swiftly.[6] The application of international obligations,

3 Most recently, see 2020 Rule of Law Report, country chapter on the Rule of Law situation in Hungary. Accompanying 2020 Rule of Law Report, *The Rule of Law Situation in the European Union*, SWD(2020) 316 final; 2020 Rule of Law Report, country chapter on the Rule of Law situation in Poland; Accompanying 2020 Rule of Law Report, *The Rule of Law Situation in the European Union*, SWD(2020) 320 final.

4 This kind of attitude and language, designed to humiliate EU officials and values, was identified by L Pech and KL Scheppele, "Poland and the European Commission, Part III: Requiem for the Rule of Law", VerfBlog, 2017/3/03, http://verfassungsblog.de/poland-and-the-european-commissionpart-iii-requiem-for-the-rule-of-law/

5 M Tushnet, "Authoritarian Constitutionalism", *Harvard Public Law Working Papers No 13–47* (2013) 72.

6 Measuring this effect is challenging (A Bozóki and D Hegedűs, "An Externally Constrained Hybrid Regime: Hungary in the European Union", *Democratization* 25(7) (2018), but EU reports (e.g., Annual reports on monitoring the application of EU law, https://ec.europa.eu/info/publications/annual-reports-monitoring-applicatio

especially in the field of human rights, which have already been embedded in both states, can also be regarded as a weak but constitutionally internalized constraint.[7] Claiming that supranational and international politics and law, which have just been depicted as having failed to protect standards and values, could be viewed as effecting a certain constraint on national governments would seem to be a paradox; but it is no more absurd than having Member States within the EU in which the remodelling of constitutionalism has gone so far that some scholars call them authoritarian regimes. We realise that this is not a strong argument, which is why we have already conducted a comparative exercise in the preceding Part of this book and mean to elaborate on compliance below.

The Hungarian FL and the 1997 Polish Constitution are the fundamental laws of the land, which sit at the top of the legal hierarchy. Laws are usually adopted by observing procedural rules, and their content is in harmony with the constitution regardless of how symbolic, ineffective, and defective it is in terms of the requirements of modern constitutionalism. The FL does not necessarily observe the principles of constitutionalism and, for instance, human rights. If the constitution cannot be considered a modern constitution and the CC is packed, the body of laws that are adopted will be in harmony with the FL but might not satisfy the requirements of modern constitutionalism. Thus, legality may be formally but not substantively observed; consequently, the law would reflect the illiberal content of the constitution. In Poland, systemic illiberal constitutional changes have been adopted and the otherwise liberal constitutional provisions have received illiberal content. Besides the apparent unconstitutional legislation and governmental actions, legal opportunism is also present when the Polish Constitution is referred to as the basic and enforceable document of the land against EU law. The informally created "invisible" constitution is rhetorically used as a basis for further change. According to the speech of Marshal-Senior Antoni Macierewicz, delivered during the first sitting of the *Sejm* (12 November 2019), the primary "legal, social and moral bases of our state order" comprise the independence of Poland, the legal recognition of relations between a man and a woman only, and protection of life in the prenatal phase too.[8] This means that, if not formally changed, the formal 1997 Constitution could ultimately neither limit political power, nor adequately guarantee human rights, which makes it a partly symbolic and ineffective constitution. On the other hand, the Hungarian FL simply assists those in power to achieve their political goals and guides society according to certain selected, overemphasised, and oversimplified ideologies and political ideas that are preferred by the political decision-makers and which please them. In Hungary, the role of Christianity, with all of its presumed implications in a society that is not famed for its religious nature, paternalism, and communitarianism, might be mentioned, amongst other things. The FL itself is used as a political instrument, as was evident during its adoption

n-eu-law_en), statistics (number of preliminary ruling procedures), and comparative analysis on the basis of indices and reports (e.g., Freedom House, WJP Project, Human Rights Watch) could assist in the exercise.

7 See Point III. below.

8 www.wprost.pl/kraj/10269223/macierewicz-wyglosil-przemowienie-marszalek-senior-mowil-o-katastrofie-smolenskiej-gender-i-konstytucji.html

process, which made it a partisan constitution, and when, for example, the Fourth, the Seventh, and Ninth Amendments were adopted.

In the unlikely event that the Polish Constitution is formally amended, it could incorporate illiberal content that is similar to that of the Hungarian FL and in harmony with the already existent illiberal and "invisible" Polish Constitution. At the same time, we expect that the Constitution may, instead, be further changed informally, and in such a way as to fill it up with illiberal content.

Under the Hungarian FL and the Polish Constitution, the legislative power is separated from the executive power, although they are supposed to cooperate in the field of legislation – as they usually do in a parliamentary system. In practice, this is not the case; the parliament is sometimes perceived as just a necessary evil in the decision-making process, and parliamentary rules and positions are used to prevent the expression of opposing views. The drafting and legislative process is characterized by formalism, disregard of substantive considerations of the theory of legislation[9] and the components of the quality of legislation,[10] and overwhelmed by political will. In Hungary, the generally accepted trends[11] in legislation, such as impact assessment, consultation, parliamentary deliberations, evidence-based legislation, and use of ICT and transparency, have not been followed, and even the barely noteworthy achievements of the 20 years between 1990 and 2010 have been significantly eroded. The packed CC is both unable and unwilling to conduct a semi-procedural review of legislation.[12] In Poland, a similar tendency may be noted, especially the abuse of accelerated procedures, non-consultation on drafts and proposals, and symbolic legislation.[13] This low quality has deteriorated further during the COVID-19 pandemic.[14]

There is firm reliance on the judicial system, regardless of the fact that its independence has intentionally been curbed. What matters is as follows: first, the usual procedural and control mechanisms are in place, that is, the constitutional and, in the majority of cases, statutory rules; this, from a merely formal and positivist perspective, and in the context of the thin concept of the Rule of Law, cannot be

9 See lately, e.g., H Xanthaki and U Karpen (eds), *Legislation and Legisprudence in Europe. A Comprehensive Guide for Scholars and Legislative Practitioners* (Hart Publishing, 2017); M Bernatt and M Ziółkowski, "Statutory Anti-Constitutionalism", *Washington International Law Journal* 28 (2019) 499–501.

10 T Drinóczi, "Legislation in Hungary" in U Karpen and H Xanthaki (eds), *Legislation in Europe: A Country by Country Guide* (Hart Publishing, 2020).

11 See, e.g., T Drinóczi, "Concept of Quality in Legislation – Revisited: Matter of Perspective and a General Overview", *Statute Law Review* 3 (2015) 225–227.

12 See, e.g., I Bar-Siman-Tov, "Semiprocedural Judicial Review", *Legisprudence* 3 (2012).

13 See more below ("Illiberal democracy"). See the 2018 report of the Supreme Audit Office assessing a drafting process at www.nik.gov.pl/plik/id,16190,vp,18712.pdf and one of the XII reports on legislation, the reports are cyclically delivered by NGO, www.batory.org.pl/upload/files/Programy%20operacyjne/Forum%20Idei/XII_Komunikat_OFL.pdf

14 T Drinóczi and A Bień-Kacała, "COVID-19 in Hungary and Poland: Extraordinary Situation and Illiberal Constitutionalism", *The Theory and Practice of Legislation* 8(1⊠2) (2020) 171–192.

criticized. Second, justice can be provided by the courts, but it is quite contrary to the principle of equality before the law, limited due to its delayed nature and its inability to restore the previous and constitutional status quo, the personal reconvergence between a public office holder and political decision-makers, and, lately, the refusal of the government to execute final court decisions[15] and deliberately misunderstand them.[16]

The constitutional interpretation and application of the Rule of Law principle have also changed. In Hungary, the scope of application of the Rule of Law has been reduced; its thinnest possible concept is enforced, while its Western value content is disregarded, due to the new FL. Its instrumental use and the authoritarian attitude of the majority of the judges of the CC are as emerging phenomena as the increased illiberal judicialization of politics.[17] Especially after 2014, judges do not embarrass the legislative power by annulling laws. Paradoxically, in some cases, for the maintenance of free speech, for instance, they use their power to establish constitutional requirements. In the case of the introduction of the crime of spreading false information during emergencies, the CC did not make its decision on the basis of the Rule of Law (unclear criminal law provision, as was argued by the petitioner). Instead, the CC recalled the previously (pre-2010) established case-law on freedom of speech and determined a constitutional requirement that guides the interpretation of the criminal offense in a way that, most probably, makes the application of the provision impossible. In Poland, the situation is similar: the scope of irregularities amounts to degradation of the Rule of Law, especially in the field of judicial independence and impartiality and human rights. The distinctive difference is, as said, that the content of the Constitution 1997 has been informally changed towards an illiberal one.[18]

These considerations are collated and visualized in Table V.1 below. In the context of this book, and especially this chapter, when we assess the Rule of Law and the degree of its implementation in Hungary and Poland, we can refer to its thin version, as described earlier.[19] That is, the thin version of the Rule of Law equals formal legality, a power exercised via law (rule by law), state actions to be subject to the law, equality before the law, and certain characteristics of the law as defined by Raz and Fuller. It can form a basis for measurements and be an object

15 The Debrecen Court of Appeals found that from 2004 to 2017, Roma students were taught separately at the Gyöngyöspata Primary School, and this segregation violated their rights, and they ordered the payment of 100 million forints (EUR 300,000) as compensation. The Prime Minster said that the Government would not pay the compensation because it would be given for nothing, i.e., it would be money received without working for it, https://hungarytoday.hu/govt-finds-court-ruling-on-school-segregation-of-romas-unfortunate-refuses-to-pay-compensation/

16 Polish legislative reaction to the ECJ's decision on the independency of the disciplinary courts.

17 See Part VI, Stability.

18 The report of Helsinki Foundation for Human Rights entitled "Instead the Rule of Law there is the Rule by Law", www.hfhr.pl/en/hfhr-report-rule-by-law-replaced-the-rule-of-law-threats-to-human-rights-in-poland-2015-2019/

19 See Part IV, Limits, point III.

of constitutional review and the interpretation process. When we look at the thick concept of the Rule of Law, the formal legality is expanded and certain substantive elements are added, mainly those that are constitutionally related to the term: they are mentioned in the same constitutional provision, appear in the jurisprudence of the constitutional courts, and ensure the enforcement of (any) constitutional rules.

Given the fact that the realization of the European Rule of Law, or, as a matter of fact, any of its concepts, similarly to that of democracy and human rights, is a matter of degree, we cannot confidently state that there is no Rule of Law in Hungary and Poland. What we can assertively claim, however, is that these states employ a different understanding of the Rule of Law as compared to the concept of the European Rule of Law. What we have in Hungary and Poland is something different: it does not equate to what it used to mean between 1990 and 2010/2015, but it has not yet been reduced to mere rule by law (power exercised via the law) without considering other components that different authors and judicial actors attach to the concept. These states employ illiberal legality.

The concept of illiberal legality and its connection to the European Rule of Law are depicted in Figure V.1 below.

The extent of non-compliance with the benchmark of the Rule of Law by the political decision-makers, in terms of quality and quantity, goes far beyond the innocent claim that honest mistakes have been made. Neither political nor constitutional dialogue managed to resolve differences in views between the Hungarian and Polish Governments and political and judicial bodies of the supranational and international communities: constitutional (adopting the FL and its major, most contested amendments) or legislative reforms (e.g., of the Polish judiciary) have been completed in the majority of cases in a manner that did not consider the opinions (or did it *ex-post facto*) of the Venice Commission, the Commission and Parliament of the EU, and many other actors, including NGOs and judicial bodies, such as the ECtHR and the CJEU. The reason for the refusal to listen may be found in different worldviews. As formulated by László Trócsányi, former Minister of Justice of Hungary, "In Europe today, we witness the clash between individualism and a mindset prioritizing community interests and the public good."[20] This position also pertains in the constitutional courts of Hungary and Poland.[21]

The political decision-makers position Hungary and Poland as defenders of "community interests and the public good", as they interpret them, which include

20 L Trócsányi, "New Challenges Facing Democracy and the Rule of Law", *Hungarian Review* 3 (2017), http://hungarianreview.com/article/20171117_new_challenges_facing_democracy_and_the_rule_of_law

21 25/2013 (X. 4) CC decision, Concurring Opinion of Béla Pokol. The CT judgment of 16 March 2017 on the Law on Assemblies suggests the subordination of the individual to the state; see I Wróblewska, "The Rule of Law: The Polish Perspective" in T Drinóczi and A Bień-Kacała (eds), *Rule of Law, Common Values and Illiberal Constitutionalism. Poland and Hungary within the European Union* (Routledge, 2021) 133–150.

Table V.1 Overview on the versions of the Rule of Law in Hungary and Poland 2020

Version	*Content*	*Hungary – realization*	*Poland – realization*
Thin/ Formal	reasonably clear, reasonably stable, publicly available general rules and standards that are applied prospectively and not retrospectively (Raz) generality, publicity, stability, prosperity, clarity, consistency of the law, the possibility of compliance with the law, and congruence between rules as announced and their actual administration (Fuller)	rather yes than no – there are issues with stability due to the inadequate preparation of laws Note the possibility of retroactive taxation in the Constitution in 2010	rather yes than no – stability is partly defective due to hasty changes of the judicial system and other legislation
	predictability (May)	rather yes than no – the constitution can easily be changed	rather yes than no – the constitution has been changed informally
Formal legality	power exercised via law (rule by law)	yes	Yes
	state actions to be subject to the law	- yes but the Constitution can easily be changed (abusive constitutionalism) - the content of the Constitution can be challenged - CC is packed; not open confrontation with power, but not always deferential	- yes but the interpretation of the Constitution is selective and arbitrary - unconstitutional interpretations and legal measures are declared constitutional - CT is packed
	equality before the law	challenged; constitutional/legal inequality	challenged; accountability depends sometimes on political agenda
	characteristics of the law	- rather yes than no - see above	- rather yes than no - see above
Rule of Law Checklist of the Venice Commission	Mixed in each element: constitutional supremacy, legality, legal certainty	- Constitution and the laws can easily be changed - plus see above	- Constitution can be changed informally - laws can easily be changed - plus see above
	equality, non-discrimination	challenged	Challenged
	prevention of abuse (misuse) of power	challenged	Challenged
	an independent judiciary	challenged	highly challenged
	access to justice	rather yes than no	rather yes than no

Source: revised version of the Table in T Drinóczi and A Bień-Kacała (eds), *Rule of Law, Common Values and Illiberal Constitutionalism. Poland and Hungary within the European Union* (Routledge, 2021) 226–227.

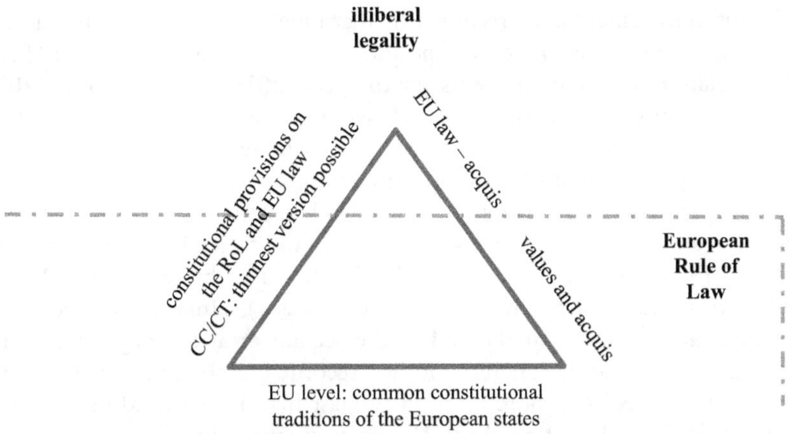

Figure V.1 Illiberal legality and the European Rule of Law – Hungary and Poland
Source: T Drinóczi and A Bień-Kacała (eds), *Rule of Law, Common Values and Illiberal Constitutionalism. Poland and Hungary within the European Union* (Routledge, 2021) 228.

the vigorous defense of the nation-state and national identity against any "foreign" concern. Each criticized step of the governments finds its justification in existing but often deliberately misinterpreted and misused political philosophical,[22] human rights,[23] and legal considerations. When invoking these thoughts, the European and the Hungarian and Polish political decision-makers, and occasionally judicial actors, talk at cross-purposes, which make it harder to resolve difficulties. When addressing these ideas in communication with the citizenry, they use a smoothly comprehensive, manipulative, and oversimplified language. The population does not have "immunity" against this political and legal "fake news" – and apparently does not need any.

2.2 In compliance with the European Rule of Law

It is a characteristic of illiberal constitutionalism that illiberal legality is not only at odds with the European Rule of Law but implements it as well.

From a quantitative perspective, an overview of the Annual Reports of the EU on monitoring the application of EU law between 2015 and 2018[24] makes us realise that neither Hungary nor Poland is the worst in terms of compliance among the EU28.[25] The Annual Reports on the EU28 differentiate between new infringement cases by Member States on 31 December of a particular year and the

22 Part VI, Stability, point II.
23 See below, point III.
24 Annual Report, n. 6.
25 The data was collected before Brexit.

number of infringement cases recorded by that time. The latter is further divided into infringements for incorrect transposition and/or bad application of EU laws and late transposition infringements for the years 2015 and 2016. Since 2017, the new late transposition infringement cases are shown separately, and in 2018 total infringement cases are broken down not only into incorrect transposition and/or bad application of EU laws and late transposition infringements, but also into infringements of regulations, treaties, and decisions. In neither of these categories can one find Hungary and Poland at the far end of the scale. If we divide the EU28 into four quarters in the diagram used by the Annual Reports (running from the least to the most number of cases), Hungary is placed, with some exceptions,[26] either at the end of the second or at the beginning of the third quarter. Poland is different: it has recorded more infringements than Hungary, and finds itself more often in the last than in the third quarter. It is worth noting that when it comes to the new category (infringement of regulations, treaties and decisions), both states are placed at the beginning of the second half of the scale.

This observation needs to be coupled with some qualitative analyses, while not forgetting the fact that there is an ongoing Article 7 procedure against both Hungary and Poland. Nevertheless, when studying Hungarian EU law compliance up to 2015, Márton Varju[27] found that the degree of compliance has generally been appropriate, even if data concerning adjudication are scarce. He detected technical problems at both the lawmaking and adjudication levels, which include late implementation, paying less attention to the details of implementation, and errors in court judgments. More substantive issues mainly related to the field of economic regulation, where the opportunities offered by the grey zone of EU economic policies are profoundly taken advantage of. Varju is hesitant as to whether Hungarian non-compliance is a trend, a systematic deficiency, or simple inadequacy. He acknowledges, however, that there are many examples of Hungarian regulatory opportunism, regulatory bad faith,[28] and obstruction in complying with EU obligations. In his view, in many cases, it is not the regulatory goal that is to be criticized but the methods of its achievement and the further consequences of the enforcement of the particular regulation. He opines that the outstanding performance of the Hungarian judges in the field of preliminary ruling procedures, especially after 2010, is due in particular to the embeddedness of EU law in the Hungarian

26 New infringement cases in 2016 (beginning of the last quarter of the diagram); new late transposition cases in 2017 and 2018 (in the first quarter of the diagram), late transpositions in 2017 (with the second least cases).

27 M Varju, "A magyar jogrendszer és az Európai Unió joga: tíz év tapasztalata" ["The Hungarian Legal System and the Law of the European Union: Experiences of Ten Years"] in A Jakab and G Gajduschek, eds, *A magyar jogrendszer állapota* (MTA Társadalomtudományi Kutatóközpont, Jogtudományi Intézet, 2016) 142–164.

28 The postponement of compliance facilitates the maximisation of the advantages originating from the violation of EU law for personal gain.

legal system. He suggests that it could also be due to the non-compliance of the lawmaker. This latter opinion, however, does not seem to be supported by the statistics provided in the Annual Reports. The number of cases has shown no great variation in any of the categories between 2011 and 2019. The number of infringement cases open at the end of each year ranged between 54 (2011) and 66 (2019), with a peak of 57 (2016); the smallest number of cases was 37 (2013). The number of new late transposition infringement cases ranged between 70 (2011), which was the peak, and 17 (2019). A drastic drop was observed in 2012 (number of cases: 26). The number of late transposition infringement cases ranged between 16 (2013) and 23 (2018), with a peak of 32 (2016); the smallest number of cases was 13 (2015).

Poland's compliance in 2015 was generally not satisfactory, but it was not the worst performer, ranking among the last five or six Member States. Jacek K Sokołowski and Dariusz Stolicki suggest that the particularities of the governmental drafting stage of the legislative process could be blamed for the late transposition infringements, but they do not exclude other possible reasons. They submit the following explanations for delayed transposition: political reasons, that is, no acceptance of the solutions imposed by the directive to be transposed, the complexity of the subject matter, and organizational failure.[29] We might note that the number of infringement cases showed considerable variation in each of the categories between 2011 and 2019. In infringement cases and new late transposition infringement cases, the trend seemed to be to decrease. The number of infringement cases open at the end of the year varied between the peak of 95 (2011) and 75 (2019); the smallest number of cases was 68 (2013). The number of new late transposition infringement cases ranged between 44 (2011), which was the peak, and 14 (2019), which also represents the smallest number of cases. The number of late transposition infringement cases ranged between 20 (2013), which was the smallest number of cases, and 26 (2019), with a peak of 39 (2016, 2017). Poland does not perform worse here than in the other categories. If we compare the country's performance with that of the EU28, we find that Poland, since 2015, has been positioned at the start of the last quarter in the category depicting the number of infringement cases as of 31 December. The figures concerning new infringement cases are unsteady, and the country shifts between the beginning of the third quarter and the beginning of the last quarter. There is a slow deterioration in the number of new late transposition cases, but Poland remains in the third quarter (it dropped back from the beginning of the third quarter to the end of it).

29 JK Sokołowski and D Stolicki, "Przyczyny opóźnień w transpozycji dyrektyw europejskich do polskiego porządku prawnego w świetle analizy ilościowej krajowego procesu legislacyjnego" ["Reasons for Delays in the Transposition of European Directives into the Polish Legal Order in the Light of Quantitative Analysis of the National Legislative Process"], *Przegląd Politologiczny* 2 (2017) 39–54.

Table V.2 Number of infringement cases in Hungary and Poland 2011–2019

		2011	*2012*	*2013*	*2014*	*2015*	*2016*	*2017*	*2018*	*2019*
Infringement cases open as of 31 December	HU	54	42	37	44	38	57	48	50	66
	PL	95	82	68	79	78	76	70	70	75
New late transposition infringement cases	HU	70	26	21	26	17	36	13	8	17
	PL	44	18	15	18	22	36	21	16	14
Late transposition infringement cases	HU	–	–	16	18	13	32	15	17	23
	PL	–	–	20	23	30	39	39	33	26

Source: authors, Annual Reports, n. 6.

II Illiberal democracy

1 The term

As we mentioned previously in Part II on Terms, we view the concept of illiberal democracy differently from Fareed Zakaria (1990s) or Viktor Orbán (2014).[30] Zakaria perceived democracy and liberalism as two separate ideals that are independent of one another but which have developed close to each other.[31] Therefore, states that previously became liberal could easily become democratic, while states that absorbed democracy first could disregard liberal rights and turn to being illiberal and democratic at the same time. Our point is, however, that both Hungary and Poland, as a result of the democratic transition of 1989/1990, created fully fledged constitutional democracies. These then became downgraded to something else in the 2010s – which we call "illiberal constitutionalism". Our views thus relate to different directions of change. As for Orbán's use of the term, for us, it expresses the main idea of how Orbán's and Kaczyński's democracy works.

In liberal constitutionalism, parliaments are the endpoint and the starting point of popular sovereignty. They are the representative body of the people, and they are created to adopt binding rules for everyone, including the people. Besides legislation, another primary role of parliaments is their oversight function. Properly conducted parliamentary business also includes participation in the two main spheres of activity, that is, legislation and oversight. As Nadia Urbinati claims, representative democracy should involve not only a simple delegation of powers, but also a social framework that allows structured debate about preferences and

30 Speech on 26 July 2014; www.kormany.hu/en/the-prime-minister/the-prime-minister-s-speeches/prime-minister-viktor-orban-s-speech-at-the-25th-balvanyos-summer-free-university-and-student-camp

31 F Zakaria, "The Rise of Illiberal Democracy", *Foreign Affaires* 76 (1997) 22; for further details, see F Zakaria, *The Future of Freedom: Illiberal Democracy at Home and Abroad* (W.W. Norton and Company, 2007).

common actions.[32] It follows that not only should the electoral processes be inclusive, fair, and democratic, supported by, amongst other things, media freedom, but the decision-making process should be as well. For the sake of democracy, it is assumed that it should not be any different during a pandemic.

As opposed to what evolved after the transition to constitutional democracy, illiberal democracy is conceptualized as a formal, manipulated, profoundly majoritarian, and non-inclusive democracy in which constitutional institutions (such as elections and connected electoral rights and principles, representation and accountability, and the central tenets of democratic lawmaking) are, to a certain extent, misused, abused, or neglected.

Hungary and Poland still feature signs of political competition. Power can be lost in elections, at least in local elections and elections to the Polish *Senat*. Therefore, as explained in Part IV on Limits, both states differentiate themselves from Russia, Turkey or Singapore, and it would not reflect the current state of affairs if we were to call them authoritarian regimes. There are, to be sure, some defective practices and power-grabbing endeavours and mechanisms in place as well. These undoubtedly lower the level of political competition and the chance for meaningful deliberation and discussion within the procedurally defective law-making procedure. These practices demolish democratic institutions, degrade democratic rights and freedoms, and detach them from what can be called a democracy. They lead the system towards majoritarian rule, and thus the concept of a substantive democracy is modified and narrowed down. The use of the adjective "illiberal" therefore seems adequate.

The application of mere majority rule can be seen in the constitution-making process in Hungary and in the legislative processes in both states.[33] In the parliamentary procedure, both the Polish and Hungarian oppositions have to face exclusion, that is, they are either outvoted or suppressed.[34] While the first can

32 N Urbinati, *Representative Democracy: Principles and Genealogy* (University of Chicago Press, 2006) 43.

33 Drinóczi, n. 10; V Kazai, "The Illiberal Challenge to the Rule of Law Principle: The Neglected Procedural Aspect (With Special Focus on Hungary)", 2019 ESIL Annual Research Forum, Göttingen (4–5 April 2019), available https://ssrn.com/abstract=3513204. As for Polish legislation, Mirosław Wyrzykowski has used the expression "anti-principle of improper law-making" as an adequate description of the legislative practices since 2015: M Wyrzykowski, "'Wrogie przejęcie' porządku konstytucyjnego" ["'Hostile Takeover' of the Constitutional Order"], http://konstytucyjny.pl/wrogie-przejecie-porzadku-konstytucyjnego-miroslaw-wyrzykowski (9.10.2020). *Idem*, "Bypassing the Constitution or Changing the Constitutional Order Outside the Constitution" in A Szmyt and B Banaszak (eds), *Transformation of Law Systems in Central, Eastern and South-Eastern Europe in 1989–2015*, Liber Amicorum in Honorem Prof. Dr. Dres. H.C. Rainer Arnold, (Gdańsk University Press, 2016). Iwona Wróblewska has listed the most significant irregularities of the legislative procedure since 2015: Wróblewska, n. 21, 143, e.g., legislative haste; abuse of special modes of law-making (separate and urgent); lack of social consultation or illusory consultation; and failure to keep proper *vacatio legis*.

34 Poland: Only 30 seconds for expressing opinion during legislative process, blocked voting on opposition amendments to bills.

obviously happen in a parliamentary democracy, the latter must be viewed as a somewhat foreign concept. There is extensive use of accelerated, symbolic, personalized, and omnibus legislation; genuine public consultations are not conducted. The overall quality of the legislation and parliamentary procedures is poor,[35] which has provided the framework within which to combat COVID-19.

During the pandemic, parliaments throughout the world have had to face a unique and complex challenge,[36] which in most cases has affected their daily operation, including lawmaking and oversight. It has also been seen that parliaments have had to adapt to the health crisis either by introducing online or combined sessions, or by taking social distancing and other precautionary rules seriously. While most parliaments have tried to overcome these difficulties, they have apparently followed a realistic and incremental approach to ensure the continuity of executive oversight, and have prioritized those mechanisms that they deem to be strategic and feasible.[37] This has not been the case in Hungary and Poland, where considerations of democratic and legislative quality have not been at the forefront of crisis management. Even if there has been some criticism regarding the type of emergency measures and the way in which they have been introduced, those measures have been supported by both the opposition and the people. The legitimacy of the emergency measures has been clear also because only a handful of issues have been submitted to the CC and CT, which is one of the consequences of the illiberal judicialization of politics, on which we elaborate in Part VI on Stability.

As said, the departure from the previous liberal constitutionalism is visible as the vector of change turns towards authoritarianism. However, the remodelling in Hungary and Poland has not reached this point so far, not even in the field of democratic deterioration (except perhaps as regards the Hungarian electoral reform in 2020), because some political pluralism and the possibility of changing the ruling majority are still available.[38] Nevertheless, in 2020, almost half of the Hungarian voters surveyed reportedly did not trust that the Government could be removed in a democratic way.[39] As a result of the changes to the electoral law submitted to and adopted by the Hungarian parliament during the second constitutional emergency (November and December 2020), this opinion might become a de facto reality in the 2022 national election. In

35 Drinóczi, n. 10.

36 These challenges include institutional, demographic, psychological, and political issues. I Bar-Siman-Tov, "Covid-19 Meets Politics: The Novel Coronavirus as a Novel Challenge for Legislatures", *The Theory and Practice of Legislation* 8(1–2) (2020) 11–48 (free online access).

37 E Griglio, "Parliamentary Oversight Under the Covid-19 Emergency: Striving Against Executive Dominance", *The Theory and Practice of Legislation* 8(1–2) (2020) 49–70 (free online access).

38 See https://freedomhouse.org/countries/nations-transit/scores

39 A Bíró-Nagy and G Laki, *Orbán 10. Az elmúlt évtized a magyar társadalom szemével*, Budapest 2020, www.policysolutions.hu/userfiles/Orban10_final.pdf, 78.

Poland, the electoral law was also reformed in the midst of the COVID-19 pandemic, right before the presidential election. The COVID-19 situation has showed a serious backsliding in democracy, which we discuss below, but this fits into the trend of steady deterioration since 2010 (Hungary) and 2015 (Poland).[40]

It seems that the conceptualization of illiberal democracy is supported by the value preferences of the population for hierarchical structures and autocratic leadership. Opposing views and considerations are not welcome, as the will of the majority, which represents the "sovereign" state and the "sovereign people (nation)", which covers only "real Poles" or "real Hungarians", should prevail. In political narrative "the nation" is composed of those who represent the traditional vision of "family", and who are Christian for Hungarians and Catholic for Poles.[41] Such a narrative disregards a constitutional perception of the nation that consists of all citizens, regardless of their nationality, and the constitutional values of human dignity and equality.

2 Electoral democracy – illiberalization

In both the Hungarian and the Polish constitutions, the formal condition of the minimalist version of democracy associated with electoral rights and procedures[42] is provided for, and it is still about "rule by the people". Against this background, both the electoral concept and its practice have been illiberalized. Nevertheless, even if Freedom House considers Hungary to be a hybrid regime, the electoral process is assessed relatively highly (9 out of 12), while Poland, a semi-consolidated democracy, scored 11 out of 12 in 2019 and 2020.[43]

2.1 Rules of elections

In Hungary, electoral illiberalization features gerrymandering, diversification of methods of casting votes, packing electoral bodies, and a non-inclusive legislative process on electoral rules.[44] There is a factual inequality regarding the ways voters

40 Zs. Csaky, *Nations in Transition: Dropping the Democratic Façade* (Freedom House, 2020), https://freedomhouse.org/report/nations-transit/2020/dropping-democratic-facade#Facade, 25.

41 See, on the concepts of heterogeneous and homogeneous nation, A Bień-Kacała, A Tarnowska and W Włoch, "The Nation, Delegation, and Constitutional Change in Poland", *Hungarian Journal of Legal Studies* 59(4) (2018) 355–377.

42 J Schumpeter, *Capitalism, Socialism and Democracy*, 2nd edn (Allen & Unwin, 1947) chs 21–23.

43 For a comparison, in 2019, Russia scored 0 and Turkey scored 5, https://freedomhouse.org/countries/freedom-world/scores

44 These irregularities have been noted by the OSCE ODIHR (2018), www.osce.org/odihr/elections/hungary/385959?download=tru, the Freedom House (2019), and scholars; A. Schmidt, "Challenges of the Illiberal Democracy in Hungary: Some Aspects to the 2018 Elections", *Polski Przegląd Politologiczny* 2 (2018) 82; T.

who are abroad on the day of the election can cast their votes. Hungarians who do not have a national address (Hungarians who are the nationals of neighbouring countries and who received citizenship based on rules that do not require a national address) can cast their votes by post. However, those who have a national address (e.g. they are only working or studying abroad – voters who have already "voted with their feet") have to go to the Hungarian Embassy.[45]

In December 2020, the amendment to the electoral law was adopted in Hungary. It pretends to ensure a fraud-free election and assure that parties having factual social support can have a national list. In fact, the amendment increases the number of single-member constituencies in which parties need to have candidates (from 27 to 71) to have their national list. In the Hungarian mixed electoral system, there are 106 single-member constituencies, from which 106 candidates can be elected in one round. The remaining 93 seats are allocated to party lists according to the D'Hondt method. This 2020 reform is the inverse of what happened before the previous elections, when it became almost effortless to become a candidate. Then, the political intention was, of course, to increase democracy, with the desired effect of the proliferation of opposition votes. Some fake parties were established, and they ran on getting financial support for the national budget and gaining votes from anti-government voters. Now, these abuses of democratic rights (fake parties and budgetary irregularities), which were created by the Fidesz-led Government itself, are sought to be prevented by the same Government. Local elections in 2019 showed that opposition parties can defeat Fidesz candidates. Because of the extra challenge introduced by the reform (2020), opposition parties in the election of 2022 would need to cooperate "officially". This means that they will be "forced" to create joint lists instead of just having a gentlemen's agreement to support each other's candidate when they feel that another party enjoys more support. Joint lists trigger different thresholds: it would not be 5 per cent of votes cast, as a minimum share of votes that a list must obtain in order to gain seats, but 10 per cent (joint list of two parties) or 15 per cent (that of three or more parties).

In Poland, there are two outstanding problems: the increased political control over electoral administration, and the state-controlled propaganda during electoral campaigns. The organs responsible for the electoral process (such as the National Electoral Council (NEC)) and validating of the elections (the newly created chamber of the SC) have been refashioned, and now they are more political than judicial bodies. As for the other aspects of electoral rights, procedures and institutional guarantees were in place in Poland – until the planned electoral reform to the presidential election of 2020, and they returned almost to "normal" by the end of the legislation process regarding this election.

The ruling majority was determined to organize the election for political gain, at any cost, on the date determined earlier in this year as 10 May 2020. That is why, at the

Drinóczi, "Dialogic Interaction and Legislation on Parliamentary Election in Hungary 2010–2014", *Osteuropa Recht* 4 (2014) 452–467.

45 Not surprisingly, the CC did not find this mechanism unconstitutional.

beginning of the COVID-19 pandemic, they did not declare a constitutional emergency but a statute-based one. From the beginning, the epidemic seemed to favour President Duda, who could still move around in his capacity as President while other candidates were more restricted. Kaczyński announced that successful crisis management could not be undertaken without winning this election.[46] Therefore, one of the first COVID-19 Acts introduced remote voting (by post) for those in quarantine and aged above 60. This could be seen as a more democratic move. Later, a constitutional amendment to increase the mandate of the current President for two years was put forward by the Deputy Prime Minister Gowin, which contradicts democratic rule. This plan, however, was not realistic, as the ruling alliance has no constitutional majority and the coalition parties could not agree on the constitutional amendment. Another controversial bill[47] on the presidential election[48] was also submitted and passed on 7 May, three days before the assigned election day, which contradicts European and international standards.[49] The Act contained rules for all-postal voting, without adequate guarantees. Its provisions on the right to vote of those living abroad were vague, as those persons could easily be excluded from voting. Additionally, there were serious concerns about the secrecy of voting. The most worrying development was, however, that on 10 May the vote was not held. On 6 May the ruling camp decided not to proceed with the election without a formal legal ground. This move was a result of political agreement by Kaczyński and his allies. Finally, the new law on the presidential election was passed and the election was organized in two rounds in June and July 2020. The rules allowed for postal voting along with voting in polling stations, and the election was organized by the NEC. The new opposition candidate had less time for electoral campaigning, but the rules were nevertheless more in line with the required standards than the earlier proposals.

All of these irregularities and manipulations could have extended the boundaries of illiberal democracy to the stage where a change to the ruling majority would have been impossible. However, there was a need to legalize and legitimize decisions on this election, that is, comply with illiberal legality, instead of using tools from the toolbox of authoritarianism. Therefore, returning to the normal illiberal practice, the ruling alliance had created an invisible constitutional rule and then ordinary legislation that allowed for the moving of the election day to the summer and the holding of reasonably free elections. Unsurprisingly, the CT, the NEC, and the newly captured SC[50] served this purpose.

In the meantime, in Hungary, the proposed change in the electoral law, in itself, will be enough to hinder even the possibility of change of the political

46 www.rmf24.pl/tylko-w-rmf24/rozmowa/news-jaroslaw-kaczynski-w-rmf-fm-wybory-10-maja-powinny-sie-odbyc,nId,4393207

47 See e.g., www.hfhr.pl/en/position-of-the-helsinki-foundation-for-human-rights/

48 https://ruleoflaw.pl/pis-pushing-elections-during-epidemic-special-law-on-postal-vote-debated-in-sejm/

49 Opinion Nr ELE-POL/373/2020 OSCE ODIHR, www.osce.org/odihr/elections/poland/450856?download=true

50 The term of office of the First President of the Supreme Court expired on 30 April 2020 and the new officeholder was appointed by the Polish President on 25 May 2020.

leadership of that country in the next election (2022), which could amount to an authoritarian turn. In both states, thus, there has been a tendency to remodel electoral rules and make it harder for the opposition to succeed. While the rulers in Poland finally backed off, in Hungary new rules have been adopted, and we now have to wait and see how, if at all, they will be used.

2.2 Freedom of the media

Freedom of the media is a key freedom in the area of people making political choices. Campaigning in democracies should be free and fair. Voters should be informed in a proper way, so that they may make free decisions on who should represent them in parliament. Media coverage should be unbiased – which presupposes independent media. Therefore, special bodies are created to provide supervision of media activities. However, in our illiberal states, the regulatory and supervisory systems have been changed. Constitutional bodies have been captured[51] and new, biased bodies have been created on the basis of statutory provisions.[52] As a result, the media may provide only vague information during elections. The electoral campaigns in both states thus seem rather to be driven by state-controlled propaganda and media bias, due to the monopolization of the media, smear campaigns, and intimidating rhetoric. The media seem to be more national than public.[53] On the other hand, private media tend to be neutral or slightly in favour of either the opposition or the Government, depending on the profile of their target audience. The internet is free, but similar trends regarding political influence can be seen there as in the printed media.

Hungarian illiberalization is more advanced in this respect[54] and, as identified by Gábor Polyák, this process rests on three pillars:

> the undermining of the independence of the organizations responsible for overseeing private and public media; the manipulation of access to the market resources necessary for media market activities; the manipulation of the information environment by controlling the access to public information and the political agenda.[55]

51 In Poland it is the National Council of Radio and TV Broadcasting: W Sadurski, *Poland's Constitutional Breakdown* (Oxford University Press, 2019) 139.

52 In Poland it is the National Media Council: M Bernatt and M Ziółkowski, "Statutory Anti-Constitutionalism", *Washington International Law Journal* 28(2) (2019) 516.

53 Sadurski, n. 51, 138–140.

54 In the Freedom House survey concerning media freedom as one of the civil liberties (so not narrowed down to electoral campaign coverage), in 2019, Hungary scored 2 and Poland achieved 3 – out of 4. In contrast, media freedom does not exist in Russia (it scored 0) and it had almost vanished in Turkey (it scored 1). No changes were detected in 2020. On Hungary, see, e.g., the Conclusions of the Joint International Press Freedom Mission to Hungary from 3 December 2019, https://rsf.org/en/news/level-media-control-hungary-unprecedented-eu-member-state

55 G Polyák, "Media in Hungary: Three Pillars of an Illiberal Democracy" in E Polonska and E Beckett (eds), *Public Service Broadcasting and Media Systems in Troubled European Democracies* (Palgrave Macmillan, 2019) 284–285.

Indeed, the electoral campaign in 2018 and 2019 did not provide voters with fully informed possibilities of choice.[56] Signs of deterioration, however, had also appeared in 2014, when political competition was more balanced even though political institutions already worked in favour of the ruling party.[57] Such deficiencies also appeared in the electoral campaign in Poland in 2019. The public television and radio stations were biased[58] and, just as in Hungary, reported more often on the activities of the ruling party connected to the campaign than those of the opposition.[59] When the public media broadcast information on the opposition, they gave them a bad name. Nevertheless, studies show that PiS voters were aware of the media bias.[60]

It was a general feature of the private media in both Hungary and Poland that they displayed a mostly balanced attitude. The private media assessed the opposition in a positive way and did not report only negatively about the ruling party.[61]

3 Procedure in parliament

There have always been issues about the quality of both the Hungarian and Polish legislative process, as there are everywhere, which is why there is, worldwide, an emerging need for legislative quality and democratic lawmaking processes, which include effective oversight mechanisms too. However, since 2010 and 2015, the Hungarian and Polish legislative process has been becoming even more exclusive, extensively symbolic and personalized, embracing a purely majoritarian approach, and using and abusing accelerated procedures.

3.1 Legislation

3.1.1 INCREASINGLY ILLIBERAL PRACTICES

The legislative process is designed in the Hungarian FL and the Polish Constitution, along with the rules of procedures of parliaments, and laws and other legal measures on legislative processes, to provide proper tools (publicity in and transparency of the process) and formal stages of lawmaking. These are supposed to ensure the quality of legislation through the provision of proper space for

56 https://freedomhouse.org/country/hungary
57 Schmidt, n. 44, 78.
58 Report of Journalist's Society, http://towarzystwodziennikarskie.pl/wp-content/uploads/2019/10/2019RaportTDParFin5.pdf, 1–2.
59 The situation did not change during the presidential campaign of 2020. See the Human Rights Commissioner's Report at www.rpo.gov.pl/pl/content/koronawirus-i-kampania-wyborcza-w-mediach
60 P Sadura and S Sierakowski, "Political Cynicism: The Case of Poland", http://politicalcritique.org/cee/poland/2019/poles-political-cynicism-research-report/, 15–16.
61 Report of Journalist's Society, n. 60, 2–3.

consideration of disagreements and divergent opinions (e.g., involvement of stakeholders and the general public, public hearings in parliaments, and time for consideration of proposals). The most important constitutional standards were translated into constitutional jurisprudence, as the CC and the CT are entitled to assess the procedural constitutionality of legislation. Both courts restrict themselves to the examination of the validity of the law, that is whether it has been produced by the organ entitled to produce it, whether it was adopted during the process prescribed by the constitutions, focusing on the majority by which it is supposed to be adopted, and whether it respects the legal hierarchy and has properly been published. According to the constitutional courts, not every procedural mistake and failure makes a statute unconstitutional, but every law should meet the constitutional criteria of the legislative process, which in Poland, for instance, comprises three hearings, *Senat* participation, and a distinction made between amendments and legislative initiatives. Neither court considers it to be its role to assess whether the law has been the subject of consultation or based on evidence, which is not what the trend shows worldwide on procedural and semi-procedural constitutional review of laws.[62] The need for evidence-based legislation was not properly recognised in the pre-2010/2015 period either. There was a lack of awareness at the level both of policy-makers and lawmakers and the constitutional courts. Laws and implementing bylaws on consultation and both ex-ante and ex-post impact assessments were passed and defectively implemented until those laws were changed (Hungary[63]) or became "obsolete" and thus disregarded in Poland.

In both states, the government should make drafts available during the drafting process – it is another duty that has been more neglected than complied with. It has never been the practice to come up with policies and versions of them, and initiate discussion of them.

Usually, where necessary, Polish bills are put out for consultation to a broad range of public bodies and NGOs and the public; but this is no longer the case in Hungary. However, in Poland, the results of those consultations may not be considered at all, as was the case regarding the draft bill on the National Council for Judiciary in 2017. The draft was broadly consulted on by many judicial bodies (e.g. the SC) or NGOs (e.g. judicial societies), but their opinions were rejected by the Government as being contrary to the idea of amendment, which resembles the situation in Hungary a couple of years ago. Drafts relating to COVID-19 are usually not put out for consultation, since there is no time for this during the pandemic, as in the case of the amendment on the public health system in July 2020. In Hungary, when the Government wants to introduce reforms on (most recently and during the statute-based emergency), for example, the legal status of medical doctors, it submits a draft without consulting the stakeholders (chamber of medical doctors), and the

62 Bar Siman Tov, n. 12; P Popelier, M M Aymanyan, and W Vanderbruwaene, eds, *The Role of constitutional Courts in Multilevel Governance* (Intersentia, 2013), especially Part IV on Constitutional courts as regulatory watchdogs.

63 Drinóczi, n. 10.

parliament adopts it within days. When the chamber is not satisfied with the law at all, the Government aims to involve them in the drafting process of the accompanying secondary legislation (which should have been prepared along with the bill). Eventually, in the case of medical doctors, it opted for modifying the law that has been just adopted. The Government has failed to properly discuss higher education reform – that resulted in a lengthy demonstration at one of the universities, which lasted until the second pandemic-related constitutional emergency was introduced at the beginning of November 2020.[64]

Public engagement has become difficult even during the parliamentary phase of the legislative procedure, especially at a time when there is the need for quick decision-making and urgent implementation. Due to the use of three hearings conducted one directly after another in the Polish parliament, it has proved almost impossible for both the parliamentary opposition and NGOs to substantially contribute to legislation.[65] Another related problem is the access to information in both parliaments. There are often technical problems in providing the text of the bill via the *Sejm* website, as this needs time while the *Sejm* operates very quickly. Accelerated legislation comes together with an increased number of new laws.[66] Passing laws quickly has become the main rule instead of remaining an exception. It has an obvious adverse effect on the quality of the law, but this phenomenon is viewed by the political decision-makers with a measure of pride. They think that more laws adopted via a rapid process are a sign of a strong and capable state.[67]

Moreover, more often than not it is almost impossible for the opposition to become familiar with a bill and responsibly reflect on it during the committee sessions. As a consequence of accelerated lawmaking, less time is spent on the debate in parliament;[68] MPs have only minutes, or at best hours, to form an opinion and formulate their own amendments. This does not favour any popular engagement either. The legislative reality has improved slightly since the 2019 election in Poland, when the PiS lost the *Senat*; there is substantial consultation and discussion of legislation during the *Senat* phase of the legislative procedure. But still, such discussion cannot turn into a proper legislative decision, as the opinion of the *Senat* may be outvoted by the *Sejm*.

64 See more in point III below.

65 Sadurski, n. 51, 132–135.

66 É Alberti et al., "Impact Assessments Public Consultation and Legislation in Hungary 2011–2014" (Budapest, 2015) www.crcb.eu/wp-content/uploads/2015/07/legislation_2014_report_150630.pdf, 83, É Alberti et al., "The Quality of Hungarian Legislation 2013–2014" (Budapest, 2015), http://ec.europa.eu/hungary/about-us/growth-and-jobs/legislation_eu_2014_report_150216_2100.pdf

67 As can be read on the website of the Hungarian Parliament, for instance, "[a]fter 1990, the National Assembly enacted 140 laws on average each year, but the most recent cycle has been much more productive (with an annual average of 215 laws in the 2010–2014 cycle)", www.parlament.hu/en/web/house-of-the-national-assembly/the-legislative-process

68 Ibid.; TA Nagy, "Parlamenti sebesség" ["Parliamentary Speed"], https://flextime.hu/cikkek/80146-Parlamenti_sebesseg.html

It is also difficult to follow passed laws and their modifications, as these can appear in the official gazettes over the course of a few days or even hours. Recently, in Poland, there was legislation that was deliberately not published as the ruling majority had passed it by mistake and wanted to amend this law.[69] Eventually, both statutes were published at the same time. So, there has also been a rising number of "junk laws, i.e., published laws with considerable faults, which have needed to be modified within one year of their publication".[70]

As mentioned previously, constitutional review cannot help. For instance, according to the jurisprudence of the CT developed before 2015, the time frame of the legislative process is not a reason for the unconstitutionality of a statute.[71] This, inadvertently, supports the apparent political demand for speedy legislation, which is meant to show the effectiveness of the political branches of government.[72] The tools of the Standing Order of the Sejm[73] are abused in this regard, despite there being no real necessity for it. Bills are passed after just a few hours in the *Sejm* and become binding law within a few days. Nevertheless, according to the same jurisprudence of the CT, the legislator should be aware of the quality of legislation, which may be lowered by the use of an accelerated procedure and not be in conformity with the Constitution. However, less care can be observed: the time allowed for deputies' speeches has been reduced to 1 minute, or even 30 seconds.[74] There is block voting on amendments (not by subject but depending on which parliamentary faction submitted them) and the content of amendments is not heard. Warnings about errors in the drafts, reported by parliamentarians and the employees of legislative offices, are being ignored.[75]

There is another "default abuse" in this illiberal legislative system: the constitutionally provided "urgent procedure"[76] has not been used to pass legislation in Poland. The Government can engage the urgent procedure only in relation to its listed bills. In fact, however, the Government often is not the initiator of politically crucial bills, as was the case regarding the remodelling of the judiciary.[77] The bills are

69 The amendment would have provided extra money to all medical personnel who treat patients with COVID-19. The Government had planned to allow extra income only to those who were ordered to work with COVID-19 patients. The regulation was extended to all medical personnel by the *Senat* and then by the *Sejm*. The ruling majority did not notice this change and voted against the intention of the Government.

70 Alberti et al., n. 66 (Impact assessment ...), 84.

71 The CT judgement of 23 March 2006 (K 4/06).

72 Especially legislation on the CT or SC and common courts.

73 The *Sejm* may decide on immediate readings without time for consideration, one reading following immediately after another.

74 Wróblewska, n. 21, 142–143.

75 Specific examples of legislative pathologies are described in detail in the Citizens' Communications of the Legislation Forum on the quality of the legislative process, http://obserwatoriumdemokracji.pl/wp-content/uploads/2016/03/XI_Komunikat_OFL.pdf

76 Art 123 of the Polish 1997 Constitution.

77 2020 Rule of Law Report, country chapter on the Rule of Law situation in Poland, https://ec.europa.eu/info/sites/info/files/pl_rol_country_chapter.pdf

submitted by the President of the Republic or private MPs. The reason, again, is the abusive and illiberal nature of the regime: in these cases, the additional requirements that government bills have to meet (e.g., a regulatory impact assessment, inter-ministerial discussions, public consultations, drafting rules) can be circumvented. This legislative trend is no different in Hungary. Mainly after 2010, important laws (such as constitutional amendments, laws governing churches, or the recently adopted overtime regulation) have been initiated by MPs. This exercise implies that these drafting processes, most probably, have not observed the standards regulating legislative quality. The reasons for this are at least twofold: either the laws have been prepared by the MPs, who have neither the infrastructure nor the human resources and skills to conduct a high-quality drafting procedure, including all the consultation and impact assessments; or the drafts have been prepared in the ministries (or somewhere else as an outsourced activity), without observing the underlying rules, and then have "unofficially" been given to the MPs belonging to the majority faction(s), for them to submit them as their own initiatives. Due to the lack of focused training and legislative and drafting skills, the quality of MPs' submissions, in terms of, for example, the implications the draft has relating to the coherency and integrity of the legal system, might be way below that of a governmental draft.

Symbolic legislation occurs when the stated purpose of the law does not coincide with a political objective that has not been publicly disclosed.[78] The legislator can also seek to confirm a system of values of a particular social group, demonstrate its power, or resolve a conflict between two or more social groups or political parties. Important to note is that the symbolic function is rarely pure and mostly combined with other functions (mainly regulatory or normative). It may also be combined with the instrumental use of law to achieve *ad hoc* political objectives.

The use of symbolic legislation increased in both Hungary and Poland after the remodelling started in 2010 and 2015. Prior to that, symbolic legislation was used only rarely, most often in relation to laws regulating the social sphere, and symbolic content was placed in preambles (e.g. in case of the law on education or support for families). Symbolism was intended to increase the regulatory and normative effects of laws – sometimes ineffectively and regardless of the requirements of lawmaking.

From the perspective of the normativity of laws, as a Rule of Law and legislative quality requirement, symbolic content is better placed in parliamentary resolutions instead of statutes. This is still the case, but more and more symbolic laws appear in the legal systems. For instance, in Poland, since 2015, at least two symbolic laws have been adopted: the Demotion Act (2018)[79] and the amendments to the Institute of National Remembrance Act of 2018 (on the defamation of the Polish

78 B van Klink, B van Beers, and L Poort (eds), *Symbolic Legislation Theory and Developments in Biolaw* (Springer International Publishing Switzerland, 2016) 1–2. In relation to the development in Poland, see A Bień-Kacała, "Illiberal Democracy in Action: Polish Kind of Symbolic Legislation", *European Studies: The Review of European Law, Economics and Politics* 6 (2019) 268–278.

79 This Act is on the deprivation of the military rank of persons and soldiers in the reserve, who, in the years 1943–1990, had betrayed the Polish *raison d'état*.

Nation). In these examples, the values represented were clearly spelled out and separated from the legal effects of the Acts. The values addressed were settlement with the past and the protection of the image of a homogeneous Polish Nation. Interestingly, the Demotion Act was vetoed by the President. Besides, according to the Marshal of the *Sejm*, there was no political intention to implement the Defamation Act, which was, as a matter of fact, partially repealed, due to a strong international reaction, and partially invalidated by the CT. This lack of implementation may be seen as limitation of political will.

Personalized legislation is a tool that helps the leading political power to secure key positions for its loyal friends. This practice, as we describe it in Part VI, Stability, could range from filling up previously judicial-type bodies with political nominees (NEC – Poland), to lifting certain preconditions for an elected position (mayor and supreme court judge – Hungary), to supporting particular foreign investments (via tax laws). This type of legislation usually pretends to have general applicability, but it has been customized for a particular situation.

3.1.2 THE LOW QUALITY OF LEGISLATION AGGRAVATED BY THE PANDEMIC

The COVID-19 pandemic confronted parliaments worldwide with many challenges: how can technology be used constitutionally; how to convene the parliament and committee sessions; how to determine the quorum; whether or not actual presence is constitutionally mandated or needed (e.g., Switzerland,[80] Georgia, the UK, Colombia[81]); whether there are any legal obstacles to organizing virtual work, whether (e.g., Kenya[82]) proper infrastructure (internet access, speech, security) is provided or not. In parliamentary businesses, it is important to involve other non-parliamentary stakeholders, as well, which proved to be challenging during the pandemic. Practice shows that the emergency, due to the fast-track legislation used to help the executive, not only curtailed participation in lawmaking,[83] but could also result in the exclusion of a parliamentary committee in decision-making on emergency matters (Brazil[84]). There has been an assumption that digital arrangements might be easier to use in a committee meeting (UK), which could enhance the possibilities for oversight.[85] Besides these and beyond the generally applied oversight mechanisms and tools, there have been various strategies in place and practices exercised for pandemic-related oversight. It is thus important to see[86] whether or not particular parliaments participated in the declaration

80 F Uhlmann and E Scheifele, "Legislative Response to Coronavirus (Switzerland)", *The Theory and Practice of Legislation* 8(1–2) (2020) 115–130 (free online access).
81 Georgia, UK, Colombia, see Bar-Siman-Tov, n. 36.
82 Ibid.
83 Griglio, n. 37.
84 VM Pinheiro, M Ilarraz and MT Mestriner, "The Impacts of the COVID-19 Crisis on the Brazilian Legal System – A Report on the Functioning of the Branches of the Government and on the Legal Scrutiny of Their Activities", *The Theory and Practice of Legislation* 8(1–2) (2020) 193–212 (free online access).
85 Griglio, n. 37.
86 Based on Griglio, n. 37.

of the emergency; whether or not oversight mechanisms were suspended or limited to written procedures in the first couple of weeks (Bulgaria); whether or not parliamentarians activated non-legislative mechanisms with several oversight tools and procedures, such as fact-finding; whether or not they could foster debate among MPs and members of government without deliberation and voting; whether or not the government explained its policies and actions on the plenary; whether or not ad hoc bodies were established for oversight (as in, e.g., France, Belgium); and whether they employ ex-ante (most advanced form) or ex-post oversight.

Against this background, we can see that neither the Hungarian nor the Polish emergency legislative regime and parliamentary functioning have fared well. As we know, in Hungary, the constitutional design on emergencies allocates a lot of power to the Government, including the power to determine the beginning and end of the emergency and governing with emergency decrees that could even be contrary to existing laws, save for the constitution. The FL, however, also demands continuous parliamentary oversight, which was, both de facto and de jure, waived by the Hungarian parliament. In Poland, the constitutional design (the presidential election) also prompted the Government to bypass the Constitution and create a new statute-based emergency, further drawing the fight against the coronavirus into the presidential elections. The question of abstract legislative quality and oversight, in these circumstances, remained less important.[87] The pandemic did bring new challenges but, at the same time, did not bring about many changes within illiberal systems of both Hungary and Poland. The relationship between the executive and legislature is still determined by populism and autocratic tendencies. Democracy is as hollowed-out as it was before the pandemic. These factors could go to show the stability of illiberal constitutionalism, which we will cover further in the Part VI on Stability.

Regardless of the fact that legislators tend to be older than the median age of the overall population,[88] in spring 2020, the introduction of online sittings and voting procedures was not seriously debated in Hungary. Nevertheless, simultaneously, no consideration was given to shutting down the parliament; the Government demanded its continuous operation. In contrast, in Poland the *Sejm* and the *Senat* provided legal grounds (Standing Orders of both chambers) for online sittings and voting during the first wave of the pandemic (March 2020). Some legal (constitutional) obstacles were discussed before amendments to both Standing Orders were passed. The Constitution provides that the *Sejm* and the *Senate* shall debate in the course of sittings. According to the generally shared view in academia, "sittings" mean meetings in person.[89] However, the idea of allowing a hybrid formula, with the majority of MPs present in the parliament buildings, prevailed. In Hungary, plenaries are held in the upper chamber (the parliament

87 For a more detailed discussion on the legislative quality, see Drinóczi and Bień-Kacała, n. 14.

88 In Hungary, in 2018, the average median age was 42.5, while the average age of the MPs was 50. In Poland, in 2020, it was 42.2 (population) and 50 (*the Sejm*) and 58 (the *Senat*) respectively.

89 www.senat.gov.pl/gfx/senat/pl/senatekspertyzy/5529/plik/oe-297.pdf

building was built when there were two chambers) and social distancing rules must be observed.

In Poland, beyond the electoral issues, the *Sejm* has chaotically passed crisis management-related omnibus legislation. The misuse of the accelerated legislative process is much more frequent than before. There is not enough time for preparation and discussion because, as it appears in the political communication of the majority, more time spent with the discussion would jeopardize the defense against the pandemic. Therefore, the opposition is forced to accept, or at least tolerate, an increasing number of accelerated procedures, and cooperate in adopting unsubstantiated bills.

The pandemic, and the two types of emergencies, has not really altered the legislative activity either. Paradoxically, while the Hungarian parliament, similarly to the other state authorities, operated under the constitutional emergency regime, it still delivered regular legislative activities. This has allowed the parliament to quickly adopt controversial laws (e.g., on the ban on changing a person's sex in official documents) and political declarations (on the rejection of the ratification of the Istanbul Convention) upon the motions of the Government, or convert personalized emergency decrees into a personalized statutes with the intention of putting opposition-led local governments into more disadvantageous positions.[90] In the new statute-based emergency regulation, which was created to replace the first constitutional emergency, and the reformed rules on constitutional emergency, oversight could have been given more importance but this did not happen.

3.2 Oversight: its diminishing importance – mainly caused by the pandemic

Oversight was not an issue, in either country, that came to the fore before the pandemic; and due to the supermajority of Fidesz in parliament, its corrupted nature was already entrenched in Hungary. This might explain why the Polish parliament may seem more active as regards oversight, but it does not mean that it is any more effective in achieving the desired result – exercising meaningful oversight.

Oversight over executive actions was waived by the Hungarian parliament itself in the Coronavirus Act (March 2020). In this Act, the parliament gave its consent to every governmental measure that had already been adopted and that would be issued in the future. That said, there was no need to establish a special committee, or to introduce new and innovative mechanisms and tools. Oversight during the constitutional emergency (May–June 2020) was no different from that pre-COVID, and the situation did not change during the statute-based emergency introduced to run to the end of 2020, which was replaced by the second

90 T Drinóczi, "Hungarian Democratic Backsliding in Light of the Recent Emergency Coronavirus Legislation", *Public Jurist*, Hong Kong University Political Science Magazine, June 2020, www.hkuglc.org/government-and-laws-committee-hku-public-jurist

constitutional emergency in November 2020 due to the rise of the number of infected persons. The less stringent statute-based emergency is called a "health crisis" and is regulated in the Health Care Act. With the termination of the constitutional emergency in July 2020, all criticized governmental decrees (e.g., on the restriction of data protection rights and the freedom of information[91]) were withdrawn, but, by that time, some of those deemed quite controversial had already been transformed into primary legislation. According to the law, the new statute-based emergency is declared and terminated by the Government on the advice of the Chief Medical Officer. It could last for six months and can be extended. The Health Care Act lays down the subjects on which emergency governmental measures can be issued. However, the parliament is not involved in decision-making on the emergency: it only has to be informed about the extension of the crisis. Thus, not even a theoretical possibility for oversight is granted; and, as we know, the Hungarian Government has a record of not ending statute-based emergencies (see, for instance, of crisis situation caused by mass migration[92]). Nevertheless, since 2010, due to the constitutional majority of the Government within parliament, talking about any meaningful practice of oversight is futile. The second constitutional emergency was introduced with similar content to the first one – with the exception that, according to law, it ceases to have effect after 90 days.

The Hungarian Prime Minister gave opening speeches, but these were nothing more than the repetition of data that had already been shared by the Operative Corps – a body that assists the Prime Minister in managing the constitutional emergency. These speeches were unsuited for information gathering or fact-finding, or initiating an informed discussion. It seems that the "oversight" was effected in a business-as-usual manner; opposition MPs had used the official question time. Especially at the beginning of the pandemic, before the declaration of the constitutional emergency, they raised issues and mentioned challenges that the government had to face. In the plenary sessions in the autumn, they spent twice as much time on questions about the pandemic as before, but no interpellation motions were brought forward.

In Poland, information on the pandemic is rarely provided by the Minister of Health or the Prime Minister in the *Sejm*. Motions of opposition are usually outvoted. The provision of information is adjusted according to the political will. For instance, the *Sejm* refused an opposition motion to hear the Minister of Health about the preparedness of the hospital system against COVID-19, but heard the Prime Minister a few days later. A procedure for a vote of no confidence against the Minister of Health was activated in June 2020 and provoked a debate on the COVID-19 situation. However, the Minister stayed in office as the opposition did not have enough votes. In June 2020, two of the opposition MPs started an investigation into the Ministry of Health in relation to, for instance, a failed contract on ventilators, as only some of the promised ventilators were delivered. The

91 Drinóczi, n. 90.

92 See more in Part VI, Stability, point I.

MPs revealed some mismanagement and irregularities, but the termination of this contract was not the direct consequence of this action. At the beginning of November, the MPs were not even permitted to enter the Ministry building.

In Poland, no constitutional or extraconstitutional special body of oversight has been created. One might suggest such a body as the National Security Council to fulfil that role – a permanent advisory organ to the President of the Republic regarding internal and external security – as it consists of some MPs (presidents of parliamentary groups, the Marshals of the *Sejm* and the *Senat*). In practice, however, the body met only twice in March 2020 for consideration of the COVID situation.

III Illiberalization of human rights

1 Steps towards illiberalization and common challenges

The human rights situation in Hungary and Poland resembles a "glass half empty and a glass half full": from a former liberal constitutionalism perspective, the glass is quite empty. However, there is still the possibility to exercise human rights, and these rights are still better protected than, or at least differently protected than, in an authoritarian state. Thus, from this perspective the glass is half full. Still, there is an apparent deterioration and illiberalization, in the sense that the scope of human rights has been narrowed, diversity has been disappearing, and inequality, exclusion, and intolerance have been increasing – a glass half empty. Human rights regimes provide for a kind of constraint on public power. Illiberalization in this field is a much slower process than the remodelling of the Rule of Law and democracy, and, as the examples of Poland and Hungary show, it has three stages:[93] dismantling institutional guarantees, "sensitization", and emergence of a new theory of human right.

The first phase occurs when the positive obligation of the state to provide an adequate legislative and institutional framework for human rights protection has been considerably weakened. This is what we have just explained in the preceding sections.

The first phase is accompanied by a decrease in the perception of the importance of human rights, which is also reflected in the behaviour of the CC and CT, in their failure to comply with court decisions and the recommendations of international institutions[94] – the second phase. The regular, reluctant direct application of international and supranational human rights obligations by ordinary judges contributes to, but does not cause, this process.[95] Furthermore, in both Hungary

93 Sadurski calls the illiberalization of human rights "redesign and recalibration", Sadurski, n. 51, 151.

94 Polish Helsinki Foundation Report, *Poland Threatening Human Rights Protection*, www.liberties.eu/en/news/hfhr-report-poland-threatening-human-rights-protections/18206

95 Zs Szabó, "Többpólusú alapjogvédelmi rendszer a gyakorlatban – a kormánytisztviselők indokolás nélküli felmentésének tükrében" ["Multilevel Protection of Human Rights in Practice – In the Light of Dismissal of Government Officials Without

and Poland, the inappropriate and "decorative" use of the case-law of the ECtHR,[96] the lack of human rights-related thinking during the judicial decision-making process, and the general failure of judges to perceive themselves as judges of human rights pose other challenges.[97] After all, just as happened in Western Europe, regular reliance on the ECtHR case-law by ordinary judges does not happen overnight but could take decades.[98] As for the Charter of Fundamental Rights of the EU,[99] scholars find that the common challenges everywhere relate to awareness, inadequate legislative responses, more restricted application, and missed opportunities for reference.[100] Beyond these, European states commonly share other challenges, such as the most common violations of the ECHR[101] and the human rights challenges that have emerged in the past decades.[102]

Concerns relating to external and internal threats have not diminished but have worsened in Europe due to populist anti-immigration and anti-refugee and anti-

Justification"], *Pro Futuro* 1 (2015) 138 (Hungarian judges do not invoke ECtHR case law but apply domestic law).

96 P. Bárd and K. Bárd, "The European Convention on Human Rights and the Hungarian Legal System", http://real.mtak.hu/65944/1/Bard_Bard_Comparative_study_on_the_implementation_of_the_ECHR_at_the_national_level_ENG_149_168_u.pdf 152; E. Csatlós, "The Application of International Law as an Instrument of Interpretation in Hungary – The Practice of the Constitutional Court and Ordinary Courts in a Comparative Approach", http://publicatio.bibl.u-szeged.hu/7049/8/2961433.pdf, 137.

97 A Kúria, "Az Alaptörvény követelményeinek érvényesülése a bírósági ítélkezésben' Joggyakorlat-elemző Csoportja2016.El.II.JGY.K.1", https://kuria-birosag.hu/sites/default/files/joggyak/alaptorveny_osszefoglalo_velemeny.pdf, 194; Szabó, n. 95, 140.

98 Bárd and Bárd, n. 96, 165.

99 O Hamulak, M Sulyok, and LN Kiss, "Measuring the 'EU'clidean Distance between EU Law and the Hungarian Constitutional Court – Focusing on the Position of the EU Charter of Fundamental Rights", *Czech Yearbook of Public & Private International Law* 10 (2009) 145–148; A. Kastelik-Smaza, "The Application of the Charter of Fundamental Rights of the EU in Poland", *Acta Universitatis Carolinae – Iuridica* 4 (2018), https://karolinum.cz/data/clanek/6410/Iurid_64_4_0101.pdf, 112.

100 See e.g., Kastelik-Smaza, n. 99, 112; M. Klamert, "The Implementation and Application of the Charter of Fundamental Rights of the EU in Austria", *Acta Universitatis Carolinae – Iuridica* 4 (2018), https://karolinum.cz/data/clanek/6409/Iurid_64_4_0089.pdf, 89, 99; A. Kustra-Rogaska and O. Hamulak, "Keeping Distance: Chapters from Randomized (Non)application of the European Court of Human Rights before the Polish Constitutional Tribunal", *Baltic Journal of European Studies* 9(4) (2019) 90; R Arnold and L Cerny, "The Application of the Charter of Fundamental Rights of the EU by the German Federal Constitutional Court with References to the Other Federal Courts", *Acta Universitatis Carolinae – Iuridica* 4 (2018), https://karolinum.cz/data/clanek/6407/Iurid_64_4_0065.pdf, 65, 77.

101 The length of the proceedings has been the main, or second biggest, cause of concern in most of the more advanced Signatory States to the ECHR, www.echr.coe.int/Documents/Stats_violation_1959_2018_ENG.pdf

102 E.g., cases before the ECtHR concerning the UK and its regulatory responses to internal and external terrorism in the 1970–1980s and after 2000 may be recalled.

Muslim agendas.[103] In the EU and in almost all its Member States, the most pressing issues and challenges, mainly because of the increase of radical right-wing populism and its "anti-everything that is not national and white (male) agenda", have recently been migration, asylum legislation, the deportation system, rising xenophobia, anti-Semitism and anti-Muslim sentiments, increasing racist intolerance and violent hate crimes, discrimination against and harassment of minorities (including the Roma population, Muslims, and sexual minorities (gender-based discrimination)), domestic violence, and violence against women. Many states have also been condemned for their inadequate attention to and judicial decisions on rape victims (Denmark, Spain, and Portugal), legislation on terrorism and related issues (surveillance, ethnic profiling, deprivation of citizenship, mainly in the UK, France, and the Netherlands), and the assassination of journalists (Malta, Slovakia).

On the other side of the coin, some priorities of some states and the EU need to be mentioned as well, such as creating a gender-neutral option in official documents (the Netherlands), protecting victims' rights (EU directive[104]), liberalizing abortion (Ireland), and stressing gender mainstreaming during the pandemic in Scotland.

Against this political and legal background, sensitivity to human rights violations, and tolerance towards "otherness", has been decreasing in society, while anti-Semitism and xenophobia are on the increase.[105] According to the Spring 2016 Global Attitudes Survey, although many Europeans were concerned with security and the economic repercussions of the refugee crisis, Hungarians made it to the top of the list, with Poland following, despite the fact that no terror attack has taken place in either of these countries and that they are not destination countries for migration and not Mediterranean countries. Hungarians scored highest in relation to statements that "refugees will increase the likelihood of terrorism in our country" (76 per cent), "refugees are a burden on our country because they take our jobs and social benefits" (82 per cent), and "refugees in our country are more to blame for crime than other groups" (43%). Poland closely followed Hungary in the first two categories (71 per cent and 75 per cent, respectively). Only in the third category was Poland placed in the middle of the list (26 per cent). To offer a comparative perspective, in those countries that do indeed have a high migrant population, and which have already suffered terror attacks, the figures are as follows: Germany: 61 per cent, 31 per cent, 35 per cent; France: 46 per cent, 53 per cent, 27 per cent.[106]

103 See e.g., Human Rights Watch World Report 2019 Events of 2018, www.hrw.org/world-report/2019, Fundamental Rights Report 2019, https://fra.europa.eu/en/publication/2019/fundamental-rights-report-2019

104 Both Hungary and Poland have taken legislative measures to advance victim's rights, which is another example of the constraint effect of the European Rule of Law.

105 Sadurski, n. 51, 157. Commissioner for Human Rights of the Council of Europe, Dunja Mijatović, Report following her visit to Hungary from 4 to 8 February 2019, Strasbourg, 21 May 2019.

106 R Wike, B Stokes, and K Simmons, *Europeans Fear Wave of Refugees Will Mean More Terrorism, Fewer Jobs: Sharp Ideological Divides Across EU on Views about Minorities, Diversity and National Identity* (11 July 2016).

After "sensitizing" society to the illiberal values and attitudes, or, rather, triggering these emotions in the population, as we explained in Part III on Identity, the third phase is most probably the emergence of a new "theory" of human rights. It has already appeared in Hungary and, at present, manifests itself in the concept that state organs can invoke their fundamental rights in proceedings before the CC. It changes the core of human rights theory, which holds that human rights are attributed to human beings, who need to be equally protected against powerholders and treated as equals. It also supports the use of the adjective "illiberal" and underscores the nature of the changes, that is, illiberalization.

2 Struggling with international and supranational obligations

2.1 International level

There is no doubt that the ECtHR has contributed to the strengthening of democracy, the Rule of Law, and human rights protection after the transition in the post-socialist countries, and its judgments have become part of their legal systems. Hungarian and Polish authors assert that both the Hungarian, even after the adoption of the FL, and Polish legal systems provide a good legal environment for the application of international law, including the international law friendliness of judges.[107] In the pre-2015 era, the Polish CT even acknowledged that the ECtHR played an essential role in determining the catalogue of fundamental rights. It also agreed that the ECHR is directly applicable as being part of the Polish legal system, having a higher legal value than statutes. This view was also held in 2015,[108] but it does not mean that the implementation has been smooth. The direct applicability of ECtHR judgments in Hungary has always been an issue to be debated, in both the ordinary courts and the CC, even if the law on the international treaties adopted in 2005 made the demand for direct applicability clear. This interpretation of the treatment of the ECtHR's judgments complies with the constitutional rules on the harmony between international and domestic law – which the FL did not change.[109] Authors thus find that in spite of these challenges,

107 R Uitz, "Nemzetközi emberi jogok és a maygar jogrend" ["International Human Rights and the Hungarian Legal Order"], https://jog.tk.hu/uploads/files/08_Uitz_Renata.pdf; E Polgári, "Az Alkotmánybíróság esete az Emberi Jogok Európai Egyezményével" ["The Constitutional Court and the European Convention of Human Rights"] *Fundamentum* 4 (2015) 6; Csatlós, n. 96, 128–133; A Wyrozumska, "The Central and Eastern European Judiciary and Transnational Judicial Dialogue on International Law" in A Wyrozumska (ed), *Transnational Judicial Dialogue on International Law in Central and Eastern Europe* (Wydawnictwo Uniwersytetu Łódzkiego, 2017) 23.

108 SK 29/04 (6 December 2004); SK 52/08 (9 June 2010); Case U 10/07 (2 December 2009); SK 32/14 (22 September 2015). I Skomerska-Muchowska, "The Dialogue of the CEE Constitutional Court in the Era of Constitutional Pluralism" in A Wyrozumska (ed), *Transnational Judicial Dialogue on International Law in Central and Eastern Europe* (Wydawnictwo Uniwersytetu Łódzkiego, 2017) 118.

109 K Bárd and P Bárd, "Összhang vagy kollízió? Hol tart Magyarország 25 évvel az EJEE-hez való csatlakozás után a strasbourgi elvárásoknak való megfelelésben?"

judgments of the ECtHR have generally been executed by the legislative power,[110] and routinely invoked by the constitutional courts and from time to time by ordinary courts.

In 2008, Eszter Polgári found that neither the Hungarian parliament nor the Government could be criticized based on a failure to meet their international obligations: legislative measures have implemented international commitments and judgments have been executed. In fact, she shows that Hungarian ordinary courts more and more invoke ECtHR jurisprudence, mainly in cases concerning children's custody, pre-trial detention, judges' disqualification for lack of impartiality, and personal lawsuits.[111] Marcin Górski, in 2017,[112] listed cases that resulted in a legislative change in Poland. In the Soviet era, based on an international agreement between the USSR and the then Polish Government, the population was evacuated without just compensation. Poland attempted to redress the situation in the early 2000s, but the regulatory scheme offered ended up at the CT and the ECtHR. After the decision of the CT in the matter and the case *Broniowski v Poland*, [113] the implementation of property rights has been secured for Bug River claimants. In *Hutten-Czapska* (2006), the ECtHR found a violation of the protection of property, because the applicant could not use their property or charge adequate rent for its lease.[114] In 2011, the ECtHR closed one of its earliest pilot judgment procedures in these rent-control cases and found the Polish actions, including changes in laws and procedures, satisfactory.

Petra Bárd and Károly Bárd have collected examples of good practice when the legal environment on the freedom of assembly, freedom of speech, political pluralism, and politicians' freedom of speech was changed as a result of CC decisions that invoked the case-law of the ECtHR. They also identified bad practice, including disregarding the case-law and cherry-picking or abusive use of the case-law.[115] These are not unusual practices though. The Polish Górski has also characterized the practice of Central and Eastern European constitutional courts as proper, decorative, or fake, and as including failed or veiled dialogue,[116] while the

["Harmony or Collision? Where is Hungary 25 Years after to Joining the ECHR in Terms of Compliance to Expectations of Strasbourg?"], 4 *Állam és Jogtudomány* (2017), https://jog.tk.mta.hu/uploads/files/2017-04-BardK-BardP.pdf, 17–18.

110 See e.g., Supervision of the execution of judgments and decisions of the European Court of Human Rights. Annual reports at www.coe.int/en/web/execution/annua l-reports,https://www.coe.int/en/web/execution/country-factsheets

111 E Polgári, "The European Convention on Human Rights and the Case Law of the European Court of Human Rights in Hungarian Judicial Practice", *Fundamentum* 5 (2008) 74–80.

112 M Górski, "The Dialogue Between Selected CEE Courts and the ECtHR", in A Wyrozumska, ed, *Transnational Judicial Dialogue on International Law in Central and Eastern Europe* (Wydawnictwo Uniwersytetu Łó dzkiego, 2017) 239–240.

113 App no 31443/96, 22 June 2004.

114 App no 35014, 19 June 2006.

115 P Bárd and K Bárd, n. 96, 148–166.

116 Górski, n. 112, 238.

Hungarian Erzsébet Csatlós draw the attention to the use of "decoration" of reasoning with irrelevant and incorrectly cited judgments of the ECtHR.[117]

The Polish and Hungarian legal systems do not allow their constitutional courts or other judicial bodies to decide on the non-execution of ECtHR judgments, which has been a legal possibility and applied practice in Russia since 2015.[118] As the Polish and Hungarian constitutions and statutes require the implementation and invocation of the ECHR and its case-law, there is no real intention to challenge the ECtHR as openly as the Russian legislative power and the Court did. Nonetheless, Kosar and Petrov mention the possibility of challenging the ECtHR shortly, "especially if the ECtHR increases the number of highly divisive judgments against these countries that would resonate with the ruling political forces and the public at large", which, according to them, is already happening.[119]

The Hungarian example of this could be in connection with the sentence of life imprisonment without the possibility of parole. This has featured in the FL since its adoption (2011),[120] and found its way into the constitution to avoid any constitutional review of this kind of imprisonment. In this case, that is, a constitutionally entrenched and, thus, politically sensitive issue, the CC and the *Kúria* followed the political lead in disregarding the ECtHR case-law (*Vinter and others* [121]), the essence of which was later repeated in *Magyar v Hungary* (2014)[122] and *TP and AT v Hungary* (2016).[123] The recommendation that review of the punishment should occur after 25 years was not accepted. Instead, in Hungary, a threshold of 40 years before the possibility of parole was introduced. When 40 years have passed, the presidential pardon procedure, which is a completely inadequate process in this regard, has to be initiated – which is viewed as the "review".

Nevertheless, as another example shows, the Hungarian parliament can explicitly express its discontent (2012) with an ECtHR decision, as in the *Fratonoló* case,[124] and then later make peace with the decision.[125] Both the *Vajna* (2008)

117 Csatlós, n. 96, 128–133.

118 The legal environment was criticized by e.g., the Venice Commission as being incompatible with Russia's obligations under international law. Final Opinion on the Amendments to the Federal Constitutional Law on the Constitutional Court adopted by the Venice Commission at its 107th Plenary Session (Venice, 10–11 June 2016), para 144.

119 D. Kosar and J. Petrov, "The Architecture of the Strasbourg System of Human Rights: The Crucial Role of the Domestic Level and the Constitutional Courts in Particular", *ZaöRV* 77 (2017), www.zaoerv.de/77_2017/77_2017_3_a_585_621.pdf, 617.

120 For a more detailed and less simplified summary, see Bárd and Bárd, n. 96, 155–157.

121 App no 66069/09, judgment of 9 July 2013.

122 *László Magyar v Hungary*, App no 73593/10, judgment of 20 May 2014. For a more detailed and less simplified summary, see Bárd and Bárd, n. 96, 155–157.

123 *TP and AT v Hungary*, App nos 37871/14 and 73986/14 (4 October 2016).

124 See the Hungarian parliamentary resolution of 2012 on the disagreement with the judgment of the ECtHR in *Fratonoló*, App no 29459, judgment of 3 November 2011. Csatlós, n. 96.

125 For a review, see Bárd and Bárd, n. 96 153–157, 162–163.

and *Fratonoló* cases (2011) were about the prohibition of the public use of the red star (a symbol of the totalitarian regime), which, according to the ECtHR, violated Article 10 ECHR (freedom of expression). The ordinary court, in the case of *Fratonoló*, chose to apply the unamended criminal provision that still criminalized the public use of a red star, instead of referring to the essence of the *Vajna* case.[126] The parliament, too, in a political statement, expressed its unhappiness with the *Fratonoló* case. Following the ECtHR judgment in the *Vajnai* case,[127] the applicant was acquitted by the Supreme Court in March 2009, but because the law was not changed, despite the adoption of a new Criminal Code in 2012, he was tried and held liable once more for wearing the red star. He submitted a constitutional complaint to the CC, which, based on the judgment of the ECtHR, annulled the criminal law provision in 2013.[128] The parliament came to terms with the *Vajna* judgment's content and amended the law accordingly[129] – without the intention of overruling the content with, for instance, a constitutional amendment.

When it comes to reliance on and invocation of the ECtHR case-law by constitutional courts, as Kosar and Petrov claim,[130] much could depend on the internal interactions among constitutional court judges and their views on the status of international law in the domestic legal system. Nevertheless, external political pressure, explicit or implicit expectations as regards both the CC and the CT, and the simple loyalty of the judges to the incumbents could be even more convincing. After all, both courts are packed.

2.2 Supranational level

The EU Charter is an applicable legal instrument in Hungary and even in Poland, despite the Polish Protocol.[131] Thus, Polish parties to litigation and courts, including the CT, apply and invoke the Charter. Polish authors agree that even if awareness of the Charter's applicability is growing, the parties to cases and the courts themselves sometimes make inadequate references, which, for instance,

126 According to the *Vajnai* judgment, the criminal conviction for using the red star is in line with the Convention if it can be proved that there was a real danger of restoring communism and that the defendant identified herself or himself with the meaning of the sign representing a totalitarian regime. For a critical assessment of the position of the Pécs Court of Appeal, see Pfv.V.20.607/2007/9. Bárd and Bárd, n. 96, 153–154.

127 *Vajnai v Hungary*, App no 33629/06 (8 July 2008).

128 4/2013 (II. 21.) CC decision.

129 The commission of the act needs to be capable of disturbing the public peace – in particular, in a way that violates the human dignity or piety of victims of dictatorial regimes – in order for it to qualify as a crime. Bárd and Bárd, n. 96, 163.

130 They identify three levels of interaction that have to be considered: the relationship with the states (macro-level), with other domestic actors that are interacting with one another (meso-level), and the micro-level interactions within the constitutional court. They claim that the most influential one is the micro-level. Kosar and Petrov, n. 119, 619.

131 https://eur-lex.europa.eu/eli/treaty/tfeu_2016/pro_30/oj

could make preliminary questions inadmissible. In Hungary, the Charter is mentioned in petitions to the CC. The CC requires reasoning why the Charter is to be applied, but many of the cases are rejected because they do not meet this requirement or other admissibility criteria.[132]

Regardless of the growing awareness of applicability, generally, when it comes to applying the Charter, both the CT and the CC, and ordinary courts[133] too, for different reasons, are reserved and apply a minimalist approach. Their detachment considerably influences the willingness to invoke the Charter and the frequency of its invocation: the Hungarian CC developed the constitutional identity model to preserve the identity of Hungary and promote national sovereignty (22/2016 CC decision);[134] and in Poland, the Charter is perceived as a mere international law instrument,[135] which by itself calls for restraint in the courts. On the other hand, the Polish judiciary, including the CT,[136] has been aware of its role as a European court, which is proved by its use of the preliminary reference procedure and willingness to start a dialogue with the CJEU. This could be seen in a case on retirement and judicial independence that affected Charter rights.[137] The retirement case was resolved, to a certain extent, which cannot be said about the issue of independence. That part of the judiciary understanding the role it plays in multilayered constitutionalism and demanding independence and seeking the help of the EU and the international community is not to be blamed for the lack of independence, and the non-compliance with the CJEU's decision by the other part of the judiciary (the CT and some chambers of the SC) and the political decision-makers.

The CC engages in "dialogue" differently.[138] It has never initiated any preliminary procedures, but in 2018, in connection with the Lex CEU[139] and the Act on foreign-funded NGOs,[140] it suspended its procedure. The rationale for this was the decision of 22/2016, which established that there should be cooperation with the CJEU. Just a reminder: this was the judgment that introduced constitutional identity into the constitutional system as a barrier against the application of EU

132 Hamulak, Sulyok, and Kiss, n. 99, 145–148; Kastelik-Smaza, n. 99, 101, 112.

133 Ordinary courts have been using preliminary ruling procedures, but here we focus more on their attitude towards the direct application of the Charter and its method.

134 Part VI, Stability, point II.

135 Kustra-Rogaska and O. Hamulak, n. 100, 99.

136 The CJEU Judgment of 7 March 2017, Case C-390/15, ECLI:EU:C:2017:174. In this case, the issue did not relate to Charter rights but was the only preliminary ruling decision at the request of the CT.

137 Joined Cases C-585/18, C-624/18 & C-625/18; Cases C-558/18 and C-563/18. However, the decisions of the CT of 20 and 21 April 2020 (U 2/20 and Kpt 1/20) changed the attitude of the CT towards EU law.

138 E. Várnay, "Az Alkotmánybíróság és az Európai Bíróság: Együttműködő alkotmánybíráskodás?" ["The Constitutional Court and the Court of the EU: Cooperating Judicial Review?"] *Állam és Jogtudomány* 2 (2019) 66–70.

139 Case C-66/18 *Commission v Hungary*, ECLI:EU:C:2020:792; Hungary does not treat foreign and national higher education institutions equally.

140 Case C-78/18, *European Commission v Hungary*, ECLI:EU:C:2020:476; Hungary infringed both the TFEU and the Charter.

law. The CC, as regards the Lex CEU and the Act on foreign-funded NGOs, argued that it needed to wait for the ruling of the CJEU on already ongoing infringement procedures. However, it simply disregarded the ongoing CJEU proceedings in those cases concerning the retirement of judges (2012)[141] and the relocation of asylum-seekers in 2016.

On the other hand, the CC did not suspend its proceedings but upheld the constitutionality of the Stop Soros law.[142] It explained that it does not exercise its power of suspension until the CJEU has decided whether or not to take the case forward. There is a lack of clarity here: the CC has not even waited for the decision on whether or not to start the judicial phase of the infringement procedure. This could raise suspicion as regards the CC's intention to ameliorate the practice, which is what it claims to be doing. Thus, at this stage, it is uncertain what precisely motivated the CC to start this practice of suspension, but we can assume that the idea of serving "two masters" lay behind it – a point on which we elaborate in Part VI on Stability.

3 The illiberal vision of human rights

The constitutional design is mostly driven by two factors. The first one comes from the fact that populist autocrats dislike "otherness", the whole of their politics being based on "us/friend/good Poles and Hungarians" and "them/enemy/bad Poles and Hungarians". Migrants, those who do not lead a life according to Catholic/Christian values or who express opposing views, and the members of the LGBTQIA+ community belong to the latter group. The second factor, which is substantially linked to the first one, is embedded in the vision of society representing both individualism and an emerging proportion holding a more communitarian view. This vision is illiberal, anti-diversity and pro-unity, populistic, formally Catholic and Christian but mainly exclusive, intolerant, paternalistic, and misogynist. And yet it still preserves some liberal remnants in both the constitutional and legal text and implementation. Liberal understanding of human rights, to a certain extent, seems to be able to rely on the otherwise (explicitly or implicitly) pressurized ordinary judges and, surprisingly, even the packed constitutional court, at least in Hungary.[143]

141 33/2012. (VII. 17.) CC decision, *European Commission v Hungary*, Case C-286/12, ECLI:EU:C:2012:687.

142 The law criminalizes activities in support of asylum applications and further restricts the right to request asylum.

143 See the decision of the CC on the spreading of false information from July 2020, in which it upheld the importance of freedom of speech in society through reasoning of a questionable quality and using a softer approach (setting a constitutional requirement) than annulling the provision. See Part VI, Stability, point II.

3.1 The design

As Fidesz has a constitutional majority in the Hungarian parliament, the illiberal vision and sentiments could easily find their way into the FL. The constitution, even in its original version of 2011, sent confusing messages[144] as to the value-orientation and the vision of the human beings whose human rights it proclaims to protect and enforce in the already curtailed system of human rights.[145] With the passing of time, the illiberal understanding of human rights and the accompanying positive obligations of the state has been boosted and made part of the FL. Even though all of this is more visible in Hungary, a similar tendency can be observed in the development of Poland's invisible illiberal constitution through continuous informal amendment practices. The 1997 Polish Constitution itself, as a visible constitution of the pre-2015 era, may be labelled a mixed constitution that juxtaposes liberal and non-liberal principles and institutions.[146] It has always shown a liberal and individualistic approach alongside a more communitarian or illiberal vision concerning the nation, family, the Catholic Church, and religion.[147] However, the pre-2015 constitution was able to maintain a healthy balance between these perspectives, which has not been removed from the text. Once we look at, for instance, the preamble, the balance is more visible than in the National Avowal in the Hungarian FL, which also serves as a preamble. The post-2015 era has nevertheless evidenced a more communitarian and paternalistic version that mostly appears in the interpretation of laws and the Constitution 1997, due to the lack of a formal constitution-amending power.

As a result, by 2020, we can say that both the Hungarian and Polish Governments had shaped an illiberal human rights regime. They only formally recognize fundamental rights, which context leads to inequality, or, using Tushnet's description, primary and secondary citizens[148] and human beings. They employ a communitarian vision towards the state, nation, and family.[149] Thus, they have come to prioritize the

144 The Fundamental Law is characterized by a large number of personal obligations, including vaguely formulated and confusing ones. The clearest example is perhaps Art O), which establishes the principles of individual responsibility and solidarity in one sentence, leaving the interpreter wondering how this rule relates to other constitutional provisions on work or the adult children's obligation toward their parents in need, or to the right to repel an unlawful attack.

145 For instance, the limited constitutional review of the CC, the change in the composition of the parliamentary nomination committee of CC judges, the decrease in the level of rights protection by the ombudsman (one Commissioner for Fundamental Rights with deputies, a data protection authority instead of the ombudsman), the abolition of the abstract ex-post norm control as *actio popularis*, and the disappearance of the rule serving as the ground for the enforcement of human right claims.

146 See Part II, Terms.

147 B Szlachta, "Aksjologia Konstytucji RP z 1997 roku. Perspektywa badacza myśli politycznej" ["The Axiology of the Constitution of the Republic of Poland of 1997: The Perspective of the Researcher of Political Thought"] *Przegląd Sejmowy* 6(143) (2017) 125–150.

148 M Tushnet, "The Possibility of Illiberal Constitutionalism", *Fla L. Rev.* 69 (2017).

149 For instance, the FL links eligibility for social allowances to the "usefulness to the community of the beneficiary's activity", bans homelessness, and defines family as a basis for survival of the nation.

rights of the community, which equates to their understanding of the majority as composed of "good citizens", over the individual, including vulnerable people and minority groups. It also means that in certain cases, they make the recognition of human rights conditional on the fulfilment of civic duties, or deny the exercise of some fundamental rights in the interests of the community.

3.2 Implementation

After the weakening of the legal infrastructure (phase one of the process), the illiberalization of human rights attacks politically and economically sensitive rights. Populist politicians not only want to seize political power, but also mean to create their own oligarchy. These oligarchs are expected to be politically loyal and financially support the political endeavours of their populist masters.[150] Illiberal populism invades the intellectual arena of society as well, because it hopes for more support from people who do not question authority but obey it. Thus, beyond the disrespected rights, such as the rights to assembly, freedom of political speech (including media and civil society), and privacy rights vis-à-vis the police and secret service forces,[151] the illiberalization of human rights also includes the area of higher education, the freedom of academia, certain economic freedoms, and the rights of women, minority groups and groups of vulnerable people, such as people of colour, the disabled, and the LGBTQIA+ community. The Hungarian treatment of asylum-seekers in the detention centres and failure to provide adequate food, the permanent discrimination against Roma people, and the criminalization of homelessness have attracted much international attention. Hungary, along with some other states,[152] has not ratified the Istanbul Convention;[153] Poland wants to withdraw; they both have opposed the EU Gender Action Plan[154] and signed the Geneva Consensus Declaration, which is an anti-abortion petition; and Poland experienced the biggest pro-life demonstration in 2020. In Poland,[155] controversies about the right to a fair trial have been increasing;[156] in both states, the LGBTQIA+ community faces increasing burdens, disrespect, and intolerance.

Nevertheless, what has not been experienced in either Hungary or Poland, despite the undisputed backsliding in human rights protection and more and more serious illiberalization, is the extent and gravity of the human rights violations seen

150 B. Magyar, *Post-Communist Mafia State ⊠ The Case of Hungary* (Noran Libro, 2016).
151 See e.g., W. Sadurski, n. 51, 150–159.
152 Bulgaria, Latvia, Lithuania, and Ireland.
153 Istanbul Convention on preventing and combating violence against women and domestic violence.
154 The Gender Action Plan (GAP) III 2021–2025 – An ambitious agenda for gender equality and women's empowerment in EU external action.
155 See K Łakomiec, "Academic Freedom(s) in the Drift Towards Authoritarianism (4/4) – Poland", https://ds.hypotheses.org/6391 (15 November 2019).
156 See e.g., "Helsinki Foundation for Human Rights Report – Poland Threatening Human Rights Protection", www.liberties.eu/en/news/hfhr-report-poland-threatening-human-rights-protections/18206

in Russia, Turkey, and Singapore, according to Freedom House.[157] Hungary and Poland are, unlike Turkey and Russia, still among the most diligent states when it comes to respecting the deadline for payments sanctioned by the ECtHR,[158] have a low record on right-to-life violations (the record in this respect is held by Russia and Turkey[159]), and an average record on violations of other conventional rights.[160] Poland is among the countries that have infringed most of the Articles of the ECHR, along with, for example, Turkey and Russia, but so did the UK and Belgium. Hungary, in this regard, shows an average record and is in the company of most of the Western and Central European states, amongst others.[161] According to the Freedom House Report 2019, in the category of civil liberties,[162] Hungary and Poland considerably outperformed Russia, Turkey, and Singapore.[163] In these states, anti-government demonstrations are banned and dispersed (in normal times, too), the politics of the government cannot be criticized, and ideologies usually disliked by illiberal regimes cannot be supported. Universities get closed and faculty members fired en masse. The regime controls the public media, blocks online sites, and bans messaging sites; journalists and editors get killed or imprisoned.

In neither Hungary nor Poland has propaganda and political repression (yet) reached a level that would result in a chilling effect on expressing opinions on sensitive topics. The efforts to stifle such opinions, as summarised by Dunja Mijatović, however, are obviously present in unnecessarily restricting legislation, intimidation, stigmatization, unjustified investigations, and funding obstacles that NGOs have to face.[164]

157 In the category of "global freedom", Russia, Turkey, and Singapore scored 20 (not free), 32 (not free), and 50 (partly free) out of 100 in 2019, respectively, while Hungary achieved 70 (the same as the previous year; partly free), and Poland 84 (free), https://freedomhouse.org/countries/freedom-world/scores,https://freedomhouse.org/country/hungary/freedom-world/2020

158 Supervision of the execution of judgments and decision of the European Court of Human Rights, 81–81.

159 Violations by Article and by States 1959–2018.

160 When one considers the proportion of violations of Articles in relation to the overall number of violations.

161 Violations by Article and by States 1959–2018.

162 Under the heading civil liberties, there are three main categories, beyond the Rule of Law. These are: (1) the freedom of expression and belief, including media freedom, freedom of academia, freedom of religion, and freedom to express opinions on sensitive topics, (2) the associational and organizational rights, including freedom of assembly, freedom of NGOs and that of trade unions; (3) personal autonomy and individual rights, such as freedom of movement, property rights, marriage, family, and protection against domestic violence, and equal opportunities and freedom from exploitation.

163 Hungary and Poland scored 43 and 49 out of 60, respectively, while, Russia scored 15, Turkey 16, and Singapore 32. This includes the scores for Rule of Law performance as well. Disregarding the scores, a state was given in the field of the Rule of Law, the results are as follows: 33, 38, 13, 13, and 25 out of 44, respectively.

164 Mijatović, n. 105, 37.

3.3 Freedom of assembly

We have already described how the right to vote and the media have been treated in Hungary and Poland. Here, we focus on the freedom of assembly. The Polish introduction of the cyclical assemblies,[165] the Hungarian constitutional amendment and the new law on assemblies have considerably limited the freedom of assembly.[166] In Poland, when it comes to competing demonstrations, the historically present assemblies are given priority, which means that others cannot be organized and opposing views cannot be expressed at the same time. In this case, the state protects cyclical events against non-cyclical and even spontaneous ones, which raises the question of ECHR compliance. This limitation, which is another example of "personalized legislation", was needed for securing undisturbed "monthenaries", organised by the PiS every month to commemorate the Smoleńsk plane crash. The political sensitivity of the cyclical assemblies ceased when there was no more political will to continue the commemoration.

What is more, one of the most worrying moments in Poland during the COVID-19 emergency in 2020 was the limitation on the right to assembly by governmental regulations. According to the Constitution, the right to assembly cannot be limited, even during a constitutional "state of natural disaster", beyond ordinary necessity and proportionality. It means that general rules should apply, and no limitation can infringe the core of this right even in a constitutional emergency, let alone the statute-based one that applied in Poland in 2020. However, the Polish authorities banned all kinds of assemblies during the spring of 2020 and did so by means of governmental regulation, which itself means that it does not conform with the Constitution, as human rights can be limited by parliamentary statute only. This unconstitutionally violates the essence of this right, which became an even more serious human rights violation as the ban was imposed during an electoral campaign.

In Hungary, the restriction of the right of assembly also followed the need for "personalized legislation". The necessity for the limitation is not the maintenance of public order but rather the convenience of certain political actors. The FL gives priority to protecting the right to privacy and home over the right of assembly – as a reaction to a demonstration held in front of the Prime Minister's home. Accordingly, the Act on assembly (2018) introduced new legal bases for limitation, formulated in vague general terms but, according to opposition politicians,[167] also aimed at making it impossible to organize a demonstration against President Erdogan.[168] It also vested the police with broad discretionary powers. Dalma Dojcsák et al., in their report, state that ordinary courts find themselves upholding the essence of the freedom of assembly, as established in the

165 A Bień-Kacała, "Gloss to the Judgement of Constitutional Tribunal of 16 March 2017 (Kp 1/17)", *Przegląd Prawa Konstytucyjnego* 4 (2017) 255–262.

166 https://njt.hu/translated/doc/J2018T0055P_20181002_FIN.pdf

167 www.europarl.europa.eu/doceo/document/P-8-2018-005174_EN.html

168 The opposition party could not demonstrate against the Turkish President in 2018, but a Budapest-wide demonstration against him was held in 2019.

jurisprudence of the CC in the pre-2010 era and years before the new assembly law was adopted. They conclude that "it seems that, according to most of the ordinary courts, the scope of protection of the fundamental right to assembly has not changed despite the new legislation", but they also warn that we still "need to see whether and how this approach will be changed as a result of delegating the judicial review of the regulatory authority's decisions to the Curia in 2020".[169]

Regardless of the restricted freedom of assembly, protests having a powerful popular backup could not be banned in either country, not even during the pandemic. For instance, in Hungary, demonstrations were able to be held against the visit of the Turkish President in 2019, and in Poland, in January 2020, thousands of people marched for the independence of the judiciary. The demonstration at the University of the Arts and Theatre (SZFE) lasted for two and a half months, and was terminated only because the second COVID-19-related constitutional emergency was introduced in November 2020. Even though Polish voters could not really engage in the presidential election campaign during the spring of 2020, they could march for days in Polish cities, expressing their discontent with the CT's October abortion decision.

3.4 Academia and higher education

The freedom of higher education institutions, their autonomy, and academic freedom have been eroded as well. Elementary education has not kept pace with the 21st century, including as regards the capability to properly function in a pandemic accompanied by lockdowns and the closing of schools. Both states have disregarded the need for good-quality education, requiring well-trained and well-paid teachers; the latter have not been consulted and their protests have not been heard. The so-called reforms in academia (*sensu lato*) have affected research institutions and universities, mainly in Hungary, while attacks at the personal level have become more frequent in Poland.

The Hungarian higher education reform started with the introduction of the chancellor system.[170] The FL provided the framework for this, which resulted in a "constitutional" restriction of the economic autonomy of the universities, claiming that the Government, as the controlling authority of the universities, has to ensure that financial resources are properly allocated. The FL also created the possibility for students to receive financial support for their university studies in exchange for subsequent national employment – which affects the freedom of accessibility and freedom of education and movement of students.

Later, the regime was not satisfied with its control of the "form" of higher education through formal measures, such as financing, but reached out to the

169 D Dojcsák et al., "The New Law on the Right to Assembly in Hungary as Applied in the Practice", http://4liberty.eu/wp-content/uploads/2020/08/The-New-Law-on-the-Right-to-Assembly-in-Hungary-as-Applied-in-Practice.pdf, 49.

170 For a brief overview, see D Gracian and G Mikut, "Requiem for a Dream: Academic Freedom under Threat in Democracies", *International Higher Education* Nr 90, Summer 2017.

"content" as well. This was the moment when conspiracy theories and the protection of the value system of Hungary collided, resulting in the termination of gender studies programs and making the functioning of the CEU impossible in Hungary: "The Hungarian government is of the clear view that people are born either men or women. They lead their lives the way they think best, but beyond this, the Hungarian state does not wish to spend public funds on education in this area."[171] This train of thought on the "nature of life" was later constitutionalized by the Ninth Amendment in 2020.[172] The CEU was forced out of the country even before that – an action that was held to be contrary to EU law by the CJEU.[173] What the Government intended to finance was further elaborated when the research institutes of the Academy of Sciences and their financial support mechanisms were reformed in such a way that the possibility for independent and cutting-edge research, especially in the field of social sciences, became questionable.[174]

The last step in the reform process was the exercise of outsourcing higher education to private funds established by law. These funds control universities and are directed by unelected boards of trustees, who happen to be loyal friends of Fidesz and government officials. During the lawmaking process creating the scheme, there were no policy papers, impact assessment, and genuine and meaningful consultation with university and student leaders and university staff. The transformation occurs only when a university already approached by the government requests it. Due to the mentioned "deliberate flaws of the preparation process", and the fast and forced nature of this transformation, there is no information about alternatives. And yet no visible resistance could be observed during the effort to place seven other universities under these kinds of boards in 2020. The reason might be that, in some cases, the collective of the university was not even aware of the transformation process as it coincided with the introduction of the first constitutional emergency. So, their university leaders decided over their heads. In January 2021, during the second constitutional emergency, other big regional universities were approached, and they had to make the decision whether or not they request the transformation within only a couple of weeks. When it came to the reorganisation of the SZFE, however, in September 2020, opposing views became loud, and students occupied the SZFE building, organised daily demonstrations, and thousands marched on the streets of Budapest to express their solidarity.[175] Repercussion followed, such as invalidation of the semester, against which students seek redress.

171 www.reuters.com/article/us-hungary-government-education/hungary-to-stop-financing-gender-studies-courses-pm-aide-idUSKBN1KZ1M0
172 See more on this in point 3.5.1. below.
173 *Commission v Hungary* Case C-66/18, ECLI:EU:C:2020:792.
174 www.france24.com/en/20190212-hungarian-researchers-rally-against-government-attack-science
175 For an overview, see P Sárosi, "David Takes on Goliath: The Struggle for Academic Freedom in Hungary", 11 October 2020, https://autocracyanalyst.net/david-takes-on-goliath-struggle-for-academic-freedom-in-hungary/

The Polish attack on the person tops in the discrediting of academics,[176] where criminal proceedings against scholars have been considered because of their scholarly opinions on legal reforms. These charges were eventually abandoned due to popular discontent. The view of historians has not always been respected, as was evidenced by the criminalization of the defamation of the Polish Nation (2006), based on which Poland intended to withdraw a national honor from the Polish historian Jan Tomasz Gross.[177] An investigation was initiated to establish whether Professor Gross had breached the Act because he claimed that Poles were complicit in Nazi war crimes. The Polish states, similarly to the Hungarian National Avowal, do not seem to respect historians' academic freedom. In both cases, we can see an attempt to set the narrative for the interpretation of historical events and the pronunciation of a unified perspective in order to manipulate the collective memory and shape national identity accordingly.

Expressing critical opinions in tweets can trigger both criminal and civil law cases, as happened with Professor Sadurski.[178] Suppressing freedom of expression seemingly has become a "daily practice" in Poland. Beyond the solidarity of the scholarly community against this kind of harassment, only the actors affected try to step up, using the legal means available. Judges, in the event of their own harassment, turn to the ECtHR,[179] and the Disciplinary Court of the Bar Association uses the preliminary ruling procedure.[180] Those who are involved in the abortion demonstrations are also harassed in political communications, as they are threatened with disciplinary action if they happen to be teachers and university lecturers. Gráinne de Búrca and John Morijn legitimately ask: "What is the point of EU and national politicians waxing lyrically about the importance of freedom of expression while refusing to speak out about flagrant abuses such as the cases

176 Łakomiec, n. 155.

177 H Reichman, "Academic Freedom Threatened in Poland", 19 February 2016, academeblog.org; Gracian and Mikut, n. 170.

178 G de Búrca, J Morijn, and M Steinbeis, *Stand with Wojciech Sadurski: His Freedom of Expression is (Y)Ours,* VerfBlog, 2019/11/18, https://verfassungsblog.de/stand-with-wojciech-sadurski-his-freedom-of-expression-is-yours/. The PiS sued him for civil defamation based on a tweet (November 2018) in which he described the PiS as an "organised criminal group". A TV station fully controlled by the PiS sued him too. The civil and criminal defamation charges are based on a tweet (January 2019) in which he described the TV station as a "Goebbelsian media company". See more in, e.g., G de Búrca and J Morijn, "Repression of Freedom of Expression in Poland: Renewing Support for Wojciech Sadurski", VerfBlog, 2020/6/03, https://verfassungsblog.de/repression-of-freedom-of-expression-in-poland-renewing-support-for-wojciech-sadurski/

179 See e.g., *Żurek v Poland*, App no 39650/18; A Bodnar, "Strasbourg Steps In", VerfBlog, 2020/7/07, https://verfassungsblog.de/strasbourg-steps-in/

180 Case C-55/20. The Disciplinary Court of the Bar Association has to deal with the freedom of expression of an advocate, a case in which they fail to see any legal ground for establishing liability. They ask the CJEU to clarify whether the EU Services Directive applies to the disciplinary liability of advocates. They also need to know how to proceed when the Disciplinary Chamber SC (last instance) is not considered to be impartial and independent. See the CJEU's judgment of 19 November 2019 in Joined Cases C-585/18, C-624/18 and C-625/18, ECLI:EU:C:2019:982.

against Sadurski?"[181] Using the preliminary ruling procedure simply puts the issue into the wrong context and fosters the assumption that there could still be a solution. But the CJEU can solve neither Rule of Law nor human rights deterioration in a Member State, unless that state's leaders are willing to cooperate. And at this point, they are not. Turning to the ECtHR could furnish some remedy, but mostly in an individual context.[182]

3.5 Human dignity and equality – the cases of "others"

3.5.1 LGBTQIA+ PERSONS – "NOT US: GOOD CATHOLIC POLES AND CHRISTIAN HUNGARIANS"

Despite the fact that Polish LGBTQIA+ people are visible in politics (former MPs Anna Grodzka and Robert Biedroń, current MEP), the official attitude towards them is still far from friendly: activists are arrested and the political narratives recognised two sexes (male and female) during the electoral campaign of 2019, with strong language being used against LGBTQIA+ people. The judgment (2019) of the CT[183] allows discriminatory market actions against people who belong to the LGBTQIA+ community. "LGBT free zone" and "LGBT-ideology free zone" stickers have been used to mark privately-owned places and objects. Anti-LGBT resolutions were enacted by some local governments in 2019 – affecting one-quarter of the territory of Poland. They claim that they do not attack LGBTQIA+ individuals but the ideology they represent.

The Polish ordinary judiciary have so far managed to stand against the discrimination and humiliation of LGBTQIA+ people. As Marta Bucholc explains, a local administrative court, based on the motion of the Commissioner for Human Rights, annulled resolutions of local governments. It did not accept the view that the exclusion of "LGBT ideology" was not equivalent to the exclusion of and discrimination against LGBTQIA+ people. But it is not only the domestic courts that reject this way of discriminatory thinking and intolerance; some members of churches are also opposed to it.[184]

The same ideology and culture war is being "fought" in Hungary, too. After making it impossible for an LGBTQIA+ person to change their sex in official documents in the summer of 2020, the Hungarian Prime Minister called the existence of the LGBTQIA+ people a provocation,[185] and amended the FL, in the midst of the

181 de Búrca and Morijn, n. 178.
182 Bodnar, n. 179.
183 K 16/17.
184 M Bucholc, "Fencing Off the Difference: On 'LGBT-Free Zones' in Poland", VerfBlog, 2020/8/26, https://verfassungsblog.de/fencing-off-the-difference/
185 The Hungarian Prime Minister consistently calls the LGBTQIA+ people homosexuals (https://24.hu/belfold/2020/10/06/orban-viktor-turelmes-homoszexualisok/) and cynically maintains the view that family and marriage can only be based, biologically, morally, and legally, on the unity of a man and a woman, even when one of its leading politicians, József Szájer, who allegedly drafted the text of the FL, was caught by Belgian police at a gay party and who attempted to escape down a drainpipe. His wife was the notorious President of the National Judicial Office, whose fight with its monitoring body (National Judicial Council) almost caused a constitutional crisis in the judiciary. They are still married, and she is the CC judge. For more on the

constitutional emergency, because of a book of fairy tales published by a lesbian association. It is an alternative storybook portraying the heroes of, among others, traditional Hungarian folk tales and fairy tales as belonging to minorities such as, for example, the lesbian or Roma communities. The book, which, in fact, is accompanied by a manual on how to use it in kindergartens, was publicly destroyed by one of the politicians, and generated debate among psychologists and the public.[186] Hungary, again, used its formal amending power to push forward its illiberal vision of family and Christian values. These were not part of the originally adopted FL, but now, for example, taking into account the subconstitutional rules as well, a single person, regardless of their sexual orientation and contrary to the previous rules, can adopt only when the Minister responsible for family matters grants special permission. When granting permission, the new constitutional rules on the protection of the child have to be strongly considered, which provide that it is the duty of the state to ensure that the upbringing of the child is based on the constitutional identity and Christian culture of Hungary. The previous loophole, which made it possible for gay couples to have a child based on the decision of the child care officer, was filled in. This course of action is clearly contrary to the endeavours of the President of the EU Commission, who would put forward a strategy to strengthen LGBTQIA+ rights, and who emphasized her commitment to the mutual recognition of family relations in the EU.[187]

3.5.2 WOMEN – "NOT US: MEN"

Another example of paternalism and exclusion is the position of women in society, including in state affairs, political communications, and their involvement in decisions about themselves. One might think of the Polish abortion case, the retirement age, and the complete lack of the understanding of gender mainstreaming in both countries, and the non-gender-neutral language that is used in the Polish Constitution and laws.[188]

The exclusion affects the position of women and their rights and opportunities. We cannot say that the Hungarian and Polish Governments, before 2010 and 2015, respectively, were pioneers in women's equality – we just have to look at the composition of representative bodies or higher judicial positions, the glass ceiling in almost every profession, and the pay gap at the national level (caused by a series of, mostly structural, reasons). While, since the transition, there has not been a

homophobia in Hungary, see L Arato, "Homophobia Is on the Rise in Hungary", www.europeandatajournalism.eu/eng/News/Data-news/Homophobia-is-on-the-rise-in-Hungary (30 October 2019); https://index.hu/kulfold/eurologus/2019/09/24/egyre_tobb_magyart_zavarnak_a_melegek/

186 https://time.com/5897312/hungary-book-lgbt-rights/

187 https://ec.europa.eu/commission/presscorner/detail/en/SPEECH_20_1655

188 The Hungarian language is a genderless language, with no grammatical gender distinctions, but it does not mean that it is gender-neutral – there is just one less thing to worry about in terms of what grammatical structure and language the law should use, and how it affects our way of thinking.

female Prime Minister or President of the CC, Hungary has only once had a female leader of the parliament. The Polish experience is slightly different: Poland has had three female Prime Ministers, three female Marshalls of the *Sejm*, and one female Marshall of the *Senat.*

Of course, the preparations for accession to the EU provided some sort of motivation as regards improvement. Nevertheless, as the European Institute for Gender Equality (EIGE[189]) noted in 2019, Poland ranked 24th and Hungary was placed 27th in the EU in the Gender Equality Index. Poland's score is 12.2 points lower than the EU average, while Hungary's scores are lower than the EU's scores in all domains.

As for positions in state bodies, the Orbán Government has handled this issue similarly to other matters: it created a façade by, for instance, appointing female Ministers and Secretaries of State. They, however, similarly to their male colleagues, do not have real power to influence policy-making – as this is not the regime's idea. What is expected from them is support for the official ideology on the role of women, which they deliver. The Minister for Family Affairs, for instance, advises women on how to be strong and fulfilled: they should not believe that they have to compete with men in life and strive for similar positions and payments.[190]

The situation of Hungarian women is very similar to that in the Polish context, where it is difficult for women to become independent political leaders as politics is dominated by the political parties associated with a powerful male leader (the "leader party" or "personal party" model). The reason for this is mainly traditional and historic, and finds its roots in actual religious belief, the position of the Catholic Church in society, and the Polish model of womanhood embodied in the ethos of the "Polish Mother". This heroic woman makes sacrifices for the wellbeing of the homeland and the family.[191] Nevertheless, cultural and social barriers and stereotypes play a role, too. In Hungary these are more to be blamed than religious beliefs – no matter how much political communications rely on Christianity. In both states, there is a close association between women's issues and family affairs, and the role of women as child-bearers has been overemphasized and their unpaid caring work overlooked. These factors have led to the instrumentalization of women as means of implementing the Government's goals regarding its demographic and immigration policies.[192]

At the same time, acts of misogyny, as a part of the "war on gender"[193] that is perceived as necessary because women obsessed with Western gender ideology do

189 eige.europa.eu

190 www.facebook.com/axiomamedia/videos/224659149173546/. The Polish Minister of Education is well known for his anti-LGBTQIA+ statements and for placing women in the role of mothers and not in the role of working persons, www.onet.pl/informacje/onetwiadomosci/przemyslaw-czarnek-ministrem-oto-jego-najslynniejsze-i-najbardziej-kontrowersyjne/4rpxnyl,79cfc278

191 K Sękowska-Kozłowska, "The Istanbul Convention in Poland" in J Niemi, L Peroni, and V Stoyanova, *International Law and Violance against Women: Europe and the Istanbul Convention* (Routledge, 2020) 261.

192 Mijatović, n. 105, 37.

193 See the opinion of Jaroslaw Gowin, Minister of Justice and in 2012 the representative of the ultraconservative wing of Civic Platform, summarized by Sękowska-Kozłowska, n. 191, 264.

not "behave and think" as men would expect, are far from being unusual behaviour by male politicians. This is the single most devastating impact of the illiberal governments and their paternalistic policies.

The lack of respect has led to a lack of consideration and gender mainstreaming in emergency legislation, which resulted in the failure to pay proper regard to the possibility of increased incidents of domestic violence at the beginning of the pandemic in spring 2020.

It has also led, for instance, to the firm conviction that Hungary and Poland have a well-functioning victim protection system, when life and NGOs show otherwise. The Polish Commissioner for Human Rights and NGOs are not so optimistic either. The Commissioner, in his alternative report in 2020, indicated many spheres in which the Istanbul Convention is defectively implemented, including, for example, housing assistance, economic violence, and social support.[194] The report was not taken into consideration and Poland intends to withdraw from the Istanbul Convention, while Hungary, as said, refused its ratification. Both countries reject the "gender ideology" that the Convention, in their view, represents. Moreover, the Convention is in apparent conflict with the traditional role model of Polish women, the "Polish Mother", even as it has also become a symbol of modern, European values worth fighting for.[195] This is another reason for rejecting it, especially as its proper implementation, to a certain extent and especially in the field of domestic violence, is counterproductive to the official political narrative – which is also present in Hungary – that the constitutional institution of the family, by definition, cannot be the locus of any violence.

As mentioned, Hungary and Poland, along with Belarus from Europe, signed the Geneva Consensus Declaration – which is an anti-abortion petition. On the other hand, and this illustrates how the regime in Hungary works, the Minister for Families was quick to confirm that the Government does not plan to amend the abortion law – which has, so far, been considered as a law that adequately balances pro-life and pro-choice considerations. In Poland, politicians, mainly elderly men, did not dare to explicitly take responsibility for their decisions on the intrusion into women's bodies but got the CT, the majority of whose members are men, to act on their behalf. They disrespected the so-called "abortion consensus" that developed in the 1990s and features quite a strict abortion law. The consensus, however, has never been stable, having always been challenged by both the pro-choice and anti-abortion forces. For example, it was legally possible to terminate a pregnancy because of "difficult living conditions" in 1996, but then in 1997 the CT found this criterion contrary to the Constitution. Before the decision of the CT in October 2020 (and even after it, as the ruling was not published until January 2021), abortion was generally banned except in three circumstances: when the woman's life or health is endangered; the pregnancy is the result of rape; there is a severe and irreversible foetal impairment. The last condition was

194 www.rpo.gov.pl/sites/default/files/raport_alternatywny_rpo_dla_grevio_czerwiec_2020.pdf

195 Sękowska-Kozłowska, n. 191, 264, 276.

challenged before the CT by the MPs associated with the PiS in 2017. The root of the case may be traced back to 2016 when the *Sejm* rejected the liberalizing abortion law bill, "Save Women". At the same time, the *Sejm* considered the parallel bill "Stop Abortion". The latter bill was dropped until April 2020 when the *Sejm* decided to proceed with it in the midst of the pandemic. The legislative procedure is still pending, but the ruling majority decided to shut down the disagreement surrounding the issue without deliberation and discussion. Therefore, the CT was abusively activated to decide on the law. On 22 October 2020, the CT de facto banned abortion during the second, more severe, wave of the pandemic. The judgment caused mass protests that lasted for over a month.[196]

Another highly debated issue is the state pension age. The CT initially recognized that the differentiation in the retirement ages of men and women (65 for men and 60 for women) conformed with the Constitution 1997. The reason for this was the additional burden on women relating to their family responsibilities. At the same time, the CT stayed flexible in relation to the same retirement age for men and women in 1999.[197] In another case in 2007, the CT upheld this view on the differentiation, pointing out social changes that could justify equalizing the retirement age in the future.[198] In 2012, it found that those factors supporting differentiation in the retirement ages in the past had become obsolete; the CT did not find any constitutional grounds for differentiating between the retirement ages of men and women.[199] Nevertheless, differentiation in the retirement ages of men (65) and women (60) was reintroduced in 2017 after a five-year period during which the retirement age was the same for both (set at 67). It means that even though the non-paid work done by women seems to be acknowledged and appreciated, it has not been accompanied by a corrective mechanism in the calculation of pensions. Thus, women, who statistically live longer, could become pensioners earlier but end up with a lower pension. There is no corrective mechanism in Hungary either, so the difference in the logic of the pension system does not really matter. In Hungary, men and women can retire at the same age, but women can choose to go take their pension after 40 years of employment. Consequently, their pension is calculated based on those 40 years as compared to the longer period of time worked by men and those women who do not want to retire after 40 years.

3.5.3 "OTHERS" – "NOT US: REAL POLES AND HUNGARIANS"

The sense of impatience and exclusion are palpable in connection with vulnerable groups of people, such as ethnic minorities, prison inmates, disabled persons, and asylum-seekers. Both governments adopt a cynical approach and pretence, in these regulatory areas, sometimes with a view to pinpointing a new group of "others" against whom the voters can unite.

196 The aftermath of the decision is discussed in Part VI, Stability, point III.
197 K 5/99.
198 K 63/07.
199 K 43/12.

The Hungarian Government tried to sabotage the payment of compensation for the segregation of Roma children, claiming that too much money would be paid without the families having to work for it.[200] Accordingly, it requested non-monetary compensation, such as education and training. The Curia, during the COVID-19 emergency, decided that monetary compensation need to be paid.[201] This train of thought might be seen in the regulatory agenda concerning the compensation system for those prison inmates whose human dignity has been violated by the overcrowded conditions. In February 2020, a statute ordered the Government to develop a new system, and also postponed the payment of compensation to those who had already been found entitled to receive it. The reform of the law adopted earlier by the Fidesz majority was needed because of the alleged prison business run by advocates and inmates, referred to as "abuse of compensation lawsuits", in order to gain millions of Hungarian forints from the Government[202] (we might add: those "unworthy" perpetrators, who wanted money without work). The deadline was set to be summer 2020, but in May this was extended to the end of the year. The Government claimed that it could not work on the new system during the pandemic, but, interestingly enough, during the second constitutional emergency, it did find time to adopt new rules. These rules make it harder for inmates to receive their compensation, which could infringe their right to property under the Convention and could also have a chilling effect on future claims against the state.[203]

In Poland, exclusion can be detected in the attitude towards disabled people, especially in connection to their 40-day long protest in 2019. As a result of the protest, the Government took action to improve their life conditions. However, these changes were only the pretence of assistance, as disabled people, for instance, received no adequate resources. Such a mode of operation was also visible in relation to protests by teachers and medical personnel (contemptuously called "young doctors"). Education and medical treatment are still underfinanced.

Campaigning against asylum-seekers, calling them "economic migrants" regardless of their motivation,[204] and using anti-Brussels propaganda too in this respect, has increased fear and intolerance in society. Actions have been communicated to the populace as a "fight for freedom", but in reality they have not met international standards. Actions against an easily identifiable "outsider group" that does not even look like "us" helps to unite the ingroup, that is, voters, which justifies and outweighs everything else, even disrespect for human dignity.

In 2017, the ECtHR found a violation of the ECHR in the case of *Ilias and Ahmed.* [205] Ilias and Ahmed were detained illegally and then forced to return to

200 https://hungarytoday.hu/govt-finds-court-ruling-on-school-segregation-of-romas-unfortunate-refuses-to-pay-compensation/
201 https://hungarytoday.hu/gyongyospata-ruling-compensation-kuria-fidesz/
202 http://abouthungary.hu/news-in-brief/prison-compensation-to-be-given-to-crime-victims.
203 https://hirklikk.hu/kozelet/a-kormany-is-beszallt-a-bortonbizniszbe/374218
204 The Hungarian version of the English term "migrant" has quickly developed a pejorative meaning in the Hungarian language.
205 *Ilias and Ahmed v Hungary*, App no 47287/15, judgment, 14.03.2017.

Serbia, without examination of their reasons for seeking asylum.[206] The Grand Chamber, at the request of the Government, re-examined the case in 2019 and, based on a newly developed test, found that the detention was not unlawful. Therefore, the applicants' right to liberty and security had not been infringed. However, it found that the authorities had violated the applicants' fundamental rights by failing to properly examine the consequences they would be facing in the event of their expulsion to Serbia.[207] The Hungarian Minister of Justice opined that the judgment was in favour of the Government, and that its border control is sovereign and legitimate,[208] so no actions, including the inadequate provision of food in the detention centres, should be criticized. Between August 2018 and March 2020, the ECtHR issued 18 emergency decisions and ordered the Hungarian Government to give food to migrants in detention in the transit zone at the southern Hungarian border.[209] In 2019, the European Commission opened new infringement proceedings for non-provision of food in transit zones.[210] According to the Hungarian Helsinki Committee, in November 2019, about 180 children were detained in the transit zones, and over the past two years, more than 1,700 detainees were minors.[211]

In April 2020, the CJEU[212] found Hungary and Poland, along with the Czech Republic, in violation of EU law because they refused to comply with the temporary mechanism for the relocation of applicants for international protection. The legal responses are still to be seen, but the Hungarian constitutional law has already been "immunized against migrants" by the constitutional identity clause. The CJEU delivered other, unsurprising decisions as well. In March 2020, it ruled that it is not compatible with EU law if an asylum request is declared inadmissible because the applicant arrives in Hungary via a country that is incorrectly listed as a safe third country. In May 2020, it stated that the transit zones in certain cases mean an unlawful deprivation of liberty. The Hungarian Government declared that it would close the transit zones – a kind of "compliance" with the ruling, which did not demand it. On the other hand, the method of initiating an asylum procedure was changed, which raises new concerns in connection to the very

206 Act CXL of 2015, www.helsinki.hu/en/ilias-ahmed-ecthr-grand-chamber-ruling/. The applicants claimed that Hungary had violated their rights under Art 3 (prohibition of inhuman or degrading treatment – in relation to reception conditions in the transit zone), Art 5 (the right to liberty and security – in relation to the rules on leaving the transit zone), and Art 13 (right to an effective remedy) of the ECHR.

207 21 November 2019. For analysis and critique of the ruling, see www.helsinki.hu/en/ilias-ahmed-ecthrgrand-chamber-ruling/. For a comparison of the two judgments, see www.echr.coe.int/Documents/Press_Q_A_Ilias_and_Ahmed_Hungary_ENG.pdf

208 https://hungarytoday.hu/hungary-confining-migrants-to-transit-zone-not-unlawful-says-european-court-ofhuman-rights/

209 www.ecre.org/hungary-continued-starvation-tactics-continued-interimmeasures/?fbclid=IwAR3sMUchN7Aai4x8KxvjAGKohQfYJzMLUDZCuyGcRSlnbwJXOI6tCN0l9y4; www.helsinki.hu/en/echr_eighth_interim_measure_denial_of_food/

210 https://ec.europa.eu/commission/presscorner/detail/en/IP_19_4260

211 www.helsinki.hu/en/ilias-ahmed-ecthr-grand-chamber-ruling/

212 Joined Cases C-715/17, C-718/17 and C-719/17, ECLI:EU:C:2020:257.

essence of asylum. Now, without valid documents issued by the Hungarian authority, asylum-seekers cannot enter into Hungary but have to submit "a letter of intent" at the Embassy abroad. The Embassy will transfer this letter of intent to the immigration authority, which will examine it and conduct an online interview with the applicant, who is requested to present himself or herself at the Embassy premises.

3.5.4 "US: MORE WORTHY TO BE MORE EQUAL" – ECONOMIC MEASURES (HUNGARY)

When it comes to the distribution of economic and financial resources, the legislature, mainly in Hungary, abuses its lawmaking power and places its members' loyal friends at an advantage. Some call this system "mafia-state", creating a network of emerging wealthy oligarchs. Corruption is not necessarily an anti-law activity, however, being facilitated by legal measures and assisted by the societal understanding of the "normal" courses of action, resulting in self-restriction in, for example, participation in public procurements. When the state intends to monopolize an activity (here, the tobacco business), it can do so even if the reform pushes former entrepreneurs out of business and allows new actors to enter. The Hungarian scheme pretended to offer equal opportunities for obtaining new licenses and the law claimed, in its preamble, that its goal was the prevention of youth smoking.

The CC, in 2014,[213] did rely on the previously developed case-law on legitimate restriction of the freedom of profession and entrepreneurship. Two elements of the case-law are important here. The first is that it distinguishes between choosing a profession, which is a subjective choice, and practising a profession, which is not a fundamental right per se. There is also a difference between subjective and objective limitations of the right to profession. The former, for example, education or training, could be more widely determined by the state, while in the case of the latter, for example, *numerus clausus*, all restrictions must undergo careful scrutiny. And yet the CC argued that the de facto objective condition for obtaining licenses (the state determines with whom it wishes to enter into a contract) was indeed a subjective condition.

This mechanism is not unusual and it brings us to the discussion of how the justiciability and the theory of human rights have started to be transformed.

4 Emerging new understanding of human rights (third phase of illiberalization)

4.1 Transforming justiciability

The above-mentioned Hungarian tobacco decision in 2014 is important not only because of how it "protects" rights and serves political purposes; it can also serve as a case study to discuss the quality of the CC's reasoning in the post-2010 era –

213 3194/2014. (VII. 15.) CC decision.

something we can also see in the case of spreading false information during an emergency.[214] The CC bases its decisions on the established case-law and then draws a conclusion that is contrary to this case-law but, at least, politically expected. It affects the overall quality of reasoning, which focuses more on the purpose of the law than on the function and role of a particular human right – an exercise for which the CC is constitutionally mandated.

The FL orders that in the course of the application of the law, courts shall interpret the text of laws primarily in accordance with their purpose and with the FL itself. This is exactly what happened in the tobacco case: the CC takes the purpose of the law for granted, without engaging in examination of whether or not the policy-maker or drafter or lawmaker has collected any evidence. The first step of evidence- or knowledge-based, and thus democratic, lawmaking is the identification and understanding of the issue, followed by deciding on how to resolve it. This cannot be done without, for example, impact assessments and meaningful and inclusive consultation. Besides, nowadays, it is not unusual for courts to ask these questions and look for evidence. But not the CC. Moreover, the constitutional majority did everything in its power to constitutionalize this practice in 2019. Now, the FL has explained what it means to say that laws need to be interpreted "in accordance with their purpose": in the course of ascertaining the purpose of a law, consideration shall be given primarily to the preamble to that law and the justification of the proposal for or for amending the law. Without the genuine preparation of drafts, including, say, impact assessments and consultation, the explanatory memorandum attached to the laws cannot offer much information. Besides, attaching informative and real justifications to the proposals has never been the strong suit of the lawmaker.

4.2 *State as a holder of fundamental rights*

As a result of one of the changes in the constitutional review process in 2019, a discussion has started in Hungary about how best to protect the fundamental rights of individuals.[215] An amendment introduced the possibility for state bodies, institutions, organs, and agencies exercising public power to submit a constitutional complaint to the CC claiming that their fundamental rights have been infringed.

Critics of the law argue against it using the most important and interrelated functions of human rights: first, the individual must be protected against the powerful, including but not restricted to those exercising state power; and, second, human rights impose a limitation on state power.

214 Part VI, Stability, point II.

215 B Orbán, "A magyarok jogainak és szabadságának védelmében" ["In Defense of the Rights and Freedoms of Hungarians"] (defending the new law); MD Szabó, "Az állampolgárt védje az alkotmány vagy az államot?" ["Whom Should the Constitution Defend: The Citizens Or the State?"]; D Karsai, "Kié az Alkotmánybíróság?" ["To Whom Does the Constitutional Court Belong?"], Index 05 December 2019 (the last two both criticizing the new law).

Those defending the law identify human rights challenges, such as the fact that it is not only the state that endangers human rights but international and supranational organizations as well, such as the CoE and the EU, the international financial system, transnational business operations, virtual platforms and the media, terrorism and cyber-threats, and mass migration. Their argument goes like this. A 21st-century state cannot be envisaged without human rights commitments. Therefore, the best way to address this challenge is to enable the state bodies to turn to the CC in the same way as individuals, who can claim that their fundamental rights have been infringed. The CC also has to be enabled to circumscribe the limits of the constitutional exercise of public power vis-à-vis international organizations in order for the function of the FL in protecting human rights and the constitutional identity of the national community to remain intact. It has to protect the proper functioning of the state bodies without infringing the protection of the rights of individuals.

This argument is confused as to the function of human rights and the connected role of the state. It pretends to keep the focus on the individual while elevating the interest of the political community, more specifically the state and its leaders. It poses the danger that this process could be used against fundamental rights under the pretense of protecting them, for example, in freedom of information cases. It has potential as well, as (opposition-led) local governments could also use this process.[216] It is just a pity that the CC is packed and that the ECtHR does not examine the CC's exercise of the constitutional complaint process, as it has been deemed to fulfil the requirement of an effective domestic remedy.[217]

216 Karsai, n. 215.
217 *Szalontay v Hungary*, Judgment 4 April 2019 (App no 71327/13).

VI Stability

How "illiberal limits" emerge and work

Based on the previous Parts, it is safe to say that, at the end of 2020, illiberal constitutionalism was still stable, deterioration remaining its permanent element, along with illiberal legality, illiberal democracy, and misunderstanding and abusive misinterpretation of human rights. The respective populations have not questioned the constitutional changes in Hungary or Poland. It seems that there is a new social contract – constitutionally entrenched in Hungary and extra-constitutional and invisible in Poland – between the leaders and the voters. This new social contract, which is based on the promise of and demand for stability and belonging, no matter how fallacious and illusory they are,[1] has not been challenged yet in elections or by more serious and influential popular discontent. Apparently, the two countries' populations still support their regimes, which, in turn, gives the people what they want: the implementation and enforcement of a new social contract that is based on a capturing mechanism and exaggerated emotional politics, wrapped up in collective narcissism and right-wing populism.

All of these things have been achieved, and stability is maintained by adoption of the following four tactics: capturing the constitution and constitutionalism, and never letting go of them, and creating an invisible constitution; illiberal judicialization of politics; pushing the limits; and eliminating exit strategies that could (have) been used to reverse the changes.

I Capturing constitutions and constitutionalism, and creating invisible constitution

For giving a real bird's-eye view and understanding the dynamics of formal and informal changes, we also need to go back to the transition and recall how the

1 Cf. the results of the Value Research: J Eichhorn et al., "How European Publics and Policy Actors Value an Open Society: Key Insight Across Countries" (Open Society European Policy Institute, 2019), http://voicesonvalues.dpart.org/images/finalreports/OSI-019-18-Key-Insights_v5.pdf; SH Schwartz and A Bardi, "Influences of Adaptation to Communist Rule on Value Priorities in Eastern Europe", *Political Psychology* 2 (1997); T Humphrey, "Democracy and the Rule of Law: Founding Liberal Democracy in Post-Communist Europe", *Colum J. E Eur. L* 2(94) (2008).

DOI: 10.4324/9781003175353-6

constitutional democracy in Hungary and Poland was developed, and contrast it with the constitutional changes after 2010 and 2015.

1 Bird's-eye view of 1989–2020: dismemberments, replacements, formal, informal, and abusive amendments

Using the terminology of comparative constitutional change, the adoption of the FL in Hungary can be considered a constitutional replacement,[2] which led to constitutional remodelling from liberal to illiberal constitutionalism. The amendment processes during the transition in 1989 and 1990 also led to a constitutional transformation from socialism to constitutional democracy (liberal constitutionalism). In this process, substantially new content was adopted through a formal amending process, while retaining the outline of the "former constitution". This transformative change to the text of the Constitution could be called "dismemberment", which sought deliberately to disassemble most parts of the socialist constitution's elemental parts. In this case, constitutional dismemberment, with formal changes, improved liberal democratic outcomes[3] not only in the text but, with the assistance of the CC, in the wider environment (i.e., constitutional culture) as well. The amendments to the FL are just amendments – but many of them are abusive. Nevertheless, unlike David S Law,[4] when we consider the constitutional nature of the Transitory Provisions, we will explain later that they were meant to be part of the FL, and that many of the new FL rules incorporated by the Fourth Amendment were a mere transposition of those contained in the Transitory Provisions.

The constitutional transition in Poland was slightly different. The constitution-making process cannot be strictly separated from the informal constitutional changes, especially until the adoption of the Small Constitution in 1992. The revision of the socialist Constitution in 1989 was an act of dismemberment, while the Small Constitution is viewed as a partial replacement of the previous socialist constitution. They were applied side-by-side until the 1997 Constitution came into force. The socialist constitution, through its revision, determined the main vector of change for Poland, that is, transformation to a constitutional democracy (liberal constitutionalism), and was the subject of the activist reinterpretation through the prism of the Rule of Law that was incorporated into its text in 1989. This activist approach, the results of which amount to informal constitutional amendment, was then limited with the enactment of the Small Constitution and the constitutionalization of the content deduced from the Rule of Law, such as, for example, the separation of powers. The second phase in Poland is connected to

2 X Contiades and A Fotiadou, "Introduction" in X Contiades and A Fotiado (eds), *Routledge Handbook of Comparative Constitutional Change* (Routledge, 2021) 14.

3 R Albert, "Constitutional Amendment and Dismemberment", *Yale J. Int'l L.* 43 (2018).

4 DS Law and R Whalen, "Comparing Amendment and Replacement" in X Contiades and A Fotiado (eds), *Routledge Handbook of Comparative Constitutional Change* (Routledge, 2021) 96.

the application of the 1997 Constitution, which replaced the former constitution. The CT took a less activist approach, as the 1997 Constitution regulates complex matters far more broadly than in the first years of the 1990s.

The formal amending process is similar in both states, as both require a supermajority. Still, due to institutional differences, that is, the Polish parliament is bicameral and the constitutional system is more inclined to use referendums in the amending process, the 1997 Constitution is more "rigid" than the Hungarian one, even though, from a comparative perspective, it is still "flexible".[5] While amending the Hungarian Constitution, that is, both the Constitution and the FL, requires only a two-thirds majority in parliament, the 1997 Constitution can be amended when supported by at least two-thirds of the Deputies to the *Sejm* and by an absolute majority of Senators. The referendum is not obligatory and may be held in relation to fundamental rules of the constitutional system, human rights, and the constitutional amendment procedure. The 1997 Constitution was amended twice with the support of the opposition but without the involvement of the Polish people. The first amendment in 2006 barred those sentenced to imprisonment by a final judgment for an intentional indictable offence from election to the *Sejm* or the *Senat*. The second amendment allowed the European Arrest Warrant to be introduced into the Polish legal system (2009).

As said, amending the constitution has always been easy in Hungary. Therefore, fixing the "granite-solid" FL to satisfy daily political purposes or whims could be quickly and effortlessly done between 2012 and 2020. The FL was amended nine times between 2012 and 2020: three times in 2012, twice in 2013, and once each in 2016, 2018, 2019, and 2020. Some of these changes were reactions to CC decisions that were protective of the old ideas of constitutionalism (e.g., Fourth Amendment); others served mere political purposes, such as those related to constitutional identity and migration (e.g., Seventh Amendment), or deregulated provisions that had become superfluous (e.g., Eight Amendment).

These amendments were supported by neither referendums nor the opposition. The exceptions are the Seventh Amendment (2018) and the Eighth Amendment (2019). The latter was also voted for by non-right-wing opposition MPs, while the former was only supported by the right-wing opposition party. There was only one short period when the constitutional majority was not secured, but it was quickly regained – when the already packed CC gave a hand in the form of an informal constitutional amendment in 2016.

5 Based on the literature, we could call the Hungarian and Polish amendment powers "weaker" and "weak" amendment powers, respectively, and the Polish design a multi-tier amendment design. See Y Roznai, *Unconstitutional Constitutional Amendments: A Study of the Nature and Limits of Constitutional Amendment Powers*, PhD thesis, The London School of Economics and Political Science (LSE), http://etheses.lse.ac.uk/915/1/Roznai_Unconstitutional-constitutional-amendments.pdf, 158–160 (calling them "strong amendment powers" when constitutions demand national elections for amendment or elections to a special constituent assembly for the purpose of adopting amendments); R Dixon and D Landau, "Tiered Constitutional Design" at https://ssrn.com/abstract=2953755, 1, 63.

As the PiS, unlike Fidesz in Hungary, could not achieve a constitutional majority, it has not been able to change the Constitution formally. Therefore, it has used an informal mechanism of constitutional change, which, beyond the CT, which rediscovered the need for another type of activism, new actors have joined. Therefore, in this section, we focus on the Hungarian illiberal, exclusive, and abusive constitution-making and amending processes.

2 Formal constitutional changes

2.1 Adoption of the FL in Hungary

In Hungary, all changes were made by the constitution-making and constitution-amending powers, which observed the established formal rules. For making any constitutional changes, a constitutional majority, that is, the support of two-thirds of MPs, was all that was required. In Hungary, there has always been a prohibition on holding a referendum on constitutional amendments,[6] which, in both the doctrinal works and jurisprudence, was extended to the adoption of the constitution. The claim that the FL could not be voted on in a referendum was based on this legal position. This was one of the reasons why neither the constitution-making process in 2010 and 2011, nor the subsequent constitution-amending processes were inclusive, in terms of popular votes. Other reasons are purely political, fuelled by the will to monopolize these processes. First, the constitutional majority repealed the four-fifths majority rule from the then applicable Constitution in 2010.[7] It was a clear message that there was no need for any political support or consensus from the opposition. Second, this attitude could later be seen in the drafting of the FL independently from the work of the parliamentary committee that was assigned the task of drafting the text of a new Constitution in summer 2010. The opposition, however, left this committee in autumn 2010 as a protest against the first unconstitutional constitutional amendments. These were submitted and adopted by the Fidesz majority regarding the possibility of retroactive taxation and the curtailment of the powers of the CC.[8]

6 It first appeared in a 2/1993 (I. 22.) CC decision, which was later incorporated into Art 8 FL.

7 A majority of four-fifths of the votes of MPs was required to pass the parliamentary resolution specifying the detailed regulations for the preparation of the new Constitution. Thus, it has never required a supermajority for the adoption of the new Constitution, as has incorrectly been asserted in scholarly works. See, e.g., T Ginsberg, *Arato on Constitution Making in Hungary and the 4/5 Rule*, I-CONnect Blog (6 April 2011), www.iconnectblog.com/2011/04/arato-on-constitution-making-in-hungary-and-the-45-rule/

8 The possibility of retroactive taxation was accompanied by an Act that was annulled by the CC in 2010; the CC did not review the constitutionality of the constitutional amendment. On the same day of annulment, a slightly different constitutional amendment and Act were submitted with the same purpose, along with the curtailment of the powers of the CC in connection to financial laws. This latter rule was later, with some modification, incorporated into the FL.

That new and independent draft of the FL was submitted and adopted by the parliament; thus, the FL became a partisan constitution.

Even though its content had already been rightly criticized, when adopted, its text did contain many fewer disputed matters than it does today. One of the reasons was that many of the controversies were grouped into an instrument known as the Transitory Provisions. The same super-majority as required for the constitution-making power adopted them as a separate instrument after voting on the FL. The Transitory Provisions, apart from introducing actual transitory provisions, completed the text of the FL. It was an unusual and unprecedented design in Hungarian constitutional law and caused many disputes, leading to the First Amendment.

2.2 *Formal amendments*

All nine amendments can be classified within the following categories that sometimes overlap: clarification, correction, addition, capture and false pretense, abuse, cosmetic changes, and repeal. Whatever the label, these techniques and tactics contributed to the capture of the constitution and constitutionalism.

2.2.1 CLARIFICATION AND CORRECTION, AND ADDITION

As a reaction to the criticism of the Transitory Provisions and their submission for constitutional review by the ombudsman, the Government proposed the First Amendment.[9] It clarified, by the addition of an additional sentence, that the Transitory Provisions were part of the FL. Accordingly, they had to be treated as part of the constitution; and, therefore, the request for their constitutional review could not be admissible. After this change, the ombudsman still upheld the petition[10] and, in 2012,[11] the CC annulled the non-transitory-provisions of the Transitory Provisions with retroactive effect (to the date of their adoption). The arguments of the CC amount to an informal constitutional amendment, to be discussed below, in point 2.3.1.

The Third Amendment (2012) reinforced the protection of the environment by adding the requirement to regulate matters affecting forests and agricultural areas in

9 It was adopted within 2 months. First amendment of the Fundamental Law of Hungary [*Hungarian Official Gazette* 2012. Issue 73, 11856].

10 The ombudsman, who apparently could not identify with the idea of having two constitutional documents in the Hungarian legal system regardless of their "constitutional quality", claimed that the provision stating that the TP are part of the FL should not be interpreted on its own but with regard to the entire FL: TP cannot overrule the provisions of the FL; neither can they make exceptions from the application of its provisions. Should the TP be able to make exceptions from the FL, the "standard" itself set by the FL would be infringed. It would question the constitutional status of the FL.

11 45/2012. (XII. 29) CC decision.

an Act adopted by two-thirds of MPs present. The Sixth Amendment (2016) created a new type of emergency – terror threat – as a reaction to terror attacks in previous years in Europe (but not in Hungary).[12] The Seventh Amendment established the Administrative Supreme Court, the design of which received much criticism.[13]

2.2.2 ABUSE AND CAPTURE

The Fourth Amendment[14] contained provisions that overruled some of the CC's decisions, including the one concerning the partial annulment of the Transitory Provisions. At that time, the CC's decisions were not (yet) in line with the political will, therefore the FL was abusively changed to incorporate content that had already been declared unconstitutional by the CC. Let us mention three examples.

The original version of the definition of "family" in Article L) provided that only a man and a woman can get married and that the family is the basis of the survival of the nation. This latter concept became the constitutional ground for annulling a legal provision of the Family Care Act in 2012. According to the decision of the CC (2012[15]), this law excluded many forms of long-standing cohabitation falling within a more dynamic sociological notion of the family than the statutory definition of "family". As a response to this ruling, the FL was amended and "enriched" with this definition: "Family ties shall be based on marriage or the relationship between parents and children." It is an even more restrictive rule than that found in the annulled law. In its explanatory memorandum, the Government assured all that it served the *acknowledgment* of the CC's decision.

A decision in 2012[16] annulled a provision of the Petty Offences Act that criminalized the state of homelessness, because it was held to be in violation of human dignity. The CC, due to the inadequate choice of the source of law, also annulled a provision of the Act on Local Governments making it possible for local governments to create criminal acts in their decrees so as to criminalize the state of homelessness. And yet the new provision in the FL stated that an Act or a decree of local government may outlaw the use of certain public spaces for habitation in order to preserve public order, public safety, public health, and cultural values. On the other hand, the FL does not oblige the state to combat homelessness: it uses

12 More on this T Drinóczi, "Hungarian Abuse of Constitutional Emergency Regimes – Also in the Light of the COVID-19 Crisis". MTA LWP 13/2020, https://jog.tk.mta.hu/mtalwp/hungarian-abuse-of-constitutional-emergency-regimes-also-in-the-light-of-the-covid-19-crisis

13 HCLU's Analysis on the Seventh Amendment of the Fundamental Law 2018, https://hclu.hu/en/articles/hclus-analysis-of-the-seventh-amendment-of-the-fundamental-law

14 Opinion on the Fourth Amendment to the Fundamental Law of Hungary Adopted by the Venice Commission at its 95th Plenary Session, Venice, 14–15 June 2013.

15 43/2012 (XII. 20.) CC decision.

16 38/2012 (XI. 4.) CC decision.

phrases like "shall strive to provide", or "shall contribute to creating" […] "the conditions for housing". This provision was "corrected" by the Seventh Amendment, which also banned homelessness.[17]

Another decision in 2013[18] annulled the provision that stipulated that in the campaign period, political advertisements may only be published in the public media; the violation of Article 10 of the ECHR was also argued on a proper ground. In return, another provision introduced into the FL makes it at the discretion of parliament how political advertisements may be published.

2.2.3 COSMETIC CHANGES AND REPEAL

The Fourth Amendment also incorporated some rules from the Transitory Provisions, for example, the rules on freedom of religion and the church, only to be modified within half a year by the Fifth Amendment. It brought about some cosmetic changes while basically withdrawing the most criticized rules on churches and other denominations, but not entirely accommodating some criticisms.[19]

The Fourth Amendment transposed the discretionary power of the President of the National Judicial Office to transfer cases from the Transitory Provisions, without the required guarantees.[20] The Fifth Amendment removed it.

The Eighth Amendment (2019) made it clear that under EU pressure and that of international institutions dealing with the evaluation of the Rule of Law status of their Member States,[21] the establishment of a separate administrative court was cancelled and therefore deleted from the FL. This simple deregulatory amendment was initiated by the opposition and accepted by the Government.

2.2.4 CAPTURE AND FALSE PRETENSE

The Seventh Amendment was a comprehensive amendment, motivated by purely political goals. It redefined the rules on refugees and asylum-seekers. It also introduced the notion of the constitutional identity of Hungary and the duty of

17 See Art XXII of the FL after the Fourth and the Seventh Amendments.
18 1/2013 (I. 7.) CC decision.
19 See, e.g., Opinion on the Fourth Amendment, n. 14.
20 T Drinóczi, "Constitutional Politics in Contemporary Hungary", *Vienna Journal on International Constitutional Law* 1 (2016) 63–98; cf. with the Opinion of the Venice Commission on the legal status and remuneration of judges, Adopted by the Venice Commission at its 90th Plenary Session (Venice, 16–17 March 2012), Opinion of the Venice Commission on the Fourth Amendment, n. 14.
21 Opinion on the Law on Administrative Adopted by the Venice Commission at its 118th Plenary Session (Venice, 15–16 March 2019).

protecting Christian culture as a constitutional basis for not implementing certain EU laws.[22] The case of the Seventh Amendment is outstanding, as it incorporated the essence of a previous CC decision on the nation's constitutional identity, which we elaborate on below, in point 3.2.2. This amendment also reinforced the protection of homes, which now provides a constitutional basis for more restrictive political rights, such as the right of assembly. As explained in the preceding Part, this was motivated by a series of demonstrations outside the house of the Prime Minister.

The Ninth Amendment is based on an imaginary threat posed to Christian values by a book of fairy tales embracing "harmful" Western ideologies, an invented need to reform the constitutional emergency regime of the FL, and, perhaps due to the aspirations regarding EU Rule of Law conditionality, an actual political need to restrict access to information on the spending of public money. In real life, the amendments, along with the subconstitutional changes, further limit the legal possibilities of LGBTQIA+ persons and single persons, regardless of their sexual orientation, in the field of establishing a family, unify the diverse emergency systems, and eliminate the involvement of anyone other than the executive in decisions concerning war. These last rules on emergencies will come into force on 1 July 2023.

3 *Informal unconstitutional constitutional changes*

3.1 Bird's-eye view of 1989–2020: differences between informal constitutional changes of the pre- and post-2010/2015 era

As can already be seen, informal constitutional change has always featured in the activities of the constitutional courts. Due to the constitutional culture, the civil law traditions, and the historical moment, strong constitutional review mechanisms and courts[23] were created around the transition. They have contributed heavily to the establishment of the new regimes, be they either liberal or illiberal, through their constitutional interpretation, and also through their power of annulment. By their interpretation[24] – which deduced new concepts from the existing text, such as legal certainty, legitimate expectation, and separation of powers from the principle of the Rule of Law (in both states), created the prevalence of indirect over direct democracy from the joint interpretation of constitutional provisions,[25] recognized new

22 See point II.9. below.

23 See JI Colón-Ríos, "A New Typology of Judicial Review of Legislation", *Global Constitutionalism* 3(2) (2014) 143–169.

24 Joel I Colón-Ríos identifies the possible manifestations of judge-made constitutional changes in common law jurisdictions in JI Colón-Ríos, "Judge-made Constitutional Changes" in X Contiades and A Fotiadou (eds), *Routledge Handbook of Comparative Constitutional Change* (Routledge, 2021) 217–230.

25 2/1993. (I. 22.) CC decision.

rights, such as the right to name from human dignity,[26] and expanded and changed the content of words[27] – they created invisible[28] constitutions.[29]

We view the practice of creating an "invisible" constitution not only as a positive aspect of constitutional change, but also as serving the creation and function of the illiberal state. Even though, descriptively, there is no difference between "good invisible" and "bad invisible" constitutions, as in both cases the constitutions are "textually amended" without actual textual change, there are at least two significant differences between the justification for and legitimacy of the use of informal constitutional changes in the pre and post 2010/2015 era.

3.1.1 ACTORS INVOLVED

The first difference is that in the pre-2010/2015 era, the major actors of informal constitutional change were exclusively the constitutional courts. No other branches of the government could get involved because their sub-constitutional actions were deemed unconstitutional and were annulled. Abusive constitutional amendments had never been a practice, which left both the jurisprudence of the CC and CT and the scholarly communities unfamiliar with the issue of unconstitutional constitutional amendments and the possibility of their constitutional review, let alone informal constitutional change.[30] This unfamiliarity was also caused by the fact that in Poland, the CT does not

26 58/2001. (XII. 7.) CC decision.

27 K 18/04, concerning Poland's membership of the EU (The Accession Treaty) expanding the meaning of "citizen", which was meant to mean Polish citizens, to EU citizens, in terms of the right to vote. In the case of the NCJ, the status of the body was changed. See further below, point 3.2.1.

28 The term "invisible constitution" is related to the Sólyom Court of Hungary. It is formulated as follows: "The Constitutional Court must continue the work of laying down the theoretical foundations of the Constitution and the rights enshrined therein, and to create a coherent system through its decisions. This system may stand above the Constitution – which is still often amended to satisfy current political interests – as an 'invisible constitution,' serving as a stable measure of constitutionality. In so doing, the Constitutional Court enjoys a latitude as long as it remains within the conceptual confines of constitutionality." 23/1990. (X. 31.) CC decision.

29 A Bień-Kacała, "Informal Constitutional Change: The Case of Poland", *Przegląd Prawa Konstytucyjnego* 6(40) (2017) 199–218; A Bień-Kacała, "Verfassungsdurchbrechung or Informal Constitutional Change: The Polish Experience", *Przegląd Prawa Konstytucyjnego* 5(57) (2020) 29–47.

30 W. Sokolewicz, "Komentarz do art. 235" ["Commentary to the Art. 235"] in L. Garlicki (ed), *Konstytucja Rzeczypospolitej Polskiej. Komentarz*, Vol II [*The Constitution of the Republic of Poland*] (Wydawnictwo Sejmowe, 2001) 4; M Masternak-Kubiak, "Dopuszczalność nieformalnej zmiany Konstytucji R P (uwagi w kontekście prawa wyborczego obywateli Unii Europejskiej)" ["Admissibility of Informal Amendment to the Constitution RP (Comments in the Context of the Electoral Law of EU Citizens)"] in B. Banaszak, M. Jabłoński, and S. Jarosz-Żukowska (eds), *Prawo w służbie państwu i społeczeństwu* [*Law in the Service of the State and Society*] (Wydawnictwo Uniwersytetu Wrocławskiego, 2012). The authors do not provide conceptualization of informal constitutional change.

have explicit competence to deliver binding constitutional interpretation *in abstracto*. This power was terminated by the 1997 Constitution itself.[31] In Hungary, the activist CC has become a criticized but, at the same time, accepted (i.e., unchallenged) phenomenon.

No event has challenged the traditional view that the CC and the CT cannot review constitutional amendments. The reason has always been that amendments are the acts of the constituent (and not a derivative) power, and once they are adopted, review is impossible, because it would mean review of the Constitution itself, which the CC/CT are not empowered to do. However, the remodelling that accompanied the preparation of the FL in Hungary did not leave unaffected either the scholarly community, which started to demand a change in the dogma on constitutional amendment,[32] or the CC. In the first few years, in spite of the commencement of the packing exercise, the CC behaved as it was supposed to in defense of constitutionalism, the Rule of Law, and human rights, but it did not step up in time against the early unconstitutional amendments (on the possibility of retroactive taxation and the curtailment of its power in 2010). Only when it was finally packed, around 2016, did its highly deferential attitude appear. Packing of the CT in Poland was more drastic and faster, not allowing any "transition time" for the CT to try to react to attacks on the then existing substantive constitutional democracy, nor for academia to wake up. In this, paralysing the CT's operation by not publishing its judgments in 2015 and 2016 played an enormous role.

After 2010 and 2015, new actors joined the CC and CT in the informal constitutional amending exercise. In Poland, because of the lack of a majority for formally amending the 1997 Constitution and the COVID-19 pandemic, both the legislative and executive powers got involved. In Hungary, the legislative power informally supplemented the constitutional emergency regime by the introduction of the crisis situation over mass migration. It also could be argued that the executive power informally changed the FL when it introduced the first pandemic-related constitutional emergency in March 2020.[33]

This brings us to another consequential difference: while in the pre-2010/2015 period any unconstitutional measures would have been annulled by the CC and CT, now those courts allow or even facilitate them. The frame is the illiberal judicialization of politics, and the technique is, as Rosalind Dixon and David

31 Nevertheless, the Polish academia has developed the concept of the interpretative judgements of the CT based on the Constitution of 1997. See more on the interpretative judgements M. Hermann, *Wyroki interpretacyjne Trybunału Konstytucyjnego z perspektywy teoretycznoprawnej* [*Interpretative Judgements of Constitutional Tribunal from a Theoretical Perspective*] (Wydawnictwo Trybunału Konstytucyjnego, 2015).

32 N Chronowski, T Drinóczi, and J Zeller, "Túl az Alkotmányon" ["Beyond the Constitution"], *Közjogi Szemle* 4 (2010).

33 See e.g., T Drinóczi and A Bień-Kacała, "COVID-19 in Hungary and Poland: Extraordinary Situation and Illiberal Constitutionalism" *Theory and Practice of Legislation* 1-2 (2020).

Landau label it,[34] abusive constitutional review in Poland and substandard quality of reasoning in Hungary.[35] We call the phenomenon of informally bringing about constitutional change by the political branches of government breaching and bypassing the constitution. These informal constitutional changes are at the same time unconstitutional and abusive. They have been achieved by the political power (the legislature and the executive) through ordinary legislation, which has led to a change of meaning of the constitution's text without a formal amending procedure and observance of the legal hierarchy. We can identify three techniques, of which we give examples in the point discussing "Practice" below: (1) bypassing the Constitution with pieces of legislation by mimicking constitutional emergency regimes at the subconstitutional level in order to be able to disregard constitutional guarantees; 2) attributing new status to certain norms, just like in the case of the judge-made informal changes; (3) bypassing and invalidating existing rules of the legislative power by acts of the executive. These techniques affect the content of the constitutional changes as well, pushing it in a more illiberal direction.

3.1.2 THE CONTENT

The second major difference between the two eras is the manifestation of informal changes resulting from the rulings of the CC and CT. The invisible constitution that emerged in the Sólyom era in Hungary or in the 1990s in Poland usually did not disengage from the actual constitutional text. For instance, the main criticism in Hungary was usually whether the CC could rule on questions that might be considered too political to be decided by an apolitical and independent body. Or whether the result of an interpretation was still in some way based on the constitutional text, as in the case of the "general right to personhood" [*általános személyiségi jog*], which, however, some doubted could have been deduced from the right to human dignity.

In illiberal constitutionalism, the result of constitutional interpretation does lead to disengagement even from the text of the partisan FL. The Hungarian informal constitutional amendment by constitutional interpretation in 2016 remains unique, though, even in the context of the activist constitutional interpretative activity of the CC engaged in before 2010 and also in 2012 and 2013. Although the CC acted in the same way after 1990, in the pre-2010 era there was never any clear and previously expressed political will regarding the "new constitutional meaning", there was at least some constitutional text on which interpretations could be based, and it was more or less clear that judges followed their "own (legal) morals". It is also true of the activity of the CT, which also changed when it attributed new status to norms, which also brought about changes in the relationship between the branches of government (judiciary, NJC – see below). In the

34 R Dixon and D Landau, "Abusive Judicial Review: Courts Against Democracy", *UC Davis Law Review* 53 (2020) 1313.

35 See below for the decision of the CC on spreading false information from July 2020.

case of both courts, in the past couple of years, it has become less clear to what extent judges profess their own moral and legal convictions and to what extent they are serving their masters.

3.2 Practice

3.2.1 INFORMAL CONSTITUTIONAL CHANGE BY THE CT: POLISH JUDICIAL REFORM AND THE RELATIONSHIP BETWEEN EU AND POLISH LAW

The most intriguing example in Poland is the judgment of the CT of 20 June 2017[36] on the reform of the judiciary, the independence of judiciary, and the impartiality of judges. The parliament intended to change the constitutional character of the National Council of Judiciary (NCJ), the terms of office of its members, and its organization. The CT delivered a legal basis for the reform. What is important is that the new interpretation of the constitutional status of the NCJ was needed before the reform commenced.[37] The reform had been criticized by many, including the ombudsman, because they feared the politicization of the NCJ and, thus, the judiciary. Therefore, it was important to have a CT judgment that would resolve the disagreement in favour of the parliamentary majority and lend a legitimizing factor to the political decision.

The change affected the selection process of judges on the NCJ, who, according to the new rules, were to be chosen by the *Sejm* and not by judges themselves. The modification of the law was adopted in December 2017, after the new interpretation of the Constitution had been provided by the CT.

Taking into consideration that the Constitution only describes the main role of the NCJ (i.e., safeguarding the independence of the courts and judges)[38] and determines its composition,[39] a reform would be legally possible. However, according to the new reading of the Constitution provided by the CT, the legislative power was authorized to create an organ almost totally different from the one functioning at that time. In its reasoning, the CT clearly departed from the previous interpretation of the constitutional status of the NCJ as an element of the independent judiciary. Moreover, the CT said that the NCJ was neither part of the judiciary nor a representative body. This latter point is substantively correct, while the former is neither substantively nor formally accurate, even if verbatim the Constitution does not list the NCJ among the organs of the judiciary. The CT, in its decision in 2017, viewed it as an authority that does not fall within the simple interpretation of the separation of powers, and placed it in between the three branches of government as an instrument of institutional balance and a forum for

36 K 5/17.
37 M. Matczak, "How to Demolish an Independent Judiciary with the Help of a Constitutional Court", VerfBlog, 2017/6/23, http://verfassungsblog.de/how-to-demolish-an-independent-judiciary-with-the-help-of-a-constitutional-court/ (31.10.2017).
38 Art 186(1) of the Polish Constitution of 1997.
39 Art 187 of the Polish Constitution of 1997.

their cooperation. After removing the NCJ from the judicial power, it realized that, stemming from its newly discovered status and powers, the same guarantees that apply to the judiciary, such as independence and impartiality, cannot apply to the NCJ.

As a consequence, the ruling majority was "constitutionally" empowered to capture the organ responsible for judicial promotion. Invoking a constitutional provision,[40] the CT pointed out that the legislator has a wide scope of discretion when it comes to determining the organizational structure of the NCJ, the remit of its activity, its modus operandi, and the procedure for electing its members. Furthermore, the change in the interpretation of the constitutional regulation regarding the term of office of the NCJ members (joint, not individual, term of office of all elected members) made it possible to end the term of office of the former members elected by the judges. The new political NCJ is free to take a part in politically loyal judges' promotion procedure. Upon the initiative of the very same NCJ, the CT approved the new provisions as constitutional in its judgment of 25 March 2019.[41]

Another example of informal constitutional change might be the CT decision that could alter the relationship between Poland and the EU. In November 2019, the CJEU delivered its ruling on Polish preliminary questions concerning the independence of the disciplinary chamber of the Polish Supreme Court (SC), and that of the NCJ.[42] It ruled, briefly, that it was doubtful that the chamber was independent, as the politicized NCJ played a role in the nomination procedure, but it left the referring court to decide on this matter. The Polish judicial and political/legislative branches interpreted the decision differently. While the former embraced the doubts raised by the CJEU concerning independence and implemented the ruling accordingly,[43] the latter, as early as December 2019, took legislative measures to disable this implementation,[44] assisted by the two newly created and already packed chambers of the SC.

In April 2020, the CT was activated to firmly consider the relations between Poland and the EU, referring to symbolically stressed sovereignty. The first ruling of 20 April 2020 related to the resolution of the non-packed chambers of the SC of 23 January 2020. The CT created its competence to the review the SC resolution by making the resolution a normative act. That allowed it in turn to settle the disputes between the *Sejm* and the SC and between the President and the SC in

40 Art 187(4) of the Constitution of 1997: "The organizational structure, the scope of activity and procedures for work of the National Council of the Judiciary, as well as the manner of choosing its members, shall be specified by statute."

41 K 12/18.

42 Judgment in Joined Cases C-585/18, C-624/18 and C-625/18, ECLI:EU:C:2019:982.

43 Rulings issued by the Supreme Court are available at https://ruleoflaw.pl/translation-of-supreme-court-rulings-applying-ecj-judgment-of-19-november-2019/

44 See the latest step in the Polish judicial reform process. The so-called Muzzle Law from 2020 forbids statements that can undermine the office of another judge; point III. below.

the second ruling of 21 April 2020. The CT said that the SC had infringed the *Sejm*'s legislative competences and the President's prerogative to appoint judges. Additionally, the CT stressed that the SC had abused its competence to implement the CJEU judgment of 19 November 2019. The Tribunal held that the SC had emphasized its primary duty of loyalty to EU law and to rulings of the CJEU, disregarding the Polish Constitution of 1997. In addition, the CT considered that the SC, using preliminary rulings, acted in breach of and in abuse of this institution. Finally, in the opinion of the CT, the SC falsely assumed the absolute binding nature of the CJEU judgments in issues that were not transferred by the Member State to the EU. This logic led the CT to assess the CJEU judgment and consider it non-binding.

The rulings of the CT are therefore a turning point in the relations between Poland and the EU, and a first step towards another informal change. While the narrative presented by the CT was visible in the political space, it has now been converted into decisions changing the Polish legal and constitutional systems. The judgments concern the foundations of the functioning of a Member State of the EU, namely, the supremacy of EU law and EU law-friendly interpretation, and the recognition of the competence of the CJEU and the preliminary rulings procedure. Without recognition of these rules, it is not possible to operate within the EU legal sphere, which is built not only on the basis of the direct application of EU law in the Polish legal order (Article 91 of the Constitution), but also in respect for binding international law, as expressed in Article 9. Stressing the importance of Article 8 of the 1997 Constitution, which recognizes the Constitution as the supreme law of the Republic of Poland, the CT disregarded Article 9 and took a confrontational stance instead of a conciliatory approach. The consequences of this position could be deeply harmful to the Polish legal system. The sovereignty of Poland and the supremacy of the 1997 Constitution have become a barrier against the EU law and EU competences.

3.2.2 INFORMAL CONSTITUTIONAL CHANGE BY THE CC: CONSTITUTIONAL REVIEW OF AMENDMENTS AND CONSTITUTIONAL IDENTITY

The 45/2012 (XII. 9.) decision on the partial annulment of the Transitory Provisions qualifies as an informal constitutional amendment for two reasons. First, it misread the text of the FL and gave it an entirely new meaning – which is contrary to the intention of the constitution-making power. If we accept the position of the CC, however, no informal amendment happened – an unconstitutional legal norm[45] was merely annulled. Second, there was a radical change in the CC's jurisprudence relating to the power of substantive review of constitutional amendments – even though the regulatory environment on formal amendments did not change at that time. What did change, as opposed to during the first 20 years of democratic Hungary, was the unprecedented political pushing of illiberal remodelling of

45 According to the CC, the Transitory Provisions "was not a formal source of law".

constitutionalism, which by 2012 still could not pack the CC. This change of heart of the CC did not go unnoticed by the political super-majority, that is, the constitution-amending power.

The reasoning of the CC leading to the partial annulment of the Transitory Provisions was as follows: it is not possible to amend the Constitution with another piece of legislation that has no constitutional rank and is clearly not a constitutional amendment, even if the "legislator"[46] calls it a part of the FL. This way, the "legislator" takes away the competence of the assumed constituent power, violates the separation of powers, and makes it impossible for the CC to conduct a substantive review of that piece of the legislation. It is essential to make it clear that at that time, the CC still followed its jurisprudence and rejected the concept of reviewing formal constitutional amendments.

The intention of the constitution-making power was the opposite. It meant the Transitory Provisions to be "part" of the content of the FL, and it expressed this in the original version of the FL and, later, in a more eloquent manner in the First Amendment.[47] This constitutional character of the Transitory Provisions was, however, systematically denied, or, rather, was not recognized at all by most academics[48] and the ombudsman himself.[49] Should the CC have considered it as part of the constitution, it would not have had the power to review it, despite its highly controversial provisions relating to constitutionalism and human rights.

As opposed to its previous practice, especially of 2010, when it could not find the competence to annul the constitutional amendment introducing the possibility of retroactive taxation, the CC in 2012 suggested that eternity clauses might be "found" in the text of the FL (e.g., the rule of law in Article B)). The CC, as a result of its interpretation of the provisions of the Rule of Law and democracy, also defined some constitutional requirements for constitutional amendments. These limits on constitutional amendment include the

46 This is the wording of the CC: despite the wording of the normative texts of the FL and the Transitory Provisions, the CC calls the power that adopted the Transitory Provisions "legislator".

47 The closing provisions of the FL read as follows: "1. The Fundamental Law of Hungary shall take effect on 1 January 2012. 2. Parliament shall adopt the Fundamental Law pursuant to Sections 19 (3) a) and 24 (3) of Act XX of 1949. 3. Parliament shall adopt the transitory provisions related to this Fundamental Law in a special procedure defined in point 2. 4. The Government shall be obliged to submit to Parliament all bills required for the enforcement of the Fundamental Law." Sections 19 (3) a) and 24 (3) of Act XX of 1949 (that is the Constitution) refer to the fact that the parliament acts as a constituent power by adopting the Transitory Provisions, which requires a two-thirds majority.

48 See e.g. L Csink and J Fröhlich, "Az Alaptörvény és az Átmeneti rendelkezések viszonya" ["The Relationship between the Fundamental Law and Transitory Provisions"] *Pázmány Law Working Papers*, No 2012/02, available at www.plwp.jak.ppke.hu/images/files/2012/2012-2.pdf

49 Drinóczi, n. 20. 78.

coherence of content and structure (the Rule of Law), constitutional legality, and proper authorization. According to the CC, these criteria should be met even by the constitution-making power, because due to the monist approach of the CC, it absorbs the constitution-amending power. It follows that in cases of non-observance, the CC could conduct a substantive constitutional review of future amendments.

The interpretation of the CC, in this case, resulted in an informal constitutional amendment. With the Fourth Amendment, the parliament acted, formally, as a constitution-amending power: it merely adjusted a "drafting mistake" of the constitution-making power (creating the Transitory Provisions as a separate instrument), the intention of which was misconstrued by the CC. Therefore, the constitution-amending power, which completely overlapped with the constitution-making power, overruled the CC's arguments made under the regime of the FL. Whatever the end-result of the constitutional interpretation was, it was clearly and undoubtedly rejected by the political power. It also rejected the idea of any real and significant restriction on its amending power. The amending power did not wish to allow substantive review competence; therefore, it explicitly empowered the CC to perform procedural review. It would thus be more difficult to justify any substantive review in the future, as only procedural review was explicitly provided for. However, decision 12/2013 (V. 24.) attests otherwise by keeping the possibility of substantive review on the agenda. The question here is whether it fits into the highly deferential policy of the CC towards this political majority.

Even more curious is the fact that by incorporating the rules of the Transitory Provisions, the amending power observed the interpretation of the CC on the limits on amending powers. It provided coherence of contents and structure when the annulled contents of the Transitory Provisions found their way into the corresponding text of the FL, for example, rules on the church.[50] It respected the limits on constitutional legality and proper authorization, when acting as a constitution-amending power as described in the FL.

The other informal constitutional amendment featured in the constitutional interpretation of the CC on the constitutional identity of Hungary in the 22/2016 (XII. 5.) CC decision. The CC declared that the constitutional identity of Hungary is based on the historical constitution, and that its protection is a duty of the state.[51] This interpretation had no legal source whatsoever in the text of the FL at that time, but the decision of the CC was preceded by the clear expression of a distinct political intention, that is, the referendum on the so-called quota decision of the European Council,[52] initiated by the Government and the failed

50 Art VII of the FL.

51 T Drinóczi, "Hungarian Constitutional Court: The Limits of EU Law in the Hungarian Legal System", 1 *Vienna J. Int'l Const. L.* 139 (2017); K Kelemen, "The Hungarian Constitutional Court and the Concept of National Constitutional Identity", 15–16 *IANUS – Diritto e finanza* 23 (2017).

52 Council Decision (EU) 2015/1601 of 22 September 2015 establishing provisional measures in the area of international protection for the benefit of Italy and Greece (OJ 2015 L 248), 80.

Seventh Constitutional Amendment. The referendum was invalid because less than the statutorily required number of voters had participated. It is true, however, that the overwhelming majority of those who did vote (98 per cent) did not want to accept the "quota decision". Therefore, it did not trigger any legal response. However, the political decision-maker decided to initiate a constitutional amendment, which was communicated as the implementation of the people's will as expressed in the referendum. This formal amendment would have constitutionalized measures that could have been activated against otherwise binding EU law. Amongst other matters, the notion of constitutional identity, based on the historical constitution and its protection as a state obligation, along with the prohibition of the settlement of alien populations in the territory of Hungary, would have been added to the constitutional text. This was the time, though, when there was no constitutional majority in parliament. This amendment thus failed. The political intention did not. The CC assisted in informally constitutionalizing one of the essential components of the failed formal amendment, that is, the constitutional identity of Hungary. The Seventh Amendment incorporated the essence of the CC decision into the FL once the necessary majority was regained. The above-mentioned provisions were resubmitted along with two other constitutional novelties (constitutional limitations to the right to assembly and the introduction of a separate administrative court system).

3.2.3 INFORMAL CONSTITUTIONAL CHANGE BY THE PARLIAMENT AND GOVERNMENT

Beyond the obvious example when the Polish *Sejm* informally changed the 1997 Constitution when it created a competence to invalidate parliamentary resolutions by which it had selected the CT judges in December 2015,[53] we give two further examples, one from each country, of how the legislative and executive powers collaborate when it comes to informal constitutional change.

In 2015, the Hungarian ordinary legislative power enacted rules governing the "crisis situation caused by mass migration", as a response to actual and existing threats, whose presence in Hungary, however, has been exaggerated. The "crisis situation caused by mass migration" does not qualify as a "special legal order" under the FL as it still does not incorporate it. However, it mirrors a "special legal order" and, without the usual constitutional guarantees, operates like such an order as far as the "deployment" of the army and fundamental rights issues are concerned. Since the initial introduction of the crisis situation, it has been extended, even though the statutory criteria have not been met since 2016.[54]

Bypassing the 1997 Constitution seems to be a useful tool in the hands of the ruling majority. The legislative power circumvented the Constitution when the COVID-19 pandemic broke out. However, the Polish ruling majority cannot be accused of acting directly contrary to the 1997 Constitution when it comes to the declaration of any

53 A Bień-Kacała, "Polish Constitutional Tribunal: A Systemic Reform or a Hasty Political Change", *DPCE Online* 1 (2016) 1–14.

54 Drinóczi, n. 12.

emergency, as no epidemic is mentioned in the Constitution but two separate acts.[55] These are the Act on a state of natural disaster and the Act on infectious diseases. The activation of any of these acts has to follow the circumstances that they prescribe. In the case of the "state of natural disaster" this is a massive infection; and in the case of a "state of epidemic", it requires the occurrence of a new infectious disease or a disease that is visibly more infectious than previously. In the midst of the COVID-19 pandemic, the most suitable action would have seemed to be the declaration of the constitutional emergency regime, that is, the "state of natural disaster". This state is based on a statute and could be activated by a governmental regulation for a constitutionally assigned period. The Act on the state of natural disaster was enacted in 2002, which means that the legal basis was prepared *ex-ante* and is separate from other legislation that covers the normal functioning of the state. The Government chose not to activate the available constitutional "extraordinary measure" but merely followed its usual train of thought and illiberal political goals. It applied the statute-based regime for the coronavirus pandemic, regardless of its direct and severe impact on society and the economy, and adopted a new law as well. In this way, in a sense, it created a new, statute-based emergency to bypass the 1997 Constitution. Combining this new law on COVID-19 and the amended Act on infectious diseases, the Ministry of Health introduced the "state of epidemic threat", a measure already existing in the legal system but adjusted to the pandemic by the Act on COVID-19 by the addition of new tools and the granting of new competences to the Government. As the crisis evolved, the "state of epidemic" was declared. The logic of the statutory regime of "state of epidemic threat" and a "state of epidemic" is similar to that of constitutionally prescribed "extraordinary measures". These statutory emergencies are also activated by governmental and local regulations. Depending on the spatial coverage of the pandemic, the *voivode*,[56] the Minister of Health, or the Government can declare them. What distinguishes the "state of epidemic" and the "state of natural disaster" is the quantity and severity of the infection. The most important difference between the constitutional and statutory emergency regimes is that the latter allows the organization of elections, such as the presidential election that was originally planned for 10 May 2020. During the "state of natural disaster" and 90 days after its termination, however, the election could not have been organized, and the President's term of office would have been extended. Therefore, the ruling majority decided not to declare a "state of natural disaster" but gradually introduce the "state of epidemic". Eventually, the election was postponed and held in two rounds in June and July 2020.

3.2.4 INFORMAL CONSTITUTIONAL CHANGE BY THE EXECUTIVE – INDEPENDENTLY

As mentioned, the greatest novelty in connection with informal constitutional changes in illiberal constitutionalism is that even the executive is able to act independently, without being constrained by anyone, including the people. While the

55 For further details, see below at point III. 3.

56 The representative of the Council of Ministers in a voivodship (territorial and administrative part of Poland).

Polish examples are definitely unconstitutional and abusive in nature, this cannot be said with certainty about the Hungarian example.

In Poland, the Prime Minister has created a legal basis for not publishing the decisions of the CT, which runs counter to the Tribunal's role in the Polish legal system and the constitutional obligation to publish judgments in the Official Journal.[57] The same was done in relation to the abortion decision of the CT (22 October 2020).

The manner in which the first pandemic-related constitutional emergency was introduced in Hungary raises the issue of an unprecedented constitutional change by the executive. Article 53 of the FL says that a "state of danger" can be declared in the event of a natural disaster (*elemi csapás*) or industrial accident endangering life and property, or to mitigate its consequences; it does not provide further explanation. The FL does not refer *expressis verbis* to a human pandemic either – constitutions usually do not mention this. It appears only in the corresponding Act on catastrophes (2011) under heading "state of danger". Under this heading, the Act groups events that can trigger Article 53 FL into three categories – (1) "natural disaster [*elemi csapás*], natural dangers"; (2) "industrial accident, civilizational dangers"; (3) other dangers – and provides for lists giving examples of each type. It includes "human pandemic" within category 3). As per the FL, the Act also contained the subject matters relating to which extraordinary measures and decrees can be issued during the "state of danger", with which the content of the governmental decrees introduced in the first weeks of the pandemic does not precisely correspond. At that time, there were five opinions on the activation of Article 53 of the FL. The first was the opinion of the Government, which claimed that the declaration of the emergency was constitutional and that each measure had been necessary. The second claimed that measures taken in normal times could have been adequate to manage the defense against COVID-19.[58] The third argued that the Act – already in 2011 – unconstitutionally expanded the meaning of the FL; therefore, the Government had declared the emergency without a constitutional basis – which is viewed as another sign of dictatorship.[59] Following this train of thought there was a fourth opinion. It also claimed the expansion of

57 See, e.g., Opinion on the Act on the Constitutional Tribunal Adopted by the Venice Commission at its 108th Plenary Session (Venice, 14–15 October 2016); Bień-Kacała, n. 29, 199. Finally, the judgments of 9 March, 11 August, and 7 November 2016 (K 47/15, K 39/16, K 44/16) were published in June 2018, with the information in the Official Journal (*Dziennik Ustaw*), however, that they were illegally delivered.

58 G Halmai and KL Scheppele, "Orbán is Still the Sole Judge of his Own Law", VerfBlog, 2020/4/30, https://verfassungsblog.de/orban-is-still-the-sole-judge-of-his-own-law/

59 G Halmai, "How COVID-19 Unveils the True Autocrats: Viktor Orbán"s Ermächtigungsgesetz", *Int"l J. Const. L. Blog*, Apr. 1, 2020, www.iconnectblog.com/2020/04/how-covid-19-unveils-the-true-autocrats-viktororbans-ermachtigungsgesetz/; A Schiffer, "Különleges jogbizonytalanság" ["Extraordinary legal uncertainty"], https://mandiner.hu/cikk/20200313_kulonleges_jogbizonytalansag (13 March 2020), KL Scheppele, "Orbán"s Emergency", https://hungarianspectrum.org/2020/03/21/kim-lane-scheppele-orbans-emergency/,https://verfassungsblog.de/pandemic-as-constitutional-moment/

the FL definition to be unconstitutional, but it acknowledged the necessity of the deviation from the too-closed system of constitutional emergency regimes. At the same time, it called for respect for constitutional principles and reconsideration of the regulatory depth of the constitutional emergency regime.[60] We believe, as the fifth, that, based on the actual threat of COVID-19 and the management of the crisis in the first four weeks, and the constitutional and statutory design of the defense against human pandemics, the actions of the Hungarian Government simply show the business-as-usual functioning of illiberal constitutionalism. Regardless of their views on the de iure elimination of the more than flawed and ineffective parliamentary oversight by the Coronavirus Act, all the state organs, the opposition, and society followed and observed the rules on emergency measures. The Government terminated the constitutional emergency in mid-June 2020, but as the COVID-19 crisis was not over, it also established a new statute-based emergency and amended the Act on catastrophes as well. The latter action could be seen as a highly flawed and questionable adjustment of the legal environment to the experienced reality of COVID-19, in terms of a constitutional emergency.

4 *The paradox of unconstitutional formal and informal constitutional amendments*

Descriptively speaking, regardless of the regimes, what is the same is that the new content developed through informal constitutional amendments has been to a varying extent distanced from the particular constitutional provision or the value system of the text. It has started to live an independent life, and the subsequent decisions of the constitutional courts and legislative and executive powers have viewed such content as binding. Formal and informal amendments together, by supporting and relying on one another, have shaped the constitutional regime. Drawing on the works on comparative constitutional change[61] and the Hungarian

60 CS Tordai, "A közjog határai a járványveszély idején" ["Limits of Public Law During the Pandemic"], https://igyirnankmi.atlatszo.hu/2020/03/16/a-kozjog-hatarai-a-jarvanyveszely-idejen/ (16 March 2020).

61 Beyond those that have already been mentioned, e.g., X Contiades (ed) *Engineering Constitutional Change* (Routledge, 2012); D Oliver and C Fusaro (eds) *How Constitutions Change? A Comparative Study* (Hart Publishing, 2016); H Krunke and S Hellqvist Frey, "Social Rights in Denmark" in K Wojtyczek (ed), *Social Rights as Fundamental Rights* (Eleven International Publishing, 2016) 119; F Sejersted, "The Norwegian Parliament and European Integration – Reflections from Medium-Speed Europe" in E Smitjh (ed), *National Parliaments as Cornerstones of the European Integration* (Kluwer Academic Publisher, 1996); C Martin, "The Legitimacy of Informal Constitutional Amendment and the 'Reinterpretation' of Japan's War Powers", *Fordham Int'l L.J.* 40(427) (2017); R Albert, "How Unwritten Constitutional Norms Change Written Constitutions", *Dublin University Law Journal* 38 (2015); R Albert, *Constitutional Amendments: Making, Breaking, and Changing Constitutions* (Oxford University Press, 2019); Y Roznai, *Unconstitutional Constitutional Amendments: The Limits of Amendment Powers* (Oxford University Press, 2017).

and Polish experiences from the pre-2010/2015 era, it is our view that in a substantive constitutional democracy (liberal constitutionalism), it is for the constituted powers (political branches of government or the constitutional courts/high courts themselves) to decide whether constitutional interpretation by any other branches that changes the literal sense of the words of the constitution, or the formerly established and applied meaning of constitutional provisions, is acceptable or not. In a constitutional democracy, in civil law jurisdiction with a strong constitutional review system, no one can challenge the constitutional interpretation of the constitutional court in any legal way. However, it is for the political branches or the courts to reject or uphold its result. Once the political branches accept the new interpretation, they can choose whether to apply it as it is, or to incorporate it into the text of the constitution. If, in the system of checks and balances, all actors, actively or tacitly, approve the new suggested meaning, that is an informal, and we might add, invisible, constitutional amendment. In a constitutional democracy, it is also normatively appealing, and it highlights the deliberative, dialogic, or collaborative and inclusive character of the regime. In this case, the constituent power – through the text – and the constituted powers – through amendments by interpretation and their application – act together. If we accept the divide between the original constitution-making power and the derived power of constitutional amendment, only a tiny step need be taken to realize that an informal constitutional amendment agreed by the constituted powers leads to a legitimate and even desirable change to the constitutional system.

Paradoxically, we could say, the same descriptive and normative claims apply in illiberal constitutionalism – regardless of whether we like the result or not. Its very core is illiberalism, therefore whatever is needed to maintain it is legitimate and desirable from the perspective of the system. The hollowed-out checks and balances can still play a part in the process, which still occurs within a European context, and to a certain extent can form an obstacle to more accelerated deterioration. We can see it in the example of the CC's ruling on the spreading of false information in constitutional emergencies vis-à-vis freedom of speech (elaborated in point II.3.2. below), and in the demonstration against the abortion decision of the CT vis-à-vis self-determination and dignity.

Given that the constitutional court did not find its competence or an eternity clause (spirit, dignity, rule of law, etc.) to review obviously unconstitutional constitutional amendments to protect Hungary's (liberal) constitutional democracy in 2010 or the FL in 2013, it was a matter of concern when it eventually managed to do so in 2016 (regarding the constitutional identity of Hungary). Regardless of the only possibility to review amendments from a procedural perspective (introduced by the Fourth Amendment), the CC could activate the constitutional identity clause and its own jurisprudence (2016) to defend the illiberal content of the FL against a possible (but not probable) future constitutional majority of the (now) opposition parties. Those who advocated the substantive review of constitutional amendments in 2010 in defense of a substantive constitutional democracy would win a battle (descriptively speaking). They would also lose the war (normatively) over this kind of reviewability of constitutional amendments, as in illiberal constitutionalism, substantive review of constitutional amendments would be used for maintaining the illiberal system against any intention to restore a substantive constitutional democracy. In Poland, this kind of capture is also a possibility, due to the illiberal judicialization of politics that would do its best to secure the illiberal invisible constitution against the formal Constitution of 1997 and future endeavours to revert to these detrimental constitutional changes.

5 *Capturing key positions*

For creating an incumbent-friendly legal environment, an empowered executive is necessary in order to capture the parliamentary majority, the constitutional courts, and other key positions. Loyal persons, preferably friends, have to be appointed. The newly elected persons are politically biased, and sometimes less qualified but politically reliable, and therefore they act as servants of the political will.

In Hungary, so-called presidentialization of the executive power has taken place since 2010. The state has been governed by the principles of statism. The centralization of political governance has prevailed even more than previously, and media-marketing governance has emerged.[62] This has led to the personalization of politics, and produced the charismatic leader in whom voters believe. In Poland, because of the different political situation in which the actual political leader is not the head of the government, the rationalized parliamentary system has been altered: substantial power is given to some Ministers, such as the Defence Minister[63] and the Justice Minister, and to the leader of the ruling party. In this construction, the Prime Minister and the President of the Republic have only secondary roles. This informal hierarchy extrapolates and affects formal rules, as it happened with Jarosław Kaczyński when he became one of the Vice Prime Ministers in October 2020.

The Hungarian reforms on the nomination of CC judges and the constitutional position of the Hungarian Prosecutor General proved to be a double-edged sword. The principal ideas behind the change to the nomination process sought to ensure the continuous functioning of the CC by avoiding previous political blockages and transforming the Court into a more juridical-type organ, which are legitimate goals. The means chosen, however, have excluded any possibility of political compromise by monopolizing the nomination process. The parliamentary committee that decides on each nomination is now formed proportionally by MPs. Previously, each parliamentary faction could send an equal number of representatives to this committee. The Prosecutor General is now elected for nine years by a two-thirds majority of parliament. The mandate terminates with the lapse of time, but the incumbent Prosecutor General can continue to act until the new Prosecutor General is elected. Extension of the mandate could serve a legitimate goal – that is, to prevent any vacancy caused by political disagreement.

62 T Sárközy, "Magyarország kormányzása 2010–2014" ["Governance of Hungary 2010–2014"] *Új Magyar Közigazgatás* 2 (2015); I Stumpf, "A kormány alkotmányos jogállása" ["Constitutional Status of the Government"], *Új Magyar Közigazgatás* 2 (2015).

63 It was especially true up until December 2017, when members of the government were changed. The current Minister of Defense is less strong and controversial.

It has another effect as well: it can keep loyal personnel in power for a very long time, which would run counter to the logic of the temporal division of power.

On the other hand, in Poland, the CT is filled by judges and a president that are PiS-friendly. Initially, as a consequence of the extreme polarization and disagreement caused by the new composition in 2015, the CT could not properly deliver any judgments. Its judges were split into two groups. New judges tended to recognize the supremacy of the political majority and reject the supremacy of the 1997 Constitution, which is supposed to be safeguarded by the CT. Others stuck to the well-established case-law and constitutional rules. This situation deteriorated after the election of the CT President (20 December 2016). The paralysis and capture of the CT ruined its reputation[64] and legitimization.[65] Putting the CT in the middle of the political conflict brings about a lack of an appropriate support that is essential to oppose political pressure. So, the neutral (as expected) organ is unjustifiably involved in the political decision-making process. This judicial reform has also resulted in a hierarchical structure and subordination of the prosecutors to the Minister of Justice, who serves simultaneously as the Prosecutor General. This has created an illegitimately strong instrument with which the ruling party is able to monitor its political opposition and civil society.[66] Because of the new law on the judiciary (2019/2020), an extremely concentration of power has been created.

As said, it is not unusual for newly elected or newly appointed persons to have remained politically biased, and sometimes for them to be less qualified than they are politically reliable. The Polish CT Judge Lech Morawski said in 2017 that he simultaneously represented the positions of the CT and the Polish Government. Likewise, the former President of the Hungarian CC declared in 2015 that the CC would be an engine of governance.[67] Others who have been appointed or

64 T Ginsberg, "When Courts Compete: A Reputational Perspective" in M Zubik (ed), *Human Rights in Contemporary World, Essays in Honour of Professor Leszek Garlicki* (Wydawnictwo Sejmowe, 2017) 61–70; and P Pasquino, "Neutrality in Constitutional Conflicts Resolution: Preliminary Observations" in ibid., 180–193.

65 Created by proper, reasonable, clear, and short (as far as the language of statements of reasons is concerned) justification. A Młynarska-Sobaczewska, "Rytualne ofiary a moralność publiczna. Analiza argumentacji Trybunału Konstytucyjnego (K 52/13) i Sądu Najwyższego USA (508 U.S. 520.1993)" ["Ritual Sacrifices and Public Morality: Analysis of Arguments of the Constitutional Tribunal (K 52/13) and US Supreme Court (508 U.S. 520.1993)"], *Państwo i Prawo* 4 (2017); and A Młynarska-Sobaczewska, "Wybór sędziów konstytucyjnych jako element legitymizacji sądu konstytucyjnego" ["Election of the constitutional judges as an element of legitimacy of the constitutional court"], *Państwo i Prawo* 5 (2018) 43–62.

66 As for the positioning of the Prosecutor General in a constitutional system, various models are available, and states opt for the versions that best fit their particular legal system. Nevertheless, there are certain criteria that should be observed, but which the Polish model does not seem to fulfil. See Council of Europe, *Compilation of Venice Commission Opinions and Reports Concerning Prosecutors* 23–26 (2015).

67 An Oxford symposium on the Polish constitutional crisis sparks public debate, Oxford University (12 May 2017), www.law.ox.ac.uk/news/2017-05-11-oxford-symposium-polish-constitutional-crisis-sparks-public-debate; Chief Justice Lenkovics on the Fidesz Constitutional Court, Part I, *Hungarian Spectrum* (18 May 2017), http://hungariansp

elected have been criticized because of their well-known personal relationship with the Hungarian Prime Minister and their loyalty to the leader of the ruling PiS party. The Hungarian CC has grown to be a partner of the governing party; the CT was first a victim of the reforms but now has also become the partner of the Polish Government.

Illiberalism also entails legally supported new patrimonialism and clientelism,[68] and state-controlled corruption, which adds up to creating a "corrupt oligarchy"[69] or mafia-state.[70] Populist leaders accumulate wealth and power for themselves and their families, their clients, and their parties.[71] According to Transparency International's Corruption Perceptions Index 2016, Hungary ranked 57th in 2016 and 64th in 2018, displaying substantial backsliding since 2012, when the FL entered into force. Hungary has dropped three points since 2015 and is the fourth most corrupt country in the EU. Poland ranked 29th in 2015 and 2016 and ranked 36th in 2018, and its scores display a slight deterioration since 2015.[72] Corruption in Hungary presents a significant risk to business, particularly in the tax administration and public procurement sectors, which suffer from high levels of corruption.[73] The possibility of corruption in Hungary is inherent in the state's legal rules and culture. It is still to be seen if Poland will keep following Hungary in dropping down the Corruption Index rankings.

This situation was one of the reasons why the EU wanted to introduce the Rule of Law conditionality mechanisms in connection to EU funds, which brings us back, on the one hand, to illiberal legality and, on the other hand, to the issue of economic fundamental rights – both of which we discussed in the preceding Part.

II Illiberal judicialization of politics

As we have already explained, the third wave of democratization brought legal constitutionalism, together with the Kelsenian theory of law and the protection of

ectrum.org/2015/07/18/chief-justice-lenkovics-on-the-fidesz-constitutional-court-part-i/

68 L Diamond, "Facing Up to the Democratic Recession", *J. Democracy* 26(142) (2015) 149; see also HE Hale, "25 Years After The USSR: What's Gone Wrong?", *J. Democracy* 27(24) (2016).

69 See J Puhl, "A Whiff of Corruption in Orbán's Hungary", *Spiegel* (17 January 2017), www.spiegel.de/international/europe/a-whiff-of-corruption-in-orban-s-hungary-a-1129713.html

70 B Magyar, *Post-Communist Mafia State: The Case of Hungary* (Central European University Press, 2016).

71 See Diamond n. 68, 149. The most visible example is Mr Misiewicz, a spokesman for the Defense Ministry, who has no professional experience; or an example from Hungary might be the case of *Baka v Hungary*, App no 20261/12 (23 June 2016).

72 Hungary scored 44 in 2019 and 55 in 2012; Poland scored 58 in 2019, 63 in 2015 (and 58 in 2012). The survey ranks some 176 countries and uses a scale of 0 (highly corrupt) to 100 (very clean). See also http://hungarianspectrum.org/tag/olaf/. For the 2019 index, www.transparency.org/en/cpi/2019/results

73 GAN Integrity, *Hungary Corruption Report* (November 2017), www.business-anti-corruption.com/country-profiles/hungary

constitutions, as the most suitable concept for the CEE countries with communist and totalitarian pasts. Due to the structural changes or the newly created constitutional settings, legal constitutionalists of the CEE region generally place more trust in judges to decide on reasonable disagreements instead of political actors and citizens. Bellamy explains that for the legal constitutionalists, it is the constitution that represents a fundamental structure for reaching collective decisions in a democratic way. The constitution is a legal document, which is binding on all and which is protected by the constitutional review mechanisms. In contrast to this, for political constitutionalists, the constitution is the democratic process itself, representing a political rather than a legal system. Thus, and since the idea emerged in the UK, the constitution is not treated as a superior norm. Disagreements are to be resolved within this political framework, which obviously rejects the idea of any kind of review conducted by apolitical, independent and non-elected but otherwise selected actors, such as judges.[74]

Illiberal constitutionalism does not really feature the previous legal constitutionalism (1989/1990–2010/2015) and is completely different from political constitutionalism.[75] As we have previously shown and, it is hoped, proved, illiberal constitutionalism is a "new" kind of constitutionalism, and worse than the one that has been evolving since the era of constitutionalization of the early 19th century. The adjective "new" obviously does not imply that Hungary and Poland would belong to the group of states representing "new constitutionalism" as characterized by Gardbaum (UK, New Zealand, Canada, etc.),[76] into which, according to Lavapuro and his co-authors, Finland also fits.[77]

Ran Hirschl,[78] basing himself on Bellamy's binary code and observing the emergence of "new constitutionalism" located in between its legal and political equivalents, found that juristocracy, as opposed to the more benevolent political processes, endangers the efficiency of redistributive politics. In this context, when legal constitutionalism seems to alternate with its political counterpart, there is a growing suspicion of the inevitable rise of juristocracy.

Although Carlos Closa criticized Hirschl's book for excellent reasons,[79] Hirschl's theory on juristocracy and the idea of political constitutionalism seem to

74 R Bellamy, *Political Constitutionalism: A Republican Defence of the Constitutionality of Democracy* (Cambridge University Press, 2007).

75 Ibid., 2–5.

76 S Gardbaum, "The Case for the New Commonwealth Model of Constitutionalism", *German Law Review* 12(14) (2013) 2230–2248.

77 J Lavapuro, T Ojanen, and M Scheinin, "Rights-based Constitutionalism in Finland and the Development of Pluralist Constitutional Review", *ICON* 2 (2011); T Ojanen, "Constitutional Amendment in Finland" in X Contiades (ed), *Engineering Constitutional Change* (Routledge, 2016) 107–109.

78 R Hirschl, *Towards Juristocracy: The Origins and Consequences of the New Constitutionalism* (Harvard University Press, 2004).

79 Closa asks many reasonable questions: "And, on a different front, it seems fair to ask if the hegemonic-preservation claim actually holds true as a general explanation for the emergence of constitutionalism. Is it plausible to claim that countries in Southern Europe, such as Spain and Portugal, develop their charters because of reasons related

be embraced by many Hungarian and Polish scholars and members of the constitutional courts.[80]

As opposed to these views, we simply argue that illiberal constitutionalism is not a political constitutionalism. We also claim that label of "juristocracy" is not the best theory to describe either the period 1990–2010/2015 or the post-2010/2015 era. Instead, its reverse form, which is the special kind of judicialization of politics theorized by Armen Mazmanyan,[81] seems to best capture this aspect and the nature of the illiberal regime of the post-2010/2015 era. The special kind of judicialization of politics in both countries means that constitutional court decisions are more often than not a product of political instruction and manipulation of constitutional law. We decided to call this phenomenon "illiberal judicialization of politics", as this term captures the nature and the core position of the constitutional court within illiberal constitutionalism.

All of this not only shows how illiberal constitutionalism works, but also underscores the fact that the system seems to be stable, or at least still has a stable position in between liberal constitutionalism and authoritarianism.

1 Bird's-eye view of legal constitutionalism and juristocracy, so ...

In Hungary and Poland, as in other CEE countries, the assurance of the implementation and the enforcement of the constitutions has been assigned to the CC (1989/1990) and CT (1982/1999[82]) respectively. Until 2010 (CC) and 2015 (CT), these bodies could exercise their wide powers independently, with *erga omnes* effect: they could provide an abstract interpretation of any provision of the

to preserving the hegemony of elites? Did the countries in Eastern Europe follow this path to protect their elites?" C Closa, "Ran Hirschl, Towards Juristocracy: The Origins and Consequences of the New Constitutionalism, Harvard University Press, 2004", ICON 4(3) (2006) 581–586.

80 See e.g., A Antal, "Politikai és jogi alkotmányosság Magyarországon" ["Political and Legal Constitutionalism in Hungary"], *Politikatudományi Szemle* 3 (2013); A Czarnota, "The Constitutional Tribunal", VerfBlog, 2017/6/03, https://verfassungsblog.de/the-constitutional-tribunal/; L Morawski, "A Critical Response", VerfBlog, 2017/6/03; G Górski and J Górska-Szymczak, "Trybunał Konstytucyjny w Sporze z Prezydentem, Rządem i Parlamentem w 2015 r." ["The Constitutional Tribunal in an Argument with the President, the Government and the Parliament in 2015"], *Przegląd Sejmowy* 5(148) (2018) 39–57; B Szmulik, "Opinia w sprawie uwag do nowelizacji ustawy z dnia 25 czerwca 2015 r. o Trybunale Konstytucyjnym przygotowanych przez Komisję Wenecką" ["Opinion on the comments to the amendment of the Act of 25 June 2015 on the Constitutional Tribunal by the Venice Commission"], *Przegląd Sejmowy* 5 (2016) 81–100.

81 In general, see, M Mazmanyan, "Judicialization of Politics: The Post-Soviet Way", *I-CON* 13(1) (2015) 200–218.

82 Under the Constitution of 1952, in 1985 the *Sejm* passed the first Law on the CT and in 1986 the CT delivered its first judgment. The Court became fully independent two years after the Constitution of 1997 entered into force, when the *Sejm* forfeited the competence to reject some of the CT judgments (Art. 239 of the 1997 Polish Constitution).

constitutions,[83] interpret specific constitutional rules that had been challenged, annul unconstitutional laws, ensure conformity of international obligations with national law, declare the unconstitutionality of legislative omissions, require parliaments to adopt the necessary legislation, and so on. These constitutional courts could annul laws with *ex nunc* and *pro futuro* effect, the latter giving parliaments the opportunity to adopt new laws, while the unconstitutional law is maintained in effect to avoid having important and essential issues unregulated. This constitutional and institutional design was the precise intention of the constitution-making and constitution-amending powers and the legislative powers in both countries. Their purpose was twofold: the removal of (older, socialist) laws that could no longer be constitutional in the new democratic context, and the preservation of the achievements of transition. This latter aim involved a political agenda that was meant to prevent earlier state parties from regaining power and thereby reversing the transition process. The rules on the effect of the constitutional courts' decisions in time were quite unusual at that time, if we compare them to the original legislative intention of other jurisdictions, for example, Belgium, Germany, Austria. In these states, due to the different focus of the constitutional review (either protecting an individual, or observing a proper division of power between the federal government and the states), the main rule has always been to ensure an *ex tunc* annulment.[84]The combined effect of the powers of the CC and CT and the rules of the effect in time have raised doubts as to the division of power between branches of government and the active role both courts took in facilitating the transition process and also later.

As we have explained above, both the CC and the CT, from the very beginning, had the power to interpret vague constitutional provisions on democracy, the Rule of Law, and fundamental rights. The CC facilitated and ensured the legality of the transition. In one of its landmark decisions in 1992, it stated that the Rule of Law could not be weighed against the Rule of Law: the CC cannot be allowed to disregard the rule of statutory limitation and get it restarted because the system has been changed.[85] Until the Polish Constitution of 1997 was adopted, the CT had delivered necessary gap-filling decisions, the essence of which was later incorporated into the new Constitution.[86] Undoubtedly, there have been many constitutional interpretations by the constitutional courts that could be seen as informal constitutional amendments. However, the political power has always

83 In Poland it was possible until 1997.

84 It was the constitutional court that in its jurisprudence developed the idea of diversion from this main rule. See P Popelier, S Verstraelen, D Vanheule, and B Vanlerberghe (eds), *The Effects of Judicial Decisions in Time* (Intersentia, 2014).

85 Interestingly, the Czech Constitutional Court came to the opposite view on the very same issue. See 11/1992. (III. 5.) CC decision and its Czech counterpart: Pl. ÚS 19/93.

86 L Garlicki, *Polskie prawo konstytucyjne* [Polish Constitutional Law] (Wolters Kluwer, 2016) 76–78; and I Wróblewska, *Zasada państwa prawnego w orzecznictwie Trybunału Konstytucyjnego RP* [The Rule of Democratic State Ruled by Law in Judgements of the Polish Constitutional Tribunal] (TNOIK, 2010) 48–50; L Sólyom, "Alkotmányértelmezés az új alkotmánybíróságok gyakorlatában" ["Constitutional Interpretation in the Practice of New Constitutional Courts"], *Fundamentum* 2 (2002) 18–20.

been free to act, provided that it has a constitutional majority (independently or with coalition partners),[87] or could enter into a compromise with the opposition, due to the importance of the issues,[88] to address them in a formal constitutional amendment. Therefore, if there was widespread disagreement about an active or dynamic interpretation by the constitutional courts, and consequent fear of "juristocracy" or "governance by constitutional courts", the constitution-amending power (the constitutional majority) could replace the interpretation of the courts with its own.[89] However, what usually occurred was that the constitutional majority respected the courts' ruling to the extent that it incorporated the essential findings into the new constitutions.[90]

Against this background, it is clear that what Hirschl asserts in connection with the reason why constitutional rights and judicial review are established in some common law states, does not simply hold true in Hungary and Poland or, even more broadly, in the former socialist CEE states. He claims that the political origin of the introduction of judicial review to protect fundamental rights was only the intention of the elite to preserve their hegemonic status ("hegemonic preservation").[91] In our region, however, the driving force was to establish a constitutional democracy that had not existed before. At the same time, one of the core assumptions was to introduce and implement human rights protection and, as a correlating duty, to join international human rights systems. Another constituent part was the protection of the constitution that was already perceived as a legal and not only a "paper" document, a political manifesto of the ruling communists. To achieve these goals and accommodate themselves among other European constitutional democracies, Hungary and Poland, by establishing their constitutional courts, created a fully-fledged constitutional review system and process. In the 1990s, the activism of these courts, for example, the doctrine of the invisible constitution of the Sólyom Court, was criticized by some scholars. They used the labelling of Hirschl, claiming that the interpretative activity and power of annulment of the CC resulted in a juristocracy in Hungary, which endangered the free political formation power in parliament. In Poland, the situation was slightly different. The CT was set up in 1982, because of the demands of lawyers and the *Solidarność* (Solidarity) movement, and its judges took office in 1986. Therefore, the rulers, around 2016 and 2017, for political reasons, falsely argued that the CT was a communist relic that preserved the communist elite. Besides, they used the

87 See a more detailed account in Drinóczi, n. 20.

88 It happened with the formal constitutional amendment on accession to NATO and the EU.

89 As occurred in 2013 in Hungary with the Fourth Amendment.

90 We might refer to the early constitutional interpretation of the CT on the Rule of Law that became part of the Small Constitution and the Constitution of 1997, or the CC on the powers of the President of the Republic and the relation between the direct and indirect exercise of popular sovereignty (referendum v representative republic) as stipulated in the former Constitution. The core of these Hungarian findings was incorporated into the FL in 2011.

91 Hirsch, n. 78, 16.

term "juristocracy" just to weaken the CT's original, that is, pre-2015, position. As opposed to this, however, what is widely acknowledged is that the jurisprudence of the CT enabled the Polish transformation process (systemic changes) by establishing and safeguarding the Rule of Law.

The features of legal constitutionalism challenge the position of parliament, which is the body of popular or national representation. Constitutional interpretations delivered by constitutional courts sometimes prevail and, allegedly, limit the will of the people. This can cause tensions between the constitutional interpretation and the will of the people, who can, however, be highly influenced by populist political parties. Therefore, the concept of political constitutionalism and the (debatable) threat the "pre-2010/2015 juristocracy" means to constitutionalism have been used in Hungary and Poland to justify the disabling and the capturing of the constitutional courts (post-2010/2015).

This attitude of the powerholders is not without precedent. Before the transition, the socialist states had started to pretend to have a prescriptive constitution that needed protection. Socialist types of constitutional courts had been established with far fewer powers as compared to their modern counterparts. To give an example, there was no power of annulment, so the parliament could just ignore the court rulings. Both in Hungary and Poland, it was the parliament that was named not only as the supreme representative body, but also, and most importantly, as the supreme organ in the state hierarchy. Both constitutional courts, during their short existence in the 1980s, were subordinated to parliaments in systems that did not recognize the principle of the separation of powers. The supremacy of the political will prevailed in these hegemony-party systems. However, after the transition, the CT and the CC functioned differently and became symbols of democratic change (along with, for example, the ombudsman and the Polish Supreme Administrative Court). From a binary perspective of political and legal constitutionalism, and disregarding another binary system of autocratic and democratic systems, the socialist constitutional courts did not obstruct the free policy formulation and lawmaking of the party and parliament. That was not their mission, but it does not mean that political constitutionalism featured during socialism either.

Thus, what was established during the transition and operated afterwards might not entirely amount to a juristocracy. Instead, it could be viewed as one of the elements of the ordinary operation of constitutional democracy, established after a socialist and autocratic period in CEE states. Moreover, the pre-2010/2015 period cannot be described either as a Third Legal Tradition that emerged after the transition period (Siems),[92] or as representing a "socialist legal tradition without socialism" (Uzalec).[93] Nevertheless, taking into consideration what has happened in the past ten and five years in Hungary and Poland, respectively, Siems' and Uzelac's views, *mutatis mutandis*, seem to be a more adequate description of

92 M Siems, *Comparative Law* (Cambridge University Press, 2014) 78–79.

93 A Uzelac, "Survival of the Third Legal Tradition", *Supreme Court Law Review* 49 (2010), (2nd) 377–396.

this period. It is because, as we have explained in the preceding Parts, Poland and Hungary use laws and institutions as instruments to protect political elites, for which they get and expect support from the CC and CT. Constitutional courts in both states started to employ the strategy of abusive constitutional review in both its weak and strong forms.[94] Another form of abusive judicial review is when the courts' process is abusively initiated, or when the reasoning of the court is apparently substandard – simply in order to be able to deliver deferential decisions. The former occurs in Poland, that is, when a case is submitted by majority members of the *Sejm* to transfer the debate to the CT instead of deliberating the issue in the representative body (e.g., abortion decision of the CT in October 2020), while the latter is more visible in Hungary – which we will show below when discussing serving two masters.

2 ... *illiberal constitutionalism is not about political constitutionalism but ...*

In the post-2010/2015 period, the almost mythical concept of the "will of the people" (or that of the Nation) to which populist politicians try to relate, has been more and more supported by scholars, first in Hungary and then in Poland. There are several scholarly works advocating the concept of political constitutionalism in their respective states.[95] Thus, one might note that even academia, to a certain extent, supports the ruling majorities in their efforts to, theoretically, justify their political actions.[96] Their arguments, however, fail to realize the differences between the foundations of legal and political constitutionalism. They also neglect to consider whether the constitutional, political, and social preconditions of political constitutionalism are present at all. These requirements encompass, amongst others, the existence of competitive elections and genuine participation in the legislative processes. In each of these accounts both Hungary and Poland exhibit more than a few defects. They do not consider either the strong Hungarian and Polish judicial review model when evaluating the type of constitutionalism applied in these states. Both the CT and CC are constitutionally mandated *expressis verbis* to annul unconstitutional laws, other normative acts, and judicial decisions. If these courts consider themselves as bodies functioning in systems in which political constitutionalism applies then they may not annul unconstitutional pieces of legislation. Instead, the constitutional courts could reinforce the efforts of the political decision-maker by using softer measures, as was openly suggested by one of the former presidents.[97] In this case, constitutional courts would indeed be

94 Dixon and Landau, n. 34, 1337–1345. The weak form refers to, e.g., upholding legal measures that amount to unconstitutional informal change (Poland), while the strong form is applied when the CC and CT act proactively with constitutional interpretation (Hungary) and by striking down legislation (Poland).

95 See n. 80.

96 For a summary, see G Halmai, "Illiberal Constitutionalism in East-Central Europe", *EUI Working Paper LAW 2019/05*.

97 Interview with Barnabás Lenkovics, President of the CC, March 2015, in Radió Kossuth. Summary can be found in Hungarian at http://nol.hu/belfold/lenkovics-az-ab-feladata-hogy-ne-blokkolja-a-kormanyzati-munkat-1519643. See also in English at http://

engines of governance by not blocking the rapid reactions of their parliaments, and would spare the prestige and authority of the parliament, which is the supreme organ of popular representation. However, they will do this at the cost of not properly performing their constitutional duty as the protectors of the constitution and constitutionalism.

It is, therefore, a misunderstanding to conceptualize the deference of the CT and the CC as the emergence of political constitutionalism and a fading of legal constitutionalism. These courts are merely supporters of the political majority in the unchanged legal setting of legal constitutionalism. Therefore, this is better viewed as legal constitutionalism "with benefits". The system upholds legal constitutionalism as a sort of façade, with its written constitution and enforcing mechanism, but the rulings of the constitutional courts, in the vast majority of cases, are nothing other than the assertion and legitimization of an openly formulated or impliedly expressed political will. This is an illiberal judicialization of politics.

3 … *illiberal judicialization of politics*

3.1 *The beginnings and emerging practice*

Both constitutional courts were affected by the first actions of illiberal remodelling. In Poland, it started in 2015 with the CT[98] and the issue of judges and anti-judges, which was followed by the appointment of the new CT president and the election of loyal justices. The packing of the CC in Hungary was also a process that ended around 2016, by which time the Court was already composed of those judges who had been nominated and elected exclusively by the Fidesz super-majority. It was not unprecedented even before 2016 for the CC to deliver deferential decisions or ones whose quality could be questioned, but this attitude and practice somewhat increased after 2016. As said, in the early years of the 2010s, the CC tried to act as a balance, which it gave up in the decision on constitutional identity (22/2016 (XII.5) CC decision), in which it constitutionalized what Fidesz wanted but, due to the temporary lack of a super-majority, could not achieve. The first sign of the judicialization of politics in Poland was the CT decision on assemblies in 2017.[99] It was an *ex-ante* constitutional review initiated by the President of the Republic, because the new rules provided that preference should be given to cyclical assemblies (to be held at repeatable specified times, e.g., every 10th day of each month) in the case of concurrent events. The CT did not find it unconstitutional and therefore helped the PiS to "constitutionally" restrict the right to assembly. This case is interesting not only because of the

hungarianspectrum.org/2015/07/18/chief-justice-lenkovics-on-the-fidesz-constitutional-court-part-i/ (18.05.2017).

98 A Bień-Kacała, "Poland Within the EU: Dealing with the Populist Agenda", *Osteuropa-Recht* 4(63) (2017) 428–443 and "Polish Constitutional Tribunal: A Systemic Reform or a Hasty Political Change", *DPCE Online* 1 (2016) 1–14.

99 Kp 1/17.

content, but also because of the procedural issues it raised. The Prosecutor General put forward a motion calling for the exclusion of certain judges from this adjudication (those who joined the CT in 2010, elected by the Civic Platform, PO majority parliament), due to alleged flaws in their election. Nevertheless, in the same case, another judge (elected in 2017) was not excluded despite the bringing of his own motion, in which he stated his previous involvement in the case. Only judges elected in 2010 were eventually excluded from this case, allowing loyal judges, including the one who asked for his own exclusion, to deliver a decision in favour of the PiS. In these circumstances, it is clear that the guiding idea of adjudication was the political loyalty of the judges. The political loyalty of the judges and the pattern of judicialization are more obvious in another judgment from 2017,[100] on the constitutional character of the NCJ. This was the case we described as one of the examples of informal constitutional change through interpretation by the CT. As a result, the CT assisted in creating a constitutionally friendly environment for the legislative agenda of curtailing the independence of the judiciary. Since then, the CT has been increasingly used, and the ideal of constitutional review has been abused by the PiS, mainly for facilitating, that is, constitutionalizing and legitimizing, the PiS policy choices on judicial reform and the abortion issue.

Due to the difference in the baseline, that is, illiberal FL in Hungary and an illiberal invisible constitution in Poland, the "abuse" is more characteristically present in Poland, while both the CC and the CT have been active in supporting the populist agenda by an activist approach to constitutional interpretation. Neither court did much as regards the emergency laws and measures introduced during the COVID-19 crisis.

The 2020 pandemic,[101] in essence, has not altered the functioning of the CT and CC; they have operated continuously, and also delivered decisions during both the constitutional (Hungary) and statute-based emergencies (Hungary and Poland). They do not have particular competences concerning emergency measures; the constitutions safeguard and demand their unfettered operation in times of emergency. When an emergency-related submission arrives, neither of the courts moves quickly. This operation of illiberal legality underscores not only the illiberal judicialization of politics, but also the attitude: the law does not dictate an accelerated procedure during an emergency, so there is no legal possibility for fast(er) decision-making on the pandemic-related issues, even though the CC and the CT are able to decide quickly. The quality of reasoning of the CC in the case of the criminal offence of spreading false information during an emergency does not explain the delay in decision-making. Let us examine why below. There we collect some of the decisions of both courts from 2020, to show that the illiberal

100 K 5/17. M. Matczak, "How to Demolish an Independent Judiciary with the Help of a Constitutional Court", VerfBlog, 2017/6/23, http://verfassungsblog.de/how-to-demolish-an-independent-judiciary-with-the-help-of-a-constitutional-court/, DOI: https://dx.doi.org/10.17176/20170623-103309 (31.10.2017).

101 Drinóczi and Bień-Kacała, n. 33, 171–192.

judicialization of politics is still a constitutional reality, which, regardless of its nature, that is, serving one or two masters, bolsters our argument on the stability of the system.

3.2 Serving two masters

The new criminal offence introduced by the Coronavirus Act 2020, criticized by many, reads as follows:

> A person who, during the period of a special legal order and in front of a large audience, states or disseminates any untrue fact or any misrepresented true fact that is capable of hindering or preventing the efficiency of protection is guilty of a felony and shall be punished by imprisonment for one to five years.[102]

The petitioner[103] argued that this new provision, due to its lack of clarity and ambiguity, did not conform with the principle of legal certainty. This is so, mainly because the individual would not know, without a doubt, what kind of speeches are not allowed, and there is no case-law available on the commission of this criminal offence during an emergency. He also claimed that it unnecessarily restricted his freedom of speech, would have a chilling effect, and hinder democratic discourse that is even more necessary during this type of emergency.

The CC, in decision 15/2020 (VI. 8.) CC, first found the case admissible. It accepted the petitioner's reasoning that the rule raised a question concerning the realization of his freedom of speech. The CC, however, did not deem the formulation of the criminal offence problematic, so it did not annul the provision based on the infringement of legal certainty. It did not find the new rule unconstitutional on the basis of the violation of the freedom of speech, either. The CC referred to the existing case-law on what constitutes "large audience", "states", "disseminates", "untrue fact", "misrepresented true fact", "hindering" and "preventing". It also reiterated the established case-law, which has emerged in the pre-2010 jurisprudence, on the difference between statements of fact and opinions, and their implications for the extension of constitutionally acceptable interference. The CC, however, failed to address the clarity of the expression "efficiency of protection", and falsely implied that the existing case-law could give guidance.

Even if the CC did not establish a violation of the Rule of Law (through the principle of legal certainty), it felt it necessary, for the advancement of the same Rule of Law and protection of freedoms, to establish a constitutional requirement for the interpretation and application of the criminal provision, which has the following content: the communication is punishable only of those facts the perpetrator, when committing the crime, knew were false or which he misrepresented;

102 http://abouthungary.hu/media/DocumentsModell-file/1585661547-act-xii-of-2020-on-the-containment-of-coronavirus.pdf
103 www.facebook.com/daniel.karsai.355/posts/10157877679272931

this kind of communication also has to be "capable of hindering or preventing the protection". What the CC did, thus, was nothing more than repeat the essence of the first part of the provision and remove two words ("efficiency of") from the second part. Thus, in this case, the CC determined a constitutional requirement in a way that, most probably, makes application of the provision impossible. The CC, however, as said, did not provide any need or justification for this "textual change". Throughout the decision, its position was that the entire new rule was necessary and precise, explaining that should an individual be prosecuted based on this provision, the ordinary court could still decide whether or not their speech was prohibited.

This decision of the CC fits into the logic of illiberal constitutionalism. The CC, due to its packed nature, did not want to embarrass the legislative power by annulling the new crime of spreading false information. At the same time, however, it also managed to maintain the importance of free speech. By setting a constitutional requirement for the application and interpretation of this crime, it changed the content of the original provision of the Criminal Code. The most probable result, in practice, is the complete opposite of what the law-maker's intention was. There is no visible political intention to overturn this CC ruling. On the other hand, in this decision, when referring to the role of ordinary courts, the CC relativized its role in the constitutional review and, by this, showed an approach that could potentially decrease the level of protection of the individual.

3.3 Serving one master only

In Poland, so far, there seems to be only one master: the PiS-led parliament and Government, who are expected to be constrained by CT decisions delivered upon the petitions submitted by PiS-related public actors, and by the invisible constitution that has also been emerging from the decisions of the CT. The opposition is reluctant to submit motions as, based on how illiberal constitutionalism operates, it expects judgments in favor of the Government.

The first group of cases that we have collected here might lead to the civil and criminal "immunization" of those officials who acted illegally while trying to combat the pandemic.

According to Article 77 (1) of the 1997 Constitution, state organs that illegally cause harm to anyone can be held liable for the damage. This provision is detailed in the Civil Code, which additionally broadens the civil liability and thus make compensation easier for an individual. And yet one of the COVID-19 bills aimed at limiting the liability of decision-makers who were trying to prevent or mitigate the harmful effects of the coronavirus but nevertheless caused damage. The bill was meant to protect Ministers who were organizing the 10 May presidential election and failed to prepare for the challenges the healthcare system had to face, that is, by ineffectively arranging the acquisition of ventilators. As the legislative action failed, the Speaker of the *Sejm* submitted a motion seeking constitutional review of the already binding legal ground (the Civil Code) for the civil liability (K 18/20). A similar case was submitted by a group of MPs too (K 23/20). This motion seeks to assess the Criminal Code provisions on the criminal liability of public officers for certain types of conduct. This provision could be used to charge officials for ineffective fighting of the pandemic and causing danger or damage to certain rights and goods.

If the CT adjudicates accordingly in its usual way within illiberal constitutionalism, the civil liability could be narrower and it would be harder for the affected individuals to enforce this constitutional provision on liability and damages. The captured CT could shift the rules of criminal liability of state officials and put individuals in a worse position than they have been in since 1997, when the Constitution introduced the favourable rules on liability and damages.

The nationwide anti-abortion protest in the autumn of 2020 is also illustrative. First, it shows that the ruling force does not want to engage in dialogue, deliberation and discussion, but, instead, abusively activates a judicial review process to close the disagreement without consideration of divergent opinions within the parliamentary debate. Second, it is connected to the operation of illiberal constitutionalism, and this is why we will review this case below in connection with "pushing the limits".

III Pushing the limits and bouncing back

1 Rules

"Pushing the limits" is a political and legal game, comprising a cynical approach to criticism and the combination of different variations of backing off: (1) taking two steps forward and one step back in advancing the illiberal system; (2) adopting cosmetic changes; (3) reaching the same result from a different angle; (4) planning on wearing down critical voices from various institutions, rendering them unable to keep pace with some major or minor but important and no less questionable changes. As a result, when these institutions have finally been able to reflect on them, many years have already passed and/or political aims been achieved. These techniques are usually used vis-à-vis the supranational and international communities, but the Polish leadership has started to play this game with its own people, too.

The rules of the game were established just after the new administrations took power in 2010 in Hungary and in 2015 in Poland. It was no different in 2020, even though the pandemic opened up new possibilities. In 2020, in the context of "pushing the limits", nothing changed. The deterioration continued to worsen, even if neither Poland nor Hungary has reached the point of taking an authoritarian turn. This is so, even if, at the beginning of the COVID-19 crisis, many, with good reason, worried about that happening.[104] It is precisely this persistence in the "pushing the limits game" that shows the stability of illiberal constitutionalism and signals the weakening influence of the EU and CoE. We have

104 G Halmai and KL Scheppele, *Don't Be Fooled by Autocrats!: Why Hungary's Emergency Violates Rule of Law,* VerfBlog, 2020/4/22, https://verfassungsblog.de/dont-be-fooled-by-autocrats

also observed a paradox: even though the system does not exclude improvement (but makes it quite unlikely), it rather features accelerated deterioration towards authoritarianism, which is, however, slowed down by the "pushing the limits" game. Authorities in both states push down the vector of changes towards authoritarianism. But, because of the game, when Hungary and Poland meet the counterforces originating in the EU, CoE or other international organizations and bodies, or come up against society (nation, people) or even the opposition, they tend to back off. Deterioration is slowed down for a while. And then, in comfortable circumstances, using variations (tools) of the game, the authorities achieve their goals with a clear move towards authoritarianism. However, if the rules of the game were lifted, the deterioration would be smooth, fast and uninterrupted.

Below, we describe variations of the "pushing the limits" game, using examples that exhibit a cynical approach to criticism and combine different variations of backing off. However, to make them clearer for readers, we decided to emphasize the leading pattern of each of the examples in hand.

2 *Techniques*

2.1 *Taking two steps forward and one step back in advancing the illiberal system*

The best Polish example of the strategy of pushing the limits by taking two steps forward and one step back is the case of the presidential election in 2020, during the pandemic. The PiS wanted to hold the election on the original date (8 May 2020) because of the political advantage they hoped they had. For this purpose, they did everything they could in the parliament, as we have explained in the part on illiberal democracy. But when they realized that constitutional changes and legislative reforms were suffering from serious constitutional and democratic flaws, and that it was impossible to hold a vote on the original date, they backed off. Eventually, they postponed the election for two months and adopted rules that were more in harmony (though not completely) with electoral standards.

The case of Białowieża Forest can also be mentioned. This case concerned tree felling in the forest, violating Directive 92/43/EEC of 21 May 1992, on the conservation of natural habitats and of wild fauna and flora, and the Directive 2009/147/EC, on the conservation of wild birds.[105] The violation of EU law may be seen as "business as usual" within the Member States as an honest mistake seems to be hard to avoid. However, in this Polish case, the violation was deliberate, with Poland evoking sovereignty of the state against its European commitments. This way the first step was taken in the push towards authoritarianism. The second step was connected to the CJEU Order of 20 November 2017.[106] The procedure was started on the application of the European Commission on 20 July 2017, which aimed at demonstrating the violation of EU law by Poland. Although the Court adopted interim measures on 27 July 2017, which banned logging in

105 Bień-Kacała, n. 98 (2017) 428–443.
106 C-441/17 R (ECLI:EU:C:2017:877)

the forest,[107] the decision was not respected and the activities continued. In the supplementary application of 13 September 2017, the Commission concluded that the actions that had been banned were still being carried out, which violated the interim measures imposed on 27 July 2017. Regardless, the Polish Government always insisted that the interim measures had been fully respected. All loggers were withdrawn from the Białowieża Forest just before the Court decided on interim measures on 20 November 2017, which is precisely one step back in "the pushing the limits" game. However, by this time, the goals of the forest management had been achieved, so the felling could be stopped. If the intention of the Polish authorities had been to abide by EU law then the actions would already have been stopped in July 2017. Therefore, the November Court decision was respected only formally, as all illegal activities had been accomplished before the decision was delivered. This could also exemplify illiberal legality.

After illustrating the "legal pushing the limits game", we now turn to the arena of politics. The issue of Rule of Law conditionality, that is, Member States showing disrespect for the Rule of Law and thus not having access to EU funds, threatening the EU budget 2021–27, offers an example.

Hungary and Poland rejected the proposed text regarding – and, to be honest, the entire idea of – Rule of Law conditionality. Their illiberal argument was that the Rule of Law is a vague, undeterminable, and mainly political concept, which the EU wants to force on Hungary and Poland because they do not comply with Western ideology, such as opening up Europe to migrants and gender ideology. In the fight against the EU (and in the Hungarian narrative, George Soros) for national self-defence, the sovereignty card was also used, and both states threatened to veto the EU budget and pandemic recovery plan, unless the EU either withdrew Rule of Law conditionality or made it much "lighter". (Since 2018, due to political disagreements, the Rule of Law conditionality rules had already been softened up as compared to the original version.) The result of such action could be that access to EU funds would be denied, due to the obvious Rule of Law violations in Hungary, but not before the next parliamentary election (2022). Being put under the pressure of Rule of Law conditionality, regardless of the softened-up rules, given the apparent willingness of the European Parliament to approve it, and the more outward intention of the EU Commission to embrace and promote the rights of LGBTQIA+ people, resulted in some arrogant counteraction, which, for instance, led to the Ninth Amendment of the FL and other laws. As we explained in the part on human rights, the Hungarian Government made a clearly illiberal statement against, mainly, trans-gender people[108] and those who are single and want to adopt child, and (as it usually does) EU law. And, the new constitutional laws define very restrictively what public money is: the income, expenditure, and pecuniary claims of the state. This makes it harder to get access to public information on spending public money.

107 EU:C:2017:622.

108 The new provision of the FL reads as follows: "the mother is a woman and the father is a man".

2.2 Adopting cosmetic changes

One might recall the controversies surrounding, for example, the Fourth Amendment to the FL, the most prominent Hungarian example of an abusive and, thus, doctrinally speaking, unconstitutional constitutional amendment. However, the case also demonstrates how "the pushing the limits" game works, in its variation "adopting cosmetic changes".

The super-majority of the Hungarian parliament enacted the statute on the right to freedom of conscience and religion and the legal status of churches, denominations, and religious communities in 2011. The content of the Act implemented the FL rules on those matters at that time. The Annex to the Act contained a list of so-called established churches, which meant that the previously adopted method – when the regional courts registered new churches during a non-litigious proceeding – became non-applicable. At that time, it was an unnecessary limitation on the freedom of religion, as previous churches lost their legal status, and only the so-called "established churches" received financial and other privileges. Even though the Constitutional Court, in its decision 6/2013. (III. 1.), declared the rules on the recognition of denominations by the parliament unconstitutional, because the parliament is a political body and not an impartial court that decides individual cases related to fundamental rights, they became part of the Fourth Amendment to the FL. This is not surprising, however, as the constitutional basis of the annulled rules could be found in the Transitory Provisions that were also annulled by the CC in its decision 45/2012 (XII. 29.) and yet found their way into the FL through the aforementioned Fourth Amendment. After concerns had been raised by the Venice Commission,[109] the Government introduced the Fifth Amendment, which again changed the rules, and it brought about some cosmetic changes while basically withdrawing the most criticized rules on the churches and other denominations.[110] In the case *Mennonita v Hungary* (2014), the ECtHR condemned Hungary based on the violation of the freedom of religion of some religious communities that were not established churches listed in the Annex to the Act and had all the privileges. In the wake of the discontent and this ruling, the Ministry of Justice promised to change the Act, but it failed to do so. A comprehensive revision of the Act took place in 2018, when more categories of "churches" and their court registry were introduced; privileges, however, were left intact.

2.3 Reaching the same result from a different angle

As we explained in the part on human rights, the fight against migration and the defence of "Christian Europe" was not only the focal point of populist rhetoric but also appeared in the law. In 2015, Hungary opposed the European Council Decision on the allocation of refugee requests,[111] which resulted in a decision

109 Opinion on the Fourth Amendment, n. 14.
110 Drinóczi, n. 20, 63–98.
111 Council Decision 2015/1601, 2015 O.J. (L 248/80) (EU).

from the CJEU upholding its validity.[112] Thus, the result desired by the Hungarian Government had not been achieved. This failure led the Government to submit its proposal for the Seventh Amendment to the FL (2018). This introduced the notion of constitutional identity, which can be used against any future European legislation the ruling political power dislikes. On the other hand, other aspects of the migration policy, in the light of the initiated infringement procedure, have been corrected, for example regarding the translation of documents. These would exemplify cosmetic changes too.

Both the ECtHR and the CJEU condemned Hungary for its treatment of refugees, for example, for misinterpreting what a safe third country means and that transit zones could mean a deprivation of liberty. The Government first pretended that the ECtHR's 2019 decision favoured it, so that its border defence was not to be criticized, but in 2020 it changed its mind. Claiming that it was implementing what the CJEU wanted, it changed the rules on how asylum requests should be submitted, and relocated the entire process far away from the physical borders of Hungary: in its Embassies. This way, the initial goal, aiming at excluding migrants from Hungarian soil, was achieved from a different angle.

The COVID-19 pandemic meant new possibilities for pushing the limits.[113] It was feared that the Hungarian constitutional state of emergency would not be terminated and that the Government would seize even more power and misuse it. The first Hungarian constitutional emergency was terminated, however, and replaced with a less stringent, statute-based emergency, as a result of which the criticized governmental decrees were withdrawn. With the termination of the constitutional emergency, Hungary backed off a little and then achieved its goal (showing a capable and strong state and successes in the fight against the "enemy", i.e., the coronavirus, to save Hungarians) from a different angle with the implementation of the statute-based emergency. It was again, as explained in the part on illiberal democracy, replaced by a constitutional emergency, due to the growing number of cases in November 2020 – in this case only for 90 days, as opposed to the first emergency, the length of which was at the Government's discretion. Another example of two steps forward (unlimited powers in the first constitutional emergency) and one step back (a time limit for the second constitutional emergency).

2.4 Wearing down critical voices with complex variations

This tactic may be linked to the Polish and Hungarian judicial reforms, as they seem to be a never-ending saga. During this long-lasting clash, all the components of the game were implemented and caused friction between the Member States and the EU. In both countries, many of the components of the heavily criticized reforms were put forward under the guise of advancements, such as the fight against corruption in Poland or addressing social issues in both countries

112 Joined Cases 643/15 & 647/15, *Slovak Republic & Hungary v Council of the European Union*, Judgement of 6 September 2017.

113 Drinóczi and Bień-Kacała, n. 33.

(retirement age), implementing constitutional changes (Hungary), and reforming the structure of the judiciary (Poland). But in reality, they more often than not compromised judicial independence. The political powers generally, and stubbornly, insisted on these reforms until they became a (greater political) liability. This is what happened with the introduction of the highly criticized Hungarian administrative judiciary, which first was postponed then given up. Sometimes a different route is taken to reach the same political goal. For instance, the de facto situation generated by early retirement in Hungary (judges were removed from their positions) did not substantially change after the decision of the CJEU[114] and the subsequent legislation enacted by the Hungarian Government (judges were reinstated to different positions much later). The Polish Government reacted slightly differently to the decision of the CJEU (2018).[115] The response to the interim decision was the urgent adoption of another law on the Supreme Court that partially reversed the effects of the reform as far as the retirement rules were concerned.[116] Nevertheless, it did not affect either the composition or the power of the NCJ. The situation was aggravated in 2020, mainly due to the CJEU's decision on the preliminary ruling question about the independence of the Polish judiciary (2019[117]): 2020 left the SC divided on whether to comply with this decision. The political sphere, quite worryingly, keeps pushing the reform, and in that it received support from the CT.[118]

This is how, in both states, the ruling majorities have achieved desired results. A variety of constant changes, bigger and smaller legislative interventions implemented in an accelerated legislative procedure, regardless of criticism from different institutions, have made it difficult for the institutions to keep pace with the changes. Moreover, Hungary and Poland keep the saga going, and as a result, when these institutions are finally able to reflect on the changes, many years have already passed and/or the political aims have been achieved.

2.5 Pushing the limits with society

In Poland, the game showed a new face at the end of 2020, which involved Polish society (the nation). In the game, the "backing off" step is taken only for a period of time, and after that steps surging forward are taken to provide a result that is in accordance with the political agenda of the ruling majority – in the case in question, tightening up the abortion law. As explained in the part on human rights, the October 2020 decision of the CT had a history going back to the endeavours to

114 Case C-286/12 *European Commission v Hungary*, ECLI:EU:C:2012:687.

115 Case C-619/18 *European Commission v Poland*, ECLI:EU:C:2019:531.

116 Decision of the Vice-President of the CJEU of 19 October 2018.

117 Joined Cases C-585/18, C-624/18 and C-625/18, ECLI:EU:C:2019:982.

118 A Bień-Kacała, "Polexit is Coming or is it Already Here? Comments on the Judicial Independence Decisions of the Polish Constitutional Tribunal", *Int'l J. Const. L. Blog*, 28 April 2020, at www.iconnectblog.com/2020/04/polexit-is-coming-or-is-it-already-here-comments-on-the-judicial-independence-decisions-of-the-polish-constitutional-tribunal

reform abortion rules according to a more pro-life agenda. As we have seen, it also involved the unwillingness of PiS politicians to openly discuss the arguments of pro-choice and pro-life advocates, and an abusively initiated CT decision, which triggered emotions. It seems that the ruling power did not expect such a strong reaction from women supported by men, nor non-partisan opposition being voiced loudly on the streets around Poland and outside of the country. As a result, the judgement was not published until the end of 2020, and the ruling majority expressed its willingness to publish it later along with new legislation on abortion. This legislative procedure was initiated by the President, who is a PiS-affiliated politician, and aims at a more liberal approach than that offered by the CT, but one that is stricter than the law that was in effect (that was affected by the decision of the CT in October 2020). Consequently, we might say that, by the end of 2020, the PiS backed off a little bit. In January 2021, however, they published the CT decision-making the strict rules on abortion applicable but have not adopted the proposed law yet (submitted by the President). The new law on abortion could still be more liberal than the CT decision – but it depends on the ongoing parliamentary process. This solution can calm the protesters to some extent, who would have to be happy with a lesser, and more uncertain, evil, and satisfy the liberalizing voices within the PiS electorate.

IV Defeating exit strategies from the hollowed-out constitutional democracy

The last way in which it seems that illiberal constitutionalism is stable, is that there does not seem to be any room for any meaningful escape strategies allowing a return to constitutional democracy. The inapplicability of these strategies has gradually revealed itself with the passing of time and the consolidation of illiberal constitutionalism. It also means that a retransformation is, unfortunately, highly doubtful, requiring something new – a technique that is outside of the box.

1 Militant democracy

The militant democracy doctrine claims that liberal democracy should maintain efficient measures to defend itself.[119] It has been connected to statutory or constitutional provisions limiting certain dangerous thoughts and extreme political parties; but it has also been acknowledged that militant democracy should respect human rights[120] and should assume that actions are taken *bona*

119 See e.g. JW Müller,, "Militant Democracy" in M Rosenfeld and A Sajó (eds), *The Oxford Handbook of Comparative Constitutional Law* (Oxford University Press, 2011) 1253–1268; A Sajó, "Militant Democracy and Emotional Politics", *Constellations* 4 (2012) 562–572; A Bień-Kacała and A Jackiewicz, "Militant Democracy. Demokracja, która sama się broni(?)" ["Militant Democracy. A Democracy that Defends Itself(?)"], *Państwo i Prawo* 8 (2017) 25–41.

120 P Macklem, "Militant Democracy, Legal Pluralism, and the Paradox of Self-determination", *I-CON* 3 (2006) 494–495.

fide when using preventive legal measures.[121] Otherwise, it can easily become an illiberal system.[122]

Nevertheless, militant democracy measures are viewed as ineffective when an extremist party is allowed to emerge in the political system.[123] On the other hand, it is challenging to find the proper balance between the rights to free speech, to association and the free formation of political parties, which articulate the will of the people, and the need for constitutional self-protection. This phenomenon brings us to the dilemma that presents itself as a paradox: if the doctrine of militant democracy, because it still affords more importance to civil and political human rights, or because the destructive intention of the party was not as visible as it has later become, could not prevent the emergence of illiberal democracy, how could the same doctrine help to defeat it? As pointed out earlier, the doctrine of militant democracy has its own in-built weaknesses in the illiberal constitutionalism. Measures such as the dissolution of extreme political parties are to be initiated and implemented by state authorities that are, to various extents, corrupted by the illiberal state. What the word "extreme" means, against which the constitutional order is to be protected, and how to interpret this constitutional order, is determined by those who have built the illiberal state, or by those who serve it. As in the illiberal constitutional setting, constitutionalism is captured, an "abusive neo-militant democracy" has emerged. Gradually, it has been taking measures for consolidating illiberal constitutionalism by handling emergencies and controlling existing and imaginary extremism. These measures go far beyond the extent a substantive constitutional democracy would use them, and it has another goal: to maintain illiberal constitutionalism.

In such circumstances, only huge and nationwide political discontent or civil disobedience may bring about change. In Poland and Hungary, however, we have not been experiencing any will to revolt. It seems that the people of Poland and Hungary are either unable or unwilling to form strong and capable civil societies, or to raise their voices against extreme views or resist aggressive political campaigns based on unfounded but popular fears for the necessary period of time.[124]

121 Sajó, n. 119, 562.

122 *Guidelines on Prohibition and Dissolution of Political Parties and Analogous Measures*, Adopted by the Venice Commission at its 41st plenary session (Venice 10–11 December 2000), at www.venice.coe.int/webforms/documents/default.aspx?pdffile=CDL-INF (2000)001-e.

123 See the case of neo-Nazi NPD, the judgment BVerfGG 17 January 2017 r (2 BvB 1/13), at www.bundesverfassungsgericht.de/SharedDocs/Pressemitteilungen/DE/2017/bvg17-004.html;jsessionid=D73C0CAD3CA98F447B2A371B748739D6.2_cid393

124 TT Koncewicz, "Constitutional Fidelity and the Polish Constitution", *Blog of the International Journal of Constitutional Law*, 11 August 2017, at www.iconnectblog.com/2017/08/constitutional-fidelity-and-the-polish-constitution. As for Hungary, see the billboard campaign on migrants and about G Soros in 2018, and the national consultation on immigration and terrorism (www.kormany.hu/download/9/a3/50000/Nemzetikonzultacio_mmkornel.docx) and the Soros Plan (to relocate migrants from Africa and the Middle East), https://bbj.hu/politics/hungarian-govt-begins-all-out-assault-on-soros_139438.

And the legal and political environments that have been created in both states do not help civil society and the public raise their voices.[125]

2 The multi-tiered amendment designs and references to transnational norms

Rosalind Dixon and David Landau propose that constitutional designers should utilize multi-tiered amendment procedures. The tiered mechanism for constitutional amendment "aims to combine the virtues of rigidity and flexibility by creating different rules of constitutional amendment for different parts of the constitution", preserve "the core of the constitution against destabilizing and antidemocratic forms of change", and "help to build a constitutional identity".[126]

In Hungary this design is not applied, since the written constitutions have always been easily amendable, provided the ruling power has enjoyed a constitutional majority. The Hungarian constitutional system has never explicitly acknowledged any eternity clauses, nor allowed the people to express their opinion on constitutional amendments via referendums. This approach to constitutional design was not even considered, and the original attitude towards a flexible constitution was not changed when the FL was adopted in 2011. Poland, however, employs more demanding procedural rules on constitutional amendments, though they are still less demanding than those of other states utilizing multi-tiered amendment procedures. A referendum on constitutional amendments is optional.[127] It is questionable whether an even more demanding tiered constitutional regime could have preserved Polish democracy and the identity of the 1997 Constitution,[128] as it has been changed through informal methods, which a formal multi-tier system, most probably, could not have avoided.

Rosalind Dixon and David Landau also propose another solution. According to them, courts should evaluate the constitutionality of constitutional changes against the standard of transnational norms in democratic constitutions.[129] If, however, the courts are packed or paralysed or corrupt, it is highly doubtful that the otherwise loyal judges would take advantage of any transnational rules as compared to the textual interpretation of the FL in Hungary or the complete neglect thereof in Poland.[130] For instance, some Hungarian judges of the CC do not even respect the rulings of the ECtHR. András Zs Varga, in his quite unfounded dissenting opinion, claims that although Hungary is obliged to

125 See, e.g., the Seventh Amendment to the Fundamental Law and the "Stop Soros" law.

126 Dixon and Landau, n. 5, 1, 63.

127 It is called when the republic, fundamental rights, and the rules on constitutional amendment are to be amended, if it is initiated by those entitled to submit constitutional amendments: Art 235.

128 As understood by T Drinóczi in "Constitutional Identity in Europe: The Identity of the Constitution: A Regional Approach", *German Law Journal* 21(2) (2020) 105–130.

129 R Dixon and D Landau, "Transnational Constitutionalism and a Limited Doctrine of Unconstitutional Constitutional Amendments", *ICON* 3 (2015) 606, 629.

130 On the other hand, the situation is not similar to that of Russia, where, since 2015, the constitutional court can overrule the decisions of the ECtHR.

execute ECtHR decisions, it is not forced to abandon its constitutional identity while doing so. Therefore, for him, the decision of the CC on the freedom of religion,[131] in which the CC directly applied one of the rulings of the ECtHR,[132] is erroneous.[133]

3 Application of the doctrine of unconstitutional constitutional amendments – and a paradox

Constitutional courts may use[134] the doctrine of unconstitutional constitutional amendments.[135] For the prevention of an illiberal or undemocratic transformation, an independent and active constitutional court is needed that is flexible and open enough to change the constitution, even informally, with a view to implementing it properly. This happened, for example, in India and Colombia. Moreover, as has already been established, both Poland and Hungary face illiberal judicialization of politics: both the CT and the CC are more the servants of the political will than independent institutions of constitutional protection. We do not expect that the CT will consider the doctrine of unconstitutional constitutional amendments. And the CT will not annul obviously unconstitutional legislation, as it has not done so before. The CC, on the other hand, opened up the Hungarian constitutional system to review of unconstitutional amendments in its decision 22/2016 (XII.5) on the constitutional identity of Hungary. Considering the possible future applicability of the unconstitutional constructional amendment doctrine in order to prevent the alteration of the identity of Hungary, the doctrine, as explained above, may serve as a double-edged sword. Not contesting at all the importance of this kind of review, which is necessary if constitutionality is to be maintained, when a constitution itself is not in line with certain international and supranational standards, even though it is bound by them, the non-standard provisions may be preserved by the constitutional courts.

131 23/2015 (VII.7) CC decision.

132 Case of *Magyar Keresztény Mennonita Egyház and Others v Hungary*, judgment 8 April 2014.

133 He considered the regulation of the FL, which differentiates between religious communities and established churches (being religious communities cooperating with the state in order to achieve goals of the community), to be a peculiarity of Hungary's constitutional history and an essential component of its constitutional identity. In his view, constitutional identity is derived from otherwise unspecified historical facts that are recognized by the FL. He listed the conditions, set by the Church Law, by which a religious community may become an established church under the heading of "constitutional identity". In his opinion, the CC had ignored the distinction between "religious community" and "established church" included in Art VII of the FL, since this CC ruling, based on the ECtHR decision, classified these criteria as conflicting with international treaties.

134 D Landau, "Abusive Constitutionalism", *UC Davis Law Review* 3 (2013).

135 Roznai, n. 61.

4 *Empowering citizens*

Overcoming the illiberal challenge would require educated and reasonable citizens. It is, however, quite a big ask, given the underfinanced education policies that Hungary and Poland pursue. Hungary has started to develop a nationalistic education and research agenda, instead of putting emphasis on liberal values and spending more public money on education. That is why developing a democratic culture that accommodates liberal values, as Gábor Halmai and others suggest,[136] appears to be a utopian ideal in a system that has already turned to illiberal constitutionalism. Advocates of a substantive constitutional democracy seem to be left with the hope that civil society might organize itself to promote and safeguard the values of liberal democracy, but it will have to do so in a legal and political environment that is far from friendly.[137] As explained in Part III on Identity, Hungary and Poland feature "top-down" societies rather than "bottom-up" communities.[138] Therefore, even the potential for civic disagreement with populist politics is highly doubtful.

5 *Emergency judicial power*

There is a more country-specific alternative, which emerged in Poland, especially in 2016 and 2017. It proposed that ordinary courts should take over the competence of constitutional review from the then paralysed CT.[139] The advocates of such an emergency judicial power correctly contend that the primary constitutional values are the supremacy of the Constitution and the separation of powers. If the CT is disabled, the ordinary courts should take over constitutional review (without, however, the power to repeal laws).[140] It is proposed that this be called "emergency judicial review".[141]

136 G Halmai, "The Decline of Liberal Democracy in Europe's Midst", at www.eurozine.com/the-decline-of-liberal-democracy-in-europes-midst/; FN Fesnic, "Can Civic Education Make a Difference for Democracy? Hungary and Poland Compared", *Political Studies* 4 (2016) 966–978.

137 See the case of the CEU and "Stop Soros" law. In Poland, for now, centralization of NGOs' financing processes has been implemented.

138 As we said in Part III on Identity, the preferred value is hierarchy instead of equality, especially in Polish society. See also A Bień-Kacała, "Równość czy hierarchiczność? Kilka słów o wartościach w państwie, prawie i społeczeństwie" ["Equality or Hierarchy? A Few Words About Values of State, Law and Society"], *Gdańskie Studia Prawnicze* 40 (2018) 17–30.

139 R Balicki, "Bezpośrednie stosowanie konstytucji" ["Direct Application of a Constitution"], *Krajowa Rada Sądownictwa* 4 (2016) 13–19; P Kardas and M Gutowski, "Konstytucja z 1997 r. a model kontroli konstytucyjności prawa" ["1997 Constitution and a Model of Constitutional Review"], *Palestra* 4 (2017) 11–30.

140 L Garlicki, "Sądy a Konstytucja Rzeczypospolitej Polskiej" [Courts and the Constitution of the Republic of Poland"], *Przegląd Sądowy* 7-8 (2016) 23–25; L Garlicki and ZA Garlicka, "External Review of Constitutional Amendments? International Law as a Norm of Reference", *Israel Law Review* 44 (2011) 343–368.

141 The statement of the CT's President Andrzej Rzepliński and unpublished judgment of 9 March 2016, K 47/15. TT Koncewicz, "On the Strategic Reading of the Constitutional Document. Mapping out Frontiers of New Constitutional Research", *Przegląd Konstytucyjny* 2 (2018) 16–45.

It is undeniable that, at the start of illiberal remodelling, constitutional democracy should and may be restored, but it is not clear whether it can be done by unconstitutional measures. The paradox here seems to be similar to that of the efficient use of militant democracy. Without a proper legal basis (regarding the competence of the courts to assess constitutionality and to set aside unconstitutional legislation), this is unconstitutional, as it affects the Rule of Law and several of its components, such as legal certainty (what the law is if a court sets aside those laws it considers unconstitutional), the transparency of the legal system and state authorities, and predictability in the functioning of state organs. Nevertheless, in a captured constitutional setting, in which the courts and the independent judiciary have already been compromised, the taking over of constitutional review by the courts may most probably be ineffective.

The advocates of emergency judicial review should try to find an answer to the question of whether "good will" aimed at overcoming unconstitutionality can make desperate measures constitutional, whether it serves the best chance of retransformation, and how it can be justified. As the CC stated in 1991 regarding the legal assessment of the transition, the Rule of Law cannot be built against the Rule of Law. In the case of emergency (danger threatening the life of the nation), state organs usually are empowered, by more or less detailed constitutional or other statutory rules, to use emergency powers. As said, that does not seem to be the case here. Moreover, once the idea of emergency judicial review is accepted, if justified and applied for restoring liberal constitutionalism, it could also potentially and legitimately be used by the already captured courts to prevent the same retransformation and to disregard laws still in line with liberal values. What could be proposed, maybe, is rather the personal empowerment and commitment of ordinary judges towards the application of EU law and international human rights law, which are both, in a stronger or weaker form, part of the Polish and Hungarian legal systems. In this way, the further rotting of the legal systems could be slowed down "from the bottom". As time has proved, this is instead what has been happening in Poland.

6 Other …

Different solutions are offered in the scholarly literature. Menocal et al., when studying Latin American and African countries, hold that potential authoritarian top-down control should be replaced by effective checks and balances and accountability to citizens.[142] In illiberal constitutionalism, however, everything is formally legal (illiberal legality): there is an established and, to a certain extent, functioning mechanism of checks and balances, which may be effective in cases of no importance to the political decision-maker. We, however, need to realize that checks and balances can only be effective to the extent that they actually shape the legal landscape so long as the political decision-maker complies. The same applies

142 AR Menocal, et al., "Hybrid Regimes and the Challenge of Deepening and Sustaining Democracy in Developing Countries", *S. Afr. J. Int'L Aff.* 15(29) (2008) 35.

to accountability and mandatory voting, which are suggested by Pap and Śledzińska-Simon.[143] Without substantive rules, which are to be adopted by those who would be subject to them, and compliance, this scheme does not seem to be feasible. According to Diamond, economic development, globalization, and the information revolution may undermine all forms of authority and empower the citizens.[144] Instead, in illiberal constitutionalism, the economy is also captured by members of the ruling party, and, because of neo-patrimonialism, an overturn is hardly imaginable. Therefore, economic development for "the others" seems to be a mere illusion. Populist nationalism as a whole is against economic globalization, tending to employ a protectionist economic policy to strengthen national companies, that is, the clientura. The information revolution may be the sole hope, but economic measures may also be applied to it, and information technology may be used for spreading populist-nationalist ideas. Any retransformation would also require educated citizens. This is, however, as mentioned, quite a big challenge.

143 AL Pap and A Śledzińska-Simon, "Mandatory Voting as a Tool to Combat the 'New Populism'", *I-CONnect Blog* (19 April, 2017), iconnectblog.com/2017/04/mandatory-voting-and-the-new-populism/
144 Diamond, n. 68, 153.

VII Conclusions

We started to write this book with the ambition of offering a comprehensive and theoretically substantiated account of the illiberal constitutionalism that has emerged and disturbingly developed in Hungary and Poland. In the Introduction, we set out our goals and reasons, along with the main content of this book. We made our case in five Parts as to the emergence and concept of illiberal constitutionalism; its underlying constitutional identity; its unique nature, which distinguishes it from modern authoritarianism; and its components, that is, illiberal legality, illiberal democracy, and illiberalization of human rights. All of these brought us to realize the stability of the system, which, besides the constraint on public power, we appreciate as one of the main elements of constitutionalism.

Now, we conclude with the following five points. These are not summaries of the Parts; instead, they convey the messages we have found it important to share and grasp, and which form the very essence of our book and thoughts about Hungarian and Polish illiberal constitutionalism.

1 Constitutionalism does not necessarily have to be liberal

There seems to be a dichotomy in the scholarly literature, which is heavily influenced by the answer to the question of whether constitutionalism is intrinsically liberal or not. We have found that there are powerful arguments on both sides, but the constitutional changes in Hungary and Poland since 2010 and 2015, respectively, led us to give more weight to the disentanglement of liberalism and constitutionalism. We propose that "constitutionalism" could be seen as less of an ideology and more of a constitutional design that could accommodate a variety of political moralities, philosophies or practices, especially in those states in which liberal constitutionalism has already been present as a political ideology and a constitutional design.

This brings us to the second point:

2 Illiberal constitutionalism is a deterioration from liberal constitutionalism towards authoritarianism but has not reached that point yet

Hungary and Poland stand out among the states in democratic decay and are noticeably different from existing (modern) authoritarian regimes. Their deterioration has

DOI: 10.4324/9781003175353-7

not, either quantitatively or qualitatively, reached the state of "authoritarianism". This, however, does not mean that no increasingly authoritarian tendencies can be observed in both countries. Hungary and Poland are still members of the EU, which, notwithstanding its failures, imposes a particular, albeit rather weak, internal constraint on the political leaderships of both countries. This existing internal constraint proves that they are still constitutionalist systems. At the same time, the deterioration of democracy, misuse of human rights, and abuse of the Rule of Law allow us to modify the Hungarian and Polish constitutionalism by adding the adjective "illiberal". Thus, there is a changed vector of development as regards both ideology and constitutional design (distancing from the original idea of liberal constitutionalism that was introduced at the beginning of the 1990s).

This brings us to the third point:

3 In an illiberal constitutional identity, the liberal and non-liberal or illiberal value orientation of the population can intermittently prevail

Hungarians and Poles have unstable constitutional identities, which may become more visible at certain historical moments, and which are prone to be combined with a desire for a charismatic leader, without, however, demanding coherence in ideology or moral philosophy. Collective victimhood, collective narcissism, and illiberal values of a given society, especially when heavily relied on and triggered by a right-wing populist autocratic leader, contribute to the formation of illiberal constitutionalism and prevent reversion of the system. The combination of all the above does not seem to be friendly to liberal constitutionalism, although it does not necessarily reject it, and could be viewed as one of the determining factors in the success of populist politics and the illiberal constitutional remodelling.

This brings us to the fourth point:

4 Illiberal constitutionalism is a coherent theory in its illiberal and weakly constrained manner

Illiberal constitutionalism, as opposed to the views of some who regard it as an oxymoron, is a coherent concept mainly because we take a less ideologically driven perspective on the term "constitutionalism".

The term "illiberal constitutionalism" indicates a process of deterioration that has not resulted (yet) in an autocracy or modern authoritarianism because there is still a weak internal constraint on public power (illiberalization of constitutionalism). Beyond this characteristic, it, as a concept, refers to a retained constitutionalist structure (as a result of the process and the existing constraints) and the combination of an unbalanced constitutional identity and a charismatic leader.

Thus, in illiberal constitutionalism, constitutional democracy, which we see as an embodiment of (liberal) constitutionalism and democracy, still exists, but its formal implementation outweighs its substantive realization. This formalized version of constitutional democracy compromises its constitutive elements. Thus, illiberal legality, illiberal democracy, and the phenomenon of the illiberalization of human rights protection emerge. In these, to a greater or weaker extent, we find some constraints on the public power in so far as they feature in the locked-in nature of EU law and international human rights commitments. Illiberal constitutionalism relies heavily on the Hungarian and Polish identities that have been moulded in such a way that they are prone to accept and support illiberal (non-liberal) visions and ideas, which makes the maintenance of liberal constitutionalism more difficult – though not impossible. They also enable the regime to defend and maintain its constitutive elements, as these are not contrary to the unbalanced constitutional identity of Hungarians and Poles.

Unless the "other side" of the unbalanced constitutional identity is successfully relied on and triggered, the established illiberal constitutionalism claims stability, which could make us only hope for the best ...

Finally, the last point:

5 Lessons learned, mostly, for others ...

What the Hungarian and Polish examples and, mostly, the lack of success of the exit strategies teach us, is that constitutional democracies that still retain their substantive status, states taking the first steps towards their democratic decay, or EU Member States on their first steps towards illiberal constitutionalism, still have choices and possibilities. They just have to heed the warning signs and strengthen their own defence mechanisms, whether that be a reinforcement of their constitutional design or raising awareness, especially among children and youth, about the values of respect, autonomy, liberty, freedom, responsibility, dignity and diversity; and they must meaningfully involve all who are affected in the decision-making processes. Finally, they have to take good care of what they have, also in the light of what the future might bring. This is especially true for the EU, the future actions of which will show whether the whole is indeed greater than its parts or, instead, that the chain is simply no stronger than its weakest link.

Bibliography

Part I

Acunha, FJG and Benvindo, JZ, "Democratic Decay in Brazil and the New Global Populism", INT'L ASS'N CONST. L. BLOG (6 June2017), https://blog-iaclaidc.org/test-3/2018/5/26/democratic-decay-in-brazil-and-the-new-global-populism.

Bozóki, A and Hegedűs, D, "An Externally Constrained Hybrid Regime: Hungary in the European Union", *Democratization* 25 (1173) (2018).

Daly, TG, "Diagnosing Democratic Decay", Conference paper, Comparative Constitutional Law Round-table, Gilbert and Tobin Centre for Public Law, UNSW Law School (7 August 2017), www.academia.edu/34052302/Diagnosing_Democratic_Decay.

Daly, TG, "Democratic Decay: Conceptualising an Emerging Research Field" (2019), https://link.springer.com/article/10.1007/s40803-019-00086-2.

Drinóczi, T and Bień-Kacała, A (eds), *Rule of Law, Common Values and Illiberal Constitutionalism. Poland and Hungary within the European Union* (Routledge, 2020).

Eichhorn, J, Kupsch, V, and Mohr, LMM, "How European Publics and Policy Actors Values an Open Society: Key Insight Across Countries" (Open Society European Policy Institute2019), http://voicesonvalues.dpart.org/images/finalreports/OSI-019-18-Key-Insights_v5.pdf.

Frantz, E and Kendall-Taylor, A, "The Evolution of Autocracy: Why Authoritarianism is Becoming More Formidable" *Survival: Global Politics and Strategy* 59 (2017) 57.

Fülöp, É, Csertő, I, Ilg, B, Szabó, Z, Slugoski, B, and László, J, "Emotional Elaboration of Collective Traumas in Historical Narratives" (2014) http://real.mtak.hu/20201/3/emotional_elaboration_of_collective_traumas.pdf.

Ginsburg, T and Huq, AZ, *How to Save Constitutional Democracy?* (University of Chicago Press, 2018).

Granat, M and Granat, K, *The Constitution of Poland: A Contextual Analysis* (Hart Publishing, 2019) 32–33.

Hajdu, T, "A magyar identitás szabadságharcos – interjú Szabó Zsolttal, az ELTE Szociálpszichológia tanszékének adjunktusával", Mindset Pszichologia (18 November 2017), http://mindset.co.hu/a-magyar-identitas-szabadsagharcos-interju-szabo-zsolttal-az-elte-szocialpszichologia-tanszekenek-adjunktusaval/.

Hanley, S, "Understanding the Illiberal Turn: Democratic Backsliding in the Czech Republic", www.tandfonline.com/doi/full/10.1080/21599165.2018.1493457.

Humphrey, T, "Democracy and the Rule of Law: Founding Liberal Democracy in Post-Communist Europe", *Colum. J. E. Eur. L.* 2 (2008) 94, 124.

Huq, AZ and Ginsburg, T, "How to Lose a Constitutional Democracy" *UCLA Law Review65* (2018) 95.

Jacobsohn, GJ and Roznai, Y *Constitutional Revolution* (Yale University Press, 2020).

Kurunmäki, J and Marjanen, J "Isms, Ideologies and Setting the Agenda for Public Debate", *Journal of Political Ideologies* 23(3) (2018) 256–282.

László, J, "Narratív pszichológia", *Pszichológia* 28 (2008), http://real.mtak.hu/2385/1/49413_ZJ1.pdf.

Lijphart, A, *Patterns of Democracy – Government Forms and Performance in Thirty-Six Countries* (Yale University Press, 2012) 192.

Lührmann A and Lindberg SI, "A Third Wave of Autocratization is Here: What is New about It?" *Democratization* 7 (2019) 1099.

Müller, J-W, *What is Populism?* (University of Pennsylvania Press, 2016) 16.

Murray, M, "Narrative Psychology and Narrative Analysis" in P.M. Camic, J.E. Rhodes, and L. Yardley (eds), *Qualitative Research in Psychology: Expanding Perspectives in Methodology and Design* (2003), 95⊠112. American Psychological Association. https://doi.org/10.1037/10595-006.

Pinheiro, VM, Ilarraz, M, and Mestriner, MT, "The Impacts of the COVID-19 Crisis on the Brazilian Legal System – A Report on the Functioning of the Branches of the Government and on the Legal Scrutiny of Their Activities", *The Theory and Practice of Legislation*, 8:1–2, 193–212.

Popp-Baier, U, "Narrative Psychology", in ALC Runehov and L Oviedo (eds), *Encyclopedia of Sciences and Religions* (Springer, 2013).

Sadłoń, W, "Differentiation, Polarization and Religious Change in Poland at the Turn of 20th and 21st century", *Przegląd Religioznawczy –The Religious Studies Review* 4(262) (2016) 33–35.

Sadurski, W, "How Democracy Dies (in Poland): A Case Study of Anti-Constitutional Populist Backsliding", *Sydney Law School Legal Studies Research Paper No 18/01* (2018) 4–8.

Sadurski, W, *Poland's Constitutional Breakdown* (Oxford University Press, 2019) 3–5.

Sadurski, W, "Constitutional Democracy in the Time of Elected Authoritarians", *International Journal of Constitutional Law* 2(331) (2020) 324–333.

Schwartz, SH and Bardi, A, "Influences of Adaptation to Communist Rule On Value Priorities in Eastern Europe", *Political Psychology* 2 (1997) 407–408.

Tushnet, M, "The Possibility of Illiberal Constitutionalism?", *Florida Law Review*, 69 (2017) 1367–1384.

Versteeg, M and Ginsburg, T, "Measuring the Rule of Law: A Comparison of Indicators", *Law and Social Inquiry* 1 (2017) 101.

Walker, G, "The Idea of Nonliberal Constitutionalism", *Ethnicity and Group Rights* 39 (1997).

Part II

Alviar, H and Frankenberg, G (eds), *Authoritarian Constitutionalism* (Edward Elgar, 2019).

Bellamy, R, "Constitutionalism", www.britannica.com/topic/constitutionalism.

Bernatt, M and Ziółkowski, M, "Statutory Anti-Constitutionalism", *Wash. Int'l L.J.* 28 (487) (2019) 505–516.

Blokker, P, *New Democracies in Crisis?* (Routledge, 2015).

Blokker, P, "Populist Constitutionalism", *VerfBlog* (4 May 2017), https://verfassungsblog.de/populist-constitutionalism/.

Blokker, P, "Populist Constitutionalism, Popular Engagement, and Constitutional Resistance", https://reconnect-europe.eu/blog/blokker-populist-constitutionalism/, 7 February 2019. Bogaards, M, "De-democratization in Hungary: Diffusely Defective Democracy", *Democratization* 8 (2018) 1491.

Bozóki, A and Hegedűs, D, "An Externally Constrained Hybrid Regime: Hungary in the European Union", *Democratization* 25(1173) (2018) 1175.

Brownlee, J, "Authoritarianism after 1989", *Harvard International Review*, 4(2010).

Bugarić, B, "A Crisis of Constitutional Democracy in Post-Communist Europe: 'Lands In-Between' Democracy and Authoritarianism", *Int'l J. Const. L.* 13(219) (2015).

Buzogány, A and Varga, M, "The Ideational Foundations of the Illiberal Backlash in Central and Eastern Europe: The Case of Hungary", *Review of International Political Economy* 25 (6) (2018) 811–828.

Castillo-Ortiz, Paolo, "The Illiberal Abuse of Constitutional Courts in Europe", *European Constitutional Law Review* 15(1) (2019) 48–72.

Chan, C, "Thirty Years from Tiananmen: China, Hong Kong, and the Ongoing Experiment to Preserve Liberal Values in an Authoritarian State", *International Journal of Constitutional Law* 17(2) (2019) 443.

Cheung, A, "'For My Enemies, the Law': Abusive Legalism", *Candidacy paper, JSD Program, NYU School of Law*, 15 January 2018.

Corrales, J, "The Authoritarian Resurgence: Autocratic Legalism in Venezuela", *Journal of Democracy* 26 (2015) 38–43.

Csaba, L, "Unorthodoxy in Hungary: An Illiberal Success Story?", *Post Communist economies*, DOI: 10.1080/14631377.2019.1641949.

Csaky, ZS, *Nations in Transition: Dropping the Democratic Façade* (Freedom House, 2020), https://freedomhouse.org/report/nations-transit/2020/dropping-democratic-facade#Facade.

Csink, L, "Rule of Law in Hungary. What Can Law and Politics Do?" in T Drinóczi and A Bień-Kacała (eds), *Rule of Law, Common Values and Illiberal Constitutionalism. Poland and Hungary within the European Union* (Routledge, 2021).

Diamond, L, "Facing Up to the Democratic Recession", *J. Democracy* 26(142) (2015).

Dixon, R and Landau, D *Abusive Constitutional Borrowing: Legal Globalization and the Subversion of Liberal Democracy* (Oxford University Press, 2021).

Drinóczi, T, "Constitutional Politics in Contemporary Hungary", *Vienna Journal on International Constitutional Law* 1 (2016) 63–98.

Elster, J, "Constitutionalism in Eastern Europe: An Introduction", *The University of Chicago Law Review* 58(2) (1991) 447–482.

Fabry, A, *The Political Economy of Hungary: From State Capitalism to Authoritarian Neoliberalism* (Springer, 2019).

Farinacci-Fernós, JM, "Post-Liberal Constitutionalism", *Tulsa L. Rev.* 54(1) (2018).

Fraenkel, E, *The Dual State: A Contribution to the Theory of Dictatorship* (Oxford University Press, 1941) 3–7.

Frankenberg, G, "Authoritarian Constitutionalism: Coming to Terms with Modernity's Nightmares" in H Alviar and G Frankenberg (eds), *Authoritarian Constitutionalism* (Edward Elgar, 2019) 18–24, 36.

Frantz, E and Kendall-Taylor, A, "The Evolution of Autocracy: Why Authoritarianism is Becoming More Formidable?", *Survival: Global Politics and Strategy* 59 (2017) 57.

Frohnen, BP, "Is Constitutionalism Liberal?", *Campbell L. Rev.* 33(529) (2011).

Gardbaum, S, "The Case for the New Commonwealth Model of Constitutionalism", *German L.J.* 14(2229) (2013).

Gingsburg, T and Huq, AZ, *How to Save Constitutional Democracy?* (University of Chicago Press, 2018).

Gyulai, A, "Reality Free of Ideology. Viktor Orbán's Realism and Illiberalism", https://ecpr.eu/Events/Event/PaperDetails/41864.

Halmai, G, "Populism, Authoritarianism, and Constitutionalism", *German Law Journal* 20 (2019).

Halmai, G, "The Making of 'Illiberal Constitutionalism' with or without a New Constitution: The Case of Hungary and Poland", in D Landau and H Lerner (eds), *Comparative Constitution Making* (Edward Elgar, 2019).

Halmai, G, "Illiberalism in East-Central Europe", *EUI Department of Law Research Paper No. 2019/05.*

Henkin, L, "Constitutionalism, Democracy and Foreign Affairs", *Indiana Law Journal* 4 (1992) 885, 886.

Howse, R, "Populism and its Enemies", *Workshop on Public Law and the New Populism*, Jean Monnet Center, NYU Law School, 15–16 September 2017.

Ip, EC, *Hybrid Constitutionalism: The Politics of Constitutional Review in the Chinese Special Administrative Region* (Cambridge University Press, 2019).

Keane, J, *New Despotism* (Harvard University Press, 2020).

Kochenov, D and Jakab, A (eds), *The Enforcement of EU Law and Values* (Oxford University Press, 2017).

Körösényi, A, Illés, G, and Gyulai, A, *The Orbán Regime: Plebiscitary Leader Democracy in the Making* (Routledge, 2020).

Landau, D, "Abusive Constitutionalism", *U.C. Davis L. Rev.* 47(189) (2013).

Landau, D, "Populist Constitutions", *The University of Chicago Law Review* 85 (2018) 521.

Law, DS, "Alternatives to Liberal Constitutional Democracy", *Md. L. Rev.* 77(223) (2017).

Levitsky, S and Way, LA, "The Rise of Competitive Authoritarianism", *Journal of Democracy* 2 (2002).

Levitsky, S and Way, LA, "The Myth of Democratic Recession", *Democracy* 26(45) (2015) 48.

Ludwikowski, R, "Supreme Law or Basic Law? The Decline of the Concept of Constitutional Supremacy", *Cardozo Journal of International & Comparative Law* 9 (2001) 253–296.

Lührmann, A and Lindberg, SI, "A Third Wave of Autocratization is Here: What is New About It?" *Democratization* 7 (2019) 1097, 1098.

Magyar, B, *Post-Communist Mafia State: The Case of Hungary* (CEU Press, 2016).

Merkel, W, Puhle, H-J, Croissant, A, and Thierry, P, *Defekte Demokratie: Band 1; Merkel et al., Defekte Demokratie: Band 2* (Verlag, 2006)

Mészáros, G, "Carl Schmitt in Hungary: Constitutional Crisis in the Shadow of Covid-19", MTA LWP 2020/17, https://jog.tk.mta.hu/mtalwp/carl-schmitt-in-hungary-constitutional-crisis-in-the-shadow-of-covid-19.

Mudde, C and Rovira Kaltwasser, C, *Populism: A Very Short Introduction* (Oxford University Press, 2017) 34.

Müller, J-W, "Populism and Constitutionalism" in C Rovira Kaltwasser, P Taggart, P Ochoa Espejo, and P Ostiguy (eds), *The Oxford Handbook on Populism* (Oxford University Press, 2017).

Müller, J-W, "The Problem with 'Illiberal Democracy'", *Soc. Eur.* (27 January 2016), www.socialeurope.eu/the-problem-with-illiberal-democracy.

Müller, J-W, *What is Populism?* (University of Pennsylvania Press, 2016) 3.

Norris, P, "Is Western Democracy Backsliding? Diagnosing the Risk", 28(2) *Journal of Democracy* (2017) 14–15.

Norris, P, "Measuring Populism Worldwide", *Harvard Kennedy School, Faculty Research Working Paper Series RWP 20–002*, 2.

Nusserger, A, "The European Court of Human Rights and the Rule of Law – A Tale of Hopes and Disillusions" in M Zubrik (ed), *Human Rights in Contemporary World. Essays in Honor of Professor Leszek Garlicki* (Wydawnictwo Sejmowe, 2017).

Pinelli, C, "Illiberal Regimes in the Perspective of Comparative Constitutionalism", *Revista di diritti comparati* 1 (2017), 5, 6.

Puddington, A, "Breaking Down Democracy: Global Strategies, and Methods of Modern Authoritarians", https://freedomhouse.org/sites/default/files/June2017_FH_Report_Breaking_Down_Democracy.pdf, June 2017.

Ruprik, J, "The Specter Haunting Europe: Surging Illiberalism in the East", *J. Democracy* 27(77) (2016) 137.

Sadurski, W, "How Democracy Dies (in Poland): A Case Study of Anti-Constitutional Populist Backsliding", *Sydney Law School Legal Studies Research Paper No 18/01* (2018).

Sadurski, W, *Poland's Constitutional Breakdown* (Oxford University Press, 2019) 25, 243.

Sanecka-Tyczyńska, J, "Prawa i Sprawiedliwości krytyka Konstytucji Rzeczypospolitej Polaskiej z 1997 r." ["Law and Justice Criticism of the Constitution of the Republic of Poland of 1997"], 4 (147) *Przegląd Sejmowy* (2018) 83–88.

Scheppele, KL, "Autocratic Legalism", *U. Chi. L. Rev.* 85(545) (2018).

Sheiring, G, www.tni.org/en/article/hungarys-regime-is-proof-that-capitalism-can-be-deeply-authoritarian.

Somer, M, "Understanding Turkey's Democratic Breakdown: Old vs. New and Indigenous vs. Global Authoritarianism", *Southeast European and Black Sea Studies* (2016).

Son, BN, *Confucian Constitutionalism in East Asia* (Routledge, 2016) 174.

Stopler, G, "Semi-liberal Constitutionalism" 8*Global Constitutionalism* (2019), 94–122.

Stubbs, P and Lendvai-Bainton, N, "Authoritarian Neoliberalism, Radical Conservativism and Social Policy Within the European Union: Croatia, Hungary and Poland" 51(2) *Development and Change* (2019) 554.

Thio, L-A, "Constitutionalism in Illiberal Polities" in *Oxford Handbook of Comparative Constitutional Law*, Online Publication Date: Nov 2012, doi:10.1093/oxfordhb/9780199578610.013.0001.

Tóth GA, "Authoritarianism" in R Grote, F Lachenmann, and R Wolfrum (eds), *Max Planck Encyclopedia of Comparative Constitutional Law* (Oxford Constitutional Law; online resource, 2017).

Tóth, GA, "Illiberal Rule of Law? Changing Features of Hungarian Constitutionalism" in M Adams, A Meuwese, and EH Ballin (eds), *Constitutionalism and the Rule of Law* (Cambridge University Press, 2017).

Tushnet, M, "Authoritarian Constitutionalism", *Cornell Law Review* 100 (2015).

Tushnet, M, "The Possibility of Illiberal Constitutionalism", *Fla L. Rev.* 69 (2017).

Tushnet, M and Bugaric, B, "Populism and Constitutionalism: An Essay on Definitions and Their Implications" (21 April 2020), http://nrs.harvard.edu/urn-3:HUL.InstRepos:42660123.

Walker, G, "The Idea of Nonliberal Constitutionalism", *Ethnicity and Group Rights* 39 (1997).

Waluchow, W, "Constitutionalism" in EN Zalta (ed), *The Stanford Encyclopedia of Philosophy* (Spring 2018 Edition), https://plato.stanford.edu/archives/spr2018/entries/constitutionalism/.

Zajadło, J, "Podwójne państwo", http://konstytucyjny.pl/jerzy-zajadlo-podwojne-panstwo/ (20.10.2020).

Zakaria, F, "The Rise of Illiberal Democracy", *Foreign Affairs* 6 (1997) 22.

Zakaria, F, *The Future of Freedom: Illiberal Democracy at Home and Abroad* (W. W. Norton and Company, 2007).

Zgut, E, "Authoritarian Regime Durability. The Bread and Butter of Hungarian and Polish Backsliding during COVID-19", https://visegradinsight.eu/authoritarian-regime-durability-hungary-poland/.

Part III

Ady, E, "Ismeretlen Korvin-kódex margójára" ["Side-note to the Unknown Korvin-Codex"] *Figyelő* (1905).

Augustyniak, P, *Homo Polacus. Eseje o polskiej duszy* [*Homo Polacus. Essays about Polish soul*] (Znak, Kraków 2015).

Bar-Tal, D, Chernyak-Hai, L, Schori, N, and Gundar, A, "A Sense of Self-perceived Collective Victimhood in Intractable Conflicts", 91 (874) *International Review of the Red Cross* (2009) 237.

Bauman, Z, *Etyka ponowoczesna* [*The Late Modern Ethics*] (Wydawnictwo Aletheia, Warszawa, 2012).

Bibó, I, Válogatott tanulmányok I–IV, Második kötet: *Eltorzult magyar alkat, zsákutcás magyar történelem* [Selected papers I–IV, 2nd vol: Distorted Hungarian character, Hungarian history with a dead end] (1948), http://mek.oszk.hu/02000/02043/html/350.html.

Bień-Kacała, A and Tarnowska, A, "Power of Authority: A Few Words About the Chief of State One Hundred Years Ago and the Present", 6(46) *Przegląd Prawa Konstytucyjnego* (2018) 125–135.

Bień-Kacała, A, "Informal Constitutional Change: The Case of Poland" 6(40) *Przegląd Prawa Konstytucyjnego* (2017), 199–218.

Bień-Kacała, A, "Równość czy hierarchiczność? Kilka słów o wartościach w państwie, prawie i społeczeństwie" ("Equality or Hierarchy? A Few Words About Values in the State, Law and Society"), *Gdańskie Studia Prawnicze* XL(2018) 17–30.

Bień-Kacała, A, "Polexit is Coming or is it Already Here? Comments on the Judicial Independence Decisions of the Polish Constitutional Tribunal", *Int'l J. Const. L. Blog*, 28 April 2020, at www.iconnectblog.com/2020/04/polexit-is-coming-or-is-it-already-here-comments-on-the-judicial-independence-decisions-of-the-polish-constitutional-tribunal.

Bień-Kacała, A, Tarnowska, A, and Włoch, W, "The Nation, Delegation, and Constitutional Change in Poland", *Hungarian Journal of Legal Studies* 4 (2018) 355–377.

Bień-Kacała, A, Tarnowska, A, and Włoch, W, "Nation – Delegation – Constitution: Reconsidering Role of Religion in Polish Identity Development", *Bratislava Law Review* 1 (2019) 6–25.

Bilewicz, M, *Być gorszymi* [*To Be Worse*] (Uniwersytet Warszawski, 2008) 43–47.

Bilewicz, M, *Między idealizacją a hiperkrytycyzmem. Polska niepamięć historyczna i jej źródła* [*Between Idealization and Hypercriticism: Poland Historical Oblivion and its Sources*] (Instytut Studiów Zaawansowanych, Warszawa, Seria ANALIZY) September 2018, 1–8.

Bíró-Nagy, A, "Illiberal Democracy in Hungary: The Social Background and Practical Steps of Building an Illiberal state", www.cidob.org/en/articulos/monografias/illiberals/illiberal_democracy_in_hungary_the_social_background_and_practical_steps_of_building_an_illiberal_state (2017) 35.

Boyd, D and Salusinszky, I (eds), *Re-reading Frye* (University of Toronto Press, 1999).

Cichocka, A and Cislak, A, "Nationalism as Collective Narcissism" *ScienceDirect Current Opinion in Behavioral Sciences* 34 (2020) 69–74.

Cieger, A, "Alkotmányosság és nemzeti identitás – a magyar történelem kontextusában. Vázlat" ["Constitutionalism and National Identity – In the Context of Hungarian History. Draft"], http://atelier.org.hu/upload/category/mta_elte_atelier/kotoerok1.3_cieger_andras.pdf.

Csordás, G, "A Farewell to Central Europe" (July 2016), www.literaturhauseuropa.eu/en/observatory/blog/a-farewell-to-central-europe.

Diamond, L, "Facing Up to the Democratic Recession", *Journal of Democracy* 1 (2015) 149.

Doliński, D and Grzyb, T, *Posłuszni do bólu: O uległości wobec autorytetu w 50 lat po eksperymencie Milgrama* [*Painfully Obedient: On the Submission to Authority 50 Years After Milgram's Experiment*] (Smak Słowa, 2017).

Drezner, DW, "The Angry Populist as Foreign Policy Leader: Real Change or Just Hot Air", *Fletcher F. World Aff.* 41 (2017) 23.

Drinóczi, T, "Concept of Quality in Legislation – Revisited: Matter of Perspective and a General Overview", *Statute Law Review* 3 (2015).

Drinóczi, T, "Hungarian Constitutional Court: The Limits of EU Law in the Hungarian Legal System" 1 *Vienna Journal on International Constitutional Law* (2017) 139–151.

Drinóczi, T, "Constitutional Identity in Europe: The Identity of the Constitution. A Regional Approach", *German Law Journal* 21(2) (2020) 105–130.

Drinóczi, T and Bień-Kacała, A, "Extra-legal Particularities and Illiberal Constitutionalism: The Case of Hungary and Poland", *Hungarian Journal of Legal Studies* 4 (2018) 338–354.

Drogosz, M (ed), *Jak Polacy przegrywają, jak Polacy wygrywają* [*How the Poles Lose, How the Poles Win*] (Gdańskie Wydawnictwo Psychologiczne, 2005).

Feischmidt, M and Majtényi, B, *The Rise of Populist Nationalism: Social Resentment and Capturing the Court in Hungary* (Central European University Press, 2019).

Forgas, JP and Lantos, D, "Understanding Populism: Collective Narcissism and the Collapse of Democracy in Hungary", www.sydneysymposium.unsw.edu.au/2019/chapters/ForgasSSSP2019%20.pdf, 28.

Fukuyama, F, "The Rise of Populist Nationalism", www.credit-suisse.com/about-us-news/en/articles/news-and-expertise/francis-fukuyama-the-rise-of-populist-nationalism-201801.html (2018).

Fülöp, É, Péley, B and László, J, "A történelmi pályához kötött érzelmek magyar történelmi regényekben" ["History-related Emotions in Hungarian Historical Novels"], http://real.mtak.hu/2385/1/49413_ZJ1.pdf, 56–77.

Fülöp, É, Csertő, I, Ilg, B, Szabó, Zs, Slugoski, B, and László, J, The Psychology of Narratives in JP Forgas, O Vincze, and J Laszlo (eds), *Social Cognition and Communication* (Psychology Press, 2014).

Fülöp, É, Csertő, I, Ilg, B, Szabó, Zs, Slugoski, B, and László, J, "Emotional Elaboration of Collective Traumas in Historical Narratives", http://real.mtak.hu/20201/3/emotional_elaboration_of_collective_traumas.pdf.

Gliszczyńska-Grabias, A and Śledzińska-Simon, A, "Victimhood of the Nation as a Legally Protected Value in Transitional States – Poland as a Case Study", https://ssrn.com/abstract=3120407, 5.

Golec de Zavala, A, Dyduch-Hazar, K, and Lantos, D, "Collective Narcissism: Political Consequences of Investing Self-Worth in the Ingroup's Image", 40(1) *Advances in Political Psychology* (2019) 46.

Granat, M and Granat, K, *The Constitution of Poland: A Contextual Analysis* (Hart Publishing, 2019) 13–14.

Gross, JT, *Neighbors: The Destruction of the Jewish Community in Jedwabne, Poland* (Princeton University Press, 2001).

Gross, JT, *Fear: Anti-Semitism in Poland After Auschwitz* (Random House, 2006).

Gross, JT, *Złote żniwa: Rzecz o tym, co się działo na obrzeżach zagłady Żydów (Golden Harvest: What was happening on the outskirts of the extermination of the Jews)* (Znak, 2011).

Humphrey T, "Democracy and the rule of law: founding liberal democracy in post-Communist Europe", *Colum J. E Eur. L* 2(94) (2008) 116.

Jacobsohn, G, *Constitutional Identity* (Harvard University Press, 2010).

Koncewicz, TT, "Unconstitutional Capture and Constitutional Recapture: Of the Rule of Law, Separation of Powers and Judicial Promises", *Jean Monnet Ctr. for Int'l & Regional Econ. L. & Just., Working Paper 3/17.*

Krastev, I and Holmes, S, "Explaining Eastern Europe: Imitation and its Discontents", *Journal of Democracy* 3 (2018) 118–122.

Ladányi, J, *Önpusztító nemzeti habitus* [*Self-destructive National Habitus*] (L'Harmattan, 2015) 19–23.

László, J, "Narratív pszichológia", *Pszichológia* 4 (2008), http://real.mtak.hu/2385/1/49413_ZJ1.pdf, 5.

Lendvai, P, *The Hungarians: A Thousand Years of Victory in Defeat* (Princeton University Press, 2004).

Leszczyński, A, *No dno po prostu jest Polska: Dlaczego Polacy tak bardzo nie lubią swojego kraju i innych Polaków* [Poland Hits Rock Bottom: Why Poles Do Not Like Their Country and Other Poles] (W.A.B., 2017) 255–264.

Michalik, E and Santorski, J, *Polska na kozetce* [*Poland on the Couch*] (Książki Burda, 2016).

Miklóssy, K and Nyyssönen, H, "Defining the New Polity: Constitutional Memory in Hungary and Beyond", *Journal of Contemporary European Studies* (2018), 5–9.

Miller-Idriss, C (2019) "The Global Dimensions of Populist Nationalism", *The International Spectator*, 54(2), 17–34, doi:10.1080/03932729.2019.1592870.

Miłosz, Czesław, *Historia literatury polskiej* [*History of Polish Literature*] (Znak, 1993) 263–264.

Müller, J-W, *What is Populism?* (University of Pennsylvania Press, 2016).

Murray, M, "Narrative Psychology and Narrative Analysis" in PM Camic, JE Rhodes, and L Yardly (eds), *Qualitative Research in Psychology: Expanding Perspectives in Methodology and Design* (American Psychological Association, 2003) 110.

Novak, B, "Setback for Orban as Opposition in Hungary Gains Ground in Elections", (14 October 2019) www.nytimes.com/2019/10/14/world/europe/hungary-elections-orban.html.

Nyyssönen, H and Metsälä, J, "Highlights of National History? Constitutional Memory and the Preambles of Post-Communist Constitutions", *European Politics and Society* 21(3) (2020), 323–340.

Petőfi, S, "The Magyar Noble", http://mek.oszk.hu/06500/06567/06567.htm#49.

Plattner, J, "Populism, Pluralism, and Liberal Democracy", *Journal of Democracy* 1(21) (2010) 88.

Pogány, I, "The Crisis of Democracy in East Central Europe: The 'New Constitutionalism' in Hungary", *European Public Law* (2013) 341–367.

Rajcsányi, G, "Viktor Orbán's Hungary: Orbanist Politics and Philosophy from a Hungarian Perspective", www.kas.de/c/document_library/get_file?uuid=8e914238-5bca-e235-e176-f8d502f4a33f&groupId=288143, 123.

Rosenfeld, M, "Constitutional Identity" in M. Rosenfeld and A Sajó (eds) *The Oxford Handbook of Comparative Constitutional Law* (Oxford University Press, 2012) 756–776.

Ruprik, J, "The Specter Haunting Europe: Surging Illiberalism in the East", *J. Democracy* 27(77) (2016) 84.

Sajó, A, "Militant Democracy and Transition Towards Democracy" in A Sajó (ed) *Militant Democracy* (2004) 217, 218.

Sajó, A, "Militant Democracy and Emotional Politics", *Constellations* 19 (2012) 563.Sajó, A, "The Constitution of Illiberal Democracy as a Theory About Society" *Polish Sociological Review* 4 (2018) 405–410.

Schmidt, A, "Challenges of the Illiberal Democracy in Hungary. Some Aspects to the 2018 Elections", *Polski Przegląd Politologiczny* 6(2) (2018) 88.

Schwartz, SH and Bardi, A, "Influences of Adaptation to Communist Rule on Value Priorities in Eastern Europe", *Political Psychology* 2 (1997) 407–408.

Skąpska, G, "Law and Society in a Natural Laboratory: The Case of Poland in the Broader Context of East-Central Europe" in M Kaase, V Sparschuh, and A Wenninger (eds), *Three Social Science Disciplines in Central and Eastern Europe: Handbook on Economics, Political Science and Sociology (1989–2001)* (Social Science Information Centre/Collegium Budapest, 2002) 597.

Spiró, G, "Két középkelet-európai mentalitás az államiság szempontjából" *Irodalmi és Társadalmi havi lap* 6(*2000*) (2007) 7.

Stambulski, M, "Nostalgic Constitutional Identity", *Journal of the Polish Section of IR* 3 (2019) 104.

Tarnowska, A, "The Sovereignty Issue in the Public Discussion in the Era of the Polish 3rd May Constitution (1788–1792)" in U Müßig (ed), *Reconsidering Constitutional Formation I, National Sovereignty, A Comparative Analysis of the Juridification by Constitution* (Springer International Publishing, 2016) 233.

Toomey, M, "History, Nationalism, and Democracy: Myth and Narrative in Viktor Orbán's Illiberal Hungary", *New Perspectives* 26(1) (2018).

Vincze, O and László, J, "A narratív perspektíva szerepe a történelemkönyvekben" ("The Role of Narratives in History Textbooks"), http://real.mtak.hu/2385/1/49413_ZJ1.pdf, 33.

Waterbury, MA, "Populist Nationalism and the Challenges of Divided Nationhood: The Politics of Migration, Mobility, and Demography in Post 2010 Hungary", *East European Politics and Societies and Cultures* 34(4) (2020) 962–983. doi:doi:10.1177/0888325419897772.

Weber, M, *The Protestant Ethic and the Spirit of Capitalism* (Routledge, 1930).

Wojciechowski, Z, *Nacjokratyzm, czyli rządy sejmikowe* (Drukarnia Uniwersytetu Poznańskiego Poznań, 1936) 20–21.

Wojciszke, B (ed), *Jacy są Polacy? Badania opinii społecznej jako źródło wiedzy psychologicznej* [*What Are Poles Like? Social Feedback Survey as a Source of Psychological Knowledge*] (Wydawnictwo Instytutu Psychologii PAN, 1995).

Wrzesiński, W, *Charakter narodowy Polaków: Z rozważań historyka* [*National Character of Poles: From the Historian's Reflections*] (Wydawnictwo Uniwersytetu Wrocławskiego, 2004).

Zajenkowska, A (ed), *Polska na kozetce: Siła obywatelskiej refleksyjności* [*Poland on the Couch: The Power of Civic Reflexivity*] (Smak Słowa, 2016).

Zamoyski, A, *The Polish Way: A Thousand-Year History of the Poles and Their Culture* (Hippocrene Books, 2012).

Zászkaliczky, M, "Eszmetörténeti szempontok a történeti alkotmányosság közép- és kora újkori magyarországi történetéhez" ["Some Considerations on the Hungarian Mediaeval and Modern History of the Historical Constitutionalism, from the Perspective of History of Ideas"] *Közjogi Szemle* 3 (2015) 14–25.

Part IV

Adams, M, Meuwese, A, and Ballin, EH (eds), *Constitutionalism and the Rule of Law* (Cambridge University Press, 2017).

Beatty, DM, "The Forms and Limits of Constitutional Interpretation", *The American Journal of Comparative Law*, 49 (2001).

Bień-Kacała, A, "Informal Constitutional Change", *Przegląd Prawa Konstytucyjnego* 6(40) (2017) 199–218.

Bogdandy von, A, MacGegor, EF, Antoniazzi, MM, Piovesan, F, and Soley, X (eds), *Transformative Constitutionalism in Latin America: The Emergence of a New Ius Commune* (Oxford University Press, 2017).

Bozóki, A and Hegedűs, D, "An Externally Constrained Hybrid Regime: Hungary in the European Union", *Democratization* 25(7) (2018).

Broberg, M, "Preliminary References as a Means for Enforcing EU Law" in Kochenov and Jakab (eds), 111.

Closa, C and Kochenov, D (eds), *Reinforcing the Rule of Law Oversight in the European Union* (Cambridge University Press, 2016).

Corrales, J, "The Authoritarian Resurgence: Autocratic Legalism in Venezuela", *Journal of Democracy* 26 (2015) 38.

Daly, TG, "Diagnosing Democratic Decay", www.academia.edu/34052302/Diagnosing_Democratic_Decay.

Drinóczi, Tímea, "The Rule of Law: The Hungarian Perspective" in Drinóczi and Bień-Kacała (eds) 119–132.

Drinóczi, T and Bień-Kacała, A, "COVID-19 in Hungary and Poland: Extraordinary Situation and Illiberal Constitutionalism" *The Theory and Practice of Legislation* 8(1–2) (2020) 171–192.

Fallon, RM, Jr, "'The Rule of Law' as a Concept in Constitutional Discourse", *Columbia Law Review* 1 (1997) 7.

Finck, DE, "Judicial Review: The United States Supreme Court Versus the German Constitutional Court", *Boston College International and Comparative Law Review* 20(1) (1997) 123–157.

Fuller, L, *The Morality of Law* (Yale University Press1969).

Ginsburg, T, "Locking in Democracy: Constitutions, Commitment, and International Law", *New York University Journal of International Law & Politics* 38 (2006) 757.

Gosalbo-Bono, R, "The Significance of the Rule of Law and its Implications for the European Union and the United States", *University of Pittsburgh Law Review* 72 (2010) 289.

Groppi, T, "Constitutional Revision in Italy: A Marginal Instrument for Constitutional Change" in X Contiades (ed), *Engineering Constitutional Change* (Routledge, 2016) 218–220.

Halmai, G, "Populism, Authoritarianism, and Constitutionalism", *German Law Journal* 20 (2019).

Henderson, L, "Authoritarianism and the Rule of Law", *Indiana Law Journal* 66 (1991) 396.

Hoffmann-Riem, W, "The Venice Commission of the Council of Europe – Standards and Impact", *European Journal of International Law* 2 (2014) 595. https://europeanlawblog.eu/2019/12/02/the-independence-of-the-disciplinary-chamber-of-the-polish-supreme-court-or-how-to-forget-about-discipline/.

Jakab, A and Bodnár, E, "The Rule of Law, Democracy and Human Rights in Hungary: Tendencies from 1989 until 2019" in Drinóczi and Bień-Kacała (eds) 105–118.

Jakab, A and Kochenov, D, "Introductory remarks" in Kochenov and Jakab (eds), 2–3.

Kochenov, D, "The EU and the Rule of Law – Naïveté or a Grand Design?", *University of Groningen Faculty of Law Research Paper Series 2018*, 510.

Kochenov, D and Jakab, A (eds), *The Enforcement of EU Law and Values* (Oxford University Press, 2017).

Krieger, H, Nolte, G, and Zimmermann, A (eds), *The International Rule of Law: Rise or Decline?* (Oxford University Press, 2019).

Krygier, M, "The Rule of Law: Pasts, Presents, and Two Possible Futures," *Annual Review of Law and Social Science* 12 (2016).

Lenaertes, K, "New Horizons for the Rule of Law Within the EU", *German Law Journal* 21 (2020) 34.

Levitsky, S and Way, LA, "The Myth of Democratic Recession", *Democracy* 26(45) (2015) 46–48.

Lührmann, A and Lindberg, SI, "A Third Wave of Autocratization is Here: What is New About It?" *Democratization* 7 (2019) 1103–1104.

Madeja, A, "The European Values and the Rule of Law" in T Drinóczi and A Bień-Kacała (eds), *Rule of Law, Common Values and Illiberal Constitutionalism. Poland and Hungary within the European Union* (Routledge, 2021) 45–76.

May, C and Winchester, A (eds), *Handbook of the Rule of Law* (Edward Elgar, 2018).

McDonald, L, "Positivism and the Formal Rule of Law: Questioning the Connection", *Australian Journal of Legal Philosophy* 26 (2001) 93.

Menocal, AR, Fritz, V and Rakner, L, "Hybrid Regimes and the Challenge of Deepening and Sustaining Democracy in Developing Countries", *South African Journal of International Affairs* 1 (2008) 15–30.

Moravcsik, A, "The Origins of Human Rights Regimes: Democratic Delegation in Postwar Europe", *International Organizations* 54 (2000) 243–244.

Nusserger, A, "The European Court of Human Rights and the Rule of Law – A Tale of Hopes and Disillusions" in Marek Zubrik (ed), *Human Rights in Contemporary World. Essays in Honor of Professor Leszek Garlicki* (Wydawnictwo Sejmove, 2017) 162–165.

Palombella, G, "Beyond Legality – Before Democracy: Rule of Law in the EU Two Level System" in Closa and Kochenov (eds).

Plattner, MF, "Populism, Pluralism, and Liberal Democracy", *J. Democracy* 21(1) (2010) 81–92.

Puddington, A, "Breaking Down Democracy: Global Strategies, and Methods of Modern Authoritarians", https://freedomhouse.org/sites/default/files/June2017_FH_Report_Breaking_Down_Democracy.pdf, June 2017.

Raz, J, "The Rule of Law and its Virtue", *Law Quarterly Review* 93 (1977).

Raz, J, "The Rule of Law and its Virtue" in J Raz (ed), *The Authority of Law: Essays on Law and Morality* (Oxford University Press, 1979).

Rosenfeld, M, "Legitimacy of Constitutional Democracy", *Southern California Law Review* 74 (2001) 1313, 1350.

Sadurski, W, *Poland's Constitutional Breakdown* (Oxford University Press, 2019) 211–213.

Scheppele, KL, "Autocratic Legalism", *The University of Chicago Law Review* 85 (2018).

Sellers, M, "What is the Rule of Law and Why it is Important?" in JR Silkenat, JRE Hickey Jr, and PD Barenboim (eds), *The Legal Doctrines of the Rule of Law and the Legal State (Rechtsstaat)* (Springer, 2014) 3–6 (the Rule of Law has a Western European origin).

Simonelli, MA, "Thickening Up Judicial Independence: The ECJ Ruling in Commission v. Poland (C-619/18)", https://europeanlawblog.eu/2019/07/08/thickening-up-judicial-independence-the-ecj-ruling-in-commission-v-poland-c-619-18/.

Tamanaha, BZ, "The History of the Rule of Law", *Singapore Journal of Legal Studies* (2012) 233.

Tóth, GA, "Illiberal Rule of Law? Changing Features of Hungarian Constitutionalism" in M Adams, A Meuwese, and EH Ballin. (eds), *Constitutionalism and the Rule of Law* (Cambridge University Press, 2017).

Tushnet, M, "Authoritarian Constitutionalism", *Cornell Law Review* 100 (2015) 72.

Varju, M, "A magyar jogrendszer és az Európai Unió joga: tíz év tapasztalata" ["The Hungarian Legal System and the Law of the European Union: Experiences of Ten Years"] in A Jakab and G Gajduschek (eds), *A magyar jogrendszer állapota* (MTA Társadalomtudományi Kutatóközpont, 2016) 143–171.

Versteeg, M and Ginsburg, T, "Measuring the Rule of Law: A Comparison of Indicators", *Law and Social Inquiry* 1 (2017) 100.

Waldron, J, "The Concept of the Rule of Law", *Georgia Law Review* 1 (2008) 59–60.

Włoch, W, "'Where the Laws Do Not Govern, There is No Constitution': On the Relationship between the Rule of Law and Constitutionalism" in Drinóczi and Bień-Kacała (eds), n. 39, 77–101.

Wróblewska, I, "The Rule of Law: The Polish Perspective" in Drinóczi and Bień-Kacała (eds), 133–150.

Zanghellini, A, "The Foundations of the Rule of Law", *Yale Journal of Law & the Humanities* 2 (2016) 216.

Zimmermann, A, "Understanding the Rule of Law: Conceptions and Perspective", http://alrf.msk.ru/understanding_the_rule_of_law_conceptions_and_perspectives.

Zinonos, P, "The Independence of the Disciplinary Chamber of the Polish Supreme Court or How to Forget About Discipline", https://europeanlawblog.eu/2019/12/02/the-independence-of-the-disciplinary-chamber-of-the-polish-supreme-court-or-how-to-forget-about-discipline/.

Part V

Alberti, É, Czibik, A, Fazekas, M, Herczog, E, Ungár, K, Bálint, S, Tóth, W, and Johannes, IJ, "The Quality of Hungarian Legislation 2013–2014" (Budapest, 2015), https://ec.europa.eu/hungary/sites/default/files/docs/body/legislation_eu_2014_report_150216_2100.pdf.

Alberti, É, Czibik, A, Fazekas, M, Herczog, E, Ungár, K, Bálint, S, Tóth, W, and Johannes, IJ, "Impact Assessments Public Consultation and Legislation in Hungary 2011–2014" (Budapest, 2015) www.crcb.eu/wp-content/uploads/2015/07/legislation_2014_report_150630.pdf, 83.

Arato, L, "Homophobia is on the Rise in Hungary", www.europeandatajournalism.eu/eng/News/Data-news/Homophobia-is-on-the-rise-in-Hungary (30 October 2019); https://index.hu/kulfold/eurologus/2019/09/24/egyre_tobb_magyart_zavarnak_a_melegek/.

Arnold, R and Cerny, L, "The Application of the Charter of Fundamental Rights of the EU by the German Federal Constitutional Court with References to the Other Federal Courts", *Acta Universitatis Carolinae – Iuridica* 4 (2018), https://karolinum.cz/data/clanek/6407/Iurid_64_4_0065.pdf, 65, 77.

Bárd, K and Bárd, Pa, "Összhang vagy kollízió? Hol tart Magyarország 25 évvel az EJEE-hez való csatlakozás után a strasbourgi elvárásoknak való megfelelésben?" ["Harmony or Collision? Where is Hungary 25 Years After Joining the ECHR in Terms of Compliance to Expectations of Strasbourg?"], *Állam és Jogtudomány* 4 (2017) https://jog.tk.mta.hu/uploads/files/2017-04-BardK-BardP.pdf, 17–18.

Bárd, P and Bárd, K, "The European Convention on Human Rights and the Hungarian Legal System", http://real.mtak.hu/65944/1/Bard_Bard_Comparative_study_on_the_implementation_of_the_ECHR_at_the_national_level_ENG_149_168_u.pdf, 152.

Bar-Siman-Tov, I, "Semiprocedural Judicial Review", *Legisprudence* 3 (2012).

Bar-Siman-Tov, I, "Covid-19 meets politics: the novel coronavirus as a novel challenge for legislatures", *The Theory and Practice of Legislation* 8(1–2) (2020) 11–48 (free online access).

Bernatt, M and Ziółkowski, M, "Statutory Anti-Constitutionalism", *Washington International Law Journal* 28 (2019) 499–501.

Bień-Kacała, A, "Gloss to the Judgement of Constitutional Tribunal of 16 March 2017 (Kp 1/17)", *Przegląd Prawa Konstytucyjnego* 4 (2017) 255–262.

Bień-Kacała, A, Tarnowska, A and Włoch, W, "The Nation, Delegation, and Constitutional Change in Poland", *Hungarian Journal of Legal Studies* 59(4) (2018) 355–377.

Bień-Kacała, A, "Illiberal Democracy in Action: Polish Kind of Symbolic Legislation", *European Studies. The Review of European Law, Economics and Politics* 6 (2019) 268–278.

Bíró-Nagy, A and Laki, G, *Orbán 10. Az elmúlt évtized a Magyar társadalom szemével*, (© Friedrich-Ebert-Stiftung – Policy Solutions, 2020), https://www.policysolutions.hu/userfiles/Orban10_final.pdf, 78.

Bodnar, A, "Strasbourg Steps In", *VerfBlog*, 2020/7/07, https://verfassungsblog.de/strasbourg-steps-in/.

Bozóki, A and Hegedűs, D, "An Externally Constrained Hybrid Regime: Hungary in the European Union", *Democratization* 25(7) (2018) .

Bucholc, M, "Fencing Off the Difference: On 'LGBT-Free Zones' in Poland", *VerfBlog*, 2020/8/26, https://verfassungsblog.de/fencing-off-the-difference/.

Búrca, G de and Morijn, J, "Repression of Freedom of Expression in Poland: Renewing support for Wojciech Sadurski", *VerfBlog*, 2020/6/03, https://verfassungsblog.de/repression-of-freedom-of-expression-in-poland-renewing-support-for-wojciech-sadurski/.

Búrca, G de, Morijn, J, and Steinbeis, M, "Stand with Wojciech Sadurski: his freedom of expression is (y)ours", *VerfBlog*, 2019/11/18, https://verfassungsblog.de/stand-with-wojciech-sadurski-his-freedom-of-expression-is-yours/.

Csaky, Z., *Nations in Transition: Dropping the Democratic Façade* (Freedom House, 2020), https://freedomhouse.org/report/nations-transit/2020/dropping-democratic-facade#Facade, 25.

Csatlós, E, "The Application of International Law as an Instrument of Interpretation in Hungary – the Practice of the Constitutional Court and Ordinary Courts in a Comparative Approach", http://publicatio.bibl.u-szeged.hu/7049/8/2961433.pdf, 137.

Dojcsák, D, Farkas, E, Fazekas, T, Hegyi, A, Kádár, A, and Szabó, M, "The New Law on the Right to Assembly in Hungary as Applied in the Practice", http://4liberty.eu/wp-content/uploads/2020/08/The-New-Law-on-the-Right-to-Assembly-in-Hungary-as-Applied-in-Practice.pdf, 49.

Drinóczi, T, "Dialogic Interaction and Legislation on Parliamentary Election in Hungary 2010–2014" *Osteurope Recht* 4 (2014) 452–467.

Drinóczi, T, "Concept of Quality in Legislation – Revisited: Matter of Perspective and a General Overview" *Statute Law Review* 3 (2015) 225–227.

Drinóczi, T, "Hungarian Democratic Backsliding in Light of the Recent Emergency Coronavirus Legislation" *Public Jurist, Hong Kong University Political Science Magazine*, June 2020, www.hkuglc.org/government-and-laws-committee-hku-public-jurist.

Drinóczi, T, "Legislation in Hungary" in U Karpen and H Xanthaki (eds), *Legislation in Europe. A Country by Country Guide* (Hart Publishing, 2020).

Drinóczi, T and Bień-Kacała, A, "COVID-19 in Hungary and Poland: Extraordinary Situation and Illiberal Constitutionalism" *The Theory and Practice of Legislation* 8(1–2) (2020) 171–192.

Górski, M, "The Dialogue Between Selected CEE Courts and the ECtHR", in A Wyrozumska (ed), *Transnational Judicial Dialogue on International Law in Central and Eastern Europe* (Wydawnictwo Uniwersytetu Łódzkiego, 2017) 239–240.

Gracian, D and Mikut, G, "Requiem for a Dream: Academic Freedom Under Threat in Democracies", *International Higher Education* Nr 90, Summer 2017.

Griglio, E, "Parliamentary Oversight Under the Covid-19 Emergency: Striving Against Executive Dominance", *The Theory and Practice of Legislation* 8(1–2) (2020) 49–70 (free online access).

Hamulak, O, Sulyok, M, and Kiss, LN, "Measuring the 'EU' clidean distance between EU law and the Hungarian Constitutional Court – focusing on the position of the EU Charter of Fundamental Rights", *Czech Yearbook of Public & Private International Law* 10 (2019) 145–148.

Kastelik-Smaza, A., "The Application of the Charter of Fundamental Rights of the EU in Poland", *Acta Universitatis Carolinae – Iuridica* 4 (2018) https://karolinum.cz/data/clanek/6410/Iurid_64_4_0101.pdf, 112.

Kazai, V, "The Illiberal Challenge to the Rule of Law Principle: The Neglected Procedural Aspect (With Special Focus on Hungary)", 2019 ESIL Annual Research Forum, Göttingen (4–5 April 2019), available https://ssrn.com/abstract=3513204.

Klamert, M., "The Implementation and Application of the Charter of Fundamental Rights of the EU in Austria", *Acta Universitatis Carolinae – Iuridica* 4 (2018), https://karolinum.cz/data/clanek/6409/Iurid_64_4_0089.pdf, 89, 99.

Klink B van, Beers, B van, and Poort, L (eds), *Symbolic Legislation Theory and Developments in Biolaw* (Springer International Publishing, 2016) 1–2.

Kosar, D and Petrov, J, "The Architecture of the Strasbourg System of Human Rights: The Crucial Role of the Domestic Level and the Constitutional Courts in Particular", *ZaöRV* 77 (2017), https://www.zaoerv.de/77_2017/77_2017_3_a_585_621.pdf, 617.

Kúria, A, "Az Alaptörvény követelményeinek érvényesülése a bírósági ítélkezésben' Joggyakorlat-elemző Csoportja2016.El.II.JGY.K.1" https://kuria-birosag.hu/sites/default/files/joggyak/alaptorveny_osszefoglalo_velemeny.pdf, 194.

Kustra-Rogaska, A and Hamulak, O, "Keeping Distance: Chapters from Randomized (Non)Application of the European Court of Human Rights before the Polish Constitutional Tribunal", *Baltic Journal of European Studies* 4(9) (2019) 90.

Łakomiec, K, "Academic Freedom(s) in the Drift Towards Authoritarianism (4/4) – Poland", https://ds.hypotheses.org/6391 (15 November 2019).

Magyar, B., *Post-Communist Mafia State ⊠ The Case of Hungary* (Noran Libro, 2016).

Nagy, TA, "Parlamenti sebesség" ["Parliamentary speed"], http://meltanyossag.hu/files/meltany/imce/kp_parlamenti_sebesseg_120228.pdf.

Pech, Land Scheppele, KL, "Poland and the European Commission, Part III: Requiem for the Rule of Law", *VerfBlog*, 2017/3/03, at http://verfassungsblog.de/poland-and-the-european-commissionpart-iii-requiem-for-the-rule-of-law/.

Pinheiro, VM, Ilarraz, Mand Mestriner, MT, "The Impacts of the COVID-19 Crisis on the Brazilian Legal System – A Report on the Functioning of the Branches of the Government and on the Legal Scrutiny of Their Activities", *The Theory and Practice of Legislation* 8(1–2) (2020) 193–212 (free online access).

Polgári, E, "The European Convention on Human Rights and the case law of the European Court of Human Rights in Hungarian Judicial Practice", *Fundamentum* 5 (2008) 74–80.

Polgári, E, "Az Alkotmánybíróság esete az Emberi Jogok Európai Egyezményével" ["The Constitutional Court and the European Convention of Human Rights"] *Fundamentum* 4 (2015) 6.

Polyák, G, "Media in Hungary: Three Pillars of an Illiberal Democracy" in E Polonska and E Beckett (eds), *Public Service Broadcasting and Media Systems in Troubled European Democracies* (Palgrave Macmillan) 284–285.

Popelier, P, Maymanyan, M, and Vanderbruwaene, W, eds, *The Role of Constitutional Courts in Multilevel Governance* (Intersentia, 2013).

Reichman, H, "Academic Freedom Threatened in Poland", 19 February 2016, academeblog.org.

Sadura, P and Sierakowski, S, "Political Cynicism: The Case of Poland", http://politicalcritique.org/cee/poland/2019/poles-political-cynicism-research-report/, 15–16.

Sadurski, W, *Poland's Constitutional Breakdown* (Oxford University Press, 2019) 139.

Sárosi, P, "David Takes on Goliath: The Struggle for Academic Freedom in Hungary", 11 October 2020, https://autocracyanalyst.net/david-takes-on-goliath-struggle-for-academic-freedom-in-hungary/.

Schmidt, A, "Challenges of the Illiberal Democracy in Hungary: Some Aspects to the 2018 Elections", *Polski Przegląd Politologiczny* 2 (2018) 82.

Schumpeter, J, *Capitalism, Socialism and Democracy*, 2nd edn (Allen & Unwin, 1947), chs 21–23.

Sękowska-Kozłowska, K, "The Istanbul Convention in Poland" in J Niemi, L Peroni, and V Stoyanova, *International Law and Violance against Women. Europe and the Istanbul Convention* (Routledge, 2020) 261.

Skomerska-Muchowska, I, "The Dialogue of the CEE Constitutional Court in the Era of Constitutional Pluralism" in A Wyrozumska (ed), *Transnational Judicial Dialogue on International Law in Central and Eastern Europe* (Wydawnictwo Uniwersytetu Łódzkiego, 2017) 118.

Sokołowski, JK and Stolicki, D, "Przyczyny opóźnień w transpozycji dyrektyw europejskich do polskiego porządku prawnego w świetle analizy ilościowej krajowego procesu legislacyjnego" ["Reasons for Delays in the Transposition of European Directives into the Polish Legal Order in the Light of Quantitative Analysis of the National Legislative Process"], *Przegląd Politologiczny* 2 (2017) 39–54.

Szabó Z, "Többpólusú alapjogvédelmi rendszer a gyakorlatban – a kormánytisztviselők indokolás nélküli felmentésének tükrében" ["Multilevel Protection of Human Rights in Practice – in the Light of Dismissal of Government Officials Without Justification"], *Pro Futuro* 1 (2015) 138.

Szlachta, B, "Aksjologia Konstytucji RP z 1997 roku. Perspektywa badacza myśli politycznej" ["The Axiology of the Constitution of the Republic of Poland of 1997: The Perspective of the Researcher of Political Thought"] *Przegląd Sejmowy* 6(143) (2017) 125–150.

Trócsányi, L, "New Challenges Facing Democracy and the Rule of Law", *Hungarian Review* 3 (2017), http://hungarianreview.com/article/20171117_new_challenges_facing_democracy_and_the_rule_of_law.

Tushnet, M, "Authoritarian Constitutionalism", *Harvard Public Law Working PapersNo*13–47 (2013), 72.

Tushnet, M, "The Possibility of Illiberal Constitutionalism", *Fla L. Rev.* 69 (2017).

Uhlmann, Fand Scheifele, E, "Legislative Response to Coronavirus (Switzerland)", *The Theory and Practice of Legislation* 8(1–2) (2020) 115–130 (free online access).

Uitz, R, "Nemzetközi emberi jogok és a maygar jogrend" ["International Human Rights and the Hungarian Legal Order"], https://jog.tk.hu/uploads/files/08_Uitz_Renata.pdf.

Urbinati, N, *Representative Democracy: Principles and Genealogy* (University of Chicago Press, 2006) 43.

Varju, M, "A magyar jogrendszer és az Európai Unió joga: tíz év tapasztalata" ["The Hungarian Legal System and the law of the European Union: Experiences of Ten Years"]', in A Jakab and G Gajduschek, eds, *A magyar jogrendszer állapota* (MTA Társadalomtudományi Kutatóközpont, Jogtudományi Intézet, 2016) 142–164.

Várnay E, "Az Alkotmánybíróság és az Európai Bíróság. Együttműködő alkotmánybíráskodás?" ["The Constitutional Court and the Court of the EU. Coopareting Judicial Review?"] *Állam és Jogtudomány* 2 (2019) 66–70.

Wike, R, Stokes, B, and Simmons, K, *Europeans Fear Wave of Refugees Will Mean More Terrorism, Fewer Job:. Sharp Ideological Divides Across EU on Views About Minorities, Diversity and National Identity* (11 July 2016), www.pewresearch.org/global/2016/07/11/europeans-fear-wave-of-refugees-will-mean-more-terrorism-fewer-jobs/.

Wróblewska, I, "The Rule of Law: The Polish Perspective" in T Drinóczi and A Bień-Kacała (eds), *Rule of Law, Common Values and Illiberal Constitutionalism. Poland and Hungary within the European Union* (Routledge, 2021) 133–150.

Wyrozumska, A, "The Central and Eastern European Judiciary and Transnational Judicial Dialogue on International Law" in A Wyrozumska (ed), *Transnational Judicial Dialogue on International Law in Central and Eastern Europe* (Wydawnictwo Uniwersytetu Łódzkiego, 2017) 23.

Wyrzykowski, M, "Bypassing the Constitution Or Changing the Constitutional Order Outside the Constitution" in A Szmyt and B Banaszak (eds), *Transformation of Law Systems in Central, Eastern and South-Eastern Europe in 1989–2015*, Liber Amicorum in Honorem Prof. Dr. Dres. H.C. Rainer Arnold (Gdańsk University Press, 2016).

Wyrzykowski, M, "Wrogie przejęcie' porządku konstytucyjnego" ["'Hostile Takeover' of the Constitutional Order"], http://konstytucyjny.pl/wrogie-przejecie-porzadku-konstytucyjnego-miroslaw-wyrzykowski (9.10.2020).

Xanthaki, H and Karpen, U (eds), *Legislation and Legisprudence in Europe: A Comprehensive Guide for Scholars and Legislative Practitioners* (Hart Publishing, 2017).

Zakaria, F, "The Rise of Illiberal Democracy" *Foreign Affaires* 76 (1997) 22.

Zakaria, F, *The Future of Freedom. Illiberal Democracy at Home and Abroad* (W.W. Norton and Company, 2007).

Part VI

Albert, R, "How Unwritten Constitutional Norms Change Written Constitutions", *Dublin University Law Journal* 38 (2015).

Albert, R, "Constitutional Amendment and Dismemberment", *Yale J. Int'l L.* 43 (2018).

Albert, R, *Constitutional Amendments: Making, Breaking, and Changing Constitutions* (Oxford University Press, 2019).

Antal A, "Politikai és jogi alkotmányosság Magyarországon" ["Political and Legal Constitutionalism in Hungary"] *Politikatudományi Szemle* 3 (2013).

Balicki, R, "Bezpośrednie stosowanie konstytucji" ["Direct Application of a Constitution"], *Krajowa Rada Sądownictwa* 4 (2016) 13–19.

Bellamy, R, *Political Constitutionalism: A Republican Defence of the Constitutionality of Democracy* (Cambridge University Press, 2007).

Bień-Kacała, A, "Polish Constitutional Tribunal: A Systemic Reform or a Hasty Political Change", *DPCE Online* 1 (2016) 1–14.

Bień-Kacała, A, "Poland Within the EU: Dealing with the Populist Agenda", *Osteuropa-Recht* 4(63) (2017) 428–443 and "Polish Constitutional Tribunal: A Systemic Reform or a Hasty Political Change", *DPCE Online* 1 (2016) 1–14.

Bień-Kacała, A and Jackiewicz, A, "Militant Democracy: Demokracja, która sama się broni(?)" ["Militant Democracy: A Democracy that Defends Itself(?)"], *Państwo i Prawo* 8 (2017) 25–41.

Bień-Kacała, A, "Informal Constitutional Change: The Case of Poland", *Przegląd Prawa Konstytucyjnego* 6(40) (2017) 199–218.
Bień-Kacała, A, "Równość czy hierarchiczność? Kilka słów o wartościach w państwie, prawie i społeczeństwie" ["Equality or Hierarchy? Few Words about Values of State, Law and Society"] *Gdańskie Studia Prawnicze* 40 (2018) 17–30.
Bień-Kacała, A, "Polexit is Coming or is it Already Here? Comments on the Judicial Independence Decisions of the Polish Constitutional Tribunal", *Int'l J. Const. L. Blog*, 28 April 2020, at www.iconnectblog.com/2020/04/polexit-is-coming-or-is-it-already-here-comments-on-the-judicial-independence-decisions-of-the-polish-constitutional-tribunal.
Bień-Kacała, A, "Verfassungsdurchbrechung or Informal Constitutional Change. The Polish Experience", *Przegląd Prawa Konstytucyjnego* 5(57) (2020) 29–47.
Chronowski, N, Drinóczi, T, and Zeller, J, "Túl az Alkotmányon" ["Beyond the Constitution"], *Közjogi Szemle* 4 (2010).
Closa, C., "Ran Hirschl, Towards Juristocracy: The Origins and Consequences of the New Constitutionalism, Harvard University Press, 2004", *ICON* 4(3) (2006) 581–586.
Colón-Ríos, JI, "A New Typology of Judicial Review of Legislation", *Global Constitutionalism* 3(2) (2014) 143–169.
Colón-Ríos, JI, "Judge-made Constitutional Changes", in X Contiades and A Fotiadou, eds, *Routledge Handbook of Comparative Constitutional Change* (Routledge 2021) 217–230.
Contiades, X, ed, *Engineering Constitutional Change* (Routledge, 2012).
Contiades, X and Fotiadou, A, "Introduction" in X Contiades and A Fotiado (eds), *Routledge Handbook of Comparative Constitutional Change* (Routledge, 2021) 14.
Csink, L and Fröhlich, J, "Az Alaptörvény és az Átmeneti rendelkezések viszonya" *Pázmány Law Working Papers*, No 2012/02, available at www.plwp.jak.ppke.hu/images/files/2012/2012-2.pdf.
Czarnota, A, "The Constitutional Tribunal", *VerfBlog*, 2017/6/03, https://verfassungsblog.de/the-constitutional-tribunal/.
Diamond, L, "Facing Up to the Democratic Recession", *J. Democracy* 29(142) (2015) 149.
Dixon, R and Landau, D, "Abusive Judicial Review: Courts Against Democracy", *UC Davis Law Review* 53 (2020) 1313.
Dixon, R and Landau, D, "Tiered Constitutional Design", 2018, at https://ssrn.com/abstract=2953755,1, 63.
Dixon, R and Landau, D, "Transnational Constitutionalism and a Limited Doctrine of Unconstitutional Constitutional Amendments", *ICON* 3 (2015) 606, 629.
Drinóczi, T, "Constitutional Politics in Contemporary Hungary", *Vienna Journal on International Constitutional Law* 1 (2016), 63–98.
Drinóczi, T, "Hungarian Constitutional Court: The Limits of EU Law in the Hungarian Legal System", *Vienna J. Int'l Const. L.* 1(139) (2017).
Drinóczi, T, "Constitutional Identity in Europe: The Identity of the Constitution. A Regional Approach", *German Law Journal* 21(2) (2020) 105–130.
Drinóczi, T, "Hungarian Abuse of Constitutional Emergency Regimes – Also in the Light of the COVID-19 Crisis". MTA LWP 13/2020, https://jog.tk.mta.hu/mtalwp/hungarian-abuse-of-constitutional-emergency-regimes-also-in-the-light-of-the-covid-19-crisis.
Drinóczi, T and Bień-Kacała, A, "COVID-19 in Hungary and Poland: Extraordinary Situation and Illiberal Constitutionalism", *Theory and Practice of Legislation* 1–2 (2020).
Eichhorn, J, Kupsch, V, and Mohr, LMM, "How European Publics and Policy Actors Values an Open Society Key Insight Across Countries" (Open Society European Policy Institute, 2019), http://voicesonvalues.dpart.org/images/finalreports/OSI-019-18-Key-Insights_v5.pdf.

Fesnic, FN, "Can Civic Education Make a Difference for Democracy? Hungary and Poland Compared", *Political Studies* 4 (2016) 966–978.

Gardbaum, S., "The Case for the New Commonwealth Model of Constitutionalism", *German Law Review* 12(14) (2013) 2230–2248.

Garlicki, L and Garlicka, ZA, "External Review of Constitutional Amendments? International Law as a Norm of Reference", *Israel Law Review* 44 (2011) 343–368.

Garlicki, L, "Sądy a Konstytucja Rzeczypospolitej Polskiej" ["Courts and the Constitution of the Republic of Poland"] *Przegląd Sądowy* 7–8 (2016) 23–25.

Garlicki, L, *Polskie prawo konstytucyjne* [*Polish Constitutional Law*] (Wolters Kluwer, 2016) 76–78.

Ginsberg, T, "Arato on Constitution Making in Hungary and the 4/5 Rule", *I-CONnect Blog* (6 April 2011), www.iconnectblog.com/2011/04/arato-on-constitution-making-in-hungary-and-the-45-rule/.

Ginsberg, T, "When Courts Compete: A Reputational Perspective" in M Zubik (ed), *Human Rights in Contemporary World, Essays in Honour of Professor Leszek Garlicki* (Kancelaria Sejmu Wydawnictwo Sejmowe Kancelaria Sejmu, 2017) 61–70.

Górski, G and Górska-Szymczak, J, "Trybunał Konstytucyjny w Sporze z Prezydentem, Rządem i Parlamentem w 2015 r." ["The Constitutional Tribunal in an Argument with the President, the Government and the Parliament in 2015"], *Przegląd Sejmowy* 5 (2018) 39–57.

Hale, HE, "25 Years After The USSR: What's Gone Wrong?", *J. Democracy* 27(24) (2016).

Halmai, G and Scheppele KL, "Orbán is Still the Sole Judge of his Own Law", *VerfBlog*, 2020/4/30, https://verfassungsblog.de/orban-is-still-the-sole-judge-of-his-own-law/.

Halmai, G, "Illiberal Constitutionalism in East-Central Europe", *EUI Working PaperLAW* 2019/05.Ord

Halmai, G, "How COVID-19 Unveils the True Autocrats: Viktor Orbán's Ermächtigungsgesetz", *Int'l J. Const. L. Blog*, Apr. 1, 2020, www.iconnectblog.com/2020/04/how-covid-19-unveils-the-true-autocrats-viktororbans-ermachtigungsgesetz/.

Halmai, G, "The Decline of Liberal Democracy in Europe's Midst", 2016, www.eurozine.com/the-decline-of-liberal-democracy-in-europes-midst/.

Halmai, G and Scheppele, KL, "Don't Be Fooled by Autocrats!: Why Hungary's Emergency Violates Rule of Law", *VerfBlog*, 2020/4/22, https://verfassungsblog.de/dont-be-fooled-by-autocrats.

Hermann, M, *Wyroki interpretacyjne Trybunału Konstytucyjnego z perspektywy teoretycznoprawnej* [*Interpretative Judgements of Constitutional Tribunal from a Theoretical Perspective*] (Warszawa, 2015).

Hirschl, R, *Towards Juristocracy: The Origins and Consequences of the New Constitutionalism* (Harvard University Press, 2004).

Humphrey, T, "Democracy and the Rule of Law: Founding Liberal Democracy in Post-Communist Europe", *Colum J. E Eur. L* 2(94) (2008).

Kardas, P and Gutowski, M, "Konstytucja z 1997 r. a model kontroli konstytucyjności prawa" ["1997Constitution and a Model of Constitutional Review"], *Palestra* 4 (2017) 11–30.

Kelemen, K, "The Hungarian Constitutional Court and the Concept of National Constitutional Identity", *IANUS – Diritto e finanza* 23(15–16) (2017).

Koncewicz, TT, "Constitutional Fidelity and the Polish Constitution", *Blog of the International Journal of Constitutional Law*, 11 August 2017, www.iconnectblog.com/2017/08/constitutional-fidelity-and-the-polish-constitution.

Koncewicz, TT, "On the Strategic Reading of the Constitutional Document. Mapping out Frontiers of New Constitutional Research", *Przegląd Konstytucyjny* 2 (2018), 16–45.

Krunke, H and Hellqvist Frey, S, "Social Rights in Denmark" in K Wojtyczek (ed), *Social Rights as Fundamental Rights* (Eleven International Publishing, 2016) 119.

Landau, D, "Abusive Constitutionalism", *UC Davis Law Review* 3 (2013).

Lavapuro, J, Ojanen, T, and Scheinin, M, "Rights-based Constitutionalism in Finland and the Development of Pluralist Constitutional Review", *ICON* 2 (2011).

Law, DS and Whalen, R, "Comparing Amendment and Replacement" in X Contiades and A Fotiado (eds), *Routledge Handbook of Comparative Constitutional Change* (Routledge, 2021) 96.

Macklem, P, "Militant Democracy, Legal Pluralism, and the Paradox of Self-determination", *I-CON* 3 (2006) 494–495.

Magyar B, *Post-Communist Mafia State: The Case of Hungary* (CEU Press, 2016).

Martin C, "The Legitimacy of Informal Constitutional Amendment and the 'Reinterpretation' of Japan's War Powers", *Fordham Int'l L.J.* 40(427) (2017).

Masternak-Kubiak, M, "Dopuszczalność nieformalnej zmiany Konstytucji RP (uwagi w kontekście prawa wyborczego obywateli Unii Europejskiej)" ["Admissibility of informal amendment to the Constitution RP (comments in the context of the electoral law of EU citizens)"] in B. Banaszak, M. Jabłoński, and S. Jarosz-Żukowska (eds), *Prawo w służbie państwu i społeczeństwu* [Law in the Service of the State and Society] (Wydawnictwo Uniwersytetu Wrocławskiego, 2012).

Matczak, M, "How to Demolish an Independent Judiciary with the Help of a Constitutional Court", *VerfBlog*, 2017/6/23, http://verfassungsblog.de/how-to-demolish-an-independent-judiciary-with-the-help-of-a-constitutional-court/, doi:10.17176/20170623-103309 (31.10.2017).

Mazmanyan, A, "Judicialization of Politics: The Post-Soviet Way", *I-CON* 13(1) (2015) 200–218.

Menocal, AR, Fritz, V, and Rakner, L, "Hybrid Regimes and the Challenge of Deepening and Sustaining Democracy in Developing Countries", *S. Afr. J. Int'L Aff.* 15(1) (2008), 29–40. DOI: doi:10.1080/10220460802217934.

Młynarska-Sobaczewska, A, "Rytualne ofiary a moralność publiczna: Analiza argumentacji Trybunału Konstytucyjnego (K 52/13) i Sądu Najwyższego USA (508 U.S. 520.1993)" ["Ritual Sacrifices and Public Morality: Analysis of Arguments of the Constitutional Tribunal (K 52/13) and US Supreme Court (508 U.S. 520.1993)"], *Państwo i Prawo* 4 (2017).

Młynarska-Sobaczewska, A, "Wybór sędziów konstytucyjnych jako element legitymizacji sądu konstytucyjnego" ["Election of the Constitutional Judges as an Element of Legitimacy of the Constitutional Court"], *Państwo i Prawo* 5 (2018) 43–62.

Morawski, L, "A Critical Response", *VerfBlog*, 2017/6/03.

Muller, Jan-Werner, "Militant Democracy" in M Rosenfeld and A Sajó (eds), *The Oxford Handbook of Comparative Constitutional Law* (Oxford University Press, 2011) 1253–1268.

Ojanen, T. "Constitutional Amendment in Finland" in X. Contiades (ed), *Engineering Constitutional Change* (Routledge, 2016) 107–109.

Oliver, D. and Fusaro, C. eds. *How Constitutions Change? A Comparative Study* (Hart Publishing, 2016).

Pap, AL and Śledzińska-Simon, A, "Mandatory Voting as a Tool to Combat the 'New Populism'", *I-CONnect Blog* (19 April 2017), iconnectblog.com/2017/04/mandatory-voting-and-the-new-populism/.

Pasquino, P, "Neutrality in Constitutional Conflicts Resolution: Preliminary Observations" in M Zubik (ed), *Human Rights in Contemporary World, Essays in Honour of Professor Leszek Garlicki* (Wydawnictwo Sejmowe, 2017).

Popelier, P, Verstraelen, S., Vanheule, D., and Vanlerberghe, B. (eds), *The Effects of Judicial Decisions in Time* (Intersentia, 2014).

Puhl, J, "A Whiff of Corruption in Orbán's Hungary", *Spiegel* (17 January 2017), www.spiegel.de/international/europe/a-whiff-of-corruption-in-orban-s-hungary-a-1129713.html.

Roznai, Y, *Unconstitutional Constitutional Amendments: A Study of the Nature and Limits of Constitutional Amendment Powers*, PhD thesis, 2014, The London School of Economics and Political Science (LSE), http://etheses.lse.ac.uk/915/1/Roznai_Unconstitutional-constitutional-amendments.pdf, 158–160.

Roznai, Y, *Unconstitutional Constitutional Amendments: The Limits of Amendment Powers* (Oxford University Press, 2017).

Sajó, A, "Militant Democracy and Emotional Politics", *Constellations* 4 (2012) 562–572.

Sárközy, T, "Magyarország kormányzása 2010–2014" ["Governance of Hungary 2010–2014"] *Új Magyar Közigazgatás* 2 (2015).

Scheppele, KL, "Orbán's Emergency", https://hungarianspectrum.org/2020/03/21/kim-lane-scheppele-orbans-emergency/,https://verfassungsblog.de/pandemic-as-constitutional-moment/.

Schiffer, A, "Különleges jogbizonytalanság" ["Extraordinary Legal Uncertainty"], https://mandiner.hu/cikk/20200313_kulonleges_jogbizonytalansag (13 March 2020).

Schwartz, SH and Bardi, A, "Influences of Adaptation to Communist Rule on Value Priorities in Eastern Europe", *Political Psychology* 2 (1997).

Sejersted, F, "The Norwegian Parliament and European Integration – Reflections from Medium-Speed Europe" in E Smitjh, ed, *National Parliaments as Cornerstones of the European Integration* (Kluwer Academic Publisher, 1996).

Siems, M., *Comparative Law* (Cambridge University Press, 2014) 78–79.

Sokolewicz, W, "Komentarz do art. 235" ["Commentary to the Art. 235"] in L. Garlicki (ed), *Konstytucja Rzeczypospolitej Polskiej. Komentarz*, Vol II [*The Constitution of the Republic of Poland*] (Wydawnictwo Sejmowe, 2001) 4.

Sólyom L, "Alkotmányértelmezés az új alkotmánybíróságok gyakorlatában" ["Constitutional interpretation in the practice of new constitutional courts"], *Fundamentum* 2 (2002) 18–20.

Stumpf I, "A kormány alkotmányos jogállása" ["Constitutional Status of the Government"], *Új Magyar Közigazgatás* 2 (2015).

Szmulik, B, "Opinia w sprawie uwag do nowelizacji ustawy z dnia 25 czerwca 2015 r. o Trybunale Konstytucyjnym przygotowanych przez Komisję Wenecką" ["Opinion on the Comments to the Amendment of the Act of 25 June 2015 on the Constitutional Tribunal by the Venice Commission"], *Przegląd Sejmowy* 5 (2016) 81–100.

Tordai, C, "A közjog határai a járványveszély idején" ["Limits of Public Law during a Pandemic"], https://igyirnankmi.atlatszo.hu/2020/03/16/a-kozjog-hatarai-a-jarvanyveszely-idejen/ (16 March 2020).

Uzelac, A, "Survival of the Third Legal Tradition", *Supreme Court Law Review* 49 (2010), (2nd) 377–396. Available at SSRN: https://ssrn.com/abstract=2498760.

Wróblewska, I, *Zasada państwa prawnego w orzecznictwie Trybunału Konstytucyjnego RP* [*The Rule of Democratic State Ruled by Law in Judgements of the Polish Constitutional Tribunal*] (TNOIK, 2010) 48–50.

Index

For Product Safety Concerns and Information please contact our EU
representative GPSR@taylorandfrancis.com
Taylor & Francis Verlag GmbH, Kaufingerstraße 24, 80331 München, Germany

www.ingramcontent.com/pod-product-compliance
Lightning Source LLC
LaVergne TN
LVHW011127300926
849160LV00008B/545

* 9 7 8 1 0 3 2 0 0 7 3 6 6 *